IRANIAN FOREIGN POLICY DURING AHMADINEJAD

Iranian Foreign Policy during Ahmadinejad

Ideology and Actions

Maaike Warnaar

IRANIAN FOREIGN POLICY DURING AHMADINEJAD
Copyright © Maaike Warnaar, 2013.

First published in 2013 by
PALGRAVE MACMILLAN®
in the United States—a division of St. Martin's Press LLC,
175 Fifth Avenue, New York, NY 10010.

Where this book is distributed in the UK, Europe and the rest of the world,
this is by Palgrave Macmillan, a division of Macmillan Publishers Limited,
registered in England, company number 785998, of Houndmills,
Basingstoke, Hampshire RG21 6XS.

Palgrave Macmillan is the global academic imprint of the above companies
and has companies and representatives throughout the world.

Palgrave® and Macmillan® are registered trademarks in the United States,
the United Kingdom, Europe and other countries.

ISBN: 978–1–137–33790–0

Library of Congress Cataloging-in-Publication Data

Warnaar, Maaike.
    Iranian foreign policy during Ahmadinejad : ideology and actions /
Maaike Warnaar.
        pages cm
    Includes bibliographical references and index.
    ISBN 978–1–137–33790–0 (hardback)
        1. Ahmadinejad, Mahmoud. 2. Iran—Foreign relations—21st century.
3. Iran—Politics and government—1997– 4. Ideology—Iran.
5. Legitimacy of governments—Iran. I. Title.

DS318.83.W37 2013
327.55—dc23   2013023470

A catalogue record of the book is available from the British Library.

Design by Newgen Knowledge Works (P) Ltd., Chennai, India.

First edition: November 2013

10 9 8 7 6 5 4 3 2 1

To my parents, all four of them.

Contents

Tables

Acknowledgments

This project goes back to a student exchange between the Political Science department at the University of Amsterdam and the School of International Relations in Islamic Republic of Iran in 2003. As a participating student, this exchange made evident to me the importance of understanding foreign policy behavior from a domestic, discursive perspective. Since I have studied Iranian foreign policy from this viewpoint, originally under the enthusiastic supervision of Paul Aarts in completion of my master's degree in Political Science and later under the stimulating supervision of Professor Raymond Hinnebusch. Their guidance and support have been indispensable in completing the dissertation that formed the basis of this book.

I am deeply indebted to many Iranians who, in the past ten years, have exchanged views with me, or who have, in other ways, been helpful during my many stays in Iran. They go by the first names of Mohsen, Mehdi, Shahriar, Mehrdad, Mehri, Sadeq, Fatemeh, Maryam, Hossein, Nasrin, Davoud, Kayhan, Behzad, Mahsa, Houman, Nasr, Yekta, and Bahareh. I want to thank in particular the generous and knowledgeable scholars who offered their views and feedback at Mofid University in Qom, the School of International Relations in Tehran, the Centre for Strategic Research in Tehran, the Middle East Strategic Centre in Tehran, the Imam Sadiq University in Tehran, and the Faculties of Law and Politics and World Studies at the University of Tehran. They have made accessible to me the various domestic perspectives on Iranian foreign policy and as such have made indispensable contributions to this study. The flaws and mistakes, of course, are all mine.

At the University of Amsterdam, I am particularly grateful to Annette Freyberg-Inan, Paul van Hooft, Peyman Jafari, Umut Kibrit, Fadi Hirzalla, Marlies Glasius, Christian Broër, Mohammad Mojahedi, Bertine Kamphuis, and Gerd Junne, all of whom provided guidance or feedback on earlier drafts. Furthermore, I would like to thank Juliette Verhoeven, Stephan de Vries, Lisalette Dijkers, and Reinoud Leenders for the stimulating environment they created with the many workshops, lectures, and seminars in the context of the Civil Society in West Asia project at the University of Amsterdam. I am indebted to my colleagues Taryn Shepperd, Mohira Suyarkulova, Beatrix Futák-Campbell, and Gladys Mokhawa at the University of St Andrews for their thoughts on identity and discourse analysis. I am grateful to Mohira Suyarkulova, Laura Khor, Hannah Brooks-Motl, Paola Raunio, and the Kleidosty family for their friendship and their hospitality during my stays in St Andrews. I am also thankful for the funding provided by Noah Lev, Stichting Vreedefonds, the Institute for Iranian Studies at St Andrews University, the British Institute of Persian Studies, and the University of St Andrews School of International Relations.

The questions and comments professors Karin Fierke and Anoush Ehteshami provided when I defended my thesis in late 2011 proved of great value in thoroughly rewriting my thesis toward this book, as did the comments by an anonymous Iranian reviewer in the United States. I want to thank the Leiden Institute for Areas Studies for facilitating me while completing this book. In particular, I would like to thank José Brittijn, Gabrielle van den Berg, Johnny Cheung, Asghar Seyed-Ghorab, Lindsay Black, Maghiel Crevel, and Koushyar Parsi for creating a welcoming and encouraging intellectual environment at LIAS.

In writing this book, I relied on the inexhaustible support of my family and closest friends. I am deeply grateful to all of them. Most of all, I want to thank my husband Tjerk Jan Schuitmaker for his patience and encouragement all the way through.

Introduction

"Iran Enters Nuclear Talks in a Defiant Mood," "Iran Expands Nuclear Fuel Production After Talks," "U.S. Imposes Sanctions on Those Aiding Iran," "Iran's Double-digit Inflation Worsens," "U.S. Adds Forces in Persian Gulf, a Signal to Iran," "Iranian Oil Minister Concedes Sanctions Have Hurt Exports," "Netanyahu Strikes Tough Tone on Possible Iran Strike"[1]: If news headlines give any indication, Iranian behavior during Ahmadinejad's presidency was marked by intransigence to Western pressure despite its apparent harmful effects. United States' and European pressure had increased over the years as the Iranian regime remained defiant, and at the end of Ahmadinejad's second term international sanctions had drastically limited the regime's options to remedy the illnesses of the Iranian economy. In addition, regionally Iran's luck was changing. When Ahmadinejad became president in 2005, the fall of the Taliban and Saddam regimes had created new options for Iran, and during the early years of Ahmadinejad's presidency, relations with Arab states seemed on the mend. The Syrian civil war, however, highlighted regional differences, narrowing the Islamic Republic's regional possibilities. Despite this, the Iranian regime kept supporting Assad's regime. It seemed that the regime's revolutionary discourse of defiance kept it from pursuing a foreign policy in line with its national interest of security and economic prosperity.

This presumed irrationality in Iran's foreign policy under Mahmoud Ahmadinejad fits conventional understanding of Iranian foreign policy: unable to come to a rapprochement with the West due to what is often considered ideological stubbornness, the Iranian regime caused its own isolation. Shireen Hunter (2010), for example, argued that the Iranian regime has been unable to adjust to the post-Cold War international system, inhibited by domestic ideology, resulting in what can consequently be called "irrational policies."[2] From her perspective, the Islamic Republic is losing the international game. Western powers, who dominate this game, perceive Iran as a rogue state and a threat to international security and have sought to isolate Iran. The Iranian regime is unable to adjust to international rules, constrained by an ideology that may serve domestic legitimacy, but which is counterproductive internationally.

However, if news lines are an indication, there is also a different story to tell: "Nonaligned Nations Back Iran's Nuclear Bid," "Russia Criticizes U.S. Iran Sanctions," "India's Support for Iran Threatens Its US Relationship," and "Russia, Turkey and Iran Meet, Posing Test for U.S."[3] These headlines refer to the Islamic Republic's attempts in coming to cooperation with rising powers in defiance of Western efforts to isolate Iran. They indicate some success in the Iranian regime's endeavors to circumvent Western pressure. Under Mohammad Khatami, the Iranian government had advocated a policy of engaging the West, but with little success. The neoconservative government announced a foreign policy reorientation, now toward the non-West, taking advantage of what it regarded as changing international tides: "Our analysis indicates that many countries disagree with the tenets of unilateralism and Western domination of the global economy," Manouchehr Mottaki, foreign minister of the Islamic Republic at the time, said in 2006. "The coalition of these forces in bilateral and multilateral settings as well as the mobilization of international organizations can bring along significant changes in the international system," he continued.[4] In other words, if from a Western perspective it seems that Iran is unable to adjust to the rules of the international game, from an Iranian perspective, the country is involved in an altogether different game, in which not the West but developing countries and rising powers make the rules. Participation in this game is essential for Iran in the context of the Iranian regime's foreign policy discourse, which represents the international order not only as unjust but also as changing. Iran under Ahmadinejad tried to ride the wave of this change, challenging US power instead of engaging it—engagement would only have been a confirmation of US power.

This book inquires into the foreign policy ideas that were current among foreign policy makers during Ahmadinejad's presidency. Particularly, it tries to answer the question how these ideas provide a context for Iranian foreign policy behavior under Ahmadinejad, building on Roxanne L. Doty's Discursive Practice Approach.[5] It offers both an analysis of Iranian foreign policy discourse as well as an inquiry into the regional and international foreign policy behavior in the light of this discourse. This book does not intend to show that ideas "matter" for Iranian foreign policy, but rather that they are constitutive of foreign policy. In other words, ideology is not considered one explanatory variable among others, but rather the primary context within which foreign policy gets shape. Particularly, this book points at how discourse has made certain foreign policy possible, even likely, whereas it has precluded other options.[6] Moreover, ideology is by itself again confirmed and reinforced through foreign policy. Following Karin Fierke (1999, 2007), this book points at a mechanism in which Iranian foreign policy is feeding back into the discourse of change by "acting as if" international change is happening. By doing so, the Iranian regime is able to take part in and also shape international developments, which challenge the status quo. Through the enactment of Iranian foreign policy discourse internationally, Iran was actively trying to shape the world in line with its own discourse: in particular, the decline of US power and challenging the notion that Iran is isolated. It aims to do so in a simultaneous effort with other developing powers and rising powers.

Who Makes Foreign Policy in Iran?

Foreign policy in Iran is not primarily made by the President and his cabinet—it is a product of negotiation and competition among various powerful individuals and institutions. Officially, in line with the 1979 Constitution, the Supreme Council for National Security is Iran's main decision-making body on foreign policy matters.[7] The council comprises the heads of the three branches of government, that is, the head of the legislative (the speaker of parliament), the head of the judiciary and the head of the executive (the president), as well as "the chief of the Supreme Command Council of the Armed Forces, the officer in charge of the planning and budget affairs, two representatives nominated by the leader, ministers of foreign affairs, interior, and information, a minister related with the subject, and the highest ranking officials from the Armed Forces and the Islamic Revolution's Guards Corps." However, decisions of the Supreme Council for National Security are effective only after the confirmation by the leader.

With the supreme leader having the final word in foreign policy issues, one would expect a high level of continuity in Iranian foreign policy. Depending on the level of analysis, there has indeed been a high level of consistency in Iranian foreign policy behavior since its birth in 1979, even when comparing the Ahmadinejad and Khatami presidencies. It is widely acknowledged that Khatami's moderate tone was not representative of, and institutionally separate from Iran's overall foreign policy behavior, and to a certain extent the same can be said for Ahmadinejad's course. There is, however, some room for maneuver for the president and his cabinet. Particularly through his speeches and his abundant international visits to Latin America, Africa, and Asia, Ahmadinejad shaped Iranian foreign policy in a quest to challenge Western attempts to isolate Iran. Moreover, during his two terms, Ahmadinejad showed increasing willingness to challenge the leader on foreign-policy-related issues, particularly with regard to the appointment of foreign policy officials. With the reformists marginalized under Ahmadinejad, the power struggle moved to the conservative camp among which one can distinguish pragmatists, who are more likely to prioritize Iran's economic needs and embrace a certain level of economic liberalization, traditional conservatives prioritizing the ideals of the Islamic revolution, and neoconservatives giving revolutionary principles a more populist and international dimension. These different outlooks have led to power struggles among foreign policy elites, and have crystallized into personal rivalries, such as between parliamentary speaker and (until October 2007) secretary of Supreme National Security Council Ali Larijani and the president.

The officials engaged in Iranian foreign policy not only share certain views but also place different emphasis. This is in line with the conception of ideology as a "battle of ideas," (Mouffe) an amalgam of competing views, which may at the same time contradict, converge, and overlap. In this study, it is what is communicated among different foreign policy makers in (re)producing a largely coherent set of foreign policy ideas that is of relevance. There are two reasons why there is much convergence and correspondence in the ideas communicated to Iran's foreign policy makers. First, the Guardian Council selects all Iran's politicians and officials, including the foreign policy elites, which means that foreign policy elites share a very similar ideological background. They are vetted particularly on their personal ideological commitment to the system of the Islamic Republic and the ideals of the 1979 Revolution. Adib-Moghaddam (2007) points at the consistency of Iran's foreign policy behavior under Khatami and Ahmadinejad and attributes this consistency to

> A culturally constituted consensus about the country's role in international affairs that is strong enough to transcend the factions of—and divisions in—Iranian politics...It functions as the guardian of identity, represents a web of shared ideals, images, norms, and institutions, and provides for the foreign policy elites a coherent, if systematically abstract, overall orientation in the conduct of international affairs.[8]

Second, even when there are disagreements among foreign policy makers, so far the supreme leader has kept a hold of his power to direct Iran's foreign policy. The main challenger to Khamene'i's power in foreign policy matters, particularly during the last years of his presidency, was Ahmadinejad. However, although Ahmadinejad since his initial election in 2005 has been able to shape Iranian foreign policy according to his own personal ideals, these views have usually complemented and rarely contradicted Khamene'i's.

Why Discourse Analysis?

Treating foreign policy ideology as an intersubjective social construct in which a somewhat hybrid group of foreign policy actors engage, and placing foreign policy within this context, means examining "how meanings are produced and attached to various subjects/objects, thus constituting particular interpretive dispositions which create certain possibilities and preclude others."[9] This study has taken discourse as the focus of analysis to unravel the production of meaning, and treats it as the manifestation of ideology in language. It borrows in particular from Doty and Hansen.[10] Discourse analysis, which has a long tradition in the social sciences, is concerned with the uncovering of "groups of related statements which cohere in some way to produce both meanings and effects in the real world."[11] Discourse does not just reflect ideology; it is "productive of subjects and their worlds."[12] While ideology is also manifest in other social practices, such as traditions, behavioral norms, or artistic and musical expression, its manifestation in (recorded) language makes it particularly researchable. Because the research at hand is inquiring into the relationship between ideology and foreign policy, the focus here will be on foreign policy discourse as a part of the political discourse used by the Iranian regime.

Foreign policy discourse does not develop overnight: it is historically constructed and refers to other, earlier discourses. It is also not static, but continuously changing as it is renegotiated. Although ruling elites operate within a discursive context and, therefore to some extent, are unable to think outside of it, they can also reshape and reorient discourse. This enables them to use the dominant ideology as a tool to secure their power—particularly and predominantly through their control of state media, censorship, and other forms of repression. As such, discourse is actively used by the ruling elite to legitimize their power, including the legitimation of the use of repression. When legitimizing the status quo, "discourses 'hook' into normative ideas and common-sense notions…This produces shortcut paths into ideas which convey messages about, for example, 'good' and 'bad'…, morality and immorality…, and acceptable and inappropriate behavior."[13] This will be investigated for the Iranian case in chapter 4.

In sum, taking as a starting point, the ontological assumption of the intersubjective construction of reality, predominantly through language, as the main locus of meaning, but letting the empirical data in a quite literal sense "speak for itself," one can see discourse as a continuum where it is simultaneously creating and recreating meaning, in some ways tilting toward recreation and sometimes tilting toward creation, the latter allowing more space for agency. In other words, although discourse is always a recreation of meaning, discourse also includes an active process of creating (new) meaning. Discourse not only then is no longer the mutual production of knowledge by a group of equals, but also a process of meaning production by groups or individuals more powerful (either because of their position or their numbers) to create this meaning to their political advantage. In this situation, groups with more power to shape the discourse are able to use discourse to shape meaning, understanding, and behavior. This means that one can both identify ways in which existing meaning is recreated, drawing on available discourse, and merely changing emphasis, while at the same time discourse is used more actively to support a (changing or unchanging) sociopolitical order, as "speech acts" through which the discourse itself shapes the world around it. Taking this as a starting point, both the view in which ideology is a battle of ideas between different participants rather than a top-down exercise by power-hungry elites, and the critical views in which discourse is used as an instrument of domination, are useful.

Plan of the Book

This is not the first work on Iranian foreign policy, not even that under Ahmadinejad. It is, however, one of the first consistently constructivist works to deal with the question of Iranian foreign policy. The first chapter traces back the steps of this constructivist approach and discusses how it fits in with other works on Iranian foreign policy and the foreign policies of Middle East states in general. It shows how the constructivist approach taken in this project engages with two theoretical points that scholars of Middle East foreign policies persistently make: the relevance of domestic circumstances for foreign policy behavior as well as the importance of ideational factors. It steers clear, however, of the holistic approaches that are common in the study of Middle East policies, but which suffer from theoretical inconsistencies. The social ontology that forms the basis of this project is combined with a social epistemology, meaning that ideas are not treated a one factor among others, but as the primary context in which foreign policy gets shape. Two case studies on Iranian foreign policy show the value of such an approach. Iran–Israel relations and the Iran–Iraq war have been studied intensively by other scholars, but explanations for Iran's behavior in both these cases are incomplete. When asking the *how possible* question, Iranian foreign policy behavior in both these cases is better understood. Answers to this question point to the historical construction of enmity through interaction between states, rather than a geopolitical rivalry inherent to the regional system. The remainder of chapter 1 elaborates on this project's constructivist approach.

Before mapping out Iranian foreign policy ideology, this book starts with a discussion of the domestic and international contexts in which the Ahmadinejad administration found itself. Chapter 2 discusses the domestic environment under Ahmadinejad in which the Iranian regime's foreign policy got shape. Central in this chapter are the related concepts of ideology and legitimacy. The first part of the chapter defines the concept of ideology and shows that it has both legitimizing and constituting functions. It is argued that, while ideology's legitimizing functions remain relevant among a core constituency, in scenarios in which regime legitimacy is waning, ideology is most important of its constituting functions. This means that even in situations of limited regime legitimacy, ideology is likely to continue to structure the regime's behavior. The remainder of the chapter discusses what this means for the Iranian sociopolitical system under Ahmadinejad. It describes and traces back the main pillars of the regime's power and shows how the regime was experiencing important challenges to its legitimacy in each of these fields. Moreover, it argues that, under these circumstances, regime ideology became more, not less, important to the Iranian regime. This was equally the case internationally, where the Iranian regime was also suffering from a legitimacy deficit. This international environment is the topic of chapter 3. The chapter starts by tracing back the enmity between the United States and Iran and shows that what is in the literature considered an irrational fear of the United States bordering on paranoia is in fact better understood in the context of the historical interaction between these states. US animosity toward Iran has caused the international environment to be generally inhospitable for the Iranian regime. However, chapter 3 also shows that US power is challenged by rising and aspiring powers, and that this has created opportunities for the Islamic Republic to find international partners.

Chapter 4 gives an elaborate account of Iranian foreign policy discourse during Ahmadinejad. It points at the main discursive mechanisms in Iranian foreign policy ideology as represented in the discourse of the president and the supreme leader. It shows that *change* is an inherent feature of Iranian foreign policy discourse. The two leaders identify the world's problems, which they blame mainly on the "bullying powers," first and foremost the United States, and also present solutions to these problems, mainly resistance against the bullying powers. According to their ideology, the world experiencing awakening: humanity is becoming aware of its capacity to be resistant against domination. The Iranian regime identifies Iran not only with "awakened nations," most importantly the Palestinians, but also the Iraqis and the Afghan people, and contrasts itself with those on the side of the United States. The main difference between the Islamic Republic and the United States is that the first is seen as moral and the second immoral. This immorality is visible in the United States' global hegemony, which is having a bad effect on humanity as a whole. Iran through the revolution has acquired an important moral role in contributing to the creation of a just, multipolar system. The power of the United States is already declining according to the regime, meaning that change toward a multipolar system is imminent.

Iranian foreign policy, in response to the domestic and international developments discussed in chapters 2 and 3, got shape in the context of this foreign policy discourse. This foreign policy behavior is the topic of chapter 5. It discusses both Iran's regional and international policies and shows, first, how foreign policy discourse made possible, even desirable these foreign policies. Secondly, it shows how the enactment of foreign policy discourse through behavior feeds back into the discourse itself, strengthening it. These two mechanisms are also the backbone of chapter 6 on the 2010 Tehran Declaration. The framing of the nuclear issue by Iranian foreign policy makers has precluded suspension of nuclear enrichment and as such cooperation with the United States on this matter. This has, however, not just limited Iran's international options, but has in another way contributed to Iran's legitimacy among developing countries and rising powers. Moreover, the Iranian regime's adherence to its antihegemonic domestic discourse has contributed to the actualization of this discourse, in that Iran has joined other nations in challenging Western domination of international politics. This made the deal with Brazil and Turkey particularly desirable, and a success for the regime in terms of its own discourse.

To be sure, the success of the Iranian regime in galvanizing legitimacy through the dissemination of the official state ideology was not the subject of this study. It is a fact that the regime is challenged by significant segments of Iranian society. Particularly since the re-election of Mahmoud Ahmadinejad in 2009, it became clear that many Iranians no longer accepted the legitimacy of president Ahmadinejad or Supreme Leader Ali Khamene'i. This, however, made regime ideology more relevant, not less. Chapter 7 deals with hardline conservative discourse on the Green Movement and elaborates on the discursive mechanisms that the regime was using to legitimize repression of the opposition. It shows that official ideology and foreign policy were important to the regime's efforts to maintain what legitimacy it had among their (popular or elite) constituency, including not only the mobilization of repressive forces, but also in an attempt to reclaim legitimacy. As such, it illustrates premise that ideology retains its relevance for Iranian foreign policy behavior even if (or perhaps even: particularly as) it is challenged. The hardline narrative on the 2009 elections identified reformists as agents of the West, in particular of the United Kingdom. This had important consequences for Iran's relations with the United Kingdom.

In the end, the main contribution of this book is to provide insight into the mutually constitutive relationship between ideology and foreign policy, particularly, how discourse forms the context of foreign policy behavior and how this discourse is confirmed and reshaped through foreign policy conduct. In other words, first, ideology has provided a context for foreign policy, in that it has precluded rapprochement with the United States and complicated relations with other Western powers, but has made possible—even desirable—a closer cooperation between Iran and rising powers. Second, foreign policy confirms and reinforces ideology as the regime through its foreign policy conduct aims at contributing to international change. This change resembled what was described and prescribed in the discourse: a change in which the power of the United States is challenged and other, alternative powers are on the rise. In other words, in a mutual effort with other states, Iranian foreign policy behavior under Ahmadinejad was aimed at challenging both the supremacy of the United States as well as the notion that Iran is isolated, confirming and actualizing its discourse. Thus, this behavior was not only made possible in the context of the regime's official, revolutionary discourse of resistance, and independence, but also confirmed it.

* * *

Under Ahmadinejad, regime legitimacy was challenged by factionalism, popular dissatisfaction, and accusations of election fraud. In addition, internationally the regime was suffering from challenges to its legitimacy, which severely limited its options to draw resources from the international environment to improve its economy or to otherwise secure the regime's power. The Iranian regime, however, was trying to turn the disadvantage of limited international legitimacy into an advantage. Domestically, the West's policies toward Iran were treated as examples of their imperialism and "bullying tactics," reinforcing the identification of Iran as both a victim and a force of resistance against injustice. Moreover, domestic calls for democratic change were treated as Western interference and Iran's reformists as agents of the West. Internationally, meanwhile, the Iranian regime tried to take on a lead role as a defender of the rights of those countries disadvantaged by Western dominance. Bolstering international legitimacy on the basis of revolutionary ideology served important international goals, as it increased Iran's international options among likeminded states as well as rising powers seeking to take an independent course. The regime's successes in this endeavor may have fed back into domestic legitimacy, at least among its own constituency.

There may be some truth to the cliché that the Iranian regime was playing chess, while their Western counterparts were playing checkers: what may be irrational in terms of a Western-dominated game, may be entirely rational within the context of the game Iranian leaders are playing. In the Iranian game, giving in to the West—known for its domination and meddling in domestic affairs—was not considered a rational option at all, but harmful to Iran's national interest. In the Iranian game, the United States no longer makes the rules. Instead, by attempts to engage other powers that take an independent course, the Iranian regime was not just trying to circumvent US power but also actively contributing to its decline. This international behavior of challenging the West was much in line with the official ideology of resistance and independence. As such, Iran's foreign policy behavior was not constrained by domestic ideology, as some have argued, but rather *made possible* by it.

Chapter 1

Studying Iranian Foreign Policy: A Constructivist Approach

Most scholarly literature on Iranian foreign policy describes the Iranian regimes as a rational actor, constrained but not motivated by ideology.[1] This view can be contrasted with works that describe the Iranian regime as primarily guided by ideological considerations, particularly a political interpretation of Shi'a Islam.[2] The discussion on Iranian "realism" versus "idealism" long characterized the academic debates on Iranian foreign policy, both inside and outside of Iran. Only recently, a third view of Iranian foreign policy behavior emerged: one based within a constructivist approach to the study of foreign policy.[3] Although still underrepresented in the academic debate, the contours of this approach are taking shape, and the insights yielded have proven invaluable in the understanding of the "how possible" of Iranian foreign policy. This chapter traces back the steps of the constructivist approach that forms the backbone of this book.

Academically, the study of Iranian foreign policy behavior takes place within a wider framework of studies on Middle East foreign policy and international relations (IR). This chapter starts with a discussion of the contending views[4] on the foreign policies and international relations of Middle East regimes.[5] This literature points at the limitations of realism in explaining the IR of the Middle East and suggests several modifications. This study takes as a starting point the epistemological issues raised by these scholars about, first, the need for inclusion of systemic, as well as domestic factors, in the analysis of foreign policy and, second, the relevance of the ideational for foreign policy. However, it argues that in both these respects, studies of IR of the Middle East have ignored the epistemological contradictions inherent to their modified forms of realism. These inconsistencies can be solved when moving the study of the IR of the Middle East into a constructivist paradigm.[6] Constructivist studies of foreign policy and IR are epistemologically diverse, but share the ontological assumption that the world that matters most for foreign policy making, is socially constructed. Constructivism in IR takes as a starting point that ideologies (including threat perceptions, identity, and norms) are social constructs that are reproduced through human action. Foreign policy behavior is made possible in the context of this ideology, reproducing it while it is produced by it. In other words, instead of treating ideology as one factor in the process of foreign policy making constructivists study foreign policy in the context of ideology. This chapter shows that studies of Iranian foreign policy point to the need for an approach that recognizes not just the relevance of ideas for foreign policy, but also acknowledges the social construction of the world relevant to foreign policy behavior, to allow for a better understanding of how Iranian foreign policy is made possible.

Foreign Policy in the Middle East

Despite the acknowledgement that the Middle East as a region "provides an important reservoir for theorizing and for contributing to broader debates in international relations,"[7] most studies of foreign relations of the Middle East take on rather traditional theoretical models. Seemingly without exception, they take on modified forms of realism, in which for many scholars the work of neo-realist Stephen Walt[8] is the starting point. The reason for this is perhaps that the Middle East "appears to be the region where the anarchy and insecurity seen by the realist school of international politics as the main feature of states systems remains most in evidence and where the realist paradigm retains its greatest relevance."[9] At the same time, most scholars of Middle East foreign policy and IR acknowledge the limitations of neo-realism. Criticisms include "a neglect of ideology and belief systems, a minimization of factors internal to states and societies, inadequate attention to economics, and, of special importance for the misrepresentation of the Middle East, a view of inter-state relations as marked by timeless, recurrent, patterns."[10] This is why studies of foreign policy in the Middle East adopted modified forms of realism as a framework for analysis.[11] In these middle-ground approaches, constructivist insights complement (neo)realist theory. The resulting approaches are "holistic and inclusionary," building on what is considered relevant in different theories.[12] The main adjustments to realism these authors offer are, first, a focus on regional and domestic determinants in addition to international, systemic determinants. Secondly, the importance of ideational factors in the shaping of foreign policy is recognized and incorporated into the framework of analysis.

The notion that the domestic "matters" for foreign policy behavior is central to the concept of omni-balancing, originally developed by Steven R. David[13] but taken up by Raymond Hinnebusch[14] to explain foreign policy behavior in the Middle East. Again, Walt's theory—to be precise, his notion of a "balance of threat"—is the starting point. According to David, decision-makers "omni-balance" between internal and external threats:

> when the primary threat is internal, a regime may align with an external power to get resources to contain it. But it could also seek to appease domestic opinion and enhance legitimacy by indulging in anti-imperialist rhetoric or irredentist campaigns. Where the primary threat is external, a regime may mobilize new domestic actors into politics to expand its power base and seek alliances with similarly threatened states.[15]

The concept of omni-balancing offers a significant improvement when compared to the one-dimensional neorealist view, which neglects the domestic realm. As such, the notion of the interconnectedness between the international and the domestic is maintained as one of the core premises underlying the approach of this study. Omni-balancing, however, merely points at the mechanism of interaction of the international and the domestic in the shaping of foreign policy that takes place at the level of the regime—omni-balancing's unit of analysis; it offers no analytical tools to study this interaction. Although the model of omni-balancing is still developing,[16] so far it has not brought us any closer to a theory on how the domestic and international are interrelated. When applied in case studies, the analysis of omni-balancing is convoluted, prone to bias, and suitable only for posthoc analyses.[17] This is particularly so, as the domestic and international factors implied in omni-balancing are not only continuously changing and reconfiguring but also interrelated. Researching omni-balancing behavior becomes even more difficult if one accepts, as the current research does, that threats and opportunities are not just "out there" but are also equally a matter of social construction.

Second, studies of foreign policy behavior in the Middle East acknowledge the importance of ideational factors such as norms, identities, and ideology in the shaping of foreign policy. Hinnebusch and Ehteshami[18] point to the importance of super- and suprastate identities, which are also central in the volume edited by Telhami and

Barnett,[19] and they also point to the importance of foreign policy role,[20] which is again the main concept in Dessouki and Korany,[21] whereas Halliday[22] prefers the term "ideology." These studies view ideational factors as the "missing link" where rationalist explanations fail to adequately explain foreign policy behavior. Telhami and Barnett, for example, who have devoted an entire volume to identity and foreign policy in the Middle East, inquire into the relevance of identity by asking the question: "Does the introduction of identity inform us about the foreign policies of Middle Eastern states in ways that we otherwise would not understand them?"[23] While this is a perfectly valid question from a rationalist point of view, adding the ideational variable to already existing variables of threats, opportunities, geopolitics, and the like implies a clear distinction between what is ideational and what is real. Threats, however, do not appear out of nothing: they usually result from perceived animosity, perhaps related to a perceived claim to a certain territory, progressively intensified by the action and reaction that accompanies mutual suspicion. Therefore, in studying foreign policy behavior in response to threats, the ideological context within which the threat is identified and responded to needs to be taken into account. This ideological context could be very different from the epistemological perspective of the researcher, further obscuring analysis. In other words, merely adding "the ideational" as one factor among many ignores the social construction of what rationalist consider "objectively material."

The main objection to constructivist approaches by conventional scholars on the Middle East is that by focusing on the ideational, constructivists have lost the material out of sight.[24] "If realism ignores values and ideas, constructivism and its outriders run the risk of ignoring interests and material factors, let alone old-fashioned deception and self-delusion."[25] These are again valid objections from a rationalist point of view, where the ideational is separated from the material. Constructivist approaches, however, do not make a distinction between the material and the ideational: after all, what rationalists treat as objective and material becomes relevant for foreign policy within a social context. Constructivism does not ignore material interests, but sees these not as objectively given but as socially constructed. As is discussed in the case studies that follow below, treating threat and material interest as objective, natural and pregiven, takes for granted their social construction. "They generally take as unproblematic the *possibility* that a particular decision or course of action could happen. They presuppose a particular subjectivity (i.e., a mode of being), a background of social/discursive practices and meanings which make possible the practices as well as the social actors themselves," in the words of Roxanne Doty.[26] This means that constructivists, in their efforts to yield insights into foreign policy behavior, ask a fundamentally different question. In the absence of an objectively defined threat or material interest, the why-question becomes irrelevant and is replaced with the questions of "how possible?"

In other words, while the above-mentioned volumes accept some of the premises of constructivism, such as its focus on the ideational, they fail to address the ontological inconsistency that rises from merely adopting these concepts: How can one reconcile the recognition of the relevance subjective understanding of the world with the objective definition of material interest? Moreover, how can one retain a positivist research agenda based on causal relations when one adopts a social ontology?[27] Last, the analytical separation between the domestic and international leaves little room for the notion that these two realms are mutually constituted. A constructivist approach, which conceptually separates the national and international but recognizes their mutual constitution, provides a more suitable approach, consistent with the ontological premises of social constructivism.

By mapping out the domestic ideological context in which foreign policy gets shape, constructivist approaches have theoretical leverage over the questions of threat perception, the identification of friends and foes, the choice of one foreign policy option over other options, as well as the timing of certain foreign policy behavior. These are all elements that rationalist studies have difficulty explaining. They take for granted the ideological context in which foreign policy is made, and which makes possible, to use Doty[28] again, certain foreign policy options, and precludes others. To be sure, the relevance of this analysis depends on the research question that is asked. If one wants to inquire, for example, into *why* Saudi Arabia has good relations with the United States, it would suffice to give a detailed analysis of Saudi Arabia's security interests.[29] This does not explain, however, why Saudi Arabia sees the United States as a potential ally in their security endeavors and not a foe (as Syria and Iran do), despite what at first sight seems an ideological clash. Nor does it explain why Saudi Arabia chose to balance with this great power against regional threats, instead of coming to regional cooperation with middle powers such as Syria, Egypt, and Iran. Moreover, it takes regional threat perception and thus preoccupation with security as given, ignoring the social construction of threat through regional interaction. Constructivism, in that way, offers a deeper understanding of foreign policy behavior than rationalism can offer.

To illustrate both the merits and the limitations of rationalist approaches, two accounts of Iranian foreign policy behavior within a neorealist tradition are discussed below: one studying Iran's involvement in two of the region's most prolonged and bloody conflicts, the Iran–Iraq War (from 1980 until 1988),[30] and one on Iranian–Israeli rivalry.[31] Both studies point toward a geostrategic competition between regional states inherent to the regional system, but take for granted the mutual constitution between ideas and material circumstances in producing perceptions of threat underlying both conflicts. Their accounts, in other words, explain Iranian foreign policy after the fact, but are unclear on how the foreign policy conducted by the Islamic Republic was made possible in the first place. To be precise, they do not show how the animosity between Iran and its adversaries was socially constructed.

Case-study One: Iranian "Miscalculations" in the War with Iraq?

Iraq invaded Iran in September 1980, a year and a half after the Iranian Revolution. Although the new Iranian regime was in the process of consolidating its power, the Iranian Revolutionary Guards and military were not only able to stop the Iraqi invasion but also to drive the Iraqi army back into their territory. At this point, which was reached in May 1982, the Iranian regime could have claimed victory and ended the war. Instead, the Iranian leadership chose to continue the war, which then turned into a war of attrition, resulting in an enormous death toll on both sides. What explains Iran's choice to continue the war after the Iraqi threat had become manageable? Walt[32] does not give an answer to this question, but he offers an explanation for the start of the war in *Revolution and War* (1996) that points to one. Walt explains how, in general, after a revolution information is scarce and revolutionary ideology may distort facts. Distorted perceptions of intent, Walt argues, result in a spiral of suspicion. In addition, both a postrevolutionary regime and its adversaries may have a false perception of advantage. The combination of these factors results in a highly volatile situation.

Walt's analysis builds on his earlier work *The Origins of Alliance* (1987), which offers a theoretical approach to foreign policy (particularly alliance behavior), taking "balance of threat" as a starting point. The level of threat that a state perceives, he argues, is dependent on the combined power of (aligned) enemies, the proximity of the threat, the offensive capabilities of the threat, and "aggressive

intentions."[33] *Revolution and War* (1996) shows how the circumstances after a revolution may inhibit this calculation. Following his
"balance of threat" hypothesis, Walt "suggests that revolutions cause
security competition by altering the perceived level of threat between
the revolutionary state and its main adversaries, on the one hand, and
by encouraging both sides to believe that the use of force can overcome the threat at an acceptable cost, on the other."[34] In other words,
Walt argues that revolutions do not only affect the distribution of
power, but they also

> alter perceptions of intent and beliefs about the relative strength of
> offense and defense. Beliefs about the intentions of other states and
> their specific capacity to do harm will exert a powerful influence on the
> foreign policy of revolutionary states, and the responses of other states
> will be similarly affected by their perception of the new regime.[35]

However, "as evidence accumulates the uncertainty that permits
exaggerated perceptions of threat to flourish declines proportionately.
Even if the new regime does not abandon its ultimate objectives, it is
likely to modify its short-term behavior in accordance with this new
information. Relations between the revolutionary states and the rest
of the system will become increasingly 'normal.'".[36] As such, when
Iraq invaded the newly established Islamic Republic of Iran in 1980,
this was "primarily a response to its fear of Iranian fundamentalism"
in combination with the perception that the instable period after the
revolution would prove a "window of opportunity."[37] He shows that
these were miscalculations: despite "poor leadership, inadequate sup-
plies, and rivalries within the revolutionary elite,"[38] the new Islamic
Republic was able to direct revolutionary enthusiasm against the Iraqi
aggressor. Although the Iraqis underestimated the Iranian threat, the
Iranians overestimated their capabilities and had had an "exaggerated
sense of its own military capabilities and ideological appeal"[39]: most
Iraqi Shi'a remained loyal to Baghdad even when Iranians carried the
war onto Iraqi territory. Another miscalculation on the Iranian side
was that their initial military success caused other states to support
Iraq, which meant they were unable to destroy Iraqi resistance.
    Walt (1996) provides a convincing explanation why the Iranian
regime chose to fight a war on Iraqi soil: the regime overestimated
its capabilities. He has more trouble explaining why the war was continued until 1988, when the Islamic Republic's new leader Ayatollah
Ruhollah Khomeini ordered a cease-fire. A possible answer is presented at the end of *Revolution and War*, where Walt (1996) admits

that revolutionary states' commitment to counterproductive strategies (he names not only the Iranian but also the Soviet and Chinese cases) was more persistent than he initially assumed:

> Although external pressures did lead all of these regimes to alter their behavior in significant ways, their tendency to cling to counterproductive strategies despite substantial cost was equally striking... One may speculate that such a tendency will be most severe when, first, the ideology in question is particularly extreme, and second, it has been formally institutionalized within a hegemonic ruling party.[40]

It seems then that ideological factors are more important than Walt's model accounts for. Michael Barnett, who has looking into regional politics in the Arab world, would go as far as to claim that Walt's work supports "not the logic of anarchy but rather the politics of identity; specifically, Walt assembles strong support for ideational rather than material forces driving... politics."[41] Particularly, Walt's focus on *perception of threat* shows that foreign policy is never based on an entirely objective calculation, but much embedded in how states perceive the international system and the friends and foes that constitute it.

Arshin Adib-Moghaddam's work[42] provides depth to this constructivist understanding of the Iran—Iraq War. Instead of taking anarchy as a given, as neorealists do, his study "takes anarchy to be constituted in a cultural context where different constructions of identity engage, compete and sometimes clash with each other."[43] He concludes that the state of anarchy that states perceived in the Persian Gulf region was a product of "exclusionary identity politics," creating rivalries between states, but that this anarchy is tempered by a regional (and international) acceptance of the notion of sovereignty as a right of individual states. The Iranian Revolution challenged this notion of sovereignty, Adib-Moghaddam explains: "The Pan-Islamic norms and institutions that were now pushed to the forefront—by necessity of their immanently transnational constitution—defied traditional forms of international sovereignty and diplomacy, hence contradicting prevailing norms and institutions of regional and global political culture."[44] This was perceived as threatening, particularly by the Iraqi regime. Moreover, as the Iranian regime was unable to close the gap between Sunni and Shi'a Islam (despite Khomeini's dogmatic adjustments), Iran's sphere of influence remained limited to Shi'a circles in Lebanon and Iraq.[45] These links were also regarded a threat to the Iraqi regime. As was already argued by Walt,[46] the threat the Iranian influence in Iraq formed to Iraqi stability was a logical cause for Saddam Hussein's decision to invade Iran, especially in the context of a favorable international climate.[47] However, that by itself is not an entirely satisfying explanation. Adib-Moghaddam[48] points out that Iraq at the time of the revolution was "wealthier and stronger than any other state in the modern history of Iraq and largely uncompromised by internal unrest," and that Iran did not pose a real threat, as it was at no stage during the early years of the revolution in the position to launch an attack. Walt (1996) would call this a case of misinformation on the Iraqi side, but Adib-Moghaddam[49] argues that there is an alternative reason for the Iraqi invasion, namely, one that should be seen in the context of "Arab nationalism, its anti-Iranian posture and the regime's internalized self-perception as the main pan-Arab force in the region."

Adib-Moghaddam[50] points out that within the official Iraqi discourse, Iraq's self-identification as the leader of the Arab world was shaped in contrast to the Iranian "other," who was presented as deceitful by nature, inferior within Islam, and expansionist. Attacking Iran was a tool in reproducing this identity:

> By reifying, institutionalising, ideologising Ba'thist Arab nationalism and anti-Iranianism as central narratives of Iraqi state identity, the meanings of these self-attributed precepts became reabsorbed into the Iraqi regime's consciousness as subjectively plausible representations of reality, morally sanctioned codes for collective behavior, rules of social discourse and a general plot for the conduct of foreign affairs.[51]

As such, Adib-Moghaddam's main contribution to the analysis of the Iran–Iraq War is that he points at a relationship between foreign policy and identity that is mutually constitutive. The identification of an outside threat was directly linked to the legitimacy of the Iraqi regime. This reality constructed by the Iraqi leadership was reified to such an extent that it seemed to have a reality of its own.[52] Suzanne Maloney[53] discusses a similar process on the Iranian side during the same Iran–Iraq War:

> The case of post-revolutionary Iran demonstrates the powerful, but paradoxical, instrumentality of identity in foreign affairs. The course chartered by the Islamic Republic illustrates that the revolutionary convulsion—particularly when it is the product of a mass movement and messianic leadership—can profoundly reconfigure the prevailing conceptualization of the nation's norms and values. In turn, those norms and values can empower a different role in the international arena.[54]

The Iran–Iraq War, "framed in both Islamist and, increasingly, nationalist terms, to generate popular support for the war effort and to consolidate the tenuous position of the clerical government," was instrumental in this endeavor,[55] and created path dependency once it was in place. This explains why Iran continued the war after it had defeated the Iraqi army and could have claimed victory.

Walt[56] also acknowledges how "the war had helped Khomeini and his supporters to consolidate their hold on power"; however, he could not explain why this consolidation did not lead to what he would call a normalization of policies. Maloney answers this question by showing how, once this identity was in place, the Iranian leadership found itself constrained by it, as "both the invocations of identity and the institutions established to advance them create path dependencies that are often exceedingly slow to adjust to the realities of holding power."[57] Consequently, "having described the war with Iraq in terms of morality and survival to mobilize popular support and military zeal, Iranian leadership this incurred a substantial cost in terms of its own legitimacy in acknowledging the futility of the war's continuation."[58] Once an identity is constructed, it creates "path dependency": "Identity is not infinitely malleable,"[59] but supports and reproduces itself.[60]

In sum, neorealist accounts fail to appreciate the importance of the mutual representations of a "threatening other" for foreign policy choices, which are not just instrumental but become constitutive of foreign policy. Constructivism offers a suitable alternative in that it allows for an understanding of foreign policy behavior as contextualized by such socially constructed shared ideas. It would be hard to judge whether the Iraqi threat had indeed subsided in 1982 to such an extent that the Iranian regime could have ended the war. What matters here, however, is not the objective calculation of threat, if such a thing is even possible, but the *perception* of this threat. From the perspective of Iranian domestic ideology, which had induced enormous revolutionary zeal among great segments of the population, the Iraqi threat continued to be real. Saddam's horrendous chemical attacks on Iranian towns, which came after Iran continued the war, confirmed this perception. There was no other reality for Iranians who lived through the horrors of the Iran–Iraq War. Understood from this context, there was nothing irrational about the Iranian regime's choice to continue the war: it was a struggle for survival.

Case-study Two: Iranian–Israeli "Strategic Rivalry"?

Treacherous Alliance: The Secret Dealings of Israel, Iran and the U.S.[61] provides a neorealist analysis of the ongoing rivalry between Iran and Israel. The book's main argument is that Iran's rivalry with Israel is a consequence of geopolitical circumstances, not ideology. According to Francis Fukuyama, on the back cover: "Trita Parsi makes a persuasive case that since the 1979 Revolution, Iran has consistently used ideology to achieve hard-headed national interest objectives, rather than sacrifice national interest on the altar of extremist ideological goals." In other words, ideology has been instrumental in achieving material goals, but has no explanatory power of its own. Parsi makes his case by showing that geopolitical—rather than ideological—shifts preceded the major transformations in Israeli–Iranian relations. The change of Iran's foreign policy toward Israel, he argued, did not result immediately from the Iranian Revolution in 1979, but followed a decade later. It was the consequence of a radical change in the balance of power in the region resulting from the collapse of the Soviet Union and the defeat of Iraq by the allied forces in 1991. Since then, the relations between Iran and Israel have changed radically from "secret collusion to overt collision," to quote Brzezinski, also on the back cover. The fact that the change in Iranian–Israeli relations did not result from the Iranian Revolution shows, Parsi argues, that ideology, though relevant for legitimation after the fact, is not the chief determining factor in Iranian–Israeli relations.[62]

However, Parsi's book does not so much give evidence of the absence of ideology in Iranian foreign policy strategy, as the Iranian preoccupation with geostrategic goals that could in itself be labeled ideological. Notwithstanding the relevance of the timing of the political shift in the late 1980s and early 1990s, Iran's response (as well as Israel's) to regional shifts can only be explained when taking into account foreign policy ideology. Enmity between Israel and Iran is not, as Parsi's account suggests, inherent to geopolitical circumstances, but a consequence of how these are perceived in the context of the ideologies that are supporting both regimes. Geopolitics, in other words, by itself cannot explain foreign policy behavior, because it fails to take into account the ideational context that is productive of and gives meaning to geopolitical circumstances.

Parsi[63] describes how after the revolution, Iranian cooperation with Israel continued despite the Iranian regime's anti-Israeli revolutionary discourse, which "was seldom followed up with action since Tehran's strategic interest . . . contradicted Iran's ideological imperatives." There were, in fact, significant changes in Iranian foreign policy behavior after the 1979 Revolution. These changes suggest that a change in regime ideology did, in fact, result in major changes in foreign policy. First, although much like the *shah* the revolutionary regime sought to increase its regional influence, the way in which the Iranian regime was trying to achieve this, changed radically. Parsi[64] describes this change as "befriending Iran's Arab neighbors, rather than balancing them through Iranian military preponderance and alliances with extra-regional states." Iran may not have been very successful in this effort, as "the Arabs...were terrified of Khomeini's political designs and Iran's attempts to export the Revolution,"[65] but the change was apparent nevertheless. Second, Parsi argues that despite their anti-Israeli discourse, the revolutionary regime continued their cooperation with Israel, again: much like the shah had done. The fact is, however, that the dealings between Israel and Iran did significantly change after the revolution. The Israeli Embassy was closed down and handed over to the Palestinian Liberation Organization (PLO), and, most importantly, the relations that did continue to exist between Iran and Israel were covert. Such relations are incomparable with the more-or-less overt alliance under the shah, and meant a major change in day-to-day regional politics.

Regime change, and with it a change in regime ideology, had major influence on Iran–Israel relations. The nature of these changes shows that they were ideologically driven.[66] When the Iraqi threat subsided in 1991, Iranian–Israeli relations further deteriorated. With the collapse of the Soviet Union and the Iraqi defeat, Parsi argued, Iran and Israel were now the main contenders for regional influence. However, a change in the regional status quo by itself does not explain the kind of rivalry that exists between Iran and Israel. In theory, Iran and Israel could have come to a form of coexistence or even cooperation. Even with the decline of the Iraqi threat, Israel and Iran continued to have common interests and shared common threats. Parsi[67] illustrates this when he says that both Israelis and Iranians today go about their lives thinking "the Arabs are out to get us." In practice, however, a socio-politically embedded ideology in both countries facilitated the other option: that of enmity. Iran's foreign policy discourse, as officially communicated by the state and the media, from the early days of the Republic has been relying on the identification of external enemies (as later chapters will show). Parsi argues how during the Iran–Iraq War, this enemy was Saddam's regime, and when the Iraqi's were defeated in the 1991 Gulf War, the Israeli enemy was there to take Iraq's place. In Parsi's words, Israel quickly transformed into "an aggressive competitor that had penetrated Iran's growing sphere of influence."[68] However, what in Parsi's book is described as "the need [of Israel and Iran] to portray their fundamentally strategic conflict as an ideology clash"[69] was a mutually reinforcing animosity based in domestic ideology, which manifested itself in strategic competition.

In sum, the portrayal of both the Iranian and Israeli regimes of one another as the ultimate enemy has facilitated a strategic clash between these two countries, and has precluded cooperation. Regional developments and the interactions between the two countries have reinforced the mutual representations of one and another as sworn enemies. These images shaped both countries' responses to the changes in the international power balance, and precluded peaceful coexistence or cooperation. The fact that Israel became Iran's strategic enemy after 1991, therefore, has as much to do with the domestic ideas in the context of which geostrategic changes were responded to, as the changes themselves, in which the mutual identification as enemy confirmed and reinforced rivalry. These two cannot be separated: historically constructed animosity is not easily deconstructed, which makes it appear natural and eternal.

Studying Iranian Foreign Policy

The two case studies discussed above show that constructivism provides insights into regional relations that rationalist approaches cannot provide, as they fail to take into account the social construction of identity and threat. Constructivism in these case studies does not just complement realism by adding the "ideational" factor—it offers a more complete alternative to realism as it recognizes the social construction of the world in which foreign policy is made. Both in the case of the Iran–Iraq War and the rivalry between Iran and Israel, constructivism has theoretical leverage because it treats foreign policy as tied up with perceptions of geopolitics, friends and foes, and regional roles. Moreover, it shows that these perceptions are not an "added factor" to objectively defined national interest, but that interests are defined only within this ideational context. Ideology as such is not merely instrumental: it is constitutive of foreign policy. This section discusses constructivist approaches to the study of foreign policy in more detail, and gives an account of what insights constructivist approaches to the study of Iranian foreign policy have so far yielded.

Constructivist Approaches

To be sure, constructivists do not hold a monopoly over the relationship between ideas and foreign policy. Important contributions have been made by scholars researching, for example, the impact of roles on foreign policy,[70] culture and security,[71] and worldviews and foreign policy.[72] In addition, the field of political psychology has made important contributions to the theorizing of the relationship between ideas and foreign policy.[73] Like constructivist approaches, political psychology points at the importance of unit-level factors in foreign policy making, in particular, the influence of domestic ideas on foreign policy. However, there are crucial differences between political psychology and constructivism, as the focus of the former is on the individual minds of decision-makers, their beliefs, and how they influence their choices, whereas the latter focuses on intersubjective meaning among social beings. The study at hand places itself in a constructivist tradition and as such is not so much interested in what individual policy makers believe as in how they act within a shared discursive space. This means that the concepts and mechanisms identified in the field of political psychology (such as perceptions, attitudes, and trust) retain their relevance in a constructivist context; however, they are treated less as psychological traits and more as intersubjective constructs.

Constructivism as an approach to foreign policy analysis (FPA) and IR is mostly concerned with questions of identity.[74] Also, political psychology focuses on the necessity for people to define the self in relation to the other. Constructivist approaches, however, focus on the *social construction* of these identities among agents. Identity relates to foreign policy in several ways, for example, not only when particular norms or expectations are attached to certain identities, but also in the identification of threats and allies. Identity in constructivism is a relational concept: "Identity is a social category that expresses not only the meaning any one actor attributes to the self; rather self-definitions are related to definitions the self gives to others and others to the self."[75] David Campbell[76] aptly describes the importance of danger and difference in constituting the identity of states. There are, however, numerous examples of less extreme constructions of difference that articulate "less-then-radical" others.[77] Identity in international relations can be based on dialogue and/or similarity, such as in the case of European identity: "The mechanisms for stabilizing and disciplining Eastern Europe, in fact, rely on the absence of a clear eastern border and the image of an open but diverse policy of which some are more members than others but in which none are identified as enemies or total outsiders."[78] As will be shown in chapter 4, mechanisms based on difference as well as those based on similarity are important for Iranian identity: the official discourse both sets Iran apart from one group of others, and identifies Iran with another group of others to reshape and reinforce its identity.

Identity is usually thought of in a spatial dimension, that is, foreign policy discourse constructs boundaries or delineations of space through identities.[79] Examples are not only "the United States" or "Iran," but also "the Middle East" and even more abstract subjects such as "humanity" or "the Ummah." However, Lene Hansen (2006) argues that constructions of identity are not only limited to spatial dimensions, but also include the temporal and the ethical. When it comes to temporal identity, the temporality of the other (e.g., backward) is constructed in relation to the temporality of the self (e.g., developed) and vice versa. Temporal identities imply the possibility of development, transformation, or change through which a (radical) other preferably becomes like the self (or the self like the other, in the case the other is temporally superior). Similarly, the temporal other can *be* the self, in the sense that the other, against which the identity of the self is constructed, can be a temporal construction of the self: the temporal other of its own past. An example is again European identity, which is constructed as overcoming its own violent past.[80] Ethical identity is constructed in terms of ethics, morality, and responsibility, through which foreign policy discourse articulates the (non) responsibility of the self vis-à-vis the other. In doing so, "a powerful discursive move is undertaken in that the issue is moved out of the realm of the strategic and 'selfishly national' and re-located within the 'higher grounds' of the morally good."[81] Each of these categories of identity, as will be shown in chapter 4, is important to Iranian foreign policy discourse.

However, that constructivism uses the concept of identity as the main locus of meaning also has its limitations. Not all ideas that are relevant to foreign policy can be comfortably implied in the term identity, particularly those that have to do with broader views of past and future, or problems and solutions, and so on. This is why this study has adopted the concept of ideology to include not only identity, but also perceptions, norms, myths, and other ideas implied here in the concept of worldview. That ideology as a central concept is less favored by constructivists is likely due to its negative connotation as a consequence of its pejorative use within a structural Marxist tradition. Telhami and Barnett,[82] for example, note that scholars of IR "typically portray ideology as an instrumental in the hands of self-interested leaders" and argue that "in contrast with ideology studies that attempt to understand how language masks social reality and occludes real interests, many studies of identity begin with the function of language in constituting social subjects and their relations." However, it seems that Telhami and Barnett, like most constructivists, do not only have an unnecessarily narrow definition of ideology, but also overstretch the concept of identity. Constructivists in their analyses often move beyond mere questions of "self" and "other" and look at how interests are socially constructed in the context of worldviews that go beyond matters of identity. In addition, threats are related to identity but cannot be equated to it: whether a state is identified as a friend or foe is related to, but not the same as saying, it is or is not a threat. Equally, myths, roles, and norms can be related to matters of identity, but matter for foreign policy on their own account. These concepts will, therefore, be treated in this research as "worldview," as such using the concepts of identity and worldview as the main elements of foreign policy ideology. Worldviews provide an understanding of how the world in which we live is made sense of: who are its main players, what are the main problems, how do we understand the past, and what are the prospects for the future? Within this understanding, identities get shape: who are we, and what sets us apart from others? Worldview and identity, though separated analytically because they deal with fundamentally different questions, are closely related, and can only be fully understood within each other's context, that is, the broader foreign policy ideology both are part of. Juxtapositions between "past and future" and "problems and solutions," for example, cannot be separated from questions of "them and us," as will become evident in later chapters.

The social construction of worldviews and identities explains certain continuity in ways of thinking and thus in foreign policy. First, because shared ideas about self and other, problems and available solutions, what is good and what is bad, do not develop or change overnight: they are the product of an on-going historical process in which meaning is continuously shaped and reshaped in social interaction. Even in authoritarian states, where the power to contribute to the creation and reproduction of meaning is characteristically highly unequal, regimes will need to base their ideology in popularly accepted ways of thinking. Second, and this is acknowledged by scholars outside the constructivist tradition, continuation is facilitated by the institutionalization of ideas. In the words of one prominent scholar of Middle East politics, once a way of thinking is "established and shapes the socialization of the next generation of policy makers, it sets standards of legitimacy and performance, which, to a degree, constrain elites, imparting a certain consistency to a foreign policy despite changes in leadership and environment."[83] When ideas become embedded in institutions, they influence policy in a pervasive way, as they "will be reflected in the incentives of those in the organization and those whose interests are served by it."[84] This creates path dependency in the sense that "once a policy idea leads to the creation of reinforcing organizational and normative structures, that policy idea can affect the incentives of political entrepreneurs long after the interest of its initial proponents have changed."[85]

Once an ideology is more or less established, these shared ideas form the context within which political actors behave and which they reproduce in their speech and behavior. This then is also the context within which foreign policy is made, and through this foreign policy behavior the dominant ideology is reproduced. Foreign policy makers act in an ideological context in which certain foreign policy is deemed possible, reasonable, or even necessary, whereas other options are (quite literally) unthinkable.[86] As such, foreign policy contributes to the reproduction of the social order by following the "script" ideology provides: "Foreign policy thus becomes a social practice that produces a social order as well as one through which individual and collective subjects themselves are produced and reproduced."[87]

Thus, ideology is constitutive of foreign policy in that it provides the discursive field in which foreign policy makers act. It defines what is considered possible and desirable in the context of the shared ideas of those who make foreign policy. Through foreign policy behavior, foreign policy actors confirm this ideology, particularly when the enactment of foreign policy means the actualization of the discourse—what is said becomes true. Examples are the self-fulfilling prophecy of paranoia and the conscious "acting as if" to create space, which are both discussed in chapter 3.[88] Foreign policy then can contribute to regime legitimacy, if the regime is able to present its foreign policy as being in line with the dominant ideology. Regime legitimacy as such is not just achieved through what Sedgwick[89] calls output legitimacy—which is mainly material benefit—but also through the reproduction of the ideology supporting the regime through foreign policy. Regimes that "do as they say" confirm their claim to power: if a leader identifies a certain threat or opportunity and then acts accordingly, he (or she) confirms their legitimacy. Moreover, by acting within this logic, a regime reproduces the ideology that supports its power: it is not mere rhetoric, but becomes real through enactment in foreign policy. In sum, ideology for foreign policy has related constituting and legitimizing functions. This means ideology is both outside of the reach of individual foreign policy makers as well as within their reach for instrumental use for the purpose of regime legitimacy—though only limitedly. Ideology is after all not static, but continuously recreated, and rulers have larger shares in this reproduction. As such regimes are able to reshape this discourse to some extent, and to the advantage of maintaining regime legitimacy. That foreign policy makers act within a discursive context on which they are dependent, but that which they are also able to shape, can perhaps be best described as a symbiosis: ideology can be reshaped only with moderation. Chapter 2 discusses further the concept of ideology.

The limitations of realism—and advantages of constructivism—that the case studies of the Iran–Iraq War and Iranian–Israeli rivalry illustrate have led some scholars to argue for a fundamental cross-fertilization between realism and constructivism, and even for novel approaches in which both approaches are combined.[90] This has produced a lively debate on the compatibility of realism and constructivism,[91] which offers a possible middle ground for researching the relationship between ideas and foreign policy. However, the debate on the compatibility between realism and constructivism is somewhat limited by the fact that both Sterling-Folker and Barkin exclude postmodern constructivism (arguably, critical and poststructuralist constructivism) from their analysis, and focus on what Karin Fierke[92] has called conventional constructivism. This book then takes an approach in which rationalism is put aside and constructivist ontology is married to a constructivist epistemology and methodology, within the tradition of what Fierke calls consistent constructivism. The more challenging theoretical endeavor would perhaps be to decide whether this book should be placed in a poststructuralist or critical constructivist tradition. Subsequent chapters will only add to the confusion, as this book borrows from both traditions, and supplements these moreover with critical discourse analysis in sociology, hermeneutics, Marxist, and post-Gramscian thought. It is up to the reader whether such eclecticism is to be excused.[93] Certainly, it is not the purpose of this book to provide a complete theory of the relationship between ideas and foreign policy, but rather to gain insight into this relationship in the Iranian case. Moreover, the aforementioned theories and approaches do share the ontological premise of a socially constructed world in which the material and ideational are mutually constitutive, and in which meaning is central to the reproduction of power relations.

Ideas and Foreign Policy in Iran

Few constructivist insights have been applied to the study of Iranian foreign policy,[94] both in Iran where the debate is dominated by a "realist" versus "idealist" paradigm,[95] as well as in the study of Iran from without. When studies of Iranian foreign policy behavior do take ideational factors into account, these are treated as a constraint on an otherwise rational foreign policy. Shireen Hunter, for example, describes how regime ideology has kept the Iranian regime from adapting to the post-Cold War era, leading to a "determination to ignore changing systemic dynamics and insist of self-defeating policies."[96] For instance, in its efforts to come to a Russian–Iranian alliance, the Iranian regime failed to realize that Russia was neither willing to engage in a global competition with the United States, nor would it want to see Iran's regional influence expanded. "More seriously," she says, "Iran did not realize that remaining at odds with the West weakened its hand in dealing with Russia. Consequently...Iran's relations with Russia, instead of leading to strategic alliance, became a fool's bargain."[97] However, later chapters will show that what Hunter describes as the inability of Iran to adapt itself to the international system, Iranian leaders motivate as an explicit *choice* for building an alternative system, and it has maximized its adaptability in terms of taking ideational resources from this environment. Moreover, rather than seeing the international system as an unchangeable fact to which it needs to adapt, Iran's foreign policy decision-makers[98] treat the international order as changeable per se. Within this context, it is not in Iran's interest to conform to the international order, as this would strengthen and not challenge it. With this worldview in mind, the Iranian regime is not so much failing to adapt to the international order, but trying to build an alternative one. This sheds light on Iranian foreign policy behavior with regard to, among other things, the nuclear issue, which Hunter herself calls "a hallmark of Iran's revolutionary ideology" through which the regime "has been striving for independence and self-sufficiency, notably in scientific and technological areas, because such self-sufficiency is necessary for political independence."[99] The nuclear issue as such is essential to the Iranian regime's efforts to break Western attempts at creating an international consensus against Iran, as will be argued in chapter 6.

   Acknowledging that Iranian foreign policy (or that of any other country) is made possible within an ideological context is one thing, to map out this ideological context another. So far, the literature on Iranian foreign policy ideology has not provided a comprehensive account of Iranian foreign policy ideas and this is where this study aims to make a contribution. To the extent that it is discussed, analysts trace back Iranian foreign policy ideas to the 1979 Revolution that marks the birth of the current Islamic Republic. Anoush Ehteshami and Mahjoob Zweiri,[100] for example, identify four fundamental principles in the Islamic Republic's 1979 constitution, which influence foreign policy: "first, rejection of all forms of external domination; second, preservation of Iran's independence and territorial integrity;

third, defense of the rights of all Muslims without allying with hegemonic powers; and, fourth, the maintenance of peaceful relations with
all non-belligerent states." In addition, Adib-Moghaddam[101] starts
with the 1979 Revolution and identifies an "Islamic utopian romanti-
cism" as the basis of Iran's strategic preferences, which inspired Iran's
revolutionary generation "with the idea that radical independence
from both superpowers would start a process at the end of which the
existing world order would be transformed." This, he says, explains
the Iranian regime's norm of "neither East nor West, only the Islamic
Republic," its decision to end its membership of Cold War institutions, its prolonged war with Iraq, its support for the PLO, its sympa-
thy with leftist movements in Latin America, and its decision to sever
ties with Apartheid South Africa.[102] Others argue that Iranian foreign
policy ideas may have changed radically after the 1979 Revolution, but
have also retained elements, which are less Islamic or revolutionary. R.
K. Ramazani,[103] for example, identifies pre-Islamic principles, Islamic-
era principles, nationalist-democratic principles, antidemocratic and
democratic principles, as well as revolutionary principles in Iranian
foreign policy ideology. In addition, Suzanne Maloney[104] points at a
"prism of competing influences" and includes Persian nationalism and
Islamism as well as revolutionary antiimperialism in her analysis, while
Ansari[105] distinguishes religious culture, national culture, and Western
culture as sources of Iranian foreign policy thought. Hunter[106] offers
yet another categorization: historical experience and anticolonial-
ism, militant Third Worldism, Islamist influences, Leftist ideas, Arab
Radicalism, and Khomeini's ideas.

What many studies of Iranian foreign policy thinking have in common is that they contrast revolutionary ideas (predominantly Iran's
Islamic identity and independence from foreign powers) with Iran's
Persian and more secular identity, compatible also with democratic
principles.[107] While the latter are associated with a more "pragmatic"
or rational foreign policy, focused on economic and strategic interest,
the former are linked to Iran's "ideological" policies of supporting
regional Islamist groups and supposed efforts to export the revolution. The discrepancy between these goals then leads to "an inconsistent and irrational foreign policy, trying to reconcile irreconcilable
goals."[108] The question remains then whether this supposed irrecon-
cilability is perceived as such by Iranian foreign policy makes. Within
Iranian foreign policy discourse what are in the literature treated as
separate and competing influences in fact may interrelate and complement each other, without ever leading to the kind of paradox or
ambiguity anticipated by outside observers. The preoccupation with a

realist paradigm has encouraged observers both in and outside Iran to label what is familiar to Western conduct as rational, and what is different as irrational, without being aware of the bias of the rationalist paradigm in which this observation is made.

There is another problem with current conceptualizations of Iranian foreign policy ideas: none of the categorizations offered in the literature so far are based on a thorough and structured investigation of Iranian foreign policy discourse. On the contrary, they are either collected from other academic texts on Iranian identity, refer to a small selection of quotes from Iranian thinkers or officials that support the categorizations offered, or are inferred from foreign policy behavior that cannot otherwise be explained. Such a reading of Iranian foreign policy ideas is, however, prone to bias and may lead to the inclusion of ideas that are in fact not directly relevant for Iranian foreign policy behavior. Brenda Shaffer's study of Iran's support for Armenia in the Nagorno–Karabakh conflict is an example of how erroneous perceptions of what constitutes Iranian foreign policy ideology results in an incorrect analysis: Brenda Shaffer[109] sees Iran's Shi'a identity as central to foreign policy ideas, only to conclude that these ideas did not influence Iran's choice to support Armenia in its conflict with Azerbaijan. After all, Azerbaijan is a Shi'a-dominated country. Iran's support for Armenia is taken as evidence that identity does not matter in foreign policy. However, not only is Shi'ism as a distinct identity of negligible importance to Iran's foreign policy ideology, as chapter 4 will show, but also protecting "oppressed" against "oppressors" is in fact one of the main pillars of this ideology. An Iranian scholar pointed out to me that Iran's support for Armenia was much in line with Iran's foreign policy ideology, in the context of which Azerbaijan was quickly identified as the aggressor against which Nagorno–Karabakh needed protection.[110] This is not to say that strategic calculations did not matter for Iran in their support for Armenia, but rather that these calculations should be understood in the context of foreign policy discourse.

One of the more elaborate and eloquent discussions of Iranian foreign policy ideology is offered by Arshin Adib-Moghaddam.[111] He refers to the thought of Al-e Ahmad, Mottahari, Shari'ati, and Khomeini in mapping out regime ideology. There is no doubt that these thinkers greatly contributed to the Iranian regime's foreign policy ideology, and inquiring into these sources gives important information about Iranian foreign policy ideas. Particularly, as Adib-Moghaddam argues himself, since this revolutionary narrative developed dynamism of its own, transcending "both the power of its makers and its agents" during the revolution, which were then institutionalized in the Islamic Republic after the toppling of the shah and today remain the pillars of Iranian foreign policy discourse. "Ultimately," he argues, "it was this process that established Iran as a revisionist power in international affairs."[112] What matters for the study at hand, however, is foreign policy ideology itself—not the thought that inspired it or the historical developments that contextualize it. Tracing the roots of current ideology back to Iranian history and political philosophy is useful, in that it gives an indication of which historical facts and which body of philosophy the regime can refer to and build on in the articulation of a dominant ideology. This is essential because it shows how ideology is the product of a genealogy, and emphasizes how it constitutes perceptions of power, shared history, and so on, which then severely limits the possibilities for instrumental use of ideology by those in power. What matters for the study at hand though is not so much what collective memories, sentiments, and bodies of literature (etc.) the regime can appeal to, but *whether it does* and *in what way*.

A final limitation of existing studies of Iranian foreign policy ideas is that these generally do not theorize on how ideology stands in relation to foreign policy behavior. Most of this literature argues, generally speaking, that Iranian foreign policy cannot be fully understood outside of the ideological context in which foreign policy is made. However, this does not move us beyond ideology as the "missing link" in otherwise rationalist explanations of foreign policy. In other words, while the literature makes evident *that* ideas matter for Iranian foreign policy, it does not show *how* and *when* they matter. This book then builds on existing literature within a constructivist tradition shows the different ways in which ideology and foreign policy are mutually constitutive, focusing primarily on discourse.[113]

Conclusion

In taking a consistent constructivist approach to the study of Iranian foreign policy, this book aims to fill at least three gaps. First, it responds to calls among prominent scholarly works on the foreign policies of Middle East states to study foreign policy in the context of domestic factors. This focus on the domestic does not mean that systemic factors are irrelevant, but that responses to international, systemic conditions get shape domestically. Second, this study expands on the insights yielded in the body of literature on Middle East foreign policies on the relevance of "the ideational" for foreign policy, by taking ideology as its main focus. However, this research does not treat ideology as an added factor to conventional approaches, but understands it as the primary context for foreign policy making. It is consistently constructivist in that it accepts the ontological premise that the social world as relevant to our studies is socially constructed and subject to constant renegotiation. Thus, contrary to approaches that treat ideology as a "straightjacket"[114] or a "playing field,"[115] in which ideology forms a boundary to otherwise rational calculations, this research's premise is that rationality does not exist outside of its ideological context. There is no separation between ideology, on the one hand, and realist calculations, on the other. This means that when Ray Takeyh[116] holds that Iranian foreign policy is driven by "great power pretensions" rather than "ideology," a constructivist would instead say that great power claims *are inherent to* the Iranian regime's foreign policy ideology (see chapter 4). Moreover, those who identify shifts between "realism" and "idealism" in Iranian foreign policy behavior actually point to shifts between a focus on economic benefit and moral roles: two competing elements within a hybrid foreign policy ideology. Morality as such is not more "ideological" than economy (or, in other words, economic policy not more "rational" than morality), as both are functional within the ideational context in which foreign policy is made. Third, this book fills a gap by offering a comprehensive account of Iranian foreign policy ideology under Ahmadinejad based on rigorous discourse analysis. So far, studies of Iranian foreign policy ideology have neither offered a comprehensive account, nor showed how it relates to foreign policy. By building on the work of Doty, Fierke, and Hansen, this book does both. In sum, this book's constructivist approach to Iranian foreign policy aims at deepening the understanding of Iranian foreign policy behavior through a focus on domestic foreign policy ideology as the main context in which foreign policy gets shape.

Chapter 2

Ideology and Legitimacy during Ahmadinejad's Presidency

The rise of the neoconservatives in Iran, culminating in the election of Ahmadinejad in 2005, meant an authoritarian turn in Iranian politics. While the political system of the Islamic Republic had authoritarian characteristics from the outset, it had experienced a period of relative cultural freedom under the reformist President Mohammad Khatami. The turn to authoritarian policies was a response to this period of relative freedom, and an attempt by conservatives to regain control. Under Ahmadinejad, increased authoritarianism was visible in particular in increased state censorship, repression, and in the systematic exclusion of reformists from governmental institutions. The regime, in its efforts to ensure its continuity in the face of calls for reform, firmly held on to its revolutionary legacy. State domination of the media made sure that the regime's preferred views were readily available to the populace. As such, under the circumstances of waning regime legitimacy, revolutionary ideology gained increased importance in the regime's struggle for survival. This chapter first explains the relevance of ideology to the functioning and survival of authoritarian regimes, and then continues by applying these insights to the increasingly authoritarian Iranian regime during Ahmadinejad's presidency.

Ideology, Legitimacy, and Repression

No government or regime, not even an authoritarian one, can function in the absence of ideology. The concept of ideology traditionally refers to "ideas bound up with power" and has a distinctly political character. It includes all ideas relevant to power relations, particularly the legitimation and reproduction of the sociopolitical order in which, inevitably, some groups have more power than others. To be sure, different scholars have formulated their personal definitions of ideology, which often do not correspond, and may even contradict each other. Moreover, scholars who use the concept of ideology may talk about essentially different things, and equally, those speaking of ideology may use different words to denote it: concepts such as culture, legitimacy, discourse, and identity may be conceptualized in such a way that they are identical to certain definitions of ideology.[1] Taking this ambiguity as given, one should keep in mind that, as Robert Cox said, a concept in the social sciences "is loose and elastic and attains precision only when brought into contact with a particular situation which it helps to explain—a contact which also develops the meaning of the concept." [2] What is required then is a definition for the purposes of the research at hand. For the purpose of this study, ideology is conceptualized as interrelated ideas (such as norms, values, perceptions, and meanings) that create, recreate, and sustain a sociopolitical order, while being recreated and sustained by this order.[3] Social practices, particularly but not exclusively through language, take a central role in this (re-)production.

The neutral definition of ideology as "ideas inherent to sociopolitical order" parts with the pejorative definition that is common in both Marxism and the everyday use of the word "ideology." Ideology here is not "the thought of the other," as "to characterize a view as 'ideological' is, it seems, already implicitly to criticize it."[4] The current conceptualization of ideology avoids assigning ideology solely to others, particularly, to see it as alien to the West, and avoids the orientalism prevalent in some studies of culture and politics in the Middle East region. There is no such thing as "the possibility of a society without ideology—whether a Marxist society where ideology seen as a bulwark of class power will no longer be necessary or a capitalist society where the self-evident norms of a rational market will impose themselves."[5] Ideology is inherent to the functioning of *any* society, including those based on Marxist, capitalist, or other labeled or unlabeled beliefs.

Four further characteristics of ideology deserve attention. First, "ideologies are usually internally complex, differentiated formations, with conflicts between their various elements, which need to be continually renegotiated and resolved."[6] This diffuse character of ideology is part of its strength: "What makes a dominant ideology powerful—its ability to intervene in the consciousness of those it subjects, appropriating and reinflecting their experience—is also what makes it internally heterogeneous and inconsistent"[7]. Moreover, ideology is not stable, but in constant transformation. In Gramscian thought, "ideology must be seen as a battle field, as a continuous struggle,"[8] quite different from "already elaborated, closed world-views. Ideological ensembles existing at a given moment are the result of the relations of forces between the rival hegemonic principles and they undergo a perpetual process of transformation."[9] Therefore, ideology

> will always be a complex ensemble whose contents can never be determined in advance since it depends on a whole series of historical and national factors and also on the relations of forces existing at a particular moment in the struggle for hegemony.[10]

Second, ideology is neither delusional nor irrational. Few would disagree that "in order to be truly effective, ideologies must make at least some minimal sense of people's experiences, must conform to some degree with what they know of social reality from their practical interaction with it."[11] More fundamentally, one could argue that it is impossible to differentiate between observable truth and ideology, as "the symbolic forms through which we express ourselves and understand others do not constitute some ethereal other world which stands opposed to what is real: rather, they are partly constitutive of what, in our societies, 'is real.'"[12] Ideology is inherent to the social realm in which people make sense of the world around them—they do not normally conceive of reality outside of this intersubjective understanding. "To view an ideology from the outside is to recognize its limits; but from the inside these boundaries vanish into infinity, leaving the ideology curved back upon itself like cosmic space."[13]

Third, ideology can to some extent be seen as a top-down tool for domination, in which ideas are imposed by the rulers on their subordinates, mobilizing meaning in the service of their own power, which is prevalent in critical studies and which lies at the basis of the idea of ideology as legitimization. The view of ideology as a tool for domination is, however, too restricted. One argument for this is that ideology, engrained in the organization of social practice and the institutionalization of power, in many ways "rules the ruler" as much as the ruled. Although rulers may have some room for maneuver, as ideologies are going through constant transformation, ideology is not infinitely malleable even by the most powerful ruler. Ideology is after all not "created out of nothing," but evolves in a historical/traditional context, needs a certain level of consistency and continuity, and is inherent to (not separate from) the sociopolitical organization and institutionalization. Regimes to a large extent draw on (and reproduce) existing structures, understandings, and sentiments. Moreover, a regime is bound by the institutions it creates to stabilize and perpetuate its own rule. According to Cox, "Institutions reflect the power relations prevailing at their point of origin and tend, at least initially, to encourage collective images consistent with these power relations."[14] This institutionalization, however, creates path dependencies, which limit the possibilities for action. Ideology as such has a structurizing effect in which power relations are reproduced not only "because meaning is mobilized in support of them, but simply because this is how things have always been done."[15] Another argument why ideology should be seen as more than a top-down tool for domination is that power "cannot be thought of in terms of one group having a monopoly of power, simply radiating power downwards on a subordinate group by an exercise of simple domination from above." Instead, it circulates between the dominant and the dominated. "The argument is that everyone—the powerful and the powerless—is caught up, *though not on equal terms*, in power's circulation. No one—neither its apparent victims nor its agents—can stand wholly outside its field of operation."[16]

Fourth, ideology is not separate from the material and institutional factors that make up a sociopolitical order, but intrinsically linked to them through a mutually constitutive relationship. Gramsci and Foucault, important theoretical differences aside, would agree that power "involves knowledge, representation, ideas, cultural leadership and authority, as well as economic constraint and physical coercion."[17] Ideology structurizes[18] and confirms the sociopolitical order, and ideology "needs" "the material and institutional structure for the elaboration and spreading of ideology" such as "schools, churches, the entire media and even architecture and the name of the streets."[19] Cox's (1981) framework proves particularly helpful here, as he incorporates material, institutional, and ideational factors in his model of sociopolitical order. Cox's model shows how the three factors of ideas, institutions, and material circumstances are interrelated. The institutional factor is important as it includes not just physical institutions such as schools and mosques, but also forms a link between the ideational and the institutional through what Fairclough[20] calls the "social practice" through which the sociopolitical order is reproduced. The material includes coercion, networks of patronage as well as relations of production—all of which have an important institutional and ideational dimension. A poststructuralist understanding would take the concept of ideology even further, and treat ideology as the context in which reality is perceived. Human beings perceive of material factors within an ideological context, which means that the social relevance of material gets shape in the context of ideology. This does not mean that material forces are not "real," but it means that their reality is not a matter of objective "being there," but of subjective perception.[21] Poststructuralists then focus on the creation of meaning, particularly representations of self and other as a context for behavior. This is an important difference with post-Gramscian thought; however, what matters here is that neither view treats the material as utterly irrelevant. On the contrary, studies of ideology show *in what way* material and institutional factors are relevant to the continuation (or challenging) of power relations. Economic despair, for example, becomes a challenge to the regime not before lower classes come to see their economic position as not only unfair, but also as changeable through collective action.[22] It is entirely possible, as is the premise of Gramsci's work, that those disadvantaged by economic structures accept the dominant ideology to such extent that they see no reason to challenge these structures and in fact contribute to their reproduction.

Ideology does not just constitute, but also legitimizes power, and in its legitimizing function, ideology also interrelates with both material and institutional circumstances underpinning the status quo. Particularly economic structures that contribute to the economic well-being of (a segment of the) people contribute to the idea that the regime is worthy of support (by this segment), and as such reinforce the ruling ideology. This makes it difficult to differentiate between belief in the system for material reasons and belief in the system for normative reasons. Arguably, individuals are more likely to accept or propagate other elements of the dominant ideology if the status quo contributes to their interest, not in the last place because people are in need of meaning beyond material incentives.[23] It should therefore be hard to determine when in a particular sociopolitical order those segments of the population that grant the regime legitimacy are motivated mainly by material enthusiasm or by a genuine belief in the system, as arguably these are two sides of the same coin. Similarly, fear may motivate the granting of legitimacy to a repressive regime as much as conviction, particularly in totalitarian states where divergence from state ideology equals treason and regime machinations isolate individuals from their peers.[24] Under such circumstances, people believe what they are required to believe for the sole reason of self-preservation, if not physically, then to avoid "mental claustrophobia."[25] Although Stalin's rule may have had its appeal to some, it is impossible to judge the extent of this appeal in a system in which no alternative views were available and which allowed no space for critical reflection. Accounts of individuals living under Stalin confirm that for many obedience out of fear and obedience out of belief were difficult to tell apart.[26]

In other words, sources of regime legitimacy cannot always be clearly distinguished. Particularly, as the survival of a sociopolitical order does not necessarily indicate the success of regime's efforts to galvanize legitimacy. In fact, regimes that suffer from a severe crisis of legitimacy may survive, either because there is no serious challenge to their power or because their repressive system is able to counter challenges. When a regime that is suffering from a legitimacy crisis nonetheless experiences no challenge to their power, the duress of everyday life could be responsible for the continuation of a sociopolitical order. People may simply be

> too exhausted after a hard day's work to have much energy left to engage in political activity, or…too fatalistic or apathetic to see the point of such activity…Ruling classes have at their disposal a great many such techniques of "negative" social control, which are a good deal more prosaic and material than persuading their subjects that they belong to a master race or exhorting them to identify with the destiny of the nation.[27]

A similar situation in which regime continuation is not dependent on legitimacy occurs when the majority of the people choose to go along with the system despite their disbelief, feigning acquiescence. According to Lisa Wedeen, so far, studies of ideology and politics "fail to distinguish between public dissimulation of loyalty or belief, on the one hand, and real loyalty and belief, on the other."[28] A similar argument is made by Scott in *Weapons of the Weak*[29]: the subordinated he discusses in his work are able to demystify the prevailing ideology, and challenge their repression through small acts of resistance. Scott uses this argument to show that Gramscian and Foucaultian approaches to power, which put much emphasis on ideology, are misleading. The ideas underpinning the power structure are not believed by the subordinates and thus, Scott implies, are irrelevant to the continuation of power. From the works of Wedeen and Scott, the conclusion could easily be drawn that material factors, such as the organization of production or physical repression, ensure the continuity of a system and that ideology here is merely the disbelieved legitimation after the fact. That conclusion is, however, drawn too quickly: even if an ideology does not successfully legitimize a sociopolitical order, it continues to structure it. Mitchell[30] in his critique of Scott's *Weapons of the Weak* shows how a dominant ideology retains its relevance for the continuation of a sociopolitical order in the absence of belief, as ideology continues to structure the people's views of the options open to them. In *Weapons of the Weak*, Mitchell argues, subordinated groups with their "small acts of resistance" expresses their disagreement with the way power is organized; however, in their everyday practice, they merely reproduce this order.

Ideology, in other words, does not lose its function in sustaining a political order when it is not (or no longer) believed: despite their disbelief in the legitimacy of the way in which power is organized, subordinated groups reproduce this order through every day practices, even through the small acts of resistance they see possible for themselves. The system as a whole—and the shared ideas that reproduce it—remains in place. When Lisa Wedeen argues that Hafez Al-Assad's power was not based on legitimacy, but rather on compliance, pointing to "the role of rhetoric and symbols in producing political power *in the absence of* belief or emotional commitment,"[31] what matters is people's conformity to the mechanism of ideology despite disbelief. The relevance of ideology to the survival of the Syrian regime was principally not for its legitimizing capacity. Rather, ideology aided social-political continuity through its enactment *despite* the absence of legitimacy. This should not come as a surprise, since the (re)production of the sociopolitical order does not merely take place through what people think or say, but particularly through what people *do*, and for which ideology provides, as it were, the "social script." Norman Fairclough calls these "interconnected networks of social practice," which constitute a social order and in which "all practices are part of production: they are the arenas within which social life is produced, be it economic, political, cultural, or everyday life." [32] Even if openly disagreeing with the way power and politics are organized, people tend to reproduce the social-political order through their acts. Ideology as such structures social practice and by doing so reproduces the status quo instead of challenging it, even in the case of limited regime legitimacy.

The relevance of ideology to authoritarian regimes seems counter intuitive: authoritarianism by definition is a reliance on a combination of repression, patronage, and/or forms of broader socioeconomic benefit. However, authoritarian states' total control of the media, the use of censorship, and interference in academic curricula suggests there is an equally important ideological component to authoritarian rule. The tools authoritarian regimes have at their disposal to maintain their powers are, first, the ability to manipulate ideology to their own advantage. State domination of the media, as well as several means of social engineering and cooptation, contributes to the persistence of one ideology, particularly as access to alternative views is limited and critical reflection is not encouraged. To a large extent, these strategies are directed at preventing the emergence of an independent civil society, partly through cooptation of emerging civil society, turning nongovernment organizations (NGOs) into government-organized nongovernmental organizations (GONGOs) and the like. In practice, this means authoritarian states are characterized by state domination of "civil" society and the media, censorship on artistic expression, state management of educational curricula, and intimidation, imprisonment, and torture of dissident academics, journalists, artists, and writers.

Second, authoritarian regimes have at their disposal repressive means, which contribute to the continuation of a sociopolitical order under circumstances of minimal regime legitimacy. The importance of coercive mechanisms for regime survival, including outright physical repression through security forces for authoritarian survival, is impossible to deny; however, political systems hardly ever rely on repression alone.[33] Repression without any form of legitimacy is short lived: the 1952 Egyptian and the 1979 Iranian revolutions both showed the failure of attempting a system based completely on coercion,[34] particularly when mobilizing the security forces that, in both cases, were unwilling to defend a regime they no longer considered legitimate. The extent to which authoritarian regimes rely on either repression or consent may vary. Louis Althusser (1970)[35] provides a useful typology when he distinguishes between an "ideological state apparatus" and a "repressive state apparatus." While the former functions primarily on the basis of consent, only retaining a certain level of repression to be able to function, the latter

> functions massively and predominantly by repression (including physical repression), while functioning secondarily by ideology. (There is no such thing as a purely repressive apparatus.) For example, the Army and the Police also function by ideology both to ensure their own cohesion and reproduction, and in the 'values' they propound externally.[36]

Authoritarian states are characterized by a reliance on repression for political survival; however, there is no such thing as an entirely repressive state. Holger Albrecht and Oliver Schlumberger[37] even emphasize the need *particularly for authoritarian regimes* to galvanize legitimacy. After all, "the lack of *democratic* regime legitimacy is, by definition, an inherent feature of every nondemocratic polity. Thus, our assumption is that the search for some form of legitimacy must be at the core of every regime-survival strategy in nondemocratic polities."[38] As long as the sociopolitical order remains unchallenged or is challenged but the repressive apparatus is strong enough to counter this threat, ideology continues to structure social practice. Ideology enables the functioning of the system—it guides social behavior, the "how things are done."

States that rely mainly on repression, cooptation, and patrimonial networks may have difficulty finding legitimacy among the broader populace. Hence, most authoritarian regimes in the Middle East today would find themselves having only minority-based legitimacy. The depth of the legitimacy crisis of Arab authoritarian regimes became visible in the uprisings, which lead to the fall of the regimes of Zine El-Abidine Ben Ali in Tunisia, Hosni Mubarak in Egypt, and Muammar Khaddafi in Libya, and to the civil war in Syria. The fact that these uprisings started only in 2011 (and not before), and so far with limited success in terms of democratic reform, shows that authoritarian regimes have a range of strategies at their disposal to ensure the continuation of their power despite structural legitimacy deficits. Such regimes are likely to try and preserve what legitimacy they have, as well as try to expand their legitimacy, as this enhances regime stability and contributes to regime survival. However, a regime that does enjoy a high level of legitimacy is also likely to seek ways to increase legitimacy, for example, through reforms or an assertive foreign policy. Legitimacy after all refers not so much to a given rule at a given moment, as to the on-going justification of this rule. These "processes of legitimation"[39] are constantly on the mind of authoritarian regimes. The Iranian regime is no exception.

Regime Legitimacy under Ahmadinejad

Ideology legitimizes and structurizes sociopolitical order. Even in situations of limited regime legitimacy, ideology retains its relevance as the "rules of the game" by which the sociopolitical order functions. Moreover, regimes may try to regain legitimacy by ideological means, particularly when regimes dominate the mass media. It is impossible to tell to which extent the Iranian regime under Ahmadinejad was granted legitimacy by the Iranian people, and to which extent state benefits and repression guaranteed compliance.[40] It is certain, however, that with the rise of the neoconservatives, Iranian politics took an authoritarian turn. There is an apparent break with the period under the reformist President Mohammad Khatami from 1997 until

2005, who tried to culturally and economically liberalize the country and propagated a dialogue among civilizations regarding foreign policy. To call the Iranian political landscape under Ahmadinejad authoritarian *pur sang* is however a simplification: there remained too much pluralism in Iranian politics, facilitated by factionalism and a large amount of government institutions. This section starts out by discussing the institutional make-up of the Islamic Republic, showing both its strengths and weaknesses with regard to regime legitimacy. It continues by describing its material sources of legitimacy, as well as obstacles to it. State domination of the economy is central in this. Last, this chapter discusses the regime's revolutionary legacy and shows its centrality to the regime's struggle for survival.

Institutional Legitimacy

The basic characteristic of authoritarianism is the limitation of personal freedom to ensure obedience to authority.[41] Authoritarian states can be autocratic, meaning ruled by one individual with absolute power, but may also be oligarchic or have elements of democratic competition. Authoritarian regimes are characterized, however, by closed circles of elites. Albrecht and Schlumberger distinguish two typical patterns of elite dynamics in authoritarian regimes: continuous elite circulation from one post to another as well as elite maintenance, keeping the same people in the same position.[42] Restricted competition and fraudulent elections make sure the pool of personnel remains stable. To a certain extent, Iranian politics fits this authoritarian profile. At the same time, the Iranian political system has democratic elements that are absent in most authoritarian states. Moreover, the label of authoritarianism does not do justice to the persistent factionalism among Iranian elites. Both the democratic elements and factionalism give make Iranian politics more diverse and less predictable than that of authoritarian states. Moreover, these dynamics give the impression that the Iranian electorate has some say in Iranian politics.

At the state level, Iran's political structure comprises several elected bodies: the *majles* (parliament), the Presidency, and the Expert Assembly, which elects the supreme leader. While theocratic institutions have the last word in most political processes, there is enough competition between the two to speak of a "dualism." Iran's officials often emphasize the popular and democratic character of the Islamic Republic, particularly after elections have taken place. The contested June 2009 elections, for example, were praised by the elites as yet another example of the trust of the nation in the political system.

During his Friday prayer sermon a week after the elections, the leader thanked the nation for participating in the ballot, which he described as "unprecedented," "magnificent," and "a great display of the people's fondness for their system."[43] Rafsanjani, during the prayers a month later, said "The people broke a record as far as presence at the ballot boxes was concerned. We all have to thank the people who participated freely in the election at a time when no other country has seen such a level of participation."[44] Similar statements have been made after other elections, restating Iran's democracy and the popularity of the political system. However, these officials ignore that democracy in Iran is institutionally limited by a nonelected overlay in the political system, as set out in the constitution of 1979 (amended in 1989),[45] comprising the Office of the Supreme Leader, the Guardian Council, and the Expediency Council.

From the point of view of the constitution, the supreme leader of the revolution is by far the most powerful person in Iranian politics. He has the authority to dictate the general policies and supervise the execution of these policies, is commander-in-chief of the armed forces, and appoints senior state officials including the commanders of the Revolutionary Guards (*sepah-e pasdaran*) and the regular army (*artesh*), the head of the Judiciary, the head of the state media, the Friday prayer leaders, and half of the members of the Guardian Council. In addition, the supreme leader has a vast network of special representatives throughout all state institutions, as well as cultural and religious institutes. He also appoints the directors of the international cultural bureaus, which are based within the embassies but operate independently.[46] However, there are some important limitations to the power of the supreme leader. First, instead of a political structure with one leader at the top, the Iranian political system consists of multiple layers and power centers: "Authority is delegated among different state institutions, thus circumventing the *velayat-e faqih* system and therefore the absolute power of the supreme leader."[47] The supreme leader as such may be powerful, but his office needs to work together with, and is dependent on, a countless number of other institutions. Second, Supreme Leader Ayatollah Ali Khamenei"'s charisma and constituency is limited, particularly when compared to his predecessor Khomeini. Particularly his religious credentials are challenged by other clerics, such as "Green Ayatollah" Ali Mohammad Dastgheib, member of the Expert Assembly, who emphasized that Khamenei was not a *marja-e taqlid* (source of emulation) when he was appointed supreme leader, but was only elevated to that status for political reasons after his appointment—an elevation that remains disputed in the clerical establishment. Although Dastgheib's views are not shared by the majority of members of the Expert Assembly, who elect and oversee the supreme leader, critics of his religious standing can seriously harm Khamenei's popular legitimacy.[48]

A third limitation to the supreme leader's power is his traditional role as a balancer. While associated with the conservative right that took over power after the death of Khomeini in 1989, Khamenei is also connected to Iran's reformist individuals and families such as Mohammad Khatami,[49] and was sympathetic to the neoconservatives, not in the last place to President Ahmadinejad himself. It seems that, much like Khomeini, Khamenei has tried to moderate the political process, shifting his weight behind one faction or another to keep a political balance. In a political system that unites different factions, all of which are loyal to the Islamic Republic, but which differ in opinion as to what its policies should be, a powerful, balancing leader proves effective in securing stability and continuity.[50] In 2005, Khamenei may have had little choice but to support the newly elected Ahmadinejad, while at the same time increasing the power of the Expediency Council (headed at the time by Ahmadinejad's rival Rafsanjani) to supervise the new government.[51] In 2007, Khamenei also appointed key figures from the pragmatic conservative camp to this council, and created the Supreme Council for Foreign Relations: an advisory foreign policy council, including the two former foreign ministers Ali Akbar Velayati and Kamal Kharazi. Conversely, he appointed the hardline Esmail Ahmadi Moghaddam to head the national police force already in July 2005, replacing the more moderate Mohammad-Bagher Qalibaf, which indicated a hardening on social freedoms.[52] This all indicates that Khamenei tried to maintain a balancing role, at least among Iran's conservative right. With the postelection developments in 2009, however, Khamenei's balancing act became a progressively more difficult enterprise. On the one hand, he denounced opposition against the election outcome and urged Iranians to stand behind their president—all in clear support of Ahmadinejad. On the other hand, Khamenei's defended pragmatic conservative Rafsanjani, who spoke out in favor of the opposition after the disputed 2009 elections, and made sure that the opposition's leadership did not face persecution.[53] Over Ahmadinejad's second term relations between the president and the supreme leader soured.

With the supreme leader as the head of the executive branch, the power of the president is limited. There is an unwritten rule that the leader chooses the ministers for the Ministries of Foreign Affairs, Petroleum, and Intelligence and Security. In turn, these ministers are loyal to the leader and follow his instructions. Under the constitution, the president oversees the foreign ministry, but in practice foreign policy is the leader's domain. Few of Iran's presidents however have willingly bowed to the supreme leader, and Ahmadinejad is no exception. In the summer of 2010, Ahmadinejad appointed four special envoys, with Esfandiar Rahim Mashaei as the head of the special envoys of Middle Eastern affairs, which was seen as a means to bypass the Foreign Ministry. Foreign Minister Manouchehr Mottaki objected, and Khamenei used strong remarks to support Mottaki— remarks that were again supported by more than a third of the majles' members in a statement to Ahmadinejad. The president's response was to change the name of "envoy" to "advisor" and the appointment of two more.[54] In December 2010, Ahmadinejad dismissed Mottaki. Ahmadinejad had already been in a dispute with the leader on the appointment of Mashaei as the first vice president in 2009. When Khamenei vehemently objected to this appointment,[55] Ahmadinejad assigned Mashaei to other important other positions, including that of chief of staff.[56]

The main limitation to Iran's democratic character does not come from the leader however, but the Guardian Council, which has both the power of vetting candidates and of veto in the legislative process that severely limits the democratic potential of the Iranian political system. Judging political candidates on the basis of their loyalty to the regime as well as their Islamic credentials, the Guardian Council until the death of Khomeini excluded mainly communists, nationalists, socialists, Kurds, and other groups whose loyalty to the regime was questioned from the political process. Since the death of Khomeini, the Guardian Council has more and more used its power to exclude the Association of Combatant Clergy (the Islamic Left) from which the reformist movement emerged from running for office.[57] The Council's role in the legislative process moreover means that the bills passed by the majles can be vetoed, and often have been vetoed, severely limiting the legislative powers of the elected representatives. The Guardian Council itself is not elected, but comprises 12 appointed members, half of whom are appointed by the leader, and the other half by the head of the judiciary at the recommendation of the majles. In cases of political stalemate between the Guardian Council and the majles, another nonelected body, the Expediency Council, is authorized to intervene.

When it comes to regime legitimacy, the combination of theocratic and democratic institutions is a mixed blessing. Iran's democratic characteristics contribute to regime legitimacy in that the electoral process has regulated factional rivalry by including an array of diverging political inclinations into one political system. Moreover, national and municipal elections in Iran provide internal and external legitimacy to a country, which boasts its democratic standing among developing countries. In addition, although the choice of candidates for elections is limited, elections have given the populace a means to express their interest even if that means voting for the opposition, casting a blank vote, or not taking part in the elections altogether.[58] However, the duality in Iran's political system also means a weakness. First, because factional rivalries combined with the theocratic overlay contribute to political stalemate. Particularly under Khatami, this has led to the disillusionment of reformist voters with the political system. Second, because it has made what is ultimately an authoritarian regime with limited public appeal vulnerable to challenges from the democratic institutions. The regime's resort to vote rigging and repression of reformism in Iran a the June 2009 elections to counter this challenge severely challenged its claims to a democratic identity.

The dualism in the Iranian political system has been accentuated by the fact that in the first 25 years of the Republic traditional conservatives dominated the theocratic institutions as well as some key ministries, while the presidency, most of the other ministries as well as the majles were in the hands of more moderate conservatives or reformists. As such the institutional make-up of the Islamic Republic facilitates factionalism. In many ways, factional rivalry in Iran's political system is not a weakness but a strength, as it gives room to a certain level of pluralism that seems to be inherent to Iranian politics. Iran's factions, which have been studied extensively elsewhere,[59] arguably go back as far as the constitutional revolution of 1905 until 1907. The 1978 coalition that ousted the shah was similarly a combination of diverging political groups. It fell apart in the aftermath of the revolution, when under Khomeini's leadership the revolution took an Islamic fundamentalist turn. In the years that followed, many of Khomeini's political opponents were eliminated. Nevertheless, the political group that was incorporated into the Islamic Republic's regime remained relatively diverse. Until today, Iran's power structure is characterized by "loose coalitions among like-minded individuals or groups and...personal patronage links."[60] These loose coalitions consist of people loyal to the idea of an Islamic state, but views on what this Islamic state should entail diverge. Less pronounced during the first decade after the revolution under the unifying leadership of Khomeini,[61] Iran's political factions have increasingly vied for influence since his death in 1989. Table 2.1 gives an overview of Iran's

Table 2.1 Political factions in Iran relevant for the period 2005–2013

	Reformists	Conservatives	
Political parties	Origin: Combatant Clerics Association (*Majma'e-ye Rohaniyun-e Mobarez*)	Traditional conservatives	Neoconservatives
	National Confidence Party (*Hezb-e E'temad-e Melli*) (Karubi), Participation Party (*Jebhey-e Mosharekat-e Iran-e Eslami*) (Khatami)	Origin: Combatant Clergy Society (*Jame'e-ye Rowhaniyat-e Mobarez*)	Alliance of Builders of Islamic Iran (*E'telaf-e Abadgaran-e Iran-e Eslami*)
Majles elections 2008 and 2012	Coalition of Reformists (*E'telaf-e Eslahtalaban*)	United Principalist Front (*Jebhe-ye Mottahed-e Osulgaran*) Broad Principalist Coalition (*E'telaf-e Faragir-e Osulgarayan*)	
Associated individuals	Mousavi (independent), Karubi, Khatami	Larijani, Rezaei, Rafsanjani, Qalibaf	Ahmadinejad, Haddad 'Adel
Political views	Political reform, rapprochement with the West	Economic Reform, pragmatic approach to foreign policy	Ideals of the revolution, firm opposition to the West

factions in the period under study in the book. To be clear, because Iranian politics is centered on individuals rather than political factions, these categories by definition overlap. Moreover, allegiances may shift depending on the topic, issue, or other circumstances.[62]

Factional politics "is conceivably the base of politics in Iran and an integral component of the political process,"[63] in that it has guaranteed a level of regime legitimacy and stability by incorporating competing views within one framework. The combination of democratic and theocratic institutions has, however, also complicated the political process. Conflicts between these institutions have been responsible not only "for enormous frictional incoherencies in the country's domestic and foreign policy" but also a recurrent condition of political stalemate.[64] This political paralysis became painfully obvious during Khatami's presidency, which has been discussed elsewhere.[65] That from 2004 onward conservatives dominated the legislative process by no means implied that the administration was now running like a well-oiled machine. Political differences between the "old guard" dominating the theocratic institutions and the "new guard" in majles prevented the neoconservatives from having much influence in their initial years. By August 2005, the new guard (united under the name *Abadgaran*) had had no major impact on policy decisions, but they had achieved budgetary increases for several traditionalist institution.[66] The fact that the marginalization of reformists did not end factionalism in Iran was clear enough when the conservatives produced three candidates in the 2005 elections (Ahmadinejad, Rafsanjani, and Larijani). Developments since then only increased divisions. The main trends among the right are pragmatist, traditional, and neoconservative, but boundaries between them are unclear, and these trends themselves are not undivided. This became apparent when the neoconservative-dominated majles rejected most of Ahmadinejad's cabinet nominees, although the "prevailing view had been that a neoconservative-dominated majles would merely rubber-stamp his nominees."[67] Four ministerial nominees, all of whom had been Ahmadinejad's close colleagues at the Municipality of Tehran, were not approved. However, the majles did agree with a budget of 40 billion[68] for the new cabinet and the use of money from the Oil Stabilization Fund for this purpose.[69]

Ahmadinejad had a harder time under the successive majles (the 2008–2012 period), which was largely dominated by traditional and pragmatic conservatives. The main disagreement between the neoconservatives and the pragmatists centered on economic policy. Associated with Qalibaf, Rezaei, and Larijani, pragmatists' roots can be traced to traditional institutions such as the bazaar, the clergy, and the original circle around Khamenei.[70] Acknowledging the challenge that the reformist movement posed to the pragmatic conservatives began to argue for a revision of the conservatives' message after their defeat in the parliamentary elections of 2000. Focusing on economic development, pragmatists favored an economic approach similar to that of Rafsanjani during his presidency: a hybrid of a market-driven economy and a certain degree of state control.[71] However, pragmatists had a hard time imposing their platform on the neoconservatives, powerful within the Revolutionary Guards, the *basij*, and other groups with a privileged status in the economy.[72] Despite this rivalry, the majority of the Combatant Clergy Society had been supporting Ahmadinejad's candidacy. By July 2009, however, Ahmadinejad was under attack from virtually every conservative group, including his own supporters.[73] His choices for the ministries and the vice presidencies were again sources of particular discontent. Conservatives who had supported Ahmadinejad's candidacy, and had even discouraged other candidates from running to increase Ahmadinejad's chances and keep the presidency within the conservative camp had done so expecting something in return. "During the election, we paid our debt to the government and to Ahmadinejad. Now, it is his turn to repay his debt by forming a strong cabinet," one MP said.[74] Ahmadinejad, however, was defiant: "The government is not indebted to any group, faction or individual," he stated.[75] After his reelection in 2009, he took a more offensive approach toward the conservatives. He refused to take part in Expediency Council meetings, probably because it was headed by his rival Rafsanjani. In addition, Ahmadinejad was criticized for his failure to enact bills passed by the majles, which sent an unprecedented amount of legal reminders to the president. He is reported to have said that he does not regard these bills as laws, and that no longer the majles, but the executive power is paramount in Iranian politics, outraging conservatives.[76]

Not only is the Iranian regime divided, but also it seems that the Iranian regime is losing its institutional legitimacy among significant segments of the people, particularly the middle and upper classes. First step in that process was the failure of the reform movement. Khatami's compliance with, rather than opposition to, the establishment meant that the conservative forces could continue their efforts to protect the status quo with any means necessary. As such, Khatami alienated from himself Iran's movement for change, which now found itself without a leader. However, the sociopolitical landscape had changed significantly under Khatami: Ahmadinejad inhered a national debate with "new and controversial dimensions" now located in "the public arena, allowing the population to evaluate and make informed judgments about the very nature of the country's Islamic system of government."[77] Adib-Moghaddam referred to this situation as "Iran's pluralistic momentum."[78] This development was not easy to reverse, even more so as disagreements among conservatives, particularly after 2007, created the space for journalists, students,[79] and intellectuals to criticize the policies of Ahmadinejad in an unprecedented manner.

The dispute over the 2009 election outcome and subsequent protests dealt another blow to the Iranian regime's democratic legitimacy. According to the official numbers, Ahmadinejad won the elections with 63 percent of the vote against 34 percent for his rival Mir-Hossein Mousavi. While support for Ahmadinejad may be larger than Western media or Iranian opposition may like to believe, few experts think that Ahmadinejad could have won by this margin without massive vote rigging.[80] The 85 percent of voters turnout showed Iranians felt they had something to choose again.[81] Although Ahmadinejad retained much support among some segments of society, the group opposing him seemed to not only have grown, but also had become increasingly politically engaged. This was evident during the well-attended campaign rallies of Mousavi, Ahmadinejad's strongest challenger,[82] and the participation in postelection demonstrations by millions of Iranian citizens.

Although the regime had a firm grip on the media, the opposition showed creativity in finding their ways around censorship, using among other things mobile phones to communicate their messages. While the regime's initial response to the opposition's silent protests against the election outcome was passive, it turned violent after the Friday Prayers one week later. The regime arrested a large group of reformist spokespeople and activists. Among the more prominent critics, around one hundred were detained in the first weeks after the elections. On television, reformists made forced confessions that "the situation in prison" had helped them "to be courageous enough" to confess their "mistakes,"[83] and stressed that the United States and other Western states were behind the protests.[84] With these efforts, the regime framed the 2009 events in favor of their own antiimperialist, revolutionary ideology. Show trials against reformist politicians, reports of rape, and torture in Iranian prisons challenged the regime's claims to democratic legitimacy.

In the face of this common threat to their power, neoconservatives loyal to Ahmadinejad and hardline conservatives loyal to Khamenei displayed unity. By the time the reformist threat was curbed however, rivalries between Khamenei and Ahmadinejad surfaced in an unprecedented manner. Although the clerics in Iran's theocratic institutions saw Ahmadinejad's populist view of Shi'a Islam as a threat to their power, rivalry between Ahmadinejad and Khamenei was not caused by a divergence in political views, but was rather a competition for political power. Various incidents illustrate this power struggle, including the before-mentioned appointment of Mashaei and dismissal of Mottaki. In August 2009, Ahmadinejad fired Intelligence Minister Gholam-Hossein Mohseni-Ejei in response to Khameneis objections to the appointment of Mashaei.[85] In May 2011, Ahmadinejad fired Intelligence Minister Heidar Moslehi, after which Khamenei reinstated the minister and told Ahmadinejad to accept this or resign.[86] Ahmadinejad in response stopped attending official meetings for ten days. In October 2011, Khamenei announced that he was considering abolishing the position of president, creating a prime minister's post instead.[87]

To sum up, in the Islamic Republic's political system, power is concentrated within a relatively diverse group of conservatives. Although constitutionally the supreme leader has the final word on all issues, in reality groups centered on various individuals compete for power. The fact that there is a certain level of diversity among these groups means that elections in Iran are not a mere façade. The Iranian populace can influence with their voting behavior the power balance between the factions. During the Ahmadinejad presidency, a shift was noticeable away from Ahmadinejad and those loyal to his government toward opposition groups (both conservative and reformists). Evidently, many Iranians were unhappy with the Ahmadinejad government. To what extent Iranians were unhappy with the Islamic Republic as a political system is hard to judge, but the 2009 election protests showed that demands for political change among large segments of Iranians was much alive. The fragmented group of conservatives in Iranian politics, particularly from 2009 onward, was preoccupied with regime security in the face of these challenges. The following section discusses the material sources that the conservative-dominated regime was able to use to curb these challenges.

Material Legitimacy

In authoritarian states, intertwined with the political elite through kinship and/or patrimonial relations, the power of the state is upheld by a moneyed minority with a vested interest in the continuation of the regime's power. In the Middle East, oil and gas rents (or in the case of nonoil states, other external financial resources) have been "crucial for regime maintenance throughout the region since the early 1970s" and used "for privileging a loyal political clientele."[88] In addition, oil money or other external revenues are used for cooptation of (civil society) organizations, by which "states successfully undermine any possible trend towards 'civility.'"[89] The regime's domination of the economy ensures that not just the political elite, but also large segments of the population have some interest in the continuation of the system, particularly as the state subsidizes basic foodstuffs, provides welfare benefits, and employs the bulk of the working population. The Iranian regime fits the frame: the domination of the economy by state-owned and revolutionary enterprises provides the regime not only with material backing but also with valuable means of social engineering. An approximate 80 percent of the workforce is employed by the state and affiliated institutions,[90] which enables the government to ensure loyalty to the regime by maintaining Islamic moral codes at the work place. In a similar way, *bonyads* (revolutionary foundations) such as the Imam Khomeini Relief Committee, which by itself provides aid to close to three million people,[91] operate as a tool of propagation: they uphold the dominant ideology and involve the public in a wide range of social and cultural activities.[92] They also facilitate "social mobility by supporting members of the lower middle classes with lay backgrounds to occupy the secondary positions in the state apparatus since the revolution," and serve to mobilize tens of thousands of people from lower classes in proregime demonstrations.[93]

Particularly relevant in the interrelation between economic and political power is the Sepah-e Pasdaran. It would have been difficult for Ahmadinejad to rally support as a relatively unknown candidate if he had not had the institutional and material support from groups with a vested interest in the system. Threatened by the calls for reform from without and within,[94] elites within the Sepah and the bonyads were happy to rally behind the candidate who propagated the revolutionary ideals underpinning the power structure. While during the Khatami years the Sepah played an important part in ad hoc crisis management, it became increasingly tied up with politics with the elections of 2003, 2004, and 2005. Influential figures within the Revolutionary Guards as well as bonyads and state-owned enterprises (SOEs)[95] provided institutional and material backing to neoconservative candidates. Intertwined with the regime, the Revolutionary Guards, the bonyads, and SOEs maintain a political structure based on vertical patron–client interests.[96] This structure consists of multiple major and minor autonomous structures. Patron–client relations are financially self-sufficient either through charity and endowment incomes, allocated budgets from the government, or both[96] (ibid., 1296).[97] Iran's vast oil and gas income provides a virtually permanent source of income for this economic structure.[98] Revolutionary institutions have replaced any independent industrial class and are, therefore, more interested in maintaining their monopoly rather than an open competition, and seem to wish to keep Iran's economy internationally isolated and under their unyielding control.[99] The liberal initiatives of Presidents Rafsanjani and Khatami posed a direct threat to the power of these institutions. Reformist attempts to limit the power of these organizations and change their lack of transparency, however, were largely unsuccessful.[100]

Reportedly, the hardline establishment[101] switched logistical support from Qalibaf to Ahmadinejad only a few days before the elections.[102] General Mohammad Baqer Zolqar, deputy commander in chief of the Revolutionary Guards stated:

> In the current complex political situation, in which both foreign pressures and internal forces were trying to prevent us from forming a fundamentalist [Osulgaran] government, we had to operate with

complexity…Fundamentalist forces, thank God, won the election thanks to their smart and multifold plan and through the massive participation of the basij.[103]

Reformist presidential candidate Mostafa Moin accused the basij of being present at polling stations to pressure people to vote for Ahmadinejad, and Moin protested against the election result.[104] Rival candidates Rafsanjani, Qalibaf, and Mehdi Karubi equally protested the involvement of the basij, with Karubi taking the unprecedented step of writing to the leader and Rafsanjani that he considered withdrawing from the elections.[105] Whether or not the support of the Revolutionary Guards and the basij for Ahmadinejad was merely a case of voter mobilization rather than direct vote rigging, the support of these organizations most likely helped to rally large segments of the lower and lower middle classes behind the president.

State domination of the economy is also the regime's Achilles heel: like most authoritarian states in the Middle East, the Ahmadinejad administration despite its resources suffered from a severe legitimacy deficit, in particular, due to its failure to efficiently manage the economy, end corruption, curb inflation, and create employment. The main socioeconomic challenges they faced were poverty, high unemployment rates, and high inflation. The growth of GDP per capita in Iran was low compared to other countries in the region, and unemployment was rapidly rising.[106] Higher economic growth was needed to create jobs, even more so while the growth of labor supply over the coming years was expected to be fairly high.[107] Inflation equally soared: According to official numbers, inflation was a little over 10 percent when Ahmadinejad became president and reached an initial peak of 30 percent in October 2008, after which it went down to a low of 7.4 percent, only to quickly rise again. Official inflation rates remained around 20 percent from January 2011 until July 2012, but inflation rose close to 40 percent toward the end of the Ahmadinejad presidency.[108] Observers believe actual inflation rates to be much higher.[109]

In the 2005 election campaign, Ahmadinejad had spoken best to the electorate's economic needs.[110] Khatami, preoccupied with cultural and foreign policy issues, had failed to address Iran's economic malaise. Ahmadinejad instead ran on an antiestablishment program, and blamed the economic malaise on the inadequate realization of the principles of the Islamic revolution.[111] This inadequacy was blamed partly on the reformist movement, which had promoted democratic ideals ill-suited to Iran.[112] Ahmadinejad promised to bring honesty back to government, to equally redistribute Iran's oil income among society, and to fight corruption and cronyism.[113] This campaign worked to the detriment of Rafsanjani who, as a billionaire and influential senior politician, personified the elitism that Ahmadinejad confronted. Ahmadinejad focused on day-to-day social and economic problems and, contrary to his rivals, displayed modesty in his campaign and personal presentation.[114]

High oil prices provided Ahmadinejad and his cabinet with a golden opportunity to structurally improve the economic situation. Despite this, the state of the Iranian economy worsened in many respects after Ahmadinejad's election. Ironically, Ahmadinejad was soon criticized for cronyism and political favoritism, appointing close associates to posts for which they were not qualified, as well as awarding billion dollar no-bid contracts to the Revolutionary Guards.[115] Numerous studies suggest that the cause of the inflation was the government's spending out of oil revenues, which lead to large liquidity injections.[116] Macroeconomic instability caused by inflation in turn caused the inability to attract foreign direct investment.[117] Cash handouts to the poor, distributed on the president's many visits around the country, as well as donations to revolutionary and religious institutions seemed to account for most of Ahmadinejad's budget.[118] According to the IMF and the Worldbank, the Iranian economy was in dire need of thorough restructuring, including greater private sector participation.[119] That, however, would threaten the economic power of the revolutionary organizations supporting the power structure. Oil income made this state-controlled economy viable, but has also made it vulnerable to fluctuations in global oil prices. Even with the creation of the Oil Stabilization Fund to smooth the impact of fluctuations, "without a continuous upward trend in oil prices the oil dependent growth process will have to come to an end."[120] Even worse, instead of increasing the balance of the Oil Stabilization Fund, Ahmadinejad depleted it. "The result is boom and bust cycles in economic performance which increase the uncertainty faced by private firms, thus further impeding private investment and job creation," the IMF noted.[121] Unemployment was around 10 percent for the total working population, and youth unemployment around 23 percent.[122] Sanctions, as later chapters will show, further aggravated Iran's economic problems.

Particularly unpopular was the subsidy reform plan the Ahmadinejad government introduced. Petrol in Iran was highly subsidized, sold at around a fifth of its real cost, but in 2007 the Iranian government withdrew these subsidies and introduced fuel rations. Violent protests were the result.[123] In November 2010, the government started what Ahmadinejad called "the biggest economic plan in the past 50 years," cutting a wide range of subsidies, including subsidies on water, electricity, and staple foods.[124] While even the opposition acknowledged that subsidy cuts were necessary, the Ahmadinejad government was harshly criticized.[125]

Ahmadinejad's economic mismanagement did not go unnoticed by the electorate and proved an important motivation to vote for opposition candidates. [126] Already in the 2006 elections, simultaneously held for the Expert Assembly and the municipal councils, the dissatisfaction of the populace with those in office became visible. Well aware of the divisions in the conservative camp, the electorate chose mainly pragmatic conservatives. The neoconservatives lost control of every municipal council they had, including Teheran, where Ahmadinejad's staunch rival Mohammad Bagher Qalibaf became mayor. The Expert Assembly elections, held every eight years, were of particular importance this time. With the reputed illness of Khamenei, and the old age of Ayatollah Ali Akbar Feyz Meshkini, chairman of the Assembly, the faction gaining control of the Assembly could decide the direction of the leadership. Although the neoconservatives were divided, their opponents were more united than ever: there was even a rapprochement between Khatami and Rafsanjani. The latter received twice as many votes as his nearest competitor, and took over chairmanship of the Assembly when Meshkini died in July 2007.[127] The election results of the 2008 legislative elections reflect the continuation of a trend in which the populace increasingly voted for opposition candidates. With the disqualification of many reformist candidates,[128] these elections were a battle between pragmatic conservatives and neoconservatives. The latter won most seats (28 percent), but were outnumbered by the various opposition groups (at least 42 percent).[129] The 2012 legislative elections again were a defeat for Ahmadinejad loyalists: out of 150, 28 elected candidates were from the reformist camp, 10 from what PressTV called "the team supporting the government," and 112 from the United Principalist Front, which were considered to be pro-Khamenei.[130]

Revolutionary Legitimacy

In their search for legitimacy, the Iranian regime can rely only limitedly on their economic achievements or their claims to democratic representation. However, the Iranian regime has powerful ways to bolster their legitimacy by spreading regime ideology. State domination of the media and censorship ensure that the regime's preferred views are also the views that are readily available to the Iranian people. Through television and other media, the regime was able to identify Iran's main problems and their causes, and present solutions that fit their agenda. These preferred views—which in this research are referred to as regime ideology—are not the product of the imagination of individual leaders, but rather come into being in the interaction among Iran's political elites, and are reproduced as they structure sociopolitical behavior. They are a social construct rather than a doctrine, meaning that there is a level of heterogeneity and inconsistency in regime ideology. Regime ideology is institutionalized in state institutions, rules, regulations, and accepted modes of behavior, ensuring a level of continuity. This means that the fate of regime ideology is tied up with the survival of the system—and vice versa. However, like in the case of the earlier mentioned Hafez al-Assad regime in Syria, what matters here is not whether regime ideology was believed during Ahmadinejad's presidency, but that it was acted upon, thereby perpetuating itself.

Regime ideology in the Islamic Republic did not emerge out of the blue, but came into being particularly through the 1979 Revolution of which the regime considers itself the product. This provides a powerful legacy that supports the regime's claims to legitimacy. To be sure, not all Iranians agree with the regime's interpretation of this revolution. The ousting of the shah was not designed as an Islamic revolution from the outset, but at the expense of competing nationalist and communist political factions Khomeini was able to turn developments to his favor. These competing groups were all but eliminated in the first years of the Islamic Republic. Before and during the revolution, Khomeini had succeeded in uniting these same groups into a coordinated effort against a mutual enemy. Ervand Abrahamian uses the word populism to describe Khomeini's prerevolutionary ideas and his political movement, "because this term is associated with ideological adaptability and intellectual flexibility, with political protest against the established order, and with socio-economic issues that fuel mass opposition to the status quo."[131] Abrahamian finds support in his argument that Khomeini was ultimately a populist in, among other things, the flexibility he displayed in his rhetoric, modifying it depending on political circumstances. In the 1970s, he "rarely mentioned doctrinal issues, especially his highly controversial concept of *velayat-e faqih*," and was unclear on specifics "especially on the question of private property."[132] Misagh Parsa notes that "While in Paris [Khomeini] declared that even Marxists would be free to express themselves under the Islamic Republic. Women, too, would be free 'to govern their fate and choose their activities'."[133] He did not live up to these promises when the Islamic Republic was established in 1979. Only then did Khomeini start to speak of an "Islamic Revolution" paving the way for an "Islamic Republic."[134] In other words, while shared ideas were important in the mobilization of diverse groups against the shah, these shared ideas were mainly directed at the shortcomings of the shah's rule, enlarging the polarization that the shah's economic and social policies had brought about and continued to encourage. At the same time, the religious character of Khomeini's thought helped to contrast his message with the secular message of the shah. His ideas did not, however, constitute a fully developed, coherent system of thought. This lack of coherence meant that different groups could identify with Khomeini's words, and was in fact the strength of his revolutionary ideology. Islamization, however, "unfolded largely after the victory of the revolution and was enforced largely from above by the Islamic state."[135]

In short, that Khomeini was able to build an alternative structure after the revolution was not so much due to the popularity of his movement: "[W]ithin a year's time, the support base of the new revolutionary regime had shrunk dramatically to an intensely loyal core base."[136] The institutionalization of the Islamic Republic depended on this loyal core, not on the much broader coalition that had toppled the shah. The newly established regime learned to rely on state domination of the media, censorship, and other methods to limit the availability of alternative views and narratives. The Cultural Revolution started in August 1979 with the introduction of restrictive press legislation "in particularly forbidding criticism of the Islamic Republic, closure of many publications...and a law attempting to restrict the foreign press."[137] Contemporary Persian and Western music was banned a month later. The Cultural Revolution continued with changes in the curricula of primary and secondary schools and universities, a central role for the Friday Prayers in advancing the revolution and maintaining unity—unity was needed to protect the country from outside interference.[138] The occupation of the US embassy by students sympathetic to Khomeini (1979 until 1980) and the invasion of Iran by Iraq in September 1980 aided regime consolidation, both of which added a sense of urgency to the postrevolutionary situation that required unison under Khomeini's leadership.

Questions of legitimacy became more urgent with the end of the devastating Iran–Iraq War in 1988 and the death of Khomeini in 1989. The pragmatism of President Rafsanjani and the moderate reformism of President Khatami broke with the antiimperialist populism of the 1980s. While foreign policy issues remained important in Khatami's message, he spoke of a *dialogue among civilizations* rather than resistance against the West. This message can be contrasted with the persistently anti-Western discourse of Khamenei during the same period.[139] The neoconservative message of Ahmadinejad, however, in many ways fell back on the antiimperialist revolutionary rhetoric of the 1980s, and was a better match with the supreme leaders' (despite political differences). It was populist in the same way in which Abrahamian described Khomeini's movement:

> A movement of the propertied middle class that mobilizes the lower classes, especially the urban poor, with radical rhetoric directed against imperialism, foreign capitalism, and the political establishment. In mobilizing the "common people", populist movements use charismatic figures and symbols, imagery and language that have potent value in the mass culture. Populist movements promise to drastically raise the standard of living and make the country fully independent of outside powers.[140]

The fact that the Ahmadinejad administration was unable to raise the standard of living made it perhaps even more dependent on antiimperialist rhetoric, which blamed outsiders for Iran's economic isolation. The regime's revolutionary legacy makes possible, even likely, this reading of current events.

Conclusion

The backbone of the Islamic Republic's regime was a hybrid ensemble of conservative groups with a vested interest in the continuation of the system. The institutional make-up of the Islamic Republic's sociopolitical system facilitates a certain level of diversity among these groups, as well as competition. The dominant ideology among conservatives can be traced back to the 1979 Iranian Revolution, and is traditionalist and antiimperialist in character. Oil rents, relatively closed circles of elites, and state domination of the media ensure that the power stays in the hands of these groups. Factionalism undermines their power to some extent; however, an interest in the continuation of the system and a loyalty to its main tenets ensures continuation. Those who deviate become marginalized.

State domination of the economy not only gives the regime powerful means of patronage and social engineering, but also makes the government responsible for Iran's economic malaise, particularly as the state manages Iran's oil income. Ahmadinejad was not able to fulfill his promise of improving Iran's dire economic situation, and this hurt his personal legitimacy as the President of Iran and that of the regime as a whole. Reliance on intelligence and security forces to curb opposition seems to contribute to regime continuation in the short run, but may have also catalyzed the erosion of its legitimacy. All of this was exacerbated by a rivalry between Iran's conservatives and neoconservatives, with the former accusing the latter of mismanagement, corruption, and adventurism.

In sum, it is clear that the Iranian regime was facing challenges to their legitimacy, some of which materialized in proreform demonstrations, others in online antigovernment activism. What we can safely say now, however, is that the Ahmadinejad government survived these challenges. Whether this is due to a popular belief in the legitimacy of the regime by a majority, loyalty of a crucial minority, apathy among Iranian citizens due to disappointment after the 2009 elections, the success of material incentives through state employment, physical or psychological repression, apathy related to the duress of everyday life under dire economic circumstances, the feigning of acquiescence by people who simply see no alternative, or a combination of these or other factors is impossible to tell. While activism continued at the margins, and small acts of resistance showed that opposition was alive, the status-quo was reproduced through everyday behavior even by Iranians who liked to see change, avoiding confrontation with the regime rather than challenging it. The dominant ideas that guide social action thereby continued to structure social practice, and reproduce the status quo even in case of limited regime legitimacy.

Chapter 3

International Legitimacy: Constraints and Opportunities

The Ahmadinejad government faced not only domestic challenges to its legitimacy, but also its international environment proved increasingly unwelcoming. The regime blamed the West for this, which it said was attempting to undermine the Islamic Republic's independence and development through its international domination. Ahmadinejad's accusing discourse marked a clear break from Mohammad Khatami's more conciliatory tone, but was in many a continuation of the revolutionary discourse of the 1980s that had remained prevalent among conservatives. The Iranian regime's preoccupation with the West was mutual. Iran already ranked high on Western security agendas as part of what George W. Bush had called the "Axis of Evil," and the Ahmadinejad government's anti-Western discourse reinforced Western suspicion of the Iranian regime. Taking progressively more intense measures against Iran in the period from 2006 to 2013, the United States and its European allies severely limited the Iranian regime's international options. Their questioning of the Iranian regime's international legitimacy became institutionally embedded in an international sanctions regime, which greatly restricted trade relations with Iran throughout the West's sphere of influence.

This chapter maps out this increasingly inhospitable international context in which the Ahmadinejad administration found itself, starting with an account of the historical construction of the hostility between Iran and the West, and the institutionalization of this animosity particularly with regard to international sanctions. It shows how sanctions were effective in limiting the Ahmadinejad administration's international options, and had a severe impact on the Iranian economy. At the same time, the international environment was not uniformly hostile to the Iranian regime. Ahmadinejad's presidency coincided with an emerging international trend in which United States' hegemony was cautiously challenged by emerging and aspiring powers. Western efforts to isolate Iran created opportunities for these powers to give shape to their autonomous course. Some of these powers criticized Western policies, while others explicitly defied Western attempts to isolate Iran, and sought friendly ties with the Islamic Republic as evidence of their independence. This created limited yet important international opportunities for the Islamic Republic.

International Legitimacy

Regime survival is dependent not only on domestic legitimacy. In an increasingly globalized world, the international community of states can seriously challenge or bolster a regime's domestic success. According to Ian Clark,[1] "The practice of legitimacy describes the political negotiation among the members of international society," which lies at the heart of the semipermanent structures of values and morality in international society. The historical construction of this normative framework means that this negotiation is not entirely "what states make of it"[2] at present, but that it is to a large extent above and beyond the consent or practice of individual states, which reproduce the framework merely because they are bound by it.[3] International legitimacy, according to Clark, is about a "rudimentary social agreement about who is entitled to participate in international relations, and also about appropriate forms in their conduct." Like in the domestic realm, legitimacy is not so much a status quo situation as a process, as "the actors within international society are engaged in endless strategies of legitimation, in order to present certain activities or actions as legitimate."[4] International legitimacy is of great importance to states, as it determines their international options. External aid, geostrategic importance, and international alliances depend on international legitimacy.[5] One could add to this list the limiting of threats, safeguarding of territorial integrity, and other matters of state and regime security.

"External legitimacy," Albrecht and Schlumberger[6] argue, "signifies the extent to which political regimes are considered legitimate by the leading external powers, that is, Western governments and international organisations." Their focus on the West as the locus of international power can be justified in the light of international dominance of the West since the end of the Cold War. Western impact on international legitimacy has been noticeable, according to Clark, in a "greater rhetorical commitment, within a broadly based section of international society, to the credentials of good governance," which are seen as "means to the wider international purpose of securing order and peace. The logic that has united these two ambitions is the assumed intimate connection between adherence to domestic legitimacy precepts and legitimate international conduct."[7] From this follows that states like Iran, which are criticized for their limited democratic legitimacy, are suffering from a lack of international legitimacy. However, Clark uses the word "rhetorical" for a reason: many authoritarian states or states that otherwise violate human rights are able to function well in international society, and moral dilemmas are conveniently ignored by Western governments that benefit from good relations with these powers. Israel and Saudi Arabia are examples.

International legitimacy, however, is not solely determined by the most dominant powers: rising and aspiring powers, in particular, are demanding their share in determining who is "in," who is "out," and on which conditions. Clark acknowledges that to a large extent international society, and with it international legitimacy, is always changing, but puts emphasis on the stability of the international structure. He does not explain how state conduct contributes to changes in what is seen as legitimate at a particular time among a particular group of states. International society, like domestic society, is continuously shaped and reshaped through social practice in conjunction with shared ideas. That international society is the social product of interaction among states and nonstate groups also means that these can consciously participate in the shaping of international society. Through their foreign policy, individual states are able to shape international society, both in behavior as well as their "speech acts." This is particularly so when states act in a simultaneous effort with citizens' initiatives, which challenge prevailing ideas. Studies such as on the end of the Cold War[8] and NATO enlargement[9] show that changes in international society do not "just happen" but are the consequence of conscious efforts by global powers as agents of change. What global powers did in this scenario was behaving *as if* change was happening. This is what Fierke calls "acting as if to create space":

> The power of "acting as if" resides in a double move, that is, in politicizing the rules of the dominant game, by flaunting them, and, at the same time, acting within the framework of a more marginal game that already has meaning within a political context.[10]

International society changes as the marginal game challenges, changes, and potentially replaces the dominant game. This was the case, Fierke argues, when the Cold War ended principally because its legitimacy was challenged by a simultaneous effort of the peace movement in the West and human rights movements in the East, creating the space for Reagan and Gorbachev to change the relationship between their countries.[11]

International legitimacy then, understood as a process, is the product of continuous negotiation among states. Legitimacy is largely derived from the dominant powers, and while Western states dominate the international community, this means Iran's options are limited. However, legitimation is an on-going process among international actors, and one in which rising and aspiring powers are increasingly asserting their influence. Nations who have been marginalized by the West are seeking legitimacy among these powers, as well as among each other through the building of alliances and a shared discourse. They can challenge the way international society is organized by providing an alternative understanding of the world, challenging the status quo. This opened up space for Iran to improve its international standing. This is, as later chapters will show, was an effort in which Iran was engaged, together with other developing countries and emerging powers, though to limited avail.

Western Hegemony: Isolating Iran

The main constraint to the Iranian regime's international legitimacy is its hostile relationship with the United States. Iranian officials speak of continuous efforts by a United States-led international coalition of states to isolate and undermine Iran. These efforts they say include international sanctions, the spread of anti-Iranian propaganda, the use of double standards, meddling in Iranian domestic affairs, and military threats (see chapter 4). While this extreme concern with the United States and other Western countries has often been referred to as paranoia, the perception of threat did not emerge out of the blue. Not only did it develop through a long history of interaction between Iran and the West, but it has been sustained in the context of a largely hostile regional and international environment. One cannot explain the pre-eminence of anti-Western rhetoric under Ahmadinejad, which can be so clearly contrasted with the approach of his predecessor Khatami, in isolation of United States' regional involvement and its obsession with Iran. When Ahmadinejad was elected president, the United States had already surrounded Iran with its military presence in Iraq and Afghanistan, and its efforts, together with other Western states, to persuade Iran to give up its nuclear development through sanctions and other isolating measures severely limited Iran's regional and international options.

The animosity between Iran and the West has often been explained in terms of conflicting strategic interests in the Middle East region.[12] However, as chapter 1 explained, strategic rivalry is not a natural condition to the international environment. Strategic rivalry emerges in interaction between states: over time rivalry becomes embedded in mutual perceptions of the other, and these perceptions on either side favor foreign policy behavior that reinforces animosity. On the Iranian side, the regime's preoccupation with the United States is best summarized as a state of securitization bordering on paranoia. Ervand Abrahamian[13] in the early 1990s described the centrality of paranoia in Iranian politics, which he defined as a hyperalertness of Iranian leaders to outside threat, their overemphasis of this threat, and the instrumentality of the fear created in uniting the people behind the regime. The notion of outside interference is particularly central to Iran's paranoid style of politics, which "treats Iranian politics as a puppet show in which foreign powers control the marionettes—the local politicians—by invisible strings."[14] While this paranoid style is shared by all sectors of Iran's political spectrum (including monarchists and communists),[15] Abrahamian described it as a particularly important characteristic to Khomeini's political views:

> [Khomeini] charged that colonial conspiracies kept the country poor and backward, exploited its resources, inflamed class antagonisms, divided the clergy and alienated them from the masses, caused mischief among tribes, infiltrated the universities, cultivated consumer instincts and encouraged moral corruption, especially gambling, prostitution, drug addiction, and alcohol consumption.[16]

These views, although with slightly different emphasis (see chapter 4), remain persistent in Iranian policies today, to such an extent that one may still speak of paranoia. Robins and Post describe paranoia as an outlook or attitude by those in power that is characterized by a set of coherent beliefs comprising the delusional blaming and suspicion of outsiders, hostility toward outsiders, centrality of the self, and a feeling of grandiosity as well as the fear of loss of autonomy.[17] The delusional element, however, should not be overstated. To be successful, leaders have to base their paranoia in the shared experience of the populace with this threat, even if they overemphasize and exaggerate this threat. This overemphasis is known as a process of securitization, constituting developments as existential threats with high priority.[18] Although paranoia is used instrumentally—it can be used to unite the people against an (internal or external) enemy, and is often an element of populist or charismatic leadership—it becomes rooted in observable fact through a self-fulfilling mechanism, in which animosity toward another state outsider is answered with animosity, confirming what the leaders already feared.[19] Suspicion, as such, is not just something projected by one state onto another, but comes into being in interaction between states.

The animosity between Iran and the West that is so central to the Islamic Republic's foreign policy today cannot be understood outside of the historical interaction between Iran and the great powers in the twentieth century. This interaction, which was mainly with Russia and the United Kingdom and later the United States, was guided by the interests of these powers, more often than not to the detriment of the interest of the Iranian nation. Particularly the United Kingdom remained subject of popular resentment, which during the Ahmadinejad presidency was visible in the many demonstrations at the UK Embassy (see chapter 7). However, in terms of its international relations, it is the animosity with the United States that demands most historical contextualization. The United Kingdom had been the dominant foreign power in Iran, when in 1953 the elected Prime Minister Mosaddeq was overthrown by a coalition between CIA and MI6.[20] The restoration of Mohammad Reza Pahlavi's power marked a change in Iran's domestic political situation in a number of ways. Historian Nikki Keddie[21] names, first of all, the United States becoming the dominant foreign power in Iran. After the overthrow of Mosaddeq, the United States was eager to support the pro-Western shah who would safeguard Iran's economic and political relations with the West. Secondly, the shah, who was deeply suspicious of his own people, became increasingly dictatorial and ever more prepared to use repressive measures. US presidents turned a blind eye on the human rights violations, at least until the late 1970s. Third, making use of an increase in oil income in the 1950s, the shah initiated a modernization program, designed to create a durable situation of prosperity. In reality, however, the "White Revolution" promoted state-dominated capitalism, and rendered the Iranian economy increasingly dependent on Western capital, Western technology, and Western consumer goods. Meanwhile, Nixon appointed the shah as the "police man" of the Persian Gulf, which meant that the shah could buy all the conventional weapons he wanted. High oil prices enabled the shah to live his dream of turning Iran into a major military power through massive purchases of American military hardware.[22] During the mid-1970s, however, the American public started criticizing the human rights situation in Iran, particularly the practices of the SAVAK (the secret police). In 1975, US President Jimmy Carter, during the final stages of his presidential campaign, had expressed concern about these violations, and also Amnesty International had turned its attention to Iran.[23] As a result, in the late 1970s, external pressure to improve the human rights situation increased, forcing the shah to change its policies. This gave opposition movements the political space to organize themselves, which contributed to the fall of the shah in 1979.

Political support from the United States, a huge oil income, an almost complete control over the economy, and an extensive network of patronage and repression, all contributed to the shah's power. Resistance against the United States thus became an important element in the revolution. Khomeini's message, which was shared by and propagated by his supporters, gained credibility through its reference to historical events, such as the 1953 coup. The ability to make reference to events like these was a powerful tool in the hands of the regime and had far-reaching consequences for Iran's political landscape in the years following the revolution. The regime equated "competition with treason, liberalism with weak-mindedness, honest differences of opinion with divisive alien conspiracies, and political toleration with permissiveness toward the enemy within," dispelling dissidents as foreign agents and legitimizing their imprisonment or execution.[24]

In the immediate aftermath of the revolution, Iran–US interactions played a decisive role in the consolidation of the Islamic regime, deeply embedding animosity toward the United States in the institutions of the Islamic Republic. The ambiguity in United States' foreign policy opened up space for Khomeini to criticize the United States. Iran's provisional government had a conciliatory attitude toward the United States, which at first was tolerated by conservatives. The United States, however, did not reciprocate to this approach, giving the conservatives the opportunity to create "a hysterical anti-US climate in Iran."[25] Two developments, in particular, contributed to the emergence of this climate. First, a group of Iranian students took over the American embassy on November 4, 1979, and held several of its diplomats hostage for 444 days. Although the seizure was not initiated by the Islamic Republican Party, but by a group of students sympathetic to Ayatollah Khomeini, none of the leading clerics opposed it.[26] The crisis undermined the liberal government, who were against the seizure.[27] The mass agitation that followed provided the ideal circumstances for the conservatives to submit their proposal for a constitution to a referendum. Moreover, in June 1981, Ayatollah Khomeini dismissed the liberal President Bani Sadr after American embassy documents were released that supposedly proved a connection between Bani Sadr and the CIA.[28]

Second, the invasion of Iran by Iraq in September 1980 both consolidated the power of the Iranian regime and reinforced the regime's suspicion of outsiders, particularly the United States. In Ramazani's words,

> [T]he Iranians saw the United States as the real instigator of the Iraqi invasion of Iran on September 22, 1980. Paranoid or not, this view of the war as having been "imposed" by the US "deputy," Saddam Hussein, to use Montazeri's characterization, was in part responsible for the Iranian decision to carry the war into Iraqi territory in July 1982.[29]

Originally, "the devastation and hardship of the lingering war, along with the prevalent corruption and lack of security and freedom, gave the opponents of the Khomeini an opportunity to resurface."[30] But later on, the war proved a blessing for the conservatives in that it helped to concentrate power among them, evolved the instrument of repression,[31] and provided the regime with a rallying cry: "Even those with strong reservations about the regime were willing to rally behind the government in a time of national emergency. It became a patriotic as well as a religious-inspired revolutionary war."[32] Moreover, it solidified the link between the conservatives and the lower classes through basij (volunteer) recruitment, increased the experience and consolidated the power of the Sepah-e Pasdaran, and kept the armed forces too busy to stage a coup.[33] Thus, through the 1979 Revolution, the seizure of the US Embassy and subsequent Iran–Iraq War, suspicion of the West became the cornerstone of the Iranian political system.

As the roots of the Iranian regime's mistrust of outsiders lie in Iran's contemporary history, the delusional element in the Iranian regime's "paranoid style" is not the mistrust of the West, but its active efforts to keep alive the memory of imperialist misconduct as part and parcel of Western policies today, as well as the purposeful cultivation of mistrust of compatriots as "agents of the West."[34] Later chapters will show that Iranian officials' references to this historical context, particularly the 1953 coup, the hostage crisis, and the Iran–Iraq War, keep this suspicion alive. However, equally important to this sustained mistrust are the many references to the then current Western policies on Iran, which confirmed the idea that the West was on an on-going mission to undermine and isolate the Islamic Republic. These Western policies were equally rooted in historically rooted mistrust, which are confirmed and reinforced by the Iranian regime's accusatory speech and its refusal to yield to Western demands.[35]

The United States cut its diplomatic ties with Iran after the hostage crisis, and although it has been suggested that Iran and the United States have since worked together clandestinely,[36] the United States and Iran only cooperated overtly again in 2001. In the first 20 years after the Iranian Revolution, the United States was a distant enemy for Iran, whose presence in the region was felt mainly through its alliances with Iran's enemies, particularly Iraq (until 1991), Turkey, and Saudi Arabia. After 2001, however, with increasing US military presence in the region, coping with the United States became of direct concern to Iran's regional policy. For the United States, Iran also become of central concern. The Bush Administration's preoccupation with the "war on terror," combined with its views of Iran as the main state supporter of terrorism, made Iran the main focal point of American strategic interest after the attacks of September 11, 2001. The United States invaded Afghanistan in 2001 and Iraq in 2003, eliminating the regimes of the Taliban and Saddam Hussein. This meant that Iran became the focus of US security concerns, particularly as Iran was actively seeking to assert its influence in both these neighboring countries. The United States' Government hardened its discourse on Iran with the 2002 State of the Union in which Iran was named as part of an *Axis of Evil*. In 2006, when Ahmadinejad became president, Iran was on top of the White House list of US security concerns.

The United States' Government has always been critical of the human rights situation in the Islamic Republic, particularly the lack of democratic freedom, but increased its efforts of promoting democracy in Iran after 2001. For example, it aimed at providing the Iranian people with news and information through organizations such as the Voice of America. The 110th Congress agreed on the allocation of 60 million US dollars for democracy promotion in Iran in 2008,[37] and after the disputed 2009 elections the 111th Congress openly and actively supported the Iranian protestors.[38] Another important concern for the United States is the Iranian regime's support for organizations that are on US State Department list of Foreign Terrorist Organizations, most importantly Hamas, Hezbollah, and Islamic Jihad. In addition, Iran was accused of supporting insurgent groups in both Afghanistan and Iraq. On the top of the list of concerns, however, was the suspicion that the Iranian regime's nuclear program is a clandestine weapons program: a concern that the United States shares with the EU. In efforts to halt Iranian nuclear development, the United States has taken the lead in isolating the Islamic Republic, granting it the status of pariah state along with North Korea. The US Government has also taken several punitive measures to encourage the Iranian regime to change its foreign and domestic policies. Unilateral sanctions already adopted in the 1990s were more strongly enforced from 2005 onward.[39]

During Ahmadinejad's two terms in office, the US confrontational approach was gaining more international support. Until 2005 the EU took a relatively conciliatory approach, using a "carrot" in the shape of a trade and cooperation agreement; however, with the failure of the EU engagement of Iran under Khatami, the EU Affairs Council changed its approach during the first years of the Ahmadinejad presidency and adopted sanctions on Iran in 2007, which were tightened in 2010, and again in 2011 and 2012.[40] This has, among other things, lead to a decrease of oil sales to European firms from mid-2012 onward.[41] Despite this, the EU was Iran's most important trading partner during most of Ahmadinejad's presidency, and its second most important at the end of his second term.[42] Germany and Italy, in particular, had profitable trade relations with Iran.[43] There was indication of a continuing willingness in these countries to trade with Iran. In early 2013, a number of German firms were reported to maintain their business relations with Iran despite the sanctions,[44] and the newly appointed Italian Ambassador to Iran was reported as saying that his country was interested in becoming Iran's main trading partner in Europe.[45] Despite this, the European trend toward weakening economic ties with Iran continued throughout the entire Ahmadinejad period.

In addition, in the United Nations, the US's approach was gaining more support, particularly after the Ahmadinejad administration resumed its enrichment activities, which had been halted during the later Khatami years. The Security Council passed four resolutions against Iran in the period from 2005 to 2013,[46] mainly designed to persuade Iran to suspend uranium enrichment and its ballistic missile programs. Permanent UNSC members Russia and China generally spoke out against sanctions that would limit their options in Iran, but this has left enough space for agreement on sanctions. Although it is hardly possible to establish to what extent the dire economic circumstances under the Ahmadinejad presidency were a consequence of misguided economic policies, of economic sanctions, or a combination of both, it is certain that sanctions had a severe economic impact.[47]

The political success of the sanctions, however, was debated.[48] If the goal of sanctions was to halt nuclear and military development, then their success was limited: the nuclear and missiles program progressed throughout Ahmadinejad's second term, despite the difficulties sanctions posed.[49] If the sanctions were meant to encourage the Iranian government to change its nuclear policies, they were equally unsuccessful: the domestic political debate, including those surrounding the factional rivalries, focused mainly on the administration's economic mismanagement, not on the nuclear program.[50] If the West hoped that sanctions would undermine the regime, they were let down, at least in the short run: analysts argued that sanctions strengthened the regime's power rather than challenging it.[51] If the economic consequences of the sanctions challenged regime legitimacy, they have equally induced great disappointment in Western governments among moderate Iranians who experience the everyday impact of the sanctions targeted at their regime. Lastly, if sanctions were meant to encourage the Iranian regime to improve its ties with the West, they instead created a greater need for the Iranian regime to look for alternative partners. Where Iran has been successful in finding these partners, this has merely limited Western options to influence Iran.

Challenging Hegemony: Befriending Iran?

Perhaps the sanctions main success was not in their economic or political, but their symbolic effect. For some countries, the increasingly tightened sanctions undermined the Iranian regime's international legitimacy, and contributed to the perception of Iran as a rogue state, excluded from the community of international states. However, among a number of non-Western powers, there was ambivalence toward the desirability and effectiveness of isolating Iran. This ambivalence toward Iran's exclusion was of particular significance as part of an international development in which rising and middle powers showed an increasingly willingness to challenge or at least question Western domination and take a more independent course. While it was too early to speak of a real decline in United States' power during Ahmadinejad's presidency, there were important developments in the way the United States was perceived globally. Not only in world opinion[52] but also among governments around the world, the United States was falling from grace. During the 1990s, only leaders of other marginalized states such as Cuba and Libya echoed the Iranian–anti-US discourse, but in the mid-2000s it became acceptable among a broader segment of states to criticize US policies and to publicly go against America's wishes. In Latin America, leftist leaders were elected who were openly opposing US unilateralism. Moreover, rising powers such as South Africa, Brazil, and Turkey more often took an independent course, sometimes going directly against American wishes. This independent course taken by middle and rising powers created opportunities for the Iranian regime to increase its international legitimacy, particularly, as the wish to take an independent course has shaped some of these aspiring powers'[53] foreign policies toward Iran, creating new opportunities that challenge the idea that Iran is isolated.

Today, the United States is the single most powerful state in the international community, and despite the serious setbacks it has faced in the last two decades, there is at present no serious challenge to that hegemony. Nevertheless, scholars and practitioners alike are anticipating the decline of American power, and the question of what a new world order will or should look like dominates foreign policy debates, particularly those taking place in aspiring powers. The anticipation of American decline is reminiscent of the anticipation of the fall of the Soviet Union in the 1980s, when activists and later politicians came to act as if the Cold War was over, creating space for this change to come about.[54] While most rising powers today still act within the space of United States' dominance, other rising and middle powers are more explicitly critical of United States' hegemony, flaunting the dominant game while acting in the space of a more marginal one[55] in which rising and middle powers make the rules. These nations seek and find the space to take a foreign policy course independent of the United States. In the eight years in which Ahmadinejad was president, the world's rising powers (this section discusses in particular Brazil, Russia, India, China, and South Africa—the BRICS) had stable but nevertheless ambivalent relations with the United States. Although preferably avoiding disagreement with the United States, particularly when this had economic or strategic consequences, these countries prioritized their independent course in establishing themselves as rising global powers.

Foreign policy officials in China, the most important rising power, never missed an opportunity to emphasize their country has no intention to replace the United States as the world hegemon. Particularly central in the foreign policy discourse of Chinese officials was the notion of a peaceful rise or peaceful development.[56] Chinese officials emphasized that China does not want to become the global hegemon: "China's rise will avoid the fate of colonialists and imperialists of the past because it will not seek external expansion, but instead will uphold peace, mutual cooperation and common development, assert the advocates of peaceful rise."[57] At the same time, Chinese official policy and scholars alike posited that the international order is moving toward multipolarity.[58] In the context of this development, they were actively reinforcing China's regional and international power. With the changes in United States' policies under Obama, the global financial crisis from 2008 onward, and the rise of the BRICS, many Chinese observers believed that the speed of multipolarization was now accelerating.[59] With the prospect of multipolarity in mind, the Chinese regime was not only maintaining stable relations with the United States as much as possible, but also asserted its international power.

The Russian regime's stance on the future of the international system was similar to the Chinese in that the United States was still regarded as an important power, however, one on the decline. Immediately after the Cold War, the dominant view of the international system in Russia was Liberal, and the main goal of Russia's international endeavors was joining the West.[60] However, after Russian politicians were left disappointed by Western policies toward Russia, particularly with the expansion of NATO, a Great Power ideology became dominant again in the mid-1990s. This evolved into an ideology with a civilizational twist: Russia is seen as one of three wings of European Civilization— the other two being Europe and the United States. These views did not reject the West, but were rather in favor of learning from the West, importing Western technology and attracting foreign investment in order to compete successfully with the West. Rather than expressing the wish of taking the place of the West, Russian officials were emphasizing the need for a more equal division of power between the West and Russia.[61]

The Indian Government was less outspoken about a need to increase its international power at the expense of that of the West, rather maintaining and strengthening its relations with the United States, which it saw as beneficial for India's rise. Ties between the United States and India had become consistently closer since the end of the Cold War. However, among the majority of Indian politicians, there was opposition to serious military partnership, and relations with the United States, in general, received opposition from leftists and nationalists. Where leftists favored relations with China over the United States, nationalists preferred a more challenging posture toward the global hegemon, which they saw as putting a strain on Indian interest. This domestic opposition meant that despite its good relations with the United States, the Indian Government needed to act prudently in upholding, let alone strengthening these ties,[62] particularly when the opposition parties accused the Indian Government of foregoing India's national interest.[63]

Neither China nor Russia or India showed an ambition to confront the US power, let alone to replace it. However, increasingly, each of these states demonstrated their economic and political power, for example, through their voting behavior at international institutions.[64] In addition, these countries voiced disagreement with United States' international policies. The Chinese Government, for example, called the United States' attempts to address the human rights situation in China a tool for foreign meddling. Also Indians were skeptical of United States' efforts in this regard, which they believed to be hypocritical, given the good relations many Western countries had with dictators around the world.[65] Likewise, Russian political groups across the spectrum saw US democracy promotion as a cover for the American ambition to expand its international influence.[66] These perceptions of United States' goals undermined United States efforts to create international support for some of their more controversial proposals, including those on Iran.

Chinese representatives on many occasions spoke out against sanctions, and confirmed Iran's right to nuclear development.[67] While they have emphasized the need to uphold the NPT in relation to Iran's nuclear development,[68] thereby insinuating deviation, they also expressed a belief in negotiations in a spirit of dialogue and cooperation.[69] Likewise, Russian governmental officials spoke out in support of Iranian peaceful nuclear development[70] and said: "Threats, sanctions and threats of pressure in the current situation, we are convinced, would be counterproductive."[71] For the Russian Government, relations with Iran were "a test and a symbol of Russia's strategic independence in its foreign policy and its ability to stand up to Western and other international pressures, something it has aspired to for a long time."[72] Also in India, "Analysts have seen India's position [on Iran] as a 'litmus test' of whether India is following an independent foreign policy, defined as independent of American interests."[73] This has led to ambiguity in India's Iran policy, with the External Relations Minister claiming India to be "extremely good friends with Iran" while simultaneously "taking positions that obviously not necessarily align themselves with the aspirations or at least perceived aspirations of Iran in recent times."[74] After a visit from Putin at the end of 2012, the Russian and Indian Governments issued a joined statement, which called for a "comprehensive and long-term settlement of the situation through exclusively political and diplomatic means by promoting dialogue," expressed discontent about unilateral sanctions, "recognized Iran's right to develop research, produce and use nuclear energy for peaceful purposes," however also emphasized the need for Iran's conformity with its international obligations, including the provisions of the relevant UN Security Council Resolutions and cooperation to the IAEA.[75]

The trends we see in the international behavior of major powers China, India, and Russia, including their ambivalence, resemble those among other BRICS members. Under Luiz Inácio Lula da Silva (from 2003 until 2010), Brazil sought an increasingly assertive role in international politics. This was coupled with an increased politicization of foreign policy. Like in Russia and China, Brazilian foreign policy actors were envisioning a new global order based on multipolarity,[76] with United States' power declining in favor of a growing role for emerging powers. In paving the way for a more equal distribution of power, the Lula administration advocated global governance reforms, particularly with regard to the UN Security Council. This indicated a break with the Cardoso administration, which had emphasized convergence with Western liberalism. Lula's foreign policy role conception translated to efforts to further institutionalize South–South relations (IBSA and BRIC) and, among other things, improved relations with the Islamic Republic. In defiance of United States' policies on Iran, the Lula administration advocated a conciliatory approach toward Iran, engaging the Iranian regime rather than contributing to its isolation. In particular, it played an important role in trying to solve the nuclear issue, which is discussed in chapter 6, and which was "heralded as an example of the increasing clout of emerging countries in a new multi-polar world."[77] Ahmadinejad made a controversial visit to Brazil in November 2009. Iran's disputed elections earlier that year and intense international pressure on Iran over its nuclear program added to the controversy. President Lula was criticized for hosting Ahmadinejad, not only internationally but also domestically. On the day of Ahmadinejad's arrival, thousands of protestors took to the streets in Rio de Janeiro and Sao Paulo. Lula defended his decision to host Ahmadinejad by emphasizing that it does not help to isolate Iran,[78] which he repeated when Hillary Clinton visited Brasilia in March 2010. Clinton was hoping to build support for a UN resolution on renewed sanctions against Iran, but Lula da Silva told her "it is not prudent to push Iran against a wall."[79] Foreign Minister Celso Amorim emphasized that Brazil had no problem going against the US's wishes: Brazil would not "simply bow to the evolving consensus" while they disagreed.[80] However, Brazil's policies under Lula were pragmatic more than anything, as it also tried to maintain good relations with the West and, for example, Israel.[81] Under Lula's successor Dilma Rousseff, long-held perceptions of Brazil as democratic and liberal became more central to foreign policy. In its advocacy of global human rights, the Dilma administration changed Brazil's voting at the Human Rights council by supporting the United States' proposal for a rapporteur to monitor the Iranian human rights situation, marking at the same time a policy shift on Iran.[82]

Among the BRICS, the South African Government was particularly outspoken[83] in its general distrust of the intentions of Western countries. South African representatives criticized the domination of the UN Security Council by the United States and the EU, and argued for increased multilateralism.[84] The South African Government also emphasized the need for negotiation on the nuclear issue.[85] Of course, the most explicit challenges to United States' power, as well as support for the Iranian regime, come from more marginalized states such as Venezuela, Cuba, Syria, and Zimbabwe. Despite the fact that these countries have little international influence, primarily due to their limited international legitimacy, they play an important role in pointing out the weaknesses of the current status quo, which contributes to the discourse of the emerging powers discussed above. The convergence of these ideals is most visible in the Nonaligned Movement (NAM), of which South Africa, India, Venezuela, Cuba, and Zimbabwe are prominent members, and to which China and Brazil have observer status. The NAM has pointed to the double standards and hypocrisy of action against Iran in the light of its nuclear program, where a blind eye is turned to known proliferators such as Israel. "It is difficult for NAM members not to conclude that the international non-proliferation agenda is driven by the West and constitutes a form of cynical neo-colonial discrimination—exactly the type of activity that the organization was set up to tackle," one scholar remarked.[86] On several occasions, the NAM expressed explicit support for Iran's peaceful nuclear ambitions.[87] In 2012, chairmanship of the NAM was transferred from Egypt to Iran. The occasion of the 16th NAM summit in Tehran was a success for Ahmadinejad and an obvious challenge to the notion that Iran was isolated.[88]

International support for the Islamic Republic's ambitions to develop nuclear capacity for peaceful purposes, as well as expressions of discontent with the sanctions,[89] was of important symbolic value. It was visible in the fact that China, Russia, and India continued their involvement with Iran as much as possible.[90] After the last round of United States' sanctions during Ahmadinejad's presidency, China,

India, and South Africa continued their imports under a temporary exemption,[91] and although Chinese investments in Iran dropped considerably in 2012,[92] Chinese oil purchases rose, as did overall oil exports.[93] The reluctance of the BRICS to abide by international sanctions showed that compliance with United States' sanctions needed persuasion, adding to the notion that the United States is pressuring nations into compliance rather than building on an international consensus against Iran. This added to the perception that the United States was using its international power to further its own interest—a concern that was often expressed by the governments of BRICS countries. While emerging powers are without exception criticizing US unilateralism and, for many of them, the unrepresentative nature of many international institutions contributed to the creation of space that, as later chapters will show, was used by the Iranian regime to further their international goals, particularly where these criticisms were combined with more assertive international roles, including the intensification of South–South relations and an independent course with regard to international issues, even if they generally followed the US lead on Iran.

Conclusion

International legitimacy creates options for states to pursue international policies for the benefit of their desired goals. For the Islamic Republic, international legitimacy is limited and with it its international options. This chapter showed how the Islamic Republic's lack of international legitimacy is tied up with its troubled relations with the West in general and the United States in particular. These relations, which are better described in terms of a deep rooted mistrust rather than outright animosity, are the result of historical interactions that were continued and even reinforced through the countries' foreign policies vis-à-vis one another during the Ahmadinejad presidency. However, as United States' power is expected to decline, emerging powers are asserting new roles for themselves. This is visible in public criticism of United States' international policies and a level of independence in the foreign policy choices of aspiring powers. This international trend created important opportunities for the Ahmadinejad administration. To some extent this was because a number of countries were actively trying to improve or at least keep relations with Iran to demonstrate their independence. This was not limited to countries such as Venezuela, which have been activists for a counter-hegemony against United States' power, but to some extent also for the BRICS. However, it was particularly the criticism of the status quo that created a space for Iran in which it could assert itself and increase its legitimacy. There is no way of knowing if international developments when Ahmadinejad was president were the first signs of a changing world order in which the international role of the United States was diminishing in favor of an increasingly role of emerging powers. What is important is that rising and aspiring powers were acting on the belief that change was on its way, thereby contributing to this (as yet potential) change. This space created opportunities for Iran, which will be explored in the coming chapters. While Iranian isolation and marginalization is part and parcel of Western hegemony, it should come as no surprise that the Ahmadinejad administration was actively trying to speed up and take advantage of global trends that challenged US power. The following chapters discuss how the Ahmadinejad administration was using Western attempts at isolating Iran to establish itself as a flag bearer of international resistance against the "arrogant powers," exploiting the space created by those criticizing the United States.

Chapter 4

A Foreign Policy Ideology of Change

Foreign policy is shaped not only in response to international develop-ments—it is within the context of regime ideology that foreign policy makers make sense of these developments and explore foreign policy options. During Mahmoud Ahmadinejad's presidency, this ideological context was characterized by a revival of revolutionary discourse, with "change" as a central theme. This ideology gained particular signifi-cance as the Iranian regime was experiencing a growing crisis of legit-imacy both domestically and internationally. In efforts to increase its legitimacy—or retain what legitimacy it had—the regime was engaged a relentless effort to communicate its own preferred views on interna-tional and domestic developments. This chapter gives a discourse analy-sis of Iranian regime's foreign policy ideology during the period in which Mahmoud Ahmadinejad was president on the basis of official state-ments[1] by President Ahmadinejad and Supreme Leader Ali Khamenei.[2] It shows how the identification of problems and solutions, juxtapositions of good and evil, narratives of the past, and expectations for the future in the regime's foreign policy ideology contributed to an elaborate and inherently consistent worldview. In line with this worldview, Iran was identified as a victim, but resistant, and undermined, yet developing, in other words: the Iranian regime's worldview of change allowed for both international and domestic developments to be framed in terms of Iran's success. Of particular relevance to this success was the immanent fall of the United States, and the awakening among the oppressed, which was expected to lead to a more equal international society.

Global Change as a Worldview[3]

To be accepted by a wider audience, worldviews need to be rooted in observable facts to a considerable extent and have inherent consistency. Any plausible portrayal of the world today, its past, and its future needs to interpret and explain observable fact in a way that people believe to be logical or common sense.[4] This common sense notion often derives from dominant worldviews being based in shared experience and a common understanding of historical developments, by which audiences recognize the present worldview's interpretation and explanation as plausible and logical. Likewise, the worldview communicated by Iran's leaders during Ahmadinejad's presidency was one that draws on the historical experiences, primarily the experiences with what has been perceived as a meddling West, and the continuous attempts by Western powers to undermine the interest of the Iranian people. In this worldview, there is a constant threat emanating from the West, which means Iranians need to remain on their guard. In many ways, the worldview present in Khamenei and Ahmadinejad's shared discourse is characterized by a dualism expressed in juxtapositions of positive and negative: the West versus Iran—a straightforward "good versus evil." This chapter starts with a discussion of three dichotomies, with on the side of the West, the oppressor, the World's problems, and the past, and on the side of Iran, the oppressed, the solutions, and the future. As will become clear however, these dichotomies are not as clear-cut as may seem on first sight. Not only is there good in the West and evil among the "rest," the promise of change implies that there is no reason to think that nations will be locked into this juxtaposition for all eternity. On the contrary, change is imminent.

Oppressors and Oppressed

A glance at the list of countries mentioned most often in Iranian foreign policy discourse (2005 until 2013)[5] gives away the centrality of the West, particularly the United States in the discourse of Iran's leaders. Iranian leaders mention the "arrogant powers" more often than any other country or group of countries, including their own.[6] They use the term "arrogant powers" to denote a group of Western states, which always not only includes the United States as their principle leader, but may also refer to European states and usually implies Israel. While the term "arrogant powers" is most recurrent, the predicates "bullying powers," "colonial powers," "domineering powers," and "hegemonic powers" are also often used. Being unspecific about which countries are implied is a discursive advantage: the broad denotations of "arrogant" or "bullying" powers make it possible to speak very negatively about a group of countries, without directly insulting one country in particular. In addition, because the countries included are not made explicit, the audience itself decides who they are thinking of when the term is used.

The arrogant powers are accused of treating the world as their own, particularly the United States that sees itself as "the headman of the global village,"[7] and are believed to have a very harmful effect on global relations. Already in the past, the narrative goes, when Western powers colonized large parts of the developing world, imperialist powers were able to impose their wishes at the expense of the development and independence of other countries. Today, most of these developing countries have political independence, but remain subjected to domination by these former colonial powers, the arrogant powers. However, it is not just the developing countries that are disadvantaged by the state of affairs: Ahmadinejad and Khamenei explicitly differentiate between Western governments and their people. They emphasize how people in the West are also harmed by the policies of arrogant powers. Exemplary is a letter of Ahmadinejad to an American mother:

> I am confident that you and the American people would not trust the pre-fabricated lies and complicated, poisonous propagandas that are made and broadcasted by inhumane, aggressive and capitalist networks. (...) I am sorry to say that the American people are kept in an absolute censorship concerning the outside world by their government (Ahmadinejad, 18 March 2007).

Similarly, Khamenei has emphasized that Western countries violate the rights of their own people, including the rights of free speech and the scientific investigation of the Holocaust by Western historians.[8]

Another subtlety in the apparent dualism is that non-Western governments are considered complicit to the oppression by arrogant powers. Arrogant powers make a habit of supporting tyrants, the discourse suggests, and are also notorious for strategies of deception. These strategies are not limited to governments: arrogant powers have also found agents among the people of other countries, even in Iran itself. This also means that while it is generally clear that the "arrogant powers" comprise a list of Western countries, the juxtaposed group does not confine to boundaries of nation states. In other words, rather than a division between the Western and non-Western world, or the Western world and the world of Islam, Iranian foreign policy discourse presents a dichotomy between arrogant powers and cooperating governments, on the one hand, and those who suffer from the domination of these powers—basically everyone else—on the other. The latter group is generally referred to as "humanity" or "mankind," which "has the deep wound caused by impious powers on his battered body,"[9] and "is tired of war, bloodshed, tension, discrimination and deception."[10] However, the problems humanity is faced with are not merely the result of arrogant powers' behavior, but to a large extent to blame on humanity itself. These problems "came about because of humanity's detachment and disregard for the message of the messengers and for following evil."[11] Human beings today have to choose whether they want to follow the guidance offered by the Holy Prophet and free themselves of their problems, or take the invitation of Satan, Khamane'i claims. In other words, "human beings are standing at a junction."[12]

Problems and Solutions

Identifying problems is a powerful discursive tool, not in the last place because it creates the opportunity to present the audience with necessary solutions and in doing so influence the course of action.[13] It is especially Ahmadinejad who, in his speeches to international organizations, presented his audience with world problems, which include poverty, oppression imposed on the majority of the global community, environmental issues, moral issues such as the status of women, the destruction of cultures, violation of human rights, and a lack of peace and security.[14] The root of these problems lies in two factors, which explicitly run through Ahmadinejad's discourse and are in line with Khamenei's worldview. The first is the status quo as it emerged after the Second World War, which "drew up a roadmap for global domination" to ensure the interest of the victors over that of the "vanquished nations," the second the immorality of these dominant powers.[15]

The status quo that Iran's leaders present is characterized by the domination of the arrogant powers at the expense of the interest of humanity. Other nations are rendered powerless in the present organization of the international system. Part of this powerlessness lies in their inability to develop under US domination. Under the circumstances that Khamenei and Ahmadinejad describe, the West always remains most prosperous and thus most economically powerful. However, the powerlessness of developing countries also has important institutional and psychological dimensions: Institutional, because as the victors of the Second World War, the arrogant powers were able to draw up international law in the aftermath of the war, thereby institutionalizing their power,[16] and psychological, because the arrogant powers have vital propaganda means at their disposal and use these to dominate the international flow of information. As such, they can actively shape world opinion.[17]

Iranian leaders' narrative on international institutions runs along the following lines: owing to arrogant powers' domination, international organizations do not function properly. Although intended to solve the world's problems, these institutions merely perpetuate them: international monetary and banking mechanisms have been turned into tools of imposition of arrogant powers, while the IAEA, for example, is merely sidestepped. However, the main problem Iranian leaders have with the UN Security Council, Khamenei remarks, is how the Security Council is used as an instrument by the arrogant powers.[18] Ahmadinejad concurs and regards the Security Council as the first among all the ineffective UN organizations. "They have created circumstances in which some powers with exclusive rights to veto in the Security Council act as judge, jury and executioner, regardless of being a defendant or respondent."[19] Under these circumstances, there is no role for the UN in promoting peace and justice.[20]

> To where should the Palestinian people take their complaints?...how can the oppressed people of Iraq ask the occupiers to compensate for the huge damages inflicted upon them? What should the people of Afghanistan do?[21]

Considering that, international law does not function properly due to domination by arrogant powers is particularly problematic as the arrogant powers are the main violators of international law. Owing to their domination of these institutions, they escape punishment.[22] This brings us to the second and perhaps more important cause of today's problems: the disregard of moral values by the arrogant powers. Today this is visible in the "exercise of political pressures by bullying powers against other governments..., maintaining as well as building up the military headquarters and forces by the big powers in different states, violation and limitation of recognized human freedoms,"[23] and other immoral behavior such as the promotion of materialism and promiscuity. Khamenei, for example, recounts:

> Presently, you can see how the United States of America, which is the pivot of the global hegemonic system, is treating human beings and human values. The killing and trampling on the honour, dignity and national identity of human beings have become a common practice for U.S. politicians, so much so that they no longer feel the wickedness of the actions.[24]

To maintain their hegemony, arrogant powers have not only a number of means at their disposal, such as military and economic threat, but also more subtle means such as psychological warfare and deception. The main aim of arrogant powers, Iranian leaders assert, is to keep other countries from progressing, so that they remain dependent. This allows arrogant powers to continue their world domination and plunder the wealth of other nations for their own benefit. For this purpose, arrogant powers create threat and insecurity in countries such as Iraq and Afghanistan to prolong their occupation, disallow Iran to develop nuclear energy, and hinder the scientific progress of other nations all together. Moreover, Iranian leaders emphasize that Western leaders use propaganda means, lies, and false promises to deceive people and governments to cooperate with them. Their propaganda means allow them to claim righteousness, deceive Western public opinion, and to spread their views among non-Western nations, even if they are based on lies and deception. The Iranian nation, thanks to its awareness, sees right through this deception and presents the reality ("undeniable truth" or "undeniable reality" is often used expressions).[25] This allows Iran's leaders to present the world with an alternative view.

In presenting an alternative worldview, Iranian leaders also question the plausibility of the worldviews presented by the West. On the one hand, they cast doubt on Western narratives such as those of the 9/11 attacks and the Holocaust, and Western views on Islam.

> By using artistic and political means and through their media they are insinuating that Islam is hostile to other nations and to other religions. This is not true...Islam is opposed to compulsion, oppression, arrogance and domination.[26]

On the other hand, they point at internal contradictions between the ideology Western leaders are presenting and the way it is applied. Not only do Western countries apply double standards when they, for example, allow Israel to develop nuclear weapons but do not allow Iran a peaceful nuclear program, but these Western countries themselves also do not practice what they preach. For instance, the arrogant powers have stockpiles of weapons of mass destruction, support terrorism in the Middle East, and violate human rights not only abroad but also at home. This double-faced nature of the arrogant powers, as Iranian leaders portray it, shows that they do not really intend to spread human rights and democracy, but are using this as a ploy to cover up their real motivations for, among other things, their presence in the Middle East.[27]

In a world in which arrogant powers are dominating humanity, Iranian leaders express the need for other nations to become aware of the current state of affairs and to become resistant against the arrogant powers. Khamenei uses the word awakening in this regard and focuses particularly on the Muslim world. He sees an Islamic revival as a direct response to the domination of the West and a sign of resistance. This resistance can only materialize if Muslim countries are no longer dependent on the arrogant powers and compensate for "today's scientific and practical backwardness and inferiority in the field of politics, industry and economy...Fortunately, some of the phenomena in the contemporary era point to the beginning of this compensating move."[28] Arrogant powers are aware of the awakening of Muslims and Muslim countries and are actively trying to undermine Islam. They do this, for example, by supporting the enemies of Islam, such as writers and artists who insulted the Prophet, and particularly by sowing discord among Muslims. They do this at the local level not only in countries such as Lebanon, Palestine, and Iraq, but also by pitting Sunni and Shi'a against each other regionally. This is particularly deceptive, Khamenei argues, as arrogant powers themselves do not differentiate between Shi'a and Sunni but regard all Muslims the same and confront them equally.[29] As such, Sunni and Shi'a have a common enemy and should unite against the arrogant powers. To become united as Muslims means becoming aware of an Islamic identity and taking the path of God.

Ahmadinejad's solutions to world problems are similar to those of Khamenei, and in many ways Ahmadinejad's view complements or overlaps with Khamenei's views. His focus however is not on Islam, but on a return to morality, which is not limited to the Muslim world. Ahmadinejad puts much less emphasis on Iran's leadership role in the Ummah, and reaches out to developing countries in Latin America, Asia, and Africa. He does so by emphasizing their shared identity not just as victims of arrogant powers, but also as the cradles of culture, civilization, and of great thinkers and prophets.[30] He describes Asia, Africa, Latin American, and the Middle East region as the direct targets of the trampling of honor, culture, dignity, and morality by the arrogant powers and emphasizes the ability of the people of these regions to resist these developments.[31] Although Ahmadinejad mentions the merits of the "great saviors of human beings like Buddha and Confucius" and emphasizes that Asians are more sincere than Westerners,[32] he mainly addresses Christians. Where Khamenei is asking for unity among Muslims, Ahmadinejad asks for unity among monotheists, and emphasizes Iran's shared identity with the Christian world.[33] According to Ahmadinejad, it is not just Islam, but morality and thus monotheism that are subjected to aggression.[34] Not only Muslims, but also Christians are called on to oppose the arrogant powers:

> If Christ was present today, undoubtedly he would have stood with the people in opposition to bullying, ill tempered and expansionist powers... Indeed, in his lifetime he waged such a fight.[35]

In other words, although Khamenei's focus is on the Muslim world, Ahmadinejad reaches out to a broader group of states by emphasizing monotheism. By doing so, he ties the world religions of Islam, Christianity, and (theoretically, but not explicitly stated) Judaism together and presents them with a common enemy: the immorality of the arrogant powers. As such he has a broader potential audience than Khamenei, who addresses only Islam, without having to compromise the religious basis of his message. Particularly, Ahmadinejad emphasizes the commonalities between these religions when it comes, for example, to their main religious personages. However, despite these differences in audiences of Ahmadinejad and Khamenei, their message is quite similar: those who value morality should become aware of what is happening and unite against their common enemy the arrogant powers.

Past and future

In the narrative of past and future, Iranian leaders' strategy of "acting as if" was most powerful. Much like at the end of the 1980s, activists and later politicians started to "act as if" the Cold War was over, creating space for this change to come about,[36] Iran's foreign policy makers were acting within the framework of a world without US hegemony. The continuous comparison of the behavior of arrogant powers today with their behavior in the past as colonial powers sends out a clear message: the behavior of the arrogant powers is unchanged, is a remnant of the past, and belongs to the past. States such as the United States are like "the people of the past," which should notice the imminent fall of empires.[37] Iranian leaders aimed to show that the changing state of affairs is an undeniable truth that even the arrogant powers are aware of and sometimes admit, but which these powers generally ignore. They have noticed that Islam is experiencing an awakening that has made Muslims aware of the deceptive slogans of the West and have become resistant. Arrogant powers now "feel they are weak in position to stand against the great movement of the Islamic Ummah. They feel they have been subjugated by the Muslim world."[38]

Ahmadinejad's UN speeches are good illustrations of the Iranian regime's "acting as if to create space" for international change: Iran is flaunting the "dominant game," which is part of the past, while acting in the space of another, more marginal one[39] that according to Ahmadinejad has the future. In September 2009, he said:

> The age of imposing the opinion of cold capitalism and forcing the style and tendencies of a particular group on the rest of the world, or expansion of global domination in the name of building the world and the era of establishing empires, have ended. The period of humiliating other nations and imposing double standards, biased policies and multifaceted discriminatory values has passed ... No longer can a group of people define democracy and freedom in their preferred terms and consider themselves the criteria of such.[40]

Furthermore, the Iranian regime's "acting as if" is not limited to merely saying things are changing. The next chapter discusses how Iran's regime through the formation of alliances and through negotiations with rising powers was literally acting as if the days of Western hegemony are over. If Western powers acknowledge their decline, Ahmadinejad emphasizes, it would not be too late for them to change:

> Is it not high time for these powers to return from the path of arrogance and obedience of Satan to the path of Godliness? ... If they answer to the invitation, they will be saved and if they don't, the same thing that befell the people of the past will befall them.[41]

In sum, Iranian leaders' dualistic worldview in which the oppressor/oppressed are juxtaposed is not static, it is not a state the world is locked into for all eternity. If anything, Iranian foreign policy discourse is one of change. Change is imminent, and states, including the arrogant powers, have the agency to change themselves: oppressors can become benevolent powers, and the oppressed can become resistant and take control of their own destiny. By doing so, these countries can change from the past, which was characterized by domination and world problems, to a bright, prosperous future. This element of change is also central in the Iranian regime's identification of Iran, which is discussed in the following section: first, as a consequence of Iran's own change through the 1979 Revolution, and secondly, as Iran's moral identity as an example for other countries that are changing or should change.

Iran's Identity of Change

Identity is a relational concept, with processes of linking and differentiation at its center. Linking happens when predicates reinforce each other, for example when Iran is identified as being simultaneously democratic, moral, and a victim of "arrogant powers," and also when the identity of the self is reinforced through identification with others: Iran is seen as democratic, moral, and a victim of arrogant powers such as the Palestinian people are seen as democratic, moral, and victims of arrogant powers. Differentiation means the radical contrasting of one set of predicates with another set. For example, the attributes associated with Iran (democratic, moral, and a victim) are contrasted with the United States (undemocratic, immoral, and aggressive). Through this juxtaposition, both sets of predicates are strengthened.

The centrality of the West and particularly the United States in Iran's foreign policy discourse under Ahmadinejad suggests that the United States is the radical other against which Iranian identity takes shape. However, as Hansen[42] suggests, identities often rely on more complex structures than self versus radical other. To fully comprehend Iran's identity, it is important to look at other more subtle constructions of difference and also similarity with the United States and other others. What is found then, first, that Iranian identity is constructed not only in *juxtaposition* with the United States: in the discourse of Ahmadinejad and Khamenei, the United States and Iran have much in common. Moreover, Iran is contrasted with itself as it was before the 1979 Revolution, providing a central temporal element to the identification of Iran. Second, Iran positions itself within a broader group of Muslim countries with a shared history and identity, and with Iran as a model state within this group. This also implies an important moral role for Iran as an example for other nations. This moral identity is than juxtaposed with a group of arrogant powers that are allied with or under the influence of the United States. This section discusses the mechanisms of linking and differentiation in the Iranian regime's construction of Iran's temporal, spatial, and moral identity.

Iran's Temporal Identity

Iran's identity as expressed by the regime derived directly from its history as a revolutionary nation and has elements of both change and continuity. Continuity can be found in the struggles of the Iranian nation against oppressors throughout history.[43] The change, however, came with the 1979 Revolution against the shah and the foreign powers supporting his rule. Through this revolution, Iranians were able to realize their potential:

> We now have attained self-confidence; we have become aware of our talents and capabilities and fulfilled our potential to a great extent; also we have made considerable progress in the scientific and industrial areas as well as in the social sphere and in the field of public affairs.[44]

The discourse of both Ahmadinejad and Khamenei is overflowing with positive self-awareness: Iranians are described as determined, strong, dignified, united, able, aware, vigilant, courageous, enthusiastic, devoted, lively—and the list continues. The revolution is described as the manifestation of these positive characteristics, some of which have according to the discourse always been inherent to the Iranian people. It is talked about as the latest and most successful stage in Iran's development toward an Islamic democracy. Through the revolution, the Iranian people toppled a decadent, corrupt, and despotic regime, established a religious democracy in which "the fragrance of serving the public based on revolutionary principles has filled the air."[45] Moreover,

> The Islamic Revolution replaced the humiliation outsiders used to impose upon this nation with self-esteem. It replaced that bitter and abject dependence with self-reliance. It replaced that total capitulation against the outsiders with resistance and authority. It turned that inherited, baseless and illogical monarchy to populistic and democratic rule. New foundations were established that earned the country a new identity.[46]

Quotes very similar to this one can be found in almost all of Khamenei's speeches and statements, although Khamenei may put emphasis on different elements of change depending on the topic and audience of his speech. The attributes associated with Iran before or after the revolution mutually reinforce each other and have many crossed links: Iran's dependency as well as the fact that it was trampled upon and exploited made it devoid of any self-confidence; the self-reliant nature of Iran after the revolution means it can defend its rights and dignity and resist outsiders; and so on.

Three elements of Iran's changed identity stand out in Khamenei's discourse and are also of particular relevance to Ahmadinejad's international discourse. These are its resistant, independent, and popular identity.[47] Both Ahmadinejad and Khamenei present an image of Iran as a nation that is still in a process of change or development. Khamenei repeatedly uses the metaphor of "path": a path Iran began treading after the revolution, led by Imam Khomeini, and on which it has been continuing since with power and strength and on which it will continue in the future. It has found its path; the path of God, repeatedly called a bright path, the path of honor, the path of independence, and a path to wealth. It will be able to tread this difficult path and will remove all obstacles on it, "and reach the peaks of honour and glory one by one, not through war and bloodshed but through patience, perseverance, prudence and firm intention, just as we have advanced and captured many such peaks so far."[48] With its change toward an independent, resistant, and popular country, Iran can look forward to a bright future. That Iran has the future is also accentuated by Khamenei's continuous reference to Iran's youth. He emphasizes the role of youngsters in government, science, and in defending the country, and praises them for their dedication, presence, and competence.

> Our youngsters, who by the favour of Allah constitute the majority of our population, may prepare themselves for the future of this country. Youngsters from all social strata, especially those belonging to the educated class, should realize that the future of this country belongs to them and is shaped by them.[49]

It is particularly Khamenei who places emphasis on Iran's changed identity as independent, resistant, and democratic through the revolution. This changed identity has an important international dimension: before the revolution, Iran played no role in international affairs; since the revolution, it is a prominent country. It is an example for other countries in a changing world. This understanding complements Ahmadinejad's discourse of Iran as a positive force internationally, resisting the arrogant powers and contributing to peace and justice. Here again, we see the element of change. In Ahmadinejad's discourse, however, the element of change is one which is projected internationally. While Khamenei speaks about the revolution, Ahmadinejad does so much less and instead emphasizes Iran's currents struggle with the arrogant powers. As such, the discourses complement each other, with Khamenei's discourse of change through the revolution gaining an international dimension within that of Ahmadinejad.

The views in the discourse on Iran's changed identity from submissive to resistant can be summarized as follows: Before the revolution, the Iranian nation was under foreign domination and had not been able to develop itself. Iran needed to become independent of these powers to develop. However, in a world where arrogant powers continue to try to dominate others, independence does not come naturally: it implies resistance against these powers. This understanding of resistance is central to Iran's identity today. It is the changed identity from a dependent nation to a resistant nation:

> Our nation had to endure complete submissiveness. The revolution changed this state of capitulation to a state of resistance and authority. It turned that state of dependence into self-reliance...New foundations were established that earned the country a new identity.[50]

As an example of the changed identity of Iran through the revolution, Khamenei refers back to the Imposed War (Iran–Iraq) and expresses with this reference the identity of resistance of Iranians:

> The epical event created by the Iranian nation in the Sacred Defence era displayed the great capabilities and potentials of the people of this divine land, especially their power of resistance and valour.[51]

Iran's changed identity since the revolution is implicitly contrasted with the unchanged nature of imperial powers, which have remained unchanged and continue to want to dominate Iran. Since the revolution, arrogant powers are trying to achieve this goal of domination through isolating and undermining Iran in every area possible.

> It is clear when you stand against bullying and domination, the world's arrogant powers will not leave you alone, but they will pose a challenge to you. This challenge has existed ever since the Islamic Revolution's victory and will continue to exist until the world's bullies and hegemonic powers give up in despair. Therefore, you should always consider yourself to be in the arena of confrontation with hegemonic powers.[52]

Iran, in other words, can be resistant because it is a victim of the world's arrogant powers. Ahmadinejad and Khamenei's statements are ridden with reference to Iran's victimized status, and emphasize that Iran is denied its progress,[53] is a victim of propaganda and psychological warfare,[54] is the object of accusation,[55] is a victim of sanctions and Security Council resolutions,[56] is a victim of military threats, aggression,[57] is denied its rights,[58] is a victim of the sowing of discord,[59] is threatened,[60] is the object of provocation,[61] and is the object of conspiracy.[62] Also mentioned are unkind treatment, political and cultural attacks, and interference in domestic affairs. Iran's identification as resistant is articulated particularly through Iran's numerous achievements despite difficult circumstances and the enemy's attempts to undermine Iran's progress:

> They tried a lot in different ways to break our nation's determination apart, but they couldn't. What is significant and really promising is the fact that within the last twenty-eight or nine years, we have been constantly moving forward. There has been no halt...Our enemies are trying a lot to stop this movement, but they have not been able to do so and will not be able to that in the future either. And they admit this fact today.[63]

For Khamenei, resistance is directly tied to the domestic achievements of Iran. In addition, Ahmadinejad emphasizes the importance of Iran's development despite the efforts of hegemonic powers. However, for Ahmadinejad resistance also has an important international dimension. On the one hand, it means defending Iran's rights in the international arena, including its right to development. On the other hand, it means standing against injustice, against the build-up of nuclear weapons, environmental pollution, bullying, and other practices of the arrogant powers.

The following quote summarizes Iran's identity of independence and development:

> If we had continued to rely on others and beg them for our basic necessities as it was the case for many years under the former regime, the situation would still be the same today and we would not be independent and self-sufficient.[64]

Iran's victimized status is particularly articulate when it comes to the discussion of Iran's development. The West's policies are aimed more than anything, Iranian leaders argue, against Iran's development. The revolution did not just change Iran from a submissive to a resistant power; it made Iranians aware of their ability to be resistant and to develop without the help of outsiders. Iranians are making efforts and take great strides toward this purpose, Khamenei emphasizes. He presents an image of development as Iran's top priority. However, Khamenei notices how Iranians are also aware that the former imperial powers are trying to undermine Iran's independence and progress. Development despite these obstructions is then framed as the manifestation of the success of both Iran's resistance and independence, even as the victory of Iran over the bullying powers.

Obstruction by the world's arrogant powers of Iran's development is aimed, in particular, at Iran's scientific progress. According to Khamenei, this is not new:

> The policies of colonial and Western countries toward Iran over the past few centuries are in need of careful study and analysis. There is strong evidence indicating that these policies have been aimed at keeping our country and nation scientifically backward and underdeveloped.[65]

Science and technological development are considered a top priority of Iran for both leaders and are mentioned more often than other areas of development by both Ahmadinejad and Khamenei. Scientific progress, according to Khamenei, "is the secret of economic, political and military power and high morale of any nation." He also emphasizes that "scientific progress will not be attained through imitation. It will be accomplished through initiative, innovation, originality and the opening of new frontiers in science."[66] The victory of Iran over the bullying power, then, is taking place particularly in the field of science and technology. Khamenei emphasizes Iran's independence in its scientific and technological development:

> You do the constructions yourselves. You acquire the knowledge yourself. You do research yourselves. Those days you were forces to accept whatever you were offered with closed eyes. These are the achievements that promote a nation to the summits of achievements and grandeur.[67]

The third pillar of Iran's temporal identity, its popularity, puts the Iranian people at the center of the stage. The Iranian Revolution is described as ultimately a popular revolution, through which the oppressed people were able to realize their potential. Iranian political discourse today continues to emphasize the centrality of the Iranian people in the revolution and since. Iran's identification as popular reinforces the identities of resistance and development to which the Iranian people are central:

> Thankfully, the Iranian nation and the Iranian youth—the revolutionary and enthusiastic youth of today—are present on the scene with a lot

of enthusiasm and with great readiness. They are ready to make efforts. You can see the results of their efforts in such fields as science, politics, technology, and different social activities.[68]

Central to the popular identity of the Islamic Republic is the emphasis on its democracy. Khamenei speaks often of Iran's democracy as a manifestation of Iran's successes. Ahmadinejad talks about the Islamic Republic as having "one of the most popular and progressive governments of the world."[69] Or, in Khamenei's words,

> The mature and sagacious conduct of the people as well as the sincerity and commitment of the authorities helped religious democracy to surpass the world democracies in terms of health of elections and to outpace the Western democracies in terms of public participation.[70]

Here also the revolution is identified as the moment of change: the former regime "regarded the country as belonging to itself and attached no status to the Iranian people,"[71] but the 1979 Revolution brought a popular administration to power that "represents the will and desires of the Iranian nation".

> Ever since the victory of the Islamic Revolution, there has been one election per year on average in this country, in which our people have displayed their freedom of choice and their power to elect their favourite officials.[72]

The Iranian people even after the revolution remains target of the arrogant powers, who are using propaganda means to deceive them and, for example, dissuade them from going to polls. Khamenei reminds the people again that they are expected not to fall for this:

> But the Iranian people, who are well aware of the objectives pursued by the enemies of Islam and Iran, will once again thwart them in their goals.[73]

As said, public participation in the elections is thus regarded as a sign of the strength of the Islamic Republic and as a clear message to the enemies of Iran.

Iran's popular identity is not as prominent in the discourse as the identities of resistance and independence. Nevertheless, it is important as a part of Iran's self-understanding as changed from a despotic to a democratic government, as well as in its identification with regard to spatial others such as the United States, which will be discussed later. First, we turn to the last aspect of Iran's change identity through the revolution: that of Islam.

There is a central role for Islam in the regime's temporal identification of Iran. When it comes to foreign policy discourse, resistance, independence, and democracy are the main characteristics of Iran's temporal identity. Islam also plays a role in this, as one would expect of a country that calls itself the Islamic Republic of Iran. Khamenei, in particular, portrays the revolution as the first step toward becoming an Islamic country "in its real sense." Through the revolution, Iranians established a popular-based Islamic system to run the country in conformity with Islam: "Religion forms the basis for the enactment and implementation of laws in the country and the people are pursuing Islamic goals and ideals."[74] Khamenei praises the peoples' efforts in this regard, although he also wants to remind them that taking part in the elections is a religious duty.

Not only Iran's popular identity but also its identity as a resistant force is supported by references to Islam. Since the establishment of an Islamic country after the revolution, Iranians have defended their revolution against national and international threats. Khamenei's references to the Iran–Iraq War that followed the revolution are used as proof of the turn the Iranian people made toward Islam. During this eight-year period, known in Iran as the Sacred Defense era, "valorous people devoted to Islam and our dear homeland . . . abandoned the comfort of their homes in order to . . . defend the frontiers of honour and dignity of their Islamic homeland," Khamenei says.[75] He also emphasizes the victory of Islam over the Ba'thist enemy Saddam. Today, Iran's Islamic identity is helping it in another battle, the one toward scientific and technological progress and development as it had done for the Islamic community in the past:

> Islam, in the first century after its advent, helped a small community of Muslims to reach the peak of world civilization, so much so that Islamic knowledge and civilization shone and prevailed in the world.[76]

The role of Islam in this is that of a religion that infuses "human beings with valour and dignity and which guides them on the path to scientific and technological progress and development." The "amazing scientific and technological progress in Islamic Iran achieved under severe economic sanctions and embargoes" is, therefore, attributed to Islam, and a clear indication of the "triumph and advancements of Islam in its struggle against its enemies in this century."[77]

In addition, Ahmadinejad frames Iran as an Islamic country, but in a less explicit way. To be sure, his repeated emphasis on change and the return of Imam Mahdi connects his broader message to Iran's Shi'a identity. His references to monotheism, faith-inspired resistance, awakening, and other such concepts give his discourse an unmistakable religious dimension. However, the Islamic identity Ahmadinejad ascribes to Iran is in the first place related to Iran's duty of bringing morality and monotheism to the world (which is also emphasized by Khamenei and is discussed later in the chapter). Instead of a distinct identity, it seems therefore that Islam is in the first place the language through which Iran's leaders express the identities of resistance, independence, and democracy than an identity by itself. To the extent it does function as a separate identity, it, on the one hand, emphasizes Iran's shared identity with other Muslim countries and, on the other, sets it apart from countries such as the United States. This relational identity will be the subject of the following section.

Iran's identity of change means a clear break from the political discourse before the 1979 Revolution: Iran's last shah liked to emphasize the continuity in Iranian history from ancient times onward.[78] To be sure, the identity of a nation with a long and glorious past is also present in Iranian discourse during Ahmadinejad. Iranians are described as an almost superior nation, whose achievements are unparalleled. These characteristics did not come about through the revolution; the revolution was merely the result of it after Iranians became aware of their true identity:

> Over many years and through ceaseless propaganda, they had turned the Iranian nation into a dependent nation, devoid of self-confidence and noble aspirations and alienated from its native culture. The Iranian people, despite their remarkable historical background, significant geographical position, great human talent and abundant natural resources, were exploited by alien powers, first by Britain and then by the United States. But the Islamic Revolution awakened our people and ended their dependency.[79]

Both Ahmadinejad and Khamenei use the language of Islam to express Iran's changed identity through the revolution; however, it is merely the *language* through which Iran's identities of resistance, development, and popularity are expressed than an identity by itself. In other words, although reference is made to Islam to develop Iran's identities of resistance, development, and popularity, it does not constitute an elaborated identity by itself in the way resistance, development, and popularity do. Islam is more relevant, however, in Iran's spatial identity as a way to contrast between Iran's moral identity and the immorality of its main others, as is discussed later in the chapter.

In sum, line with the regime's worldview of change, Iran's temporal identity according to the regime is one of change. Through the Iranian Revolution, Iran became a changed nation: from submission, dependence, and despotism, it turned into a resistant, self-reliant, and popular nation. Iranian leaders talk about Iran not only as a changed country but also as a country that is able to contribute to change internationally. Iran invites other countries to change and directs its calls particularly to the developing world. Despite their ability to change, the arrogant powers have not changed, and do not seem to be inclined to change either. They are attributed an identity of intransigence and seems permanently located in (particularly, moral) backwardness. The following section discusses the juxtapositions in the spatial identity of Iran as articulated by Khamenei and Ahmadinejad.

Iran's Spatial Identity

The subject positioning present in Iranian foreign policy discourse is contextualized by the dualistic worldview that was described above, through which Iranian leaders identified Iran's problems and solutions, combined with an element of blaming by differentiating between culprits (oppressors) and victims (the oppressed). This is also related to clear notions of past and future with an explicit element of change. Within this dualistic worldview, a subject position is made possible between Iran and its temporal, spatial, and ethical "others." The regime's identification of Iran in relation to other countries to a large extent relies on the dichotomy between changed/unchanged. It is, however, not a mere juxtapositioning of "us" versus "them" or a self-identification in relation to a radical other. Particularly relevant to Iranian identity are others that resemble Iran. While those countries resembling Iran have changed or are currently changing (e.g., through the Islamic awakening), Iran's enemies remain unchanged and greatly resemble Iran's past. This section explores the Iranian regime's identification of Iran with regard to these two groups of countries.

Iran shares certain elements of its identity with (groups of) countries that find themselves victim to the arrogant powers, particularly the sowing of discord, colonial domination, and propaganda. Whether these countries put up resistance against the arrogant powers or not, Iran shares with them this victimized status. These countries can be found in the Islamic world, the Arab world, and, though less often mentioned by Khamenei, the continents of Asia, Africa, and Latin America. Only a few of the countries in this group share Iran's resistance against (and victory over) arrogant powers and, in doing so, show a stronger resemblance to Iran. These countries are Palestine, Iraq, Afghanistan, and Lebanon.[80]

The discourse on Palestine, Iraq, Afghanistan, and Lebanon reinforces Iran's identity of a resistant nation, by portraying this resistance as a shared struggle against a common enemy.[81] Iran is, however, different from these countries in that it is no longer the victim of the atrocities these countries go through today. In other words, on the one hand, all five countries are the victim of military aggression and the sowing of discord by arrogant powers, find their rights violated, and all have lost martyrs in their struggles. In addition, they are all the scene of victory over the arrogant powers and share an identity of success. On the other hand, Palestine, Iraq, Afghanistan, and Lebanon share characteristics of suffering, massacre, oppression, and displacement, which Iran does not endure anymore. These characteristics all derive from the domestic circumstances of conflict these countries are in. While Iran does not share these specific signs with the four nations, it does share with these nations the common enemy of the arrogant powers—the main culprit in all four scenarios.

Here also we see that the concept of change is key. For Khamenei, an important moment of change for Palestine was the victory of Hamas in the 2006 Parliamentary elections, which he presents as a defeat for the arrogant powers.[82] In addition, Iraq changed from a country "in which a bloodthirsty leader brutalized its people with the encouragement of the United States" to a country whose "proud people humiliated the pompous America," and Lebanon from a country "that the Zionists could easily encroach upon" to one that defeated the Israeli army.[83] Palestine, Iraq, and Lebanon changed from passive victims to actively resistant people, in line with what both Khamenei and to a lesser extent Ahmadinejad call the awakening of Muslim nations. Afghanistan is an exception to this: although it shares many characteristics with the other three as a victim of the arrogant powers, it is not attributed the same agency in resisting these powers.

Not just Palestine, Lebanon, Iraq, and Afghanistan are in the process of change—the entire Muslim world is awakening according to Khamenei. However, there is much room for improvement when it comes to the behavior of the Ummah, in general, and the Arab world, in particular.[84] Both the Arab world and the Muslim world at large are criticized for being silent and indifferent about the atrocities committed by the arrogant powers, of failing to put these powers to justice through international law, and of cooperating with them. The latter is seen as treachery and betrayal, which may partly be explained not only by blackmail and bullying on the side of Western powers, but also weakness, laziness, irrationality, indolence, and ignorance of Muslim nations.[85] The Muslim and Arab world, therefore, should and can change—just as Iran has.[86] The most important change that Khamenei presents as necessary for the Ummah is to become united. Iranian leaders try to influence the perception of a Sunni–Shi'a divide by claiming that this division is imposed by arrogant powers.[87] As such, they try to create space for cooperation by acting as if there is no difference between Shi'a and Sunni, particularly as they share a common enemy: the confrontation of Islam and morality by the West. Khamenei tries to create space for cooperation with other Muslim states by acting as if they were naturally united and the arrogant powers are trying to undermine this. In doing so, Iran effectively equates cooperation with the West as going against the unity of the Ummah and against Islam.

Khamenei talks about the Ummah and the Arab World much more than Ahmadinejad does. Ahmadinejad has a broader focus and talks about Africa, Asia, and Latin America—continents generally ignored in Khamenei's discourse. Like the Ummah in Khamenei's discourse, the countries on these continents share many characteristics with Iran, such as its historical encounter with imperialism:

> The imposition of colonial regimes, plundering the enormous resources of this rich and vast continent, along with the imposition and propagation of racism, degradation of indigenous culture and trampling the rights of the hard working, talented and noble African nations continued for centuries. Albeit, the people of the continent and their revolutionary leaders were able to force out such adversaries and establish independent nations.[88]

Its human capacity,

> Each of the Asian countries is home to treasures of knowledge which stands as the great capital of great human society…We shall break the inhuman monopoly of science and technology exercised by some bullying powers.[89]

And its victimized status,

> In Latin America, people find their security, national interests and cultures to be seriously endangered by the menacing shadow of

alien domineering governments, and even by the embassies of some empires.[90]

Moreover, Ahmadinejad ties the experiences of these continents and those of the Ummah and Arab world together as to create one common fate:

> Unfortunately the humanity has witnessed that in all long wars, like the Korean and Vietnam wars, the war of the Zionists against Palestinians and Lebanon, war of Saddam against the people of Iran and ethnic wars of Europe and Africa, one of the members of the Security Council was one of the belligerents or supported one party against the other, usually the aggressor, or the conflict itself.[91]

Identifying humanity as a witness here is a powerful discursive tool to make this sound like an objective truth. In addition, it adds to the "arrogant powers" versus humanity dichotomy. Ahmadinejad also talks of the oppression imposed on the majority of the global community, "especially on the people of Iraq, Palestine, Africa, Latin America, and Asia" and calls for the ending of "interferences in the affairs of Iraq and Afghanistan, [the] Middle East, African nations, Latin America, Asia and Europe."[92] Again here Ahmadinejad is tying the fate of the developing world to Iran and is juxtaposing it with an oppressive, meddling West. In short, while Khamenei addresses the Ummah, as one would expect of a religious leader, and Ahmadinejad's main focus is on Asia, Africa, and Latin America, as one would expect of a president who travels to these regions regularly, there is a convergence in their discourses in the sense that both aim to appeal to larger audience outside the country by constructing a shared identity.

Despite the importance of similarity in Iranian foreign policy discourse, the juxtaposition of Iran with the United States is undoubtedly the most central to the regime's perception of Iran's spatial identity. The "arrogant powers" is the term most commonly used to denote the group of Iran's ultimate "others."[93] They are central to the worldview communicated by Iranian leaders in that they are the cause for current problems and stand in the way of proper solutions. For the regime's identification of Iran, it is particularly interesting to see how the countries implied in this group are talked about separately, that is, as nation states like Iran. One could argue that the negative identification with another is most effective when there is a basic similarity to that other.[94] After all, a more refined identification is possible only through a process of (implicit) comparison with another, which to make comparison possible needs to share some attributes, in this case, being a nation. The representation of the other as defining the boundaries of the self, the others as the what-we-are-not, is after all more convincing when that other shares at least some basic characteristics with the self. If there would be no basic similarity, the comparison would fall short. When it comes to nation-states, the United States proves the most elaborate other against which the Iranian regime's identification of Iran takes place. This should be no surprise as the United States has been Iran's main enemy since the revolution. There are a number of key characteristics, which the United States and Iran share and which make them particularly well matched. Both countries are considered prominent nations in the world, both countries are aware of the international state of affairs, both country are strong and powerful, both have international responsibilities, both claim to advocate democracy, and both are the object of challenge and threat— usually each other's. In other words, according to the discourse, both countries have an international role to play, but are challenged as such by the other. It could even be argued that the role that Iran attributes to the United States as the headmen of the West is the kind of role Iran would seek for itself among Muslim and/or developing nations. At any rate, the identification of Iran as a juxtaposition against the United States is aided by the fact that these two countries, to Iran, are in fact highly comparable.

When comparing the discourse on Iran and the United States, what stands out is that the United States has remained unchanged: it is arrogant, immoral, incapable, un-Islamic, aggressive, and so on. The United States, according to Iranian leaders, is able to change, but it has not. It has been, in fact, invited to change, but has chosen to ignore this invitation. As such, the contrast between Iran and the United States also remains unchanged. The representation of the United States in Iranian discourse reinforces the elements of Iran's identity by presenting it with antonyms: Iran is moral, the United States is immoral, Iran is democratic, the United States is undemocratic, and each of these categories implicates subsigns such as honest/dishonest, stronger/weaker (than it seems), loved/hated, and nuclear nonproliferation/proliferation.

The identification of Iran in contrast to the United States is not just through juxtaposition, but also through causal relations. In Iranian foreign policy discourse, the United States is the culprit, whereas Iran is the victim—and not just that, Iran is defending what the US attacks, and is actively resistant against the United States. The culprit/victim dichotomy is more than a simple differentiation such as democratic/

undemocratic, moral/immoral in that culprit and victim cannot exist independently, as one is the consequence of the other. As such, the representation of the United States in Iranian foreign policy discourse does not only make possible Iran's identification as its opposite (moral, democratic, etc..) but also makes possible its identity as resistant and an example to other countries. Iran can only be resistant and defensive if there is something to be resisted; Iran can only defend the victims if there is a culprit. Table 4.1 gives an overview of these juxtaposed signs.

Table 4.1 Juxtaposing Iran and the United States

Iran	The United States
Victim of...	Is...
Accusation	Accusing
Aggressions	Aggressive
Provocation	Provoking
Double standard policy	Applying double standards
Sowing of discord	Sowing discord
Conspiracy	Conspiring against Iran
Chemical weapons	Supporting chemical warfare
Blackmail	Blackmailing
Terrorism	Supporting terrorism
Saddam	Supported Saddam
Interference	Interfering
Propaganda	Using propaganda
Plotting	Plotting
Denied its rights	Denying other their rights
Defending...	
Independence	Making others dependent
Democracy	Undermining democracy
Unity	Sowing discord
Human rights	Violating human rights
Islam	Fighting Islam
Natural resources	Plundering natural resources
The oppressed	Oppressing
Cooperation	Supporting conflict
Peace	Obstructing peace
Palestine	Defending Israel
Fighting...	
Arrogance	Arrogant
Environmental pollution	Polluting the environment
Tyranny	Supporting tyrants
Aggression	Aggressive
Imposition	Imposing
Military aggression	Militaristic
Occupation	Occupying

This dichotomy between victim/culprit also means that the United States' failure is Iran's success and vice versa. Directly, when the United States is trying to undermine Iran but fails to do so, the United States is sowing discord but Iran remains united, the United States is seeking to dominate Iran but Iran cannot be dominated, and indirectly, when the United States is "bogged down in a quagmire" in Iraq. While at first sight the situation in Iraq or Iran's domestic political developments have little to do with the relationship between Iran and the United States, by implication in the broader dualistic discourse is does. This indirect linking of United States' failure to Iran's success and vice versa runs through all of the discourse and ties in with the broader worldview of dualism. This dualistic view is reinforced by the identification of the United States as a power, which has failed, is defeated, and is stuck, whereas Iran is successful, victorious, and progressing. This also means that the United States, unchanged, belongs to the past, while Iran, changed, has the future.

Due to the fact that, for an ultimate juxtaposition, some basic similarity is needed implies that Israel cannot be Iran's ultimate other: in Iranian foreign policy discourse, there is nothing quite like Zionism. Normally referred to as the Zionist regime and often as the "usurper regime," Israel is the embodiment of evil. Zionism is not merely the opposite of what Iran claims or aims to be—its evilness goes beyond juxtaposition. For much of the attributes of the Zionist regime (atrocities, savagery, and usurpation), there are no straightforward antonyms. However, Zionism is not just Israel; it is not a nation state such as Iran or the United States. Zionism is a global network of domination by a small group. While the United States is presented as a country with human qualities, Zionists have a number of inhuman characteristics. In addition, although the United States has capacity for change, Zionism is unable to do so. That Zionists are unlike others becomes evident when looking at the qualities foreign policy discourse attributes exclusively to Israel: atrocities, savagery, bloodthirstiness, inability to change, artificiality, genocide, slavery, and usurpation. In addition, the "usurper regime" is spilling the blood of women and children, supported and protected by the West, and even dominating and teaching the West. Moreover, more than any other country, Israel is associated with aggression, brutality, assassination, criminal acts, destruction, massacre, and occupation. Its invincibility, however, is a myth according to Iran's leaders and its defeat and collapse imminent.[95]

The difference between Israel and Iran is so stark that comparing the two is like comparing apples and oranges. This means that the

othering of Israel does not contribute in the same elaborate way to
Iranian leaders' identification of Iran as the othering of the United
States does. However, the identification of Israel as something beyond
human does shape Iran's self-understanding, as well as its position
among other states. Nations such as Iran, and particularly Palestine,
get an explicitly human face: they are mothers, children, and youth,
which are innocent, have homes, who are in need of protection, and
who suffer immensely. The United States, Israel, and other arrogant
powers are not attributed these human qualities and are in fact called
both inhuman and inhumane. Iranian leaders, as discussed earlier, do
try to make a separation between the governments and the people.
For example, in response to worldwide demonstrations against Israel's
Gaza attacks, Khamenei notices people in the West have "not been
fully subjugated to the forces of evil,"[96] and he also emphasizes that
there are Muslims living in Europe even if they suffer under Europe's
political conditions.[97] Although Zionism is called inhuman, both
Ahmadinejad and Khamenei mention Jews as the rightful inhabitants
of Palestine alongside Muslims and Christians.[98] As for settlement of
the Israeli-Palestinian issue, both Khamenei and Ahmadinejad promote a one-state solution in which these groups live together peace-
fully. Both emphasize that the current state of Israel should (and will)
disappear. Nowhere do Iranian leaders imply an active role for Iran in
Israel's defeat or collapse; the collapse of Israel is presented as an inevitable but natural course of events.[99] What is explicitly stated, however, is that solutions to the conflict should be fair and reasonable and
that according to what are called Iran's Islamic principles, "neither
throwing the Jews into the sea nor putting the Palestinian land on fire
is logical and reasonable."[100]

While the identification of Israel falls short because of the extreme
identification of Israel, European countries simply have too few points
of reference in contrast to which Iranian identity gets shape. Generally
implied in the term arrogant powers, there are a few characteristics that
Europe, in general, and Britain, in particular, share with the United
States and Israel. These countries are all three explicitly associated
with sowing discord, possession of nuclear weapons, propaganda and
psychological warfare, violation of human rights, and plotting. Britain
is more explicitly implied in the term arrogant powers than the rest
of Europe. Its imperial past in Iran is not easily forgotten. However,
while the United Kingdom is referred to as an unchanged imperialist power, Europe, in general, is discussed in a milder tone. Europe
obtained science earlier than others,[101] is wasting less energy than the
United States,[102] is a victim of meddling by outside powers,[103] has

Muslim citizens,[104] suffered from wars in the twentieth century,[105] and Europeans are turning toward Islam.[106] In other words, Europe (bar the United Kingdom) is a part of the West that is regarded more positively. In some ways, European countries are even considered a victim to the arrogant powers, particularly of domination by the United States and global Zionism. In this sense, European countries share parts of Iran's identity. Although these similarities are subtle, they also speak from the fact that Europe, like the Muslim world, obtained science early on, and that Europe has Muslims among their population. To be sure, Iran has its problems with Europe when it comes to issues such as the cartoon affair[107] and the position of Muslims in Europe in general; however, it is emphasized that Europe and Iran are on speaking terms and the similarities between Iran and Europe to a certain extent aid Iran's positive identification.

Iran's Moral Identity

Iran's changed identity within a changing world follows a central role for Iran as an example for other nations. Palestine, Iraq, and Lebanon are all changing toward an identity, which is similar to that of Iran, particularly one that is awakened and resistant and in the case of Iraq and Palestine also democratic. Iran in this way is ahead of the others: it is no longer oppressed by the arrogant powers. The Iranian Revolution changed this, and Iran is this sense is "the first flag bearer of the Islamic awakening."[108] This identity of Iran as an example is even more strongly present in the discourse on the broader Ummah and the Arab world[109]:

> The bright path that was opened by the Iranian nation's movement—the path that originated from the Iranian people's religious faith and votes and emerged as a religious democracy—is still appealing and attractive. Today, other Muslim nations and their intellectuals are studying the slogans chanted and the developments taking place in the Islamic Republic; they are closely following developments in this country.[110]

Iran can be this example, as it shares many characteristics with the Ummah and to some extent with the Arab world. All are victims of the arrogant powers and have the capacity and the responsibility to act against this. The suggestions it has for change in the Ummah[111] implicitly emphasize Iran's identity as a role model for other states, as these suggestions all resemble attributes Iran already assigns to itself. However, Iran's identity as an example for other countries is not only implicit but also made explicit. Khamenei claims Iran is already witnessing the results of this:

> The Iranian nation is witnessing the great results of its revolution in the Islamic world one by one. It is witnessing that this sapling is now bearing fruit, and such results are going to increase in the future.[112]

To be an example to others, Iran needs to get rid of the stigmatized image presented of Iran by the arrogant powers: Iran as an uncooperative force supporting terrorism, for example. Building on the identification of arrogant powers as deceiving through propaganda, Iranian leaders aim to neutralize the accusations made against them. The United States, for example, "instead of paying attention to the main cause of their failure" is accusing Iran "of confronting the United States in Iraq." The same happened in Palestine, Khamenei argues, and again Iran was blamed: "They say Iran has entered Gaza and besieged Israel!"[113] Considering that Western countries "try to attribute any freedom and justice seeking movement in any part of the world to Iran" is not the only issue; Western governments also claim to oppose Iran's pursuit of nuclear weapons, "as if the Islamic Republic were seeking to build nuclear weapons!"[114] Iranian leaders portray their own nation as nonaggressive: it has never attacked another country, and is explicitly against nuclear proliferation as an advocate of a world without nuclear weapons.[115] Iranian leaders are explicitly against violent action too, including against Israel, except in defense.[116] Most other allegations made against Iran, such as its uncompromising stance in the nuclear issue, are not explicit in the discourse, but implicit in Iran's overstatement of its positive characteristics and behavior: Iran is following international law, is in favor of cooperation, and is ready for constructive measures.

To add credibility to the positive image Iranian leaders present of Iran's behavior, and to further discredit those presented by the West, Iranian leaders reverse many of the accusations leveled against them by the West. When it comes to terrorism in the Middle East, for example, Iranian leaders accuse or at least suspect the United States and Israel. In response to attacks on Shi'a pilgrims at Karbala, Iraq, Khamenei said:

> The growth of terrorism weeds and venomous plants in Iraq will indeed be recorded in the log of American crimes. The American and Israeli intelligence bodies are the prime suspects.[117]

Moreover, the arrogant powers do not only own nuclear weapons but also used them, they use censorship[118] on their own people and prevent the proper investigation of historical events,[119] they undermine democracy and support tyrants,[120] and they are the ones responsible for terrorism in the Middle East.[121] Quite the opposite of the allegations leveled against Iran by the West, the discourse presents the audience with a moral identity for Iran. Iran is portrayed as a benevolent force, which stands by the oppressed and aims to actively contribute to a better future for humanity and for Iran. Khamenei and Ahmadinejad both emphasize Iran's moral duties in promoting justice and friendship, its support for the oppressed, and the need for Iran to defend its own rights. In all of this, Iran's behavior is talked about as nonaggressive, cooperative, and constructive.[122]

As Iranian leaders promise the world a bright future if it turns away from the current status quo toward morality and justice, they talk about Iran as having a central role in promoting moral values and in doing so contribute to international positive change. This morality, according to Khamenei, is an important pillar of Iran's revolutionary identity:

> The Islamic Republic of Iran has been established on the principles of promoting religious and spiritual values, promoting global justice, holding all human beings in high regard and standing against the bullying and domination of hegemonic powers.[123]

Iranian leaders express Iran's international moral obligations in this regard. The articulation of moral responsibility is a particularly powerful discursive tool.[124] Contrasted against the self-interested nature of the United States, it gives Iran moral supremacy. Iranian leaders consider it the Iranian nation's duty to stand by the oppressed and to confront oppression. While other nations around the world are also mentioned and explicit assistance is offered, for example, to African nations, the main focus is on the Middle East. Iran's role in the Middle East goes beyond Iran's moral obligation: as Iran is part of the Middle East, it has a natural role in the region—a role for Iran that is also confirmed by the arrogant powers themselves.[125] Iran as such is very different from the United States, which invaded the Middle East "from several thousands kilometres away" and do not understand the Middle East.[126] Iran instead is "genuinely concerned" with the Middle East, and has important views on the region.[127] Iran's concerns are mainly with Afghanistan, Iraq, Lebanon, and Palestine—and the latter features more prominently than any other country, which again confirms the importance of this country for Iranian identity. In Khamenei's words,

> Our Islamic Revolution has most seriously advocated the cause of Palestine. No country and no government and no nation have supported the Palestinian nation and their resistance and intifada as earnestly as the Iranian nation and government and our Islamic system have done. We have extended both moral support and material assistance to the Palestinian nation. We have done whatever we could.[128]

Khamenei speaks about the assistance Iran gives to the Palestinians as a duty of all Muslims. If other Muslims countries lack the courage to support the Palestinians, he says, instead of criticizing Iran, they should appreciate Iran for doing this.[129]

Both Ahmadinejad and Khamenei speak of Iran and Iranians in a way which may sound unrealistically positive. Credibility is added to this positive discourse in two ways. First, Khamenei adds some nuance by emphasizing that Iran is on a path toward development and a bright future, but that currently it has its shortcomings. Iran is not yet a perfect Islamic government, for example, as it is currently not free of corruption, hypocrisy, misconceptions, and narrow mindedness. Secondly, Ahmadinejad and particularly Khamenei emphasize that Iran is regarded positively by other nations:

> The fact of the matter is that in the present world and in the arena of the international relations and with respect to the balance of the world's great powers, our country Iran and our nation and our government are regarded by other nations and governments and by the international political circles as deserving respect, or rather as worthy of being taken seriously and held in high regard.[130]

Khamenei notices how Iran receives the attention of the world's analysts, in which it is looked at as an example by other Muslim countries, that it is seen as aware and vital, that the world is witnessing Iran's enthusiasm, and that it is loved, appreciated, and even envied.[131] Ahmadinejad adds that Iran astonishes the world and is seen as a country with capacity.[132]

Discussion and Conclusion

To a large extent, this research has built on the literature on discourse and foreign policy, particularly Hansen (2006) and Doty (1993). What was very useful in Hansen is her emphasis on elaborate forms of identification, also emphasized by Fierke (2007), and particularly her method of linking and differentiation. Building on this conception of elaborate identity construction produced interesting insights for the study of Iranian foreign policy discourse during Ahmadinejad. First, the regime's identification of Iran happened mainly in juxtaposition to the United States as Iran's main "other" as well as to the arrogant powers in general—which always imply the United States but may include other Western countries particularly the United Kingdom. Iran's most radical other, however, was Israel, or even "global Zionism," which is attributed inhumane (even inhuman) characteristics that in terms of evilness far exceed those attributed to the United States. Precisely because of this radicalness, Israel is less relevant for Iran's self-identification as it does not provide grounds for an elaborate juxtaposition. The characterization of the United States does provide this possibility, in the sense that US predicates are explicit opposites of Iran's predicates: The United States is immoral, Iran is moral, the United States is aggressive, Iran is peaceful, and so on. As such, the characterization of the United States in many way as a country *like* Iran—even in the sense that it is able to change but it does not, and is aware of what is going on in the world but chooses to ignore this, and knows what morality is but nevertheless applies double standards—provided a much more elaborate ground for Iran's self-identification than Israel does.

Hansen's division between temporal and spatial other proved useful as the element of change inherent to the Iranian regime's foreign policy discourse: the regime contrasted the Iranian nation's identity today with its identity in the past, that is, before the 1979 Revolution. Then it was tyrannical, now it is democratic; then it was submissive, now it is resistant, and so on. This element of change was also shared by some of Iran's spatial others, and it is against these "positive others" that Iran's identity is confirmed. As such, Iranian identity was not only juxtaposed with others who are differ from the self, as Hansen shows, but also through linking with others who are in many ways similar to the self. It is a positive identification in the case of Palestine, Iraq, Afghanistan, and Lebanon, as the regime showed how these nations have become resistant to the arrogant powers. The Palestinian case is most important here, with Palestinians described as the ultimate victims, which deserve the admiration and protection of other oppressed countries, particularly the Muslim world. The very human and vulnerable identity of Palestinians is particularly powerful when contrasted with the inhuman nature attributed to Israel. There is, however, also a broader group of others who are similar to Iran as they are also the victims of the arrogant powers, and they were called on by the Iranian regime to change, that is, to become aware of their position, return to morality, and become resistant. This is how Iran's identity as an example for others, particularly in terms of morality, gets shape. These others-like-the-self then are crucial to Iran's self-identification.

The relevance of these positive spatial others and Iran's negative temporal other, however, did not limit the relevance of the United States as Iran's most important other, but rather inflated it. Iran's identity of change, which it shares with its positive others, is only relevant because of the situation in the past, in which Iran, Iraq, and the Palestinians were passive victims of the arrogant powers. It is the resistance against the United States and Israel that characterizes the identity of these countries in the discourse. Positive linking then does not only take place between the predicates of a single self or other,[133] in Iran's case its morality, democracy, resistance, and so on but also between the self *and* the other: Iran's morality and that of the Palestinians, Iran's democracy and that of the Iraqi's, and so on.

The following chapters will discuss how the regime's discourse of change stood in relation to Iranian foreign policy behavior. They show how Iranian foreign policy was made possible in the context of the discourse presented in the chapter and how through its enactment, foreign policy confirmed the ideology that supports the regime. Chapter 5 gives an account of the developments in Iran's foreign relations during the Presidency of Ahmadinejad, aims to show how these are connected to Ahmadinejad's message of global change, and his ability to sell this message abroad—thereby contributing to the actualization of this change. Chapters 6 and 7 provide two case studies in which the relationship between discourse and foreign policy is explored: the nuclear issue and Iran's hardliners response to Iran's Green Movement. The case studies show how foreign policy was made possible within a discursive context and vice versa: how foreign policy confirmed the regime's preferred views.

Chapter 5

Iranian Foreign Policy Behavior 2005–2013

In the fall of 2006, the Centre for Scientific Research and Middle East Strategic Studies in Tehran held a round table meeting on the foreign policy of the Ahmadinejad administration. Foreign Minister Manouchehr Mottaki (2005 until 2010) was invited as a guest speaker. During this meeting, the foreign minister identified a shift in Iranian foreign policy behavior under the new administration, which he argued was a response to two developments. The first development was the failure of the previous administration to come to a constructive dialogue with the West on an equal basis; and the second the increase of Western unilateralism and, with it, international opposition to this development. After the fall of the Soviet Union, he recounted, the Non-aligned Movement lost much of its impetus and assertiveness, while the West pursued unilateral global domination. The rise of China, India, and Russia added to the intricacies of the global system, but did not prevent Western global domination. After the events of September 11, 2001, the United States pursued unilateralism in an even more determined way, Mottaki explained. When the Iranian reformist government initiated a dialogue with the West, the West did not reciprocate. Since then, Mottaki said, "a revision of Iranian foreign policy has become essential," and the Ahmadinejad administration "has sought a new approach in Iran's standing with the Western world based on the teachings of the Islamic Revolution and the Late Leader of the Revolution." Part of this new approach was a focus on regionalism, while another was concerned with global developments, he said. By taking this new approach, the Iranian regime was contributing to recent "serious process of political activism" against Western unilateralism in the Non-Aligned Movement (NAM), the Arab League, and the Organization of the Islamic Conference. Mottaki said the regime would pursue this activism, among other things through expansion of relations with countries with similar global concerns.[1]

Iranian foreign policy behavior under Ahmadinejad showed much resemblance to what the foreign minister described: the Ahmadinejad administration simultaneously tried to expand its regional relations and enhance its standing among Arab countries, while also assuming a lead role in global antihegemonic initiatives among developing countries and rising powers. This chapter will discuss this foreign policy behavior and places it in the context of the foreign policy discourse discussed in the previous chapters. By doing so, it points at mutually constitutive relations between the Iranian regime's ideology, on the one hand, and its foreign policy, on the other. In particular, it shows how the Iranian regime is acting on the premise of international change and is finding international partners to actualize this change. The identification of Iran as a benevolent power, which is contributing to international justice, and an example to others in its resistance against the malevolent "arrogant powers," is central to this change. This chapter shows that the regime's foreign policy discourse during the Ahmadinejad presidency made possible, even probable, Iran's "activist" foreign policy behavior during this same period. In addition, it shows how the regime was not merely responding ad hoc to changing regional and international circumstances within the context of this discourse, but was actively trying to shape these in line with their discourse.

Regional Policies

Chapter 4 showed the centrality of the region in the foreign policy discourse of the Iranian regime during Ahmadinejad's presidency. There are many points of identification between Iran and several countries in the Arab world, particularly Iraq, Afghanistan, Lebanon, and Palestine. The Iranian regime sees an important role for Iran as an example to these states, which are currently the "victim of arrogant powers," but which have awakened and become resistant—much like Iran in 1979. This important role for Iran as a regional example coincided with a time in which regional conditions had significantly improved for Iran during the years prior to Ahmadinejad's presidency. With the removal of the Saddam and Taliban regimes in 2001 and 2003, respectively, the United States had contributed to the increased influence of Iran within both of these countries. Initially, the presence of the United States in Iran's neighboring countries of Afghanistan and Iraq had presented Iran with a security dilemma, but the Islamic Republic grew more confident as the efforts in both countries presented major challenges to the United States. By the time Ahmadinejad came to power, it had become evident that their influence in Afghanistan and Iraq came naturally for Iran, which had not only cultural–historical ties with both countries, but also the economic means to exert its influence. Iran's regional influence beyond Afghanistan and Iraq was, however, limited. In the regime's foreign policy discourse, the Arab world (with the exclusion of Iraq, Lebanon, and Palestine) was accused of cooperating with the oppressors and being indifferent to the suffering of Palestinians. In line with this discourse, the regime sought to increase regional cooperation as a way to unite against the arrogant powers. As a first step in this endeavor, the regime's main regional aim was to improve ties with the Arab States.

The Ahmadinejad administration's regional policy of improving ties with Iran's Arab neighbors was geared in particular toward changing the image of Iran as a meddling power preventing the Palestinian-Israeli conflict from being solved and stirring conflict in both Lebanon and Iraq. In other words, the Iranian regime tried to present a positive, cooperative image of itself, much in line with its foreign policy discourse of cooperation. Already in the first year of Ahmadinejad's presidency, numerous delegations were sent to Arab countries in an effort to create an image of Iran as a positive regional force, willing to come cooperate. In October 2005, Foreign Minister Mottaki made his first trip to five Persian Gulf countries: Kuwait, Bahrain, Oman, the United Arab Emirates, and Qatar, aimed at broadening cooperation with these countries in all fields and to promote security and stability.[2] These visits were followed by further visits to regional states including Kuwait, the United Arab Emirates, and Libya, as well as a rare official visit to Jordan in May 2006.[3] President Ahmadinejad traveled to Kuwait, the first visit there by a high-ranking Iranian official in more than 25 years, in March 2006. Earlier that month, the president's special envoy visited Qatar, Bahrain, and the United Arab Emirates.[4] Moreover, Ali Larijani, secretary of the Supreme National Security Council visited Oman, Qatar, and Saudi Arabia in April and May 2006, and later that year went to Yemen, Egypt, and Algeria.[5] Also in May, Rafsanjani, the Chair of the Iranian Expediency Council, visited Syria and Kuwait.[6] All of these visits were geared toward improving cooperation on regional security and stability, as well as to convince the Arab states that Iran was not pursuing nuclear weapons.

However, Iran's efforts to improve regional ties had not only the United States, but also America's main allies in the region worried.

The Gulf[7] countries, in particular, expressed concern about Iran's rising regional power, and Saudi Arabia took on the most assertive role in curbing this Iranian influence. Suspicion of Iran's intentions complicated the prospects for an improvement of ties. Arab governments saw Ahmadinejad's championing of the Palestinian cause as an attempt to get support on the Arab street, enlarging divisions between the pro-Palestinian Arab masses and their pro-Western rulers.[8] Miscommunication exacerbated the suspicion of Iran's intentions. Three examples from the early years of Ahmadinejad's Presidency illustrate this. When Qatar's emir Sheikh Hamad bin Khalifa al-Thani visited Iran in April 2006, the emir, seeking diplomatic goodwill, said he hoped Iran's national soccer team, during the 2006 World Cup in Germany, would bring pride to the "Arabic Gulf" region. Iranian officials insist on the use of "Persian Gulf," as it was historically called, and Ahmadinejad corrected the emir. Iran's insistence on the denomination "Persian Gulf" is politically sensitive, however, and was interpreted as a sign of Iranian expansionism. While this incident took place, Larijani was in Dubai, trying to ease concerns raised a month earlier when Iranian Interior Minister Mostafa Pourmohammadi warned his nation had "control over the biggest and most sensitive energy route of the world." This remark was interpreted among the Gulf countries as a threat that Iran might close the Strait of Hormuz and strangle Arabs' economic life's blood.[9] In addition, on a visit to Bahrain in March 2007, Mottaki suggested that Persian Gulf stability would be best achieved through cooperation of regional states, not by reliance American forces. His message was also interpreted as an ambition by Iran to replace the United States as a regional superpower, instead of as a genuine attempt on the Iranian side to come to cooperation on equal terms.[10]

Gulf countries such as Saudi Arabia have a motive to cultivate the perception of regional Iranian threat, both to curb Iran's influence, with the aid of the United States, as well as to legitimize the repression of their own Shi'a minority, which they claim is supported by Iran to destabilize the Saudi monarchy. The United States also added to the perception of an Iranian threat to encourage and legitimize Arab states' security alliances with the West. Zweiri[11] notes how the "nuclear programme has been used to mobilise Arab states against the 'Iranian threat,'" while "there is no mention of the Israeli threat to Arab national security. This perspective is creating the basis for a coalition between the 'moderate' states (Egypt, Jordan, Saudi Arabia and even the other GCC countries) with Israel to face the emerging Iranian threat." As long as the United States and these Arab states depend on each other for their security against a perceived shared threat, the US government creates obstacles for any rapprochement between these states and Iran, while Gulf countries prevent a rapprochement between Iran and the United States. This has given the United States and its Arab allies incentives to cultivate the perception of an Iranian threat in the absence of conclusive evidence that the Iranian regime is, in fact, undermining regional security. This is not to say that Iran poses no threat to the interest of the United States in the region—their perceived interests clearly collide—but instead that the perception of an Iranian threat cannot be seen outside of the construction of dangers by regional states and the United States. As such, the actual danger may lie in the self-fulfilling prophecy that arises when mutual threat perceptions lead to the build-up of tensions, as they have done before in the region.[12] Smaller Gulf states are aware of this risk and have at times downplayed the Iranian threat. This is particularly the case for Bahrain, which is seen as a vulnerable country, and as the United States's "last frontier against Iran."[13] While allying with the United States, Bahrain tries to maintain good relations with Iran. Bahraini officials have expressed concern over Mubarak's remarks about Iran's influence through Shi'a groups throughout the region, which could aggravate tensions between Sunnis and its own large Shi'a minority. Other regional officials expressed similar concern over the possibility of US military action and stressed they favor diplomatic options in dealing with regional security.[14] This explains why the Ahmadinejad administration sought to improve ties with the Gulf states, which was welcomed by these smaller Gulf countries.

Saudi Arabia, however, which saw its influence in Iraq and Lebanon threatened by the growing Iranian influence, curbed this challenge by stressing a "Persian threat," and thus emphasizing Iran's Shi'a identity and suggesting an Iranian hand in regional sectarian conflicts. Saudi newspapers even called Iran "more dangerous than Israel itself" and warned that the "Iranian revolution has come to renew the Persian presence in the region."[15] Saudi journalists accused Iran of meddling in Iraq, the Palestinian territories, and Lebanon and destabilizing the region.[16] While the Iranian regime was indeed asserting its influence in these countries and benefiting from high oil prices, successfully so, there was little evidence, however, of the Iranian regime inciting the kind of violence that the United States and Saudi Arabia claimed it did. In fact, most suicide bombers in Iraq were Sunni and many came from Saudi Arabia, whereas the Shi'a forces that aligned with Iran were the same ones upon which Washington depended.[17] The Iranian regime's goals were to increase its options by improving ties, not by creating instability. As one journalist noted "Iran fears a spill over of Iraq's political problems on its own large Kurdish, Sunni and Arab minorities in the events of a full-scale civil war. It was also burdened with a refugee problem as more than 2 million people fled wars in neighbouring Iraq and Afghanistan."[18] Nevertheless, the Iranian regime was interested in building alliances with parties that could strengthen their influence, including insurgent groups. Many political groups in the region, particularly the ones otherwise marginalized by pro-Western Arab regimes, shared Iranian discourse on a meddling West. These groups offered the Iranian regime a potential network of reprisals and as such work as a deterrence strategy against possible US aggression.[19] However, Iran's support of militant groups in the region does not mean that these groups acted as Iran's puppets, nor that the Iranian regime was able to solve conflicts through their proxies.[20] The reason that the influence of Iran on these regional players is often overrated may be partly due not only to the goals of the United States and Saudi Arabia, but also to the Iranian regime's boasting of its good relations with these groups. The Iranian regime certainly benefits from the impression that it has influence in many of the regional conflicts, which fits their discourse of regional cooperation and resistance to outsiders.

The fall of the Saddam regime provided the Iranian regime with an opportunity to build ties with the Arab world beyond their traditional allies. Historical ties with the Shi'a majority in Iraq aided the identification of the Iraqi government as a brother to the Iranian regime, despite the horrifying legacy of the Iran–Iraq War. Ironically, in the case of Iraq, the United States' government and the Iranian regime found themselves on the same side: that of the Shi'a-dominated Iraqi government, where Arab states including Syria and Saudi Arabia expressed the need to back the Sunni minority. Relations between the Ahmadinejad and Talabani governments were positive. Iran's efforts to build ties with neighboring Iraq started from the fall of Saddam and continued after Ahmadinejad became president. When president of Iraq Jalal Talabani visited Tehran in November 2005, heading a high-ranking political and economic delegation, Ahmadinejad assured him that there were no limits to Iranian cooperation with Iraq, and pledged that Iran would help end insurgency.[21] Relations between Iran and Iraq intensified in the period 2005–2009, with "the Islamic Republic engaged in an ambitious expansion of commercial connections, media, tourism, and cross-border migration, together with major investments in power plants, schools, hotels, and the reconstruction of the southern Iraqi cities such as Basra, Karbala and

Najaf."[22] Meanwhile, it was not Iranian but Saudi interests in Iraq that conflicted with the United States. A Saudi analyst said at the time that if the United States would retreat from Iraq, Saudi Arabia would back the Sunnis against what he saw as Iranian-backed Shi'a militias butchering Sunnis.[23] In practice, however, Iran was able to increase its influence in Iraq mainly because of US support for the Shi'a-dominated government.

Aside from having good relations with Iraq, the Iranian regime remained reliant on its traditional allies in the Middle East that shared with Iran, the United States, and Israel as enemies. Ahmadinejad's administration bolstered ties with Iran's regional ally Syria. In the fall of 2005, Iran and Syria found themselves in a similar position: Iran was criticized for Ahmadinejad's anti-Israeli remarks, particularly as they had been translated as a call to "wipe Israel off the map." This had prompted United Nations Secretary General Kofi Annan to cancel his planned visit to Iran. Syria was equally under pressure from the UN that fall, as the Security Council had adopted a resolution urging Syria to fully cooperate with the UN investigation of the murder of Lebanese expremier Rafiq Hariri, or face international action. Tehran expressed its support for Syria, and Ahmadinejad assured his Syrian counterpart that he would soon make a visit to Damascus.[24] Ahmadinejad first visited Syria in January 2006. This visit was described by a Syrian newspaper as helping the region to move "away from suspicious, foreign interventions and dictates that seek to turn the region into alienated and non-cooperating peoples, tribes, sects and clans that fight and kill one another,"[25] indicating a shared Syrian-Iranian concern with foreign (read: the United States) meddling in the region.

The Iranian regime's interests in Syria coincided with its interests in Lebanon and the Palestinian territories. On his trips to Syria, Ahmadinejad usually met with leaders from Palestinian groups, including Islamic Jihad and Hamas, and with Hezbollah's leadership. Iran's oil money means that Tehran had a lot to offer to these marginalized groups, which were otherwise largely cut off from financial aid. Syria, in particular, needed Iranian aid after Hariri's assassination, when Saudi Arabia and Egypt withdrew their support.[26] Moreover, as both Syria and Iran are under American blockage, their economic cooperation serves their mutual interest. In addition, Syria's economic liberalization made it interested in foreign investment, which Iran is able to supply.[27] Iran's engagement in the region fuelled accusations by Saudi Arabia and the United States that the Islamic Republic was destabilizing the region. As the situation in Iraq deteriorated, the United States did not only blame Iran, but in response also sought to strengthen the Sunni factions and insurgents in Iraq, which led to the attack on the Shi'a Askariya shrine in Samarra in February 2006.[28] Iran's influence in the Palestinian territories was also a concern to both the United States and the Saudis. Worried that with Iran involved, the Middle East peace process would never progress, Jordan, Egypt, and Saudi Arabia held consultations to form an "Arab Quartet" as a way of weakening the influence of Iran and Syria. "We say let's solve the Palestinian issue and deprive the extremists of these cards," a Jordanian official said, tellingly.[29] Meanwhile, Iran and Saudi Arabia found themselves on opposite sides in Lebanon, as Iran backed the Shi'a movement Hezbollah, and Saudi Arabia the pro-Western Sunni-led government of Faoud Siniora, putting a serious strain on their barely improved relations.

Nevertheless, Ahmadinejad was adamant to improve ties with Saudi Arabia and continued his efforts to come to cooperation with this country. In January 2007, Iran and Saudi Arabia mediated an agreement to end violence in Lebanon and facilitated a Palestinian summit in Mecca where Palestinian factions agreed to a government of national unity.[30] Mistrust between Saudi Arabia and Iran complicated their cooperation, particularly in the light of accusations that Iran was converting Sunni to Shi'ism in Sunni-dominated countries, particularly in Morocco and Algeria. Saudi clerics, even the moderate ones, adopted an anti-Shi'a tone in response to what they saw as Iran's rising influence among Shi'a.[31] Ahmadinejad visited Saudi Arabia in March 2007 to discuss with King Abdullah the sectarian and political battles in the region. King Abdullah, who greeted Ahmadinejad at the airport, seemed pleased with the Iranian initiative to cooperate on regional issues. He invited Ahmadinejad to *hajj*, which he carried out in December that year. Nevertheless, tensions between Iran and Saudi Arabia continued. In May 2008, Saudi Arabia accused Iran of a coup in Lebanon, as Hezbollah again clashed with the government.

While the Saudi Arabian regime and the United States government pointed at Iran as the main instigator behind regional tensions, the Iranian regime accused the United States. When in January 2006 two bombings in the south-western Iraqi city of Ahvaz killed nine people, Iran's president blamed "the occupiers of Iraq," meaning the United States and Britain,[32] which the Iranian regime also blamed for the attack a month later on the Askariya shrine in Samarra, central Iraq.[33] Accusations toward the United States, the United Kingdom, and Israel continued in line with the discourse that the United States is the "real terrorists."

The Ahmadinejad administration insisted meanwhile that Iran's relations with the Arab states including Saudi Arabia were good, and that US interference in the region has created difficulty for these relations. Nevertheless, the Iranian regime's overtures to Saudi Arabia produced little result. In July 2007, the US government announced that it would sell sophisticated weapons to Saudi Arabia and five other Persian Gulf countries. Iran criticized this, claiming that these sales harmed the good relations among the countries of the region, and that the Persian Gulf instead needed security and stability.[34] In early 2009, the Arab countries response to a remark by an Iranian official that Bahrain was historically an Iranian province showed that the suspicion of Iran continued to run deep among Persian Gulf states. Morocco went as far as to sever ties with the Iranian regime over this misunderstanding. One analyst observed that the comment was intentionally taken out of context and exaggerated to show that Iran was expansionist.[35] Shi'a in Kuwait, Saudi Arabia, and Bahrain present a similar analysis, complaining that their governments are using the excuse of Iran's rising influence to increase their oppression.[36] When Saudi Arabia launched an offensive in Yemen in November 2009, Mottaki publicly warned that no one should interfere in Yemen's internal affairs. The Yemini government responded by accusing the Iranian regime of interference in Yemen, escalating tensions between the Shi'a rebels and the Yemeni government. It did not provide any evidence to support this assertion.[37] In December 2009, Iran accused Saudi Arabia of seizing an Iranian nuclear expert who was on pilgrimage in Mecca, and handing him over to Washington.[38] At the same time, the Iranian regime has been careful to maintain good relations with Saudi Arabia as much as possible. The 2010 "wikileaks" were taken as evidence of the United States' hegemonic goals in the region, including regime change in Iran, but at the same time Ahmadinejad downplayed Arab hostility toward Iran (such as Saudi King Abdullah's remark that the United States should "cut off the head of the snake," implying a military strike on Iran) as "propaganda": "We are friends with the regional countries and mischievous acts will not affect relations," he said.[39]

The Iranian regime had little more success with other Arab countries. When Arab governments were silent on the Israeli attacks on Gaza in December 2008, this highlighted the differences between the Iranian and the Arab regimes. Iran was very critical of their silence, and its own stance on the Palestinian issue contributed to Ahmadinejad's popularity among the Arab masses. Particularly Egypt was irritated with this Iranian charm offensive, and the Gulf countries accused Iran of interfering in Arab affairs.[40] When US Secretary of State Hillary Clinton visited the region in March 2009, she told reporters that she was struck by the extent to which the Iranian regime meddles in the regions' affairs and the depth of the fear of Iran. She specifically mentioned that the Iranian regime was making efforts to undermine the Palestinian Authority by calling for resistance against Israel among Palestinians.[41]

Thus, the foreign policy behavior of the Ahmadinejad administration until the Arab Spring started in December 2010 shows a persistent effort to increase Iran's influence in the region. High oil prices and regional changes after the US invasions created some opportunities for this endeavor, while United States' dominance was the main obstacle. What explains the Iranian regime's persistence in improving ties with the Arab world, despite little success? Rationalists would explain Iran's behavior in terms of power politics: a quest for influence with a geostrategic rivalry between Iran and Saudi Arabia as the main obstacle. A quest for influence, however, is not objectively given but socially constructed. How, in other words, was the Ahmadinejad administration's regional behavior made possible? Chapter 4 showed the centrality of resistance and independence to the Iranian regime's foreign policy discourse, and much of Iranian foreign policy behavior in the Middle East can be explained in this context. The United States, the main other for the Iranian regime, is identified as the culprit in the Middle East: with its hegemonic goals, it has come from far away to dominate the region by creating discord among the countries and the ethnic groups living there. This policy of "divide and rule" implies that conflict in the Middle East is not inherent to interactions between Arabs and Persians, or Sunni and Shi'a—ultimately, according to the regime, all these share the same goals of creating a peaceful and prosperous region that they could (and would) achieve if it was not for United States meddling in the region. This understanding of regional relations makes it possible, even desirable, for Iran's foreign policy makers to initiate dialogue with their neighboring Arab states. According to the official discourse, Arab states (like other parts of the Muslim world) were led astray by the hegemonic powers, and Ahmadinejad goes as far as to claim that supposed anti-Iranian remarks by Arab leaders are fabrications of Western propaganda. Moreover, while foreign powers have emphasized differences between Sunni and Shi'a, in Iranian official discourse this difference is downplayed. Chapter 4 showed how Khamenei repeatedly calls for the Muslim world to be united against the one threat that they all share: the bullying powers. This is in line with Ahmadinejad's efforts to improve ties among the Gulf states and, preferably, come to regional security arrangements.

The dominant discourse among Iranian foreign policy makers, however, also complicated relations in that it emphasized Iran's moral superiority. Iranian leaders (particularly Khamenei) criticized the Arab world for being silent and indifferent in face of the violence committed against their Palestinian and Lebanese brothers, and the Muslim world, in general, is accused of betrayal, cooperation with the West, of humiliating themselves and the Muslim community, as well as ignorance. This tension in the Iranian official discourse was also visible in the regime's attempts to improve regional relations. Its insistence on support for the Palestinian case hampered the possibility to come to good relations with the Arab states, which are seen as potential allies. However, the discourse expressed the hope for, and even anticipates, change in the shape of an awakening, which according to Iran's leaders already took place in some parts of the Arab world: in Lebanon, Palestine, and Iraq. These countries, which have been victim to Western plots more than any other country in the region, became resistant and as such are an example to other countries in the region, including Iran itself. Iran's leaders did not only identify their country with these three Arab nations, but also tie its own fate to it: they attribute to Iran an explicit role in defending the rights of these nations—as should the other regional powers. The implied regional role for Iran, as well as its tone of moral superiority that is so central in its discourse, rubbed Arab leaders the wrong way. Particularly, as Arab states are wary of Iranian expansionism and have motives to exaggerate a perceived Iranian threat to form a united front with the United States changing its regional image therefore proved hard for the Iranian regime.

These were the conditions under which the Iranian regime was operating in the region when the Arab Spring started in December 2010. Needless to say, to the Iranian regime, these developments were evidence of the anticipated awakening in the Muslim world.[42] Regime changes in the Arab world (bar Syria) were welcomed by the Iranian regime. Much like the 1978–1979 Iranian Revolution, the regime claimed, the Arab uprisings were evidence of resistance to dictatorial regimes and Western domination.[43] The regime even claimed these regional successes were an effect of Iran's exemplary behavior.[44] However, contrary to the hope that the Iranian regime expressed, the Arab Spring did not lead to a more favorable view of Iran. In fact, renewed Arab nationalism highlighted Sunni–Shi'a differences that formed an obstacle to improved relations with the Arab world. These differences came to the fore in particular in the Syrian civil war, where Iran and the Arab world found themselves supporting opposite sides.

Perhaps the only positive effects of the Arab Spring for Iran were the somewhat improved ties with Egypt. Relations with Iran were already on the mend before the Egyptian regime change, and Qolam Ali Haddad 'Adel, spokesman of the Iranian majles, and the supreme leader's advisor, Ali Akbar Nateq Nouri, made a historical visit to Egypt in early 2010 to talk about the normalization of ties.[45] After the Egyptian regime change, relations rapidly improved. In August 2012, Iran hosted the NAM summit, and on this occasion President Mohamed Morsi came to Iran. He made it explicit that it was his intention to improve ties between the two countries. Ahmadinejad visited Cairo during the Organization of Islamic Cooperation (OIC) summit in Cairo in February 2013 expressing the same intention.[46] At the end of Ahmadinejad's presidency, Egypt and Iran seemed well on their way to reestablishing diplomatic ties[47] and there was promise of increased economic cooperation.[48] However, the Egyptian government's room for maneuver in engaging Iran was limited. Domestically, it faced opposition against improved relations with the Shi'a state,[49] and the Egyptian government seemed careful not to upset its good relations with the United States and Saudi Arabia. Morsi's first visit after he became President was in fact to Saudi Arabia, reciprocating Saudi Arabian offers of financial aid to the new Egyptian government.[50] Regime change in Egypt temporarily brought normalization of ties, but hardly increased the Iranian regime's regional options. Because the Egyptian and Iranian governments supported opposite sides in the Syrian conflict made their differences all too obvious.[51]

Syria, Iran's only loyal state ally in the region, became the scene of a civil war did not only complicate relations with Egypt, but meant that Iran was losing touch with the entire Arab world. Not just because the weakening of the Assad regime made Iran lose an important Arab partner, and a buffer that kept Israel and the United States at bay,[52] and as Syria functions as a gateway to Iran's allies Hezbollah and Islamic Jihad, the civil war also hampered Iran's relations with these groups. Most importantly, however, the conflict in Syria aggravated the regional tensions that the Ahmadinejad administration had tried to downplay in the preceding years. Iranian officials widely regarded the Syrian conflict as heavily influenced by Saudi Arabia and the United States, which were both supporting the Syrian opposition. Observers in Iran regarded this as an attempt by Saudi Arabia to increase its regional influence.[53]

For many Arabs, the Syrian civil war was a conflict between Sunni and Shi'a groups, and Iran's sustained support for Assad was seen an attempt to keep in place a "Shi'a crescent" through which Iran could continue its supposedly destabilizing influence. This made it difficult for governments of Sunni-dominated countries to keep friendly ties with Iran.

First, relations with Hamas became more difficult, particularly after its open support of the Syrian opposition in early 2012.[54] Closer links between Hamas and Egypt were also a potential challenge to Iran's influence in the Gaza strip. Already before the Egyptian regime change, Egyptian authorities reopened the Rafah border crossing and President Mubarak himself started mediation between Fatah and Hamas. After the 2011 regime change and with the Muslim Brotherhood having close relations with Hamas, relations between Hamas and the Egyptian Government greatly improved. This occurred, despite the fact that Morsi's Government upheld the peace treaty with Israel. However, relations chilled when in the summer of 2012 a border attack killed 16 Egyptian soldiers,[55] and Egypt and Hamas struggled to keep good relations in the face of accusations that Hamas was destabilizing Egypt.[56] However, even if Egypt did not replace the Islamic Republic as Hamas main supporter, relations between Iran and Hamas by the end of Ahmadinejad's presidency had somewhat cooled.

Second, relations between Iran and Turkey soured as a consequence of the Syrian civil war. Relations had first improved during Ahmadinejad's presidency, with growing trade links and mutual visits to boost economic ties. At the end of Ahmadinejad's first term, Turkey imported a third of its gas consumption from Iran and agreed to invest in Iran's gas industry.[57] Moreover, when international sanctions limited the possibilities for trade in the later years of the Ahmadinejad presidency, Turkey found creative ways to import it.[58] However, conflicting interests made sustained regional cooperation difficult. The Syrian War was not the first area in which these conflicting interests came to the surface. First, Turkish and Iranian interest in Iraq diverged, as Ankara tried to keep good relations with the Kurdish north while having tense relations with the Shi'a dominated government.[59] Second, Turkey's collaboration with United States' goals in the Middle East, which remain central to its regional policy despite an apparent reorientation under the AKP, made relations with Iran difficult. In September 2011, Turkey agreed to the installation of a NATO missile defense shield aimed at countering ballistic missile threats from Iran,[60] which the Iranian regime criticized for being "managed by America and the Zionists."[61] When the conflict in Syria erupted, this created further rifts in Iranian-Turkish relations, as Turkey supported the Syrian opposition.[62]

Meanwhile, relations with the Iraqi administration also became more difficult. Especially, the 2010 parliamentary elections in Iraq, which brought with it changes in Iran–Iraq relations. In these elections, the parties that presented themselves as trans-sectarian and nationalist won most seats and the pro-Iranian Islamic Supreme Council of Iraq (ISCI) lost a significant amount. The Shi'a camp had fractured due to intra-Shi'a rivalry, partly as a result of Iranian pressure on these groups to unite.[63] This meant that after the 2010 elections, Iraqi politics was more self-confidently nationalist at the expense of Tehran's influence over sectarian groups in Iraq.[64] While Shi'ism provided a common identity between the Iraqi majority and the Iranian regime, Iraqi nationalism was historically articulated in contrast to a Persian other and may prove less compatible with warm relations between Baghdad and Tehran.[65] Because the Iraqi government did not support the Bashar al-Assad regime in Syria, defying Iran's strategic interest, and thus showing Iraq's new found confidence and independence from Tehran.[66]

All in all, the regional changes that the Iranian regime witnessed with such positive expectations in December 2010 brought uncertainty for Iran. Although relations with Egypt somewhat improved, the conflict in Syria highlighted the Sunni-Shi'a divide, the conflicting interests between Iran and Turkey, the changing relations with Iraq as well as the deep-seated mistrust between Saudi Arabia and Iran. The prospect of closer ties between Hamas and Egypt, on the one hand, and the closing corridor to Hezbollah and Islamic Jihad, on the other, further isolated Iran in the Middle East, giving room to Egypt to take on a more assertive regional role. Meanwhile Iran–Western tensions in the Middle East were building up, particularly in and around the Persian Gulf. In the summer of 2012, in response to United States sanctions, the Iranian government threatened to close the Strait of Hormuz, through which 20–40 percent of world oil traveled.[67] Other threats on the Iranian side included preemptive strike to safeguard Iran's interest.[68] This aggressive rhetoric contrasts with the Ahmadinejad administration's emphasis on regional cooperation, but is in line with the regime's insistence on protecting its perceived national interest. Why the Iranian regime did not yield to United States' demands in the face of international sanctions can only be explained in the context of international developments, to which the following section turns.

International Policies

What is perhaps most striking about the Iranian regime's foreign policy behavior under Ahmadinejad is its insistence on nuclear development despite the international sanctions, which decreased Iran's international options substantially during Ahmadinejad's presidency. Instead of giving in to Western demands, the Iranian regime has sought alternative partners in its nuclear efforts. This foreign policy behavior, to which chapter 6 turns, is in line with Iran's broader foreign policies under Ahmadinejad, geared toward cooperation amongst like-minded states in an effort to circumvent United States unilateralism and build an alternative power structure. In line with the anti-Western tone of the regime's official discourse, the regime's main message was not one of aggression—something which the regime associates with the United States—but one of peace and cooperation. In some ways, the discourse shows resemblance to that of Mohammad Khatami, who during his presidency (from 1997 until 2005) aimed at establishing a "dialogue among civilizations." Unlike under the Khatami administration, however, Iran's foreign policy under Ahmadinejad was not so much concerned with getting out of the Iranian-Western impasse through an Iranian-European dialogue, evading this deadlock by finding alternative partners. The Ahmadinejad administration emphasized that when it came to improving ties between Iran and the West, the ball was in the West's court, and it welcomed Western initiatives in this regard. In the context of the Iranian regime's discourse, south–south cooperation was more desirable than a settlement with the West. Particularly, as Iran's isolated position contributed to the regime's identification of Iran as a resistant country, and a leading power in the fight against Western hegemony. Western policies such as sanctions and democracy promotion, which chapter 3 described, confirm the image of the West as, among other things, meddling in other country's internal affairs and undermining their technological development. The Iranian regime portrayed itself as advancing not simply its own interest, but also those of all developing states against the bullying West. The regime, as such, tried to recast the image of Iran from an outcast to a flag bearer of resistance among oppressed nations. Moreover, it actively sought new alliances not only to circumvent international isolation, but also to challenge Western hegemony.

Iranian foreign policy makers tried to expand their country's influence much in line with the regime's foreign policy discourse of resisting

Western hegemony and positioning itself as a positive international force. Circumstances were particularly favorable for Iran: a combination of high oil prices coupled with challenges to the United States' power (see chapter 3) made it possible for Iran to pursue an active foreign policy. High oil prices facilitated "check-book diplomacy," particularly as the same high oil prices[69] made developing countries more in need of assistance.[70] The Ahmadinejad administration tried to ride this wave, voicing concerns, which other developing countries might share but were afraid to voice for fear of upsetting the United States or its allies. Using international organizations such as the D8, NAM, and the OIC as a platform, Ahmadinejad denounced the West's hegemonic policies, and criticized it for depriving non-Western states of influence and development.

The Iranian regime was relatively successful in galvanizing support for Iran's nuclear program among developing countries, breaking what the United States would like to be an international consensus against Iran's nuclear ambitions. Turning the nuclear issue into a matter of Third World pride, Ahmadinejad claimed that the United States was determined to prevent the developing world from technological development. This was the message he delivered at the D8 Summit in Bali in May 2006, attended by member states Bangladesh, Egypt, Indonesia, Iran, Malaysia, Nigeria, Pakistan, and Turkey. Following closed-door talks, the D8 issued a statement supporting the development of nuclear energy for peaceful purposes, in clear support of Iran's ambitions.[71] When he visited Indonesia, Ahmadinejad received a warm welcome, his public speeches were greeted with standing ovations,[72] and Indonesian President Susilo Bambang Yudhoyono suggested that a broader summit, rather than just pressure from Western nations, was required to solve the nuclear issue.[73] In March 2008, during a visit of Yudhoyono to Tehran, Iran and Indonesia signed five memoranda of understanding, including an agreement to build a 6 billion US dollar oil refinery in Indonesia.[74]

Ahmadinejad had similar success at the Non-Aligned Movement, which met in September 2006 in what Mottaki called "a dissenting voice against unilateralism."[75] The 118 NAM member states met in Havana, Cuba, and Raúl Castro criticized the United States' "irrational pretensions for world dominance,"[76] echoing statements made by both Ahmadinejad and Hugo Chavez at the UN earlier that month. At the UN General Assembly, several representatives had voiced their discontent with the veto rights of the five permanent members at the UN Security Council—also a point repeatedly made by Chavez and Ahmadinejad.[77] Although the UN speeches of these two leaders were quickly denounced by most diplomats, particularly that of Chavez who had called the United States "the devil," "in quieter moments officials and diplomats said they feared that he was reaching a receptive audience of poor countries that felt exploited and bullied by the United States."[78] This pattern was repeated at other international institutions. The 2012 NAM conference particularly important in sending off the message that Iran was not isolated, as it was hosted by Iran.[79] Ahmadinejad took the opportunity to express what he saw as an important task for the NAM: "I believe that the wishes of the founders of the Non-Aligned Movement can be summarized in the realization of the idea of joint global management,"[80] in line with the idea of multipolarity and global equality.

Among the developing states, the Ahmadinejad administration had some success in Africa and Latin America with beginning cooperation. Iran started development projects in, among other countries, Nigeria, Senegal, and Sudan.[81] In addition, Ahmadinejad found an ally in President Mugabe, Zimbabwe's fierce critic of the United States. When Zimbabwe held presidential elections in March 2008, and the West feared vote rigging, Iran and China were among the few foreign teams allowed in.[82] Iran rehabilitated an oil refinery in Zimbabwe,[83] and in April 2010 Robert Mugabe assured Ahmadinejad of Zimbabwe's continuous support of "Iran's just cause on the nuclear issue."[84] On one of Ahmadinejad's last tours, which took place in April 2013, he visited Benin, Ghana, and Niger to boost cooperation.[85] In Niger, a uranium-rich country, Ahmadinejad stressed the common belief of the two governments, and stated that "the two countries have abundant talents and potentials which they can jointly utilize to facilitate each other's progress."[86]

Ahmadinejad was most successful in Latin America where he quickly found friends in Hugo Chavez and the newly elected presidents of Nicaragua (Daniel Ortega), Ecuador (Rafael Correa), and Bolivia (Evo Morales). Ahmadinejad visited each of these countries several times,[87] and used these visits as opportunities to express his grievances against the United States, which were then echoed by these leaders on their visits to Tehran.[88] Relations with Venezuela were most extensive and Ahmadinejad developed a close personal relationship with Hugo Chavez. In fact, when Chavez passed away in March 2013, the Iranian government announced a day of national mourning.[89] In the early years of Ahmadinejad's presidency, the Islamic Republic initiated numerous developmental projects in Venezuela, including the building of ten flour factories, low-income housing, and factories assembling tractors and bicycles.[90] Iranian car factories were built in the city of Maracay and in Caracas.[91] These projects were expanded in the years that followed. Iran and Venezuela also cooperated in the oil field, for example, by pressing for export cuts within OPEC to push oil prices up at a time when they were low.[92] Iran helped Venezuela in exploring oil as well as uranium.[93] Moreover, the two countries made plans for a joint oil trading company, and had the ambition to price oil in Euros instead of dollars to weaken US influence in the international oil market.[94] In January 2007, Venezuela bought four oil tankers from Iran in an effort to expand its fleet,[95] and in March 2007 they strengthened ties with a direct Caracas-to-Tehran flight,[96] which was suspended after some time.[97] Relations between Iran and Venezuela were further intensified during the rest of the Ahmadinejad presidency, despite setbacks, including international sanctions.[98]

Ahmadinejad also intensified relations with Bolivia, South America's poorest country, in the fields of health, basic foodstuffs, and humanitarian assistance.[99] The Iranian government promised to help Bolivia build a nuclear power plant, trained Bolivian petroleum experts, and helped finance a military training center at the initiative of Venezuela. All of this was intended to decrease the region's dependency on Western aid and training.[100] The administration also expanded Iran's cooperation with Nicaragua. In August 2007, Nicaragua agreed to trade bananas, coffee, and meat in exchange for Iranian help in the field of infrastructure and funding for, among other things, a farm equipment factory, a health clinic, 10,000 houses, and a deep-water port. They had already agreed on the building of a hydroelectric power station by Iran, with another three plants in the pipeline.[101] In May 2009, Hillary Clinton warned that Iran was building a huge embassy in Managua, the capital of Nicaragua, and said "You can only imagine what it is for."[102] Since Ahmadinejad's first election, Iran opened six embassies in Latin America: in Colombia, Ecuador, Uruguay, Bolivia, Chile, and Nicaragua. No superembassy was erected however in Managua. Moreover, Iran's efforts to increase international cooperation often did not materialize. The proposed investments in Nicaragua, such as the ocean port, hydroelectric plants, and a tractor factory, never came, nor did many other projects in Latin America. Furthermore, the Iranian majles was not always willing to ratify the agreements made by Ahmadinejad's administration.[103] Nevertheless, Iran's involvement in Latin America, which was widely considered to be America's "back yard," had important symbolic value, even if these countries had little to offer to Iran in economic terms. In terms of trade, relations with Argentina and Brazil were significant. Brazil and Iran intensified cooperation in this area[104] and Brazil ranked eight among Iran's major import partners in 2011.[105] Brazil and Iran also cooperated in the field of petroleum, as Iran was benefitting from Brazilian expertise in deep-water exploration.[106] Ahmadinejad's controversial visit to Brazil in November 2009 was intended to bolster ties, as he arrived in Brazil together with 200 Iranian businessmen. Trade with Argentina also grew sharply from 2006 onward, with Argentina ranking 11th on the list of Iran's most important import partners in 2011.[107]

Iran's efforts to circumvent Western efforts to isolate the country were also effective in the nuclear field. In Latin America, Venezuela, Nicaragua, and Bolivia all expressed support for Iran's (peaceful) nuclear program. Ortega went as far as to claim that "Even if they want nuclear power for purposes that are not peaceful, with what right does (the U.S.) question this?"[108] Although less outspoken, Brazil has also been supportive of Iran's ambitions to become a peaceful nuclear power. Lula da Silva flew to Tehran in early 2010 to meet with Ahmadinejad to discuss the nuclear issue and explore the options for a diplomatic solution. Both Khamenei and Ahmadinejad praised Lula for his mediating role.[109] Not only Brazil but also Turkey positioned itself as an independent player when it joined the negotiations in Teheran. Turkey's role was not unexpected: in November 2008, Prime Minister Recep Tayyip Erdoğan had already offered for Turkey to be a mediator between Iran and the new Obama administration, which considered talks with Iran.[110] He also said that Iran had already asked, under Bush, for Turkey's help in improving relations between Iran and the United States.[111] Like Brazil, Turkey preferred negotiations with Iran over sanctions, and believed there was enough goodwill on the Iranian side to be hopeful. The Tehran Declaration that Brazil, Turkey, and Iran signed in May 2010 was presented as a victory by all parties involved, but the US government, and particularly Hillary Clinton, saw it as an attempt by Iran to avoid renewed sanctions.[112] More than anything, the Tehran Declaration showed that rising powers were ready to take on a role in international affairs independent from the United States, and that Iran was happy to contribute to this development.

From the viewpoint of Iran's official foreign policy discourse, Russia and China were more favorable partners for the Islamic Republic than the United States or European Union. Despite Iran's troubled history with the former Soviet Union, these countries did not share the stigma of "arrogant" or "hegemonic" powers. In fact, China and Russia do not take a prominent position in the discourse either in a positive or negative sense. To be clear, historically speaking, Russia's interactions with Iran have been similar to those of the United Kingdom and the United States, and anti-Russian sentiments run deep in Iranian society, and they come easily to the surface.[113] However, the regime chose not to tap into these sentiments, and Iranian officials went out of their way to show their understanding for Russia's ambivalent behavior toward Iran:

> Put yourself in the place of a Russian official. No matter how much Russia believes that Iran is in the right—and of course in their minds Russian leaders know that we are in the right...they will not say that publicly because they will mainly think of their own position [interests].[114]

It is interesting to see how much of a small role Russia plays in Iran's otherwise anti-imperialist discourse.[115] Iranian officials seem to make the conscious choice not to tap into anti-Russian sentiments in their political discourse. While Russia has a complicated history in Iran, China is perhaps the better alternative. As one official put it,

> China is a country which has no negative history against our national interest. Also, no colonialist past has been observed and it has usually carried out its commitments to Iran. Therefore, the expansion of ties with China is in Iran's interest.[116]

Russia and China are desirable partners for Iran, because of their large economies, their permanent membership in the UN Security Council, and because both countries are less concerned about Iran's human rights record and support for organizations that the West deems terrorist. Moreover, as previously demonstrated, Iran's options in the Middle East are limited, and an eastward glance is the logical alternative, particularly as Iran has long historical ties with Asia. These historic ties gave symbolic value to the expansion of Asian-Iranian relations under Ahmadinejad. In fact, already in 1996, Iran and Turkmenistan symbolically reopened the Silk Road with the opening of a railroad, which effectively connected Iran with Eastern China.[117] Ahmadinejad tried to promote its Asian identity and encouraged inter-Asian cooperation. Under Ahmadinejad, Iran has acquired observer status in the South Asian Association for Region Cooperation (SAARC) and was engaged in both the Asian Cooperation Dialogue (ACD) and in the setting up of the Asian Parliamentary Assembly (APA) whose headquarters are in Tehran.[118] Iran has been trying to get full membership into the Shanghai Cooperation Organization where it was granted observer status in 2005—a position that was denied to the United States in the same year.[119]

Iran's successes in Asia were mostly in the field of economic cooperation. Iran's main oil buyers since the 1979 revolution have already shifted from Western buyers to predominantly Asian buyers.[120] After 2004, China became one of the main investors in Iran's energy sector, with a historic agreement of a 100 billion dollar investment by Sinopec in 2007, with the aim of securing China's long-term supply of oil.[121] In addition, economic relations with Russia have been good, and until the sanctions of 2010, Russia provided Iran with arms while sanctions prevented Iran from acquiring its weapons from Western sellers. Politically, however, Iran's relations with China and Russia are a mixed blessing. China and Russia have at times expressed support for Iran's pursuit of peaceful nuclear technology, watering down, and (in the case of Russia) occasionally voting against sanctions in the UNSC. Russia was cooperating with Iran in the construction of the Bushehr power plant, and agreed to supply fuel for this plant for ten years in March 2009. Iran's relations with both powers are however ambivalent: they supported UNSC sanctions on Iran on several occasions, and even when they were watering down these sanctions, this seemed to have been mainly to protect their own economic and business interests in Iran.[122] China and Russia faced little competition in Iran while Western embargoes were maintained, and as such gain from the hostility between Iran and the West.[123] However, as sanctions tightened, these relations became more difficult to maintain (see chapter 3).

The failure of the Tehran Declaration in June 2010 was a tipping point, after which the regime's efforts to circumvent US efforts to isolate Iran became less and less successful. The UN Security Council adopted new sanctions in June 2010. Nonpermanent members Turkey and Brazil voted against the resolution, and Lebanon abstained. Ahmadinejad, who was in China at the time, accused the United States of bullying and intimidating the countries on the Security Council and emphasized that Iran's relations with China were good.[124] However, Russia ended its sale of air defense missiles to Iran, which now fell under the sanctions, and also made clear at the Shanghai Cooperation Organization's annual summit that it would not permit any country under UN sanctions to join the security organization.[125] Brazil meanwhile ended its role as mediator in the nuclear issue, after the United States had rejected the deal that it had brokered together with Turkey. "We got our fingers burned by doing things that everybody said were helpful and in the end we found that some people could not take 'yes' for an answer," a disappointed Celso Amorim said.[126] Between 2010 and 2012, Ahmadinejad continued his efforts to intensify south–south ties, but as sanctions were further tightened, options were limited.

All in all, the Iranian regime's international charm offensive had mixed results. Like in the Middle East, elsewhere in the world, the Ahmadinejad administration had trouble coming to extensive cooperation with countries that benefit more from relations with the West than they believe they can from relations with Iran. Hence, the Iranian regime's options were largely limited to those countries, which share criticism of the United States, such as Syria, Venezuela, and to some extent Nicaragua, Bolivia, and Ecuador. Despite this, in terms of Iran's foreign policy discourse, the Iranian regime's international accomplishments in the period 2005–2013 were significant. Not only did international developments in this period tie in neatly with the Iranian regime's image of a dominating West, which increased pressure on Iran over its nuclear program, but it also found this perception resonated among various states in different corners of the world. Much in line with what Khamenei would call "awakening," developing countries showed awareness of the state of Western domination they were living under and became "resistant." These countries then were part of the solution and the future, which the Iranian regime proposed, while the West (the problem) was part of the past. Moreover, Iran was able to contribute to this development, challenging the United States in a joint effort with other defiant states. Iran's international policies are a textbook example of "acting as if to create space": Iran politicizes the rules of the dominant game, while acting in a framework of a more marginal game.[127] Iran's nuclear policy under Ahmadinejad, as will be discussed in the next chapter, was one of the acts of defiance toward the dominant game, and its relations with other marginalized powers shows also defiance toward the dominant rules of what constitutes a legitimate power. According to Iranian foreign policy makers, the West—and particularly the United States—was becoming marginalized. Their dollars and their UN resolutions according to Ahmadinejad were "worthless pieces of paper."[128] Because not only the traditional "rogue" states, but also rising middle powers such as Turkey, South Africa, and Brazil expressed their concerns about American unilateralism; this added to the Iranian regime's ability to challenge the West and create an alternative space, based on south–south relations, under the premise that Iran neither wants nor needs a restoration of relations with the United States.

In many ways, Iran's economic isolation merely increased during Ahmadinejad's presidency. This was mainly due to the intransigence of both the United States and Iran in the nuclear issue, which the next chapter discusses, and subsequent international sanctions. As Western pressure on Iran persisted, increasingly limiting other countries' dealings with Iran, the Iranian regime was backed into a corner. Toward the end of Ahmadinejad's presidency, relations with important economic partners were made increasingly difficult, and while the regime was denying this,[129] it felt the effect of international sanctions. However, at the same time, these made a negotiated settlement of the nuclear issue more difficult: in the context of regime discourse, bowing to Western pressure was not an option. The regime's threats to close the Strait of Hormuz and even of preemptive strikes to safeguard what is regarded the Iranian national interests both show that the regime was trying to assert its resistance and independence. It should be clear by now that the Iranian regime's views of Iranian identity could hardly be brought in line with surrender to Western coercive measures. If the United States or other governments wanted to stop Iran from developing nuclear weapons, then they needed to understand that the Iranian regime sees nuclear development as central to Iran's independence and development, and that yielding to Western demands would be a humiliation in terms of its foreign policy discourse.

Conclusion

In the context of the Iranian regime's discourse of international change and the identification of Iran as independent and developing, Ahmadinejad's two terms in government were a success for the regime. Acting on the premise that the United States is an international bully, seeking to undermine the development of alternative powers such as Iran, the Iranian regime was able to assert its moral superiority by resisting United States' demands. Meanwhile, it sought alternative partners to both circumvent ad undermine United States' attempts at isolating Iran. Despite these successes, things were far from optimal for the Iranian regime in the international environment at the end of Ahmadinejad's presidency. Iran may not be as isolated as the United States would like it to be, but that does not mean Iran's isolation from the West does not severely limit its options. What is important here, however, is that the Ahmadinejad administration, instead of trying to reverse its isolation, was trying to take maximum advantage of it, turning this weakness into Iran's main international strength. The regime's revolutionary discourse was central to this endeavor, through its analysis of the current state of affairs it points to the inherent changeability of the international system, saying: things do not have to be this way. In the context of this discourse, giving in to Western demands is irrational; rationality is to build alliances that secure Iran's independence and development, building a future in which the United States no longer makes the rules. Chapter 6 takes a closer look at the nuclear issue and discusses its discursive context and shows how this precluded a negotiated settlement with the United States. It also shows how the Iranian regime was not just losing, but also gaining from the nuclear issue, by challenging the United States and creating global space for itself among developing and rising powers, while defending what is considered a cause for the entire developing world.

Chapter 6

"Nuclear Power Is Our Right!": The 2010 Tehran Declaration

Most studies on the Islamic Republic's nuclear development focus on the Iranian regime's assumed intentions to build nuclear weapons, the strategic motivations that guide this program or the kind of threat a nuclear Iran would pose to the region.[1] When these studies acknowledge, there is an important ideological component to Iran's nuclear program; they see this as a constraint on Iran's rationality, which only adds to the concerns about the prospect of a nuclear Iran. This chapter takes a different approach, and places Iran's nuclear development in the context of the Iranian regime's foreign policy discourse. The previous chapters argued that foreign policy discourse, as the framework within which foreign policy makers understand international developments, forms the context in which foreign policy decisions are made. This context makes certain foreign policy possible, even favorable, while precluding other options. Within the Iranian regime's ideological context under Ahmadinejad, Iranian intransigence toward Western demands in the nuclear issue was not only a possibility, but even an advantage for the regime, as it confirms the revolutionary ideology that underpins their claim to power. Moreover, the nuclear issue made it possible for the regime to act within an international space in which United States' power is challenged by rising powers, increasing Iran's international options and challenging the notion that it is isolated.

This chapter starts with an overview of the main developments in the nuclear issue, focusing in particular on the developments that led to the 2010 Tehran Declaration. It then summarizes the Iranian regime's official discourse on the nuclear issue. It shows how this discourse was not an ad hoc response to international developments to secure Iran's "objective national interest," or a post hoc justification of irrational policies: the regime's nuclear discourse was rooted in its broader foreign policy discourse, had a high level of internal consistency, and got plausibility from its placement within historical as well as contemporary international developments. Moreover, the case study of the Tehran Declaration not only shows that discourse makes foreign policy possible, but also shows how the Iranian regime's foreign policy behavior fed back into the discourse by "acting as if" to create international space. Through its cooperation with Turkey and Brazil, Iran was able to contribute to the actualization of a worldview in which Western hegemony is increasingly challenged by rising powers. In other words, although the 2010 deal with Turkey and Brazil did not resolve the nuclear issue between Iran and the West, it was a major success for the Iranian regime in terms of its own foreign policy views.

The Nuclear Issue

The European Union and the United States' Government time and again express their concerns about the Islamic Republic's lack of democracy, its human rights violations, its stance on Israel, and its support of regional militant groups, but nothing seems to worry the United States and the EU more than Iran's nuclear program. Iran's nuclear development started in the 1950s, and was immediately under suspicion of being a covert military program to acquire nuclear weapons. As Mohammad Reza Pahlavi, the shah at the time, had warm relations with the United States, these worries were, however, less urgent than under the current regime.[2] Even after the establishment of the Islamic Republic Iran's nuclear development was not high on the West's agenda, but concern rose when in 2002 an opposition group in exile, the *Mujahedin-e Khalq* (MEK or MKO), revealed that the Iranian regime had been constructing nuclear enrichment facilities. In subsequent years, the US government implemented punitive measures in the form of sanctions to persuade the Iranian regime to stop its nuclear activities, while the EU sought to engage Iran through negotiations between Iran and the EU3 (Germany, France, and the United Kingdom). The EU's conciliatory approach seemed successful at first, as the reformist Iranian Government came to a number of promising agreements with the EU3, and in fact suspended enrichment activities. In 2004, Iran and the EU3 reached the Brussels Agreements, in which both parties expressed the commitment to establish a long-term relationship including a Trade and Cooperation Agreement. However, owing to US pressure, changes in Iran's domestic politics and discrepancies between what Iran had reported to the IAEA and what the IAEA had found in Iran, the Brussels Agreement was never implemented. In November 2004, the Paris Agreement was reached in which the Iranian regime voluntarily suspended enrichment, but Tehran left this agreement in July 2005 and resumed enrichment activities.

After Iran resumed its enrichment, the European stance on the nuclear issue toughened. The elections of Sarkozy in France, Brown in the United Kingdom, and Merkel in Germany contributed to the hardening of the atmosphere between the partners,[3] as did the election of Ahmadinejad in August 2005. Ahmadinejad presented himself as the champion of the nuclear program, which he saw as a test case for Iran's independence and self-determination. Iran's case was referred to the UN Security Council in 2006, after which Iran held negotiations with the 5+1 (the five permanent UNSC members plus Germany) and the EU's chief foreign policy official Javier Solana. The United States joined the negotiations in 2009, and together with the IAEA and Russia proposed a deal in which Iran would send its low-enriched uranium to France via Russia for transformation into fuel, which would then be returned to Iran. Divergence in goals between Islamic Republic and US officials made negotiations hard, whereas the US Government was seeking to halt Iranian nuclear development, to the Iranian negotiators the continuation of peaceful nuclear development was not negotiable. The US Government, meanwhile, continued its efforts to implement stronger sanctions on Iran anticipating that negotiations would be unsuccessful. The Iranian regime at the same time felt hesitant about cooperation with France and Russia in a nuclear deal, as France had in the past proven to be an unreliable supplier. Therefore, Iran insisted that a fuel swap should be simultaneous and take place on own soil, but the US delegation rejected this. When no agreement was reached, Iran declared in early 2010 that it would enrich its own uranium to 20 percent. This caused concern in the United States, Europe, and Russia, and the United States picked up the pace of implementing sanctions on Iran.[4]

Unable to come to a negotiated settlement with Iran by itself, the US Government encouraged talks between Iran and Brazil and Iran and Turkey. The Tehran Declaration, which Turkey and Brazil announced on May 17, 2010, is a revision of the nuclear fuel swap proposal by the United States, France, and Russia in 2009. The 2010 Tehran Declaration aimed at circumventing the problem of Iran's mistrust of Russia and France by using Turkey as the middleman. It read: "Iran agrees to deposit 1,200kg LEU [low-enriched uranium] in Turkey," and "upon the positive response of the Vienna Group (U.S., Russia, France, and the IAEA), further details of the exchange will be elaborated through a written agreement and proper arrangement between Iran and the Vienna Group that specifically committed themselves to deliver 120kg of fuel needed for the Tehran Research Reactor (TRR)."[5] The Tehran Declaration was received with skepticism by the Vienna Group, and did not prevent the UNSC from adopting new sanctions just three weeks after the declaration was signed. Nevertheless, the Tehran Declaration was a success to the Iranian regime and can be considered a milestone in the nuclear issue. Particularly, as will be argued below, because the negotiations with Brazil and Turkey provided Iran with foreign policy options much in line with their domestic discourse, thereby actualizing their discourse and actively challenging the authority of the United States.

A Shared Discourse on the Nuclear Issue

Iran's official discourse on the nuclear issue under Ahmadinejad was marked by a high level of internal consistency. The information that different policy makers shared overlapped to a great extent, and where emphasis differs, official statements usually mutually reinforced or complemented each other.[6] From the careful analysis of the discourse of these officials[7] emerges an inherently consistent narrative according to which the Iranian regime is pursuing peaceful nuclear energy, which it is entitled to under international law, and in which Iran is cooperative and open for dialogue. According to the same narrative, the West was deliberately undermining Iran's progress, but to no avail, as Iran was making progress in the nuclear field and with or without the help of others would succeed in becoming a self-sufficient nuclear power.

Iran's Rights

The official discourse on the nuclear program to a large extent got shape outside Iran's borders, at press conferences and international meetings. As such, it seems that much of the discourse was a direct response to international accusations of Iran's noncompliance, and aims to counter these accusations by emphasizing that Iran's program is for peaceful purposes and insisting on Iran's rights under the NPT. That is, Iran's right to nuclear development is the most recurrent statement in the Ahmadinejad adminstration's official discourse on the nuclear issue.[8] It is repeatedly stated that under the NPT and IAEA, members who are committed to their obligations have the right to nuclear development, and there is no reason why Iran should be an exception to this.[9] This incessant referral by Iran's officials to its rights under the NPT suggests that Iran's insistence on indigenous nuclear development is mostly a matter of principle: Iran wants to develop in the nuclear field, not because it needs to but because it *should be allowed to* under international law. As such, Iran's progress in its nuclear development is a political statement by itself, conveying a message of defiance and self-reliance. There is much to say for this reading of Iran's insistence on nuclear development, as Iranian leaders emphasize that nuclear development is a source of pride for Iran,[10] and that the demand for nuclear development is first and foremost a popular demand.[11] Iran's officials, however, claim that to Iran, the issue is in fact not political: it is vital to Iran's economic and technological development. First of all, Iran is in need of nuclear energy. This claim may seem unfounded for a country with oil and gas reserves far beyond domestic needs, but Iranian officials emphasize they cannot rely on oil forever.[12] They claim that Iran, like other countries, tries to limit its dependence on oil by looking into alternative energy sources.[13] Secondly, it is said that Iran needs nuclear development as a part of its scientific and technological development.[14] Officials give examples of Iran's nuclear developments in the field of medicine.[15] In sum, Iran is said to be simply pursuing its national interest in the nuclear issue, and Western attempts to halt Iran's nuclear progress are an assault on its national interest.

Iran Is Cooperative

Iran's officials rarely missed an opportunity to explicitly state that Iran's nuclear program has peaceful purposes.[16] The main reason they give for Iran's nondeviation toward military use is that the Iranian regime is against nuclear weapons for religious reasons.[17] An image of Iran's nuclear program as positive, beneficial, and peaceful is instilled by the peaceful purposes that are named for Iran nuclear program, such as clean energy and medicine, as well as the use of the word "civilian" to denote these uses.[18] Moreover, Iranian officials point to objective evidence that Iran's nuclear program is peaceful. First, they refer to reports by the IAEA that confirm Iran's cooperation as well as the peaceful nature of Iran's program.[19] When the IAEA does not confirm Iran's compliance, this is dismissed as bias due to US pressure on the organization.[20] Officials also emphasize Iran's commitment to the NPT[21] and international law,[22] and state that the cooperation between Iran and the IAEA has not only been constructive in the past,[23] but will also continue.[24]

Iranian officials insist that negotiations on the nuclear issue must continue, as is consistently stated in the discourse. Although in the

earlier discourse Iranian officials emphasized that Iran had taken con-
fidence-building measures to solve the nuclear issue, and was offering
objective guarantees of nondeviation,[25] closer to 2010 the discourse
emphasized that the IAEA and Iran have solved their issues, and that
the IAEA confirms the peaceful nature of Iran's development.[26] To
Iran the nuclear file is therefore closed, officials say, and negotiations
that remain are only about how Iran and international partners can
come to cooperation in the field of nuclear development.[27] Iranian
officials state that Iran has the capacity to become self-sufficient in its
nuclear development,[28] but that they would prefer partnerships with
other countries.[29] Iranian officials propose a fuel swap, which would
have Iran enrich uranium to a certain percentage domestically, and get
uranium with a higher level of enrichment in return.[30]

West Is Undermining Iran

The understanding of Iran as a peaceful and cooperative power, which
is only following its national interest in its wish to develop in the
field of science and technology, is further strengthened by discrediting the objectives of the West in questioning Iran's peaceful program.
To start, and as previously said, Iranian officials emphasize that Iran's
nuclear development takes place within the framework of international law, that it is a committed member of the NPT and that the
IAEA has confirmed that there are no signs of deviation of Iran's program toward military purposes. The, therefore false, accusations made
by the West contradict international law and are discrediting international organizations such as the IAEA.[31] There is no legal framework
for referral of the Iranian case to the UN Security Council, officials
agree, or for sanctions against Iran.[32] In fact, the pressure the West
has been putting on the UNSC means this institution cannot function properly.[33] Western countries have also pressured the IAEA to
the same effect and as such Western countries are undermining the
credibility of the UN altogether,[34] Iranian officials state. As Iranian
officials claim there is no legal basis for the nuclear issue, they insist
the West has politicized it: the West knows Iran's program has peaceful purposes, officials claim, however, tries to keep the issue on the
international agenda by blatantly lying about Iran's nuclear program
and making up false accusations.[35] This politicization serves the interest of Western countries, which try to keep Iran from developing and
to that purpose are depriving it of know-how and technology, they
argue.[36] To this end, Western powers use their well-known bullying
tactics (see chapter 4), including an extensive propaganda campaign or

"psychological operation" to discredit Iran,[37] pressuring international organizations and other countries, and threatening other countries' security.[38] What is particularly troublesome to Iranian officials, and evident of the West's bad intentions, is the double-standards policy Western governments maintain: although Iran's nuclear development is under scrutiny, much of these Western countries have developed and in the case of the United States have even used nuclear weapons themselves.[39] Moreover, they do nothing about the development of nuclear weapons by Israel, which is in fact a nonparty to the NPT, and is threatening regional states.[40]

If the West is only interested in undermining Iran, it does not come as a surprise to Iranian officials that negotiations with the EU or the United States have so far been unproductive.[41] Iranian officials also emphasize that although they are in favor of continuing negotiations, it is the West that pulled out.[42] The West is not interested in resolving the conflict, officials conclude, as Western countries offer no ground for negotiations.[43] Negotiations should have no preconditions, Iranian officials insist, such as suspension of nuclear research or enrichment.[44] Moreover, the West should offer objective guarantees that they will live up to their proposals.[45] Iran has learned from the past, officials say, and knows from experience that Western states do not live up to their promises.[46] France, the United Kingdom and Germany unilaterally ceased cooperation with Iran that had started before the revolution, and Iran's purchased equipment was neither delivered nor refunded.[47] Nevertheless, Iranian officials express a willingness to continue talking to the West,[48] and even claim to understand the predicament the West is in. After all, after years of obstructing the nuclear program, it is hard for the West to find a face-saving way out of this situation.[49] Iran offers solutions to these problems, officials claim, and offer a way out for the West by becoming a partner to Iran's nuclear program, which would be a mutually beneficial cooperation.[50]

Iran Will Succeed Nevertheless

Iranian officials under Ahmadinejad emphasized that Iran's nuclear development will continue despite international threats and sanctions. These have no effect, Iranian officials repeatedly state, and are even counterproductive.[51] Iran does not only have the capacity to become a nuclear power, but also the will, as nuclear development is a demand from the Iranian people themselves, they say.[52] Often it seems that the officials act as if Iran's nuclear development is out of their hands, and that it is not the Iranian regime, but the Iranian people's wish the West is going against. Officials emphasize that this is not the first time in history that the West is going against the Iranian nation's will, and that they should by now have learned from past experience.[53] Iranians are not scared of sanctions or other threats, they say, but are steadfast when it comes to defending their right to nuclear development. It is due to the steadfastness and dedication of the Iranian people that Iran has been able to make steady progress in this field, according to the officials.[54] Iran has shown self-sufficiency in its nuclear development, which has made Iran independent from international partners.[55] This does not mean that Iranian officials would not like international cooperation, officials emphasize,[56] but that their program will survive without it. It is stressed that Iran's progress in the nuclear field is something to be exceptionally proud of, [57] not just for Iranians but also for the Muslim world and the international community.[58] In fact, Iran's nuclear development should be an example to other countries—a scenario the West is trying to prevent.[59]

Iran Fights Global Nuclear Proliferation

Iran's discourse on the nuclear issue is not just about Iran's wish to develop nuclear capacity for civilian purposes, but it is also about global nuclear proliferation. Reversing the accusations made against itself, the Ahmadinejad adminstration pointed at the West as the main culprit. After all, it is the West that has not only developed nuclear weapons, but has also employed them during the Second World War. [60] Although Iran has not itself been a victim of Western nuclear threat, Iranian officials effortlessly place Iran in the camp of the victims. At one time recounting the atrocities of the Iran–Iraq War, particularly the chemical attacks of Iraq on Iran that have left many Iranians permanently injured both physically and psychologically, and at another describing the nuclear effects of the nuclear attacks in today's generations of Hiroshima and Nagasaki, Iranian officials relate to the victims of nuclear weapons. The link between the atrocities committed by the West in Japan, on the one hand, and the Iran–Iraq War, on the other, are further strengthened by the emphasis placed on the fact that the West provided Saddam Hussein with chemical weapons.[61] In both the case of Hiroshima/Nagasaki and the Iran–Iraq War, the West is held accountable for the use of WMDs.

The fact that the West has developed nuclear weapons shows that science is not in safe hands under Western domination, Ahmadinejad argues. "Making nuclear, chemical and biological bombs and weapons of mass destruction is another result of misuse of science and research by great powers," he said during a speech at Columbia University in 2007.[62] In fact, it shows that the West is using their domination over science to achieve their own goals. They need not do so, as technological advancement can be used for beneficial purposes, such as in the field of medicine. In Khamenei's words, "Nuclear technology is not sinful in itself. The sin is committed by those who alter the aim of this technology to destroy human beings. The same goes for other advanced technologies such as nano-technology..."[63] Both he and Ahmadinejad agree that there is no rational use for developing nuclear weapons: "How can these weapons be used to protect global security?" Ahmadinejad asked.[64] Western countries have developed nuclear weapons despite "obvious ethical, intellectual, human, and even military realities" and "the strong and repeated urge by the global community to dispose of these weapons"[65] makes them backward and irrational.[66]

* * *

In sum, under Ahmadinejad the nuclear issue was framed as as a situation in which the West seeks to maintain its dominance over science and technology, so to dominate other countries. This means that Iran's fight against nuclear proliferation can be seen as a manifestation of Iran's resistance against this Western domination of science. The discourse on the nuclear issue builds on and reinforces Iran's broader foreign policy ideology. It reflects the same worldview in which the West is using powers to dominate others. The West is using its propaganda means as well as its ability to pressure other nations and international institutions to further its own interest, which is to stay ahead of others in terms of development. The nuclear case is an illustration of Iran's identity of resistance and independence, particularly as the nuclear discourse revolves around the notion that Iran is pursuing its national interest of scientific and technological development. Iran is resisting the West not just on its own behalf, but also on behalf of humanity, which does not agree with the Western approach. It is emphasized that unlike the immoral West, Iran is willing to share its knowledge with other nations to the betterment of mankind. The contrast with the West, particularly the United States, is elaborated by the juxtapositions of the characteristics in table 6.1, which complement and reinforce each other.

Table 6.1 lists how the discourse on the nuclear issue is building on the dualistic worldview that is inherent to the discourse of the Iranian regime, where the world's problems are caused by the oppressors at

Table 6.1   The nuclear issue—Iran and the West juxtaposed

The West	Iran
Oppressor	*Oppressed*
Is threatening	Is a victim of threats
Is using propaganda	Is the victim of propaganda
Is accusing	Is falsely accused
Is using WMDs	Is a victim of WMDs
Unchanged	*Changed*
Cannot be trusted	Has learned from the past
Aims to dominate	Is independent
Immoral	*Moral*
Offers no ground for negotiation	Is ready for negotiations
Is dominating science	Shares knowledge with others
Is using "double standards"	Is following international law
Is using WMDs	Is against WMDs
Is using nuclear technology to build WMDs	Is using peaceful nuclear technology
Is using censorship	Promotes free scientific investigation
Is threatening other countries	Has peaceful intentions
Cannot be trusted	Is building confidence
Failure	*Success*
Threats have no effect	Is making progress

the expense of the oppressed. Iranian foreign policy discourse, however, also has an important element of change: Iran has learned from the past and has become independent, whereas the United States still cannot be trusted and aims to dominate. Moreover, when it comes to their respective foreign policies, the West's immorality, its dominating and threatening behavior, and its use of double standards are central. Conversely, Iran shares its knowledge with others instead of monopolizing science, follows international law instead of using it as a tool for domination, and is peaceful and cooperative instead of threatening.

The Tehran Declaration

Iran's official discourse on the nuclear issue under Ahmadinejad, as described above, shows much continuity and consistency over the years and among foreign policy actors. Its relevance for understanding Iranian foreign policy behavior in the nuclear issue is twofold. First, the discourse served as the context in which Iran's foreign policy behavior on the nuclear issue got shape, including the developments that lead to the Tehran Declaration in May 2010. It precluded cooperation with the West on a less than equal basis, but made possible (at least on the Iranian side) the cooperation with other powers such as

China, Russia, Turkey, and Brazil. Second, Iran's behavior and particularly the signing of the Tehran Declaration confirmed and reinforced the regime's discourse, particularly as it challenged the idea of Iran's international isolation, confirmed US bullying, and contributed to cooperation with rising powers, challenging US dominance.

Central in Iranian officials' nuclear discourse is the perception of the unwillingness of the West to come to a settlement. It is believed that the West would prefer Iran not to develop nuclear capability altogether—whether for civilian or other use. Settlement of the nuclear issue with the West becomes highly problematic in this context: Iran's main motivation is its technological development. Moreover, the discourse precludes any settlement in which the regime would give in to the United States' demands without equal reciprocation. The discourse of resistance, and the prediction of Iran's victory over the bullying powers, thus precludes a settlement that would improve Iran's relations with the United States, but harm the premises of its discourse of resistance and independence. This is not to say that a settlement is precluded under all circumstances or forever. On the contrary, discourse changes over time, in particular, in response to international developments. However, Western demands of suspension combined with the Iranian discourse of development and resistance precluded a negotiated settlement under the Ahmadinejad administration. Giving in to the West would simply be unacceptable to the Iranian regime as it would compromise its main goals. Moreover, the nuclear issue is framed as a demand by the Iranian people, which means that in the context of Islamic Republic's popular identity, the regime sees it as its mission to follow through in the nuclear program.

As nuclear negotiations with the West reached a stalemate, the Iranian regime needed to find alternative partners in its nuclear development, preferably outside of the West's circle. Iranian officials under Ahmadinejad expressed the wish to come to cooperation with anyone, propagating cooperation and the sharing of technology. They reached out, in particular, to Russia and China. There are many reasons why China would appear a suitable partner in Iran's nuclear development. China's interests seem to match those of Iran: China's growing need for energy resources have resulted in growing economic ties between the two countries, China's foreign policy ideology of noninterference and respect for state sovereignty are a good match with Iran's antiimperialist discourse, and Iran's isolation from the West means China faces little competition in Iran. As such, "Tehran is increasingly viewing a rising China as not only a trade partner, but as a means to further distance itself from Western demands for nuclear transparency."[67] Iran's officials emphasize the trade relations between China and Iran as well as convergence of worldviews: "Iran and China's common views over international evolutions provide a favorable ground for the expansion of relations between the two countries at the regional and international levels and the formation of Iran-China strategic cooperation," Jalili[68] said in April 2010. China, however, unwilling to jeopardize its good relations with the United States was not very forthcoming in developing ties beyond energy and trade.[69]

Cooperation with Russia and China was made possible in the context of Iran's foreign policy discourse, particularly as it was largely neutral regarding these powers. This neutrality is remarkable when it comes to Russia, considering Russia's long history of interference in Iranian affairs. Seeing Russia as a partner rather than an imposing power facilitated cooperation between Russia and Iran, for example, in the development of the Bushehr power plant, as well as cooperation in the fields of energy and trade, including arms trade. However, the Iranian regime was unable to come to full-blown cooperation with Russia. Since 2010, it encountered increasing resistance from both Russia and China regarding their nuclear development, and this had an effect on cooperation in other fields.

The Iranian regime had some success in finding partners among the smaller rising powers. In terms of Iran's discourse of resistance, cooperation, and equality, particularly with regard to the Ummah and Latin America, cooperation with smaller rising powers such as Turkey and Brazil is favorable. As such, Turkey and Brazil's willingness to work with Iran on a settlement of the nuclear issue in 2010 came as a blessing for the regime. The fact that Turkey and Brazil are considered equal partners for Iran may have contributed to a greater flexibility on the side of Tehran in the negotiations: the Tehran Declaration greatly resembles the US proposal half a year earlier, including a swap on Turkey's soil and not, as Iran insisted earlier, on Iranian soil. Mottaki[70] emphasized cooperation with Turkey, which was a logical step since trade between the two countries had already grown significantly during Ahmadinejad's presidency. He also mentioned that the presidents of both countries supported the talks, and he called it a chance for all parties to build trust. Mottaki confirmed Iran's flexibility toward Turkey, stating that a nuclear swap outside of Iran's borders could be considered a trust building gesture.

What was particularly favorable in terms of Iran's nuclear discourse was that both Turkey and Brazil explicitly shared and confirmed the Iranian regime's outlook: "You must be sure that Ankara's views on nuclear weapons are similar to those of Iran. Ankara and

Tehran are both against the use of nuclear weapons[71] for military purpose," Turkish Foreign Minister Ahmet Davutoğlu said in April 2010.[72] Brazilian statements showed similar convergence with the Iranian regime's view of the situation. When Ahmadinejad "thanked the Brazilian president's stance in support of Iranians' rights and the position he adopts for improving the world," and reminded the audience that together Brazil and Turkey can overcome the injustice of the domineering powers, Lula was quoted in reply: "Brazil regards its ties with Iran as strategic as it believes one can act stronger with each other's help."[73] When the Tehran Declaration was signed, Lula said "Diplomacy emerged victorious today," in a radio interview, and later on Brazilian radio: "It showed that it is possible to build peace and development with dialogue." Brazilian Foreign Minister Celso Amorim said the Declaration "contains all the elements for an agreement to trade uranium for fuel elements," and that it should be sufficient to avoid new sanctions.[74]

Much to the contrary of what Iran, Brazil, and Turkey had hoped, the Tehran Declaration did not prevent the adoption of UN Security Council Resolution 1929 on June 9, 2010, which introduced new sanctions on Iran. Secretary of State Hillary Clinton had already called it "as convincing an answer to the efforts undertaken in Tehran over the last few days,"[75] pointing to the agreement with Brazil and Turkey, which she regarded "a transparent ploy to avoid Security Council action."[76] Turkey and Brazil as nonpermanent members had voted against the UN sanctions, and Lebanon had abstained. In response to the Resolution's adoption, Iranian officials directed their criticism particularly at Russia and China. "China is gradually losing its respectable position in the Islamic world and by the time it wakes up, it will be too late," Salehi said, adding "There was a time when China branded the U.S. as a paper tiger. I wonder what we can call China for agreeing to this resolution."[77] Ahmadinejad[78] lashed out against Russia, accusing it of considering itself master of the world, of going against global public opinion, and of politicizing the issue. "If Russia comes and speaks in a two-faced manner, it is not acceptable for us," Ahmadinejad said.

This Iranian response was to be expected and is much in line with its discourse. What was interesting, however, is that Turkey and Brazil's statements, to a considerable extent, echoed the Iranian discourse. Lula da Silva called the resolution a "Pyrrhic victory" and said the move "weakened the UN Security Council."[79] In an official statement, Ahmet Davutoğlu expressed disappointment, stating that "Turkey is worried that the UN Security Council's decision...will hurt diplomatic efforts and the window of opportunity for a peaceful settlement of the issue on Iran's nuclear program."[80] Earlier, Erdoğan had made an appeal to the international community to support the declaration, stating that those countries that "are speaking against nuclear weapons unfortunately are the ones still possessing nuclear weapons." Also in line with the Iranian regime's discourse, he wondered "Are we speaking about the law of supremacy or are we talking about the rule of law and the supremacy of the law?" He also underlined that "the ones who are mistrustful of this process are not the ones who are living in the region."[81]

With the Tehran Declaration, Iran could not avoid new sanctions, but was nevertheless a success for the Iranian regime in terms of its discourse in several ways. First, the Tehran Declaration and the subsequent votes against sanctions by Turkey and Brazil effectively put these countries on the side of Iran, and Iranian officials used this as evidence that there is no world consensus against their country. Ahmadinejad[82] noted that "Each of these three countries [Brazil, Turkey and Iran] carries a few nations behind it in the political arena," which are looking for a different international model. "They would not dare say so, of course. In reality, Turkey and Brazil are standing shoulder to shoulder with Iran." Second, that the UNSC adopted sanctions, despite the Tehran Declaration, supported the notion that the US government is pressuring other countries to take a tough stance on Iran. It aids the understanding of the world with the bullying West, on the one side, and justice seeking humanity, on the other. Similar views are present in the discourse of Brazil and Turkey, as mentioned. Ahmadinejad claimed that the Tehran Declaration had become a criterion: "Those who are in favor of law and justice, are supporting this declaration, but those who are has evil intentions and wants to cause trouble and domineer the world have adopted a biased approach." He emphasized the lawful nature of the agreement: "One cannot find any faults with the statement. Any moderate and rational individual would say these are reasonable statements."[83]

Last, and most importantly, the Tehran Declaration can be seen as the enactment of a worldview in which new powers are on the rise, while the power of the West is shrinking. "Acting as if," the Tehran Declaration challenged the international status quo at the expense of the Western camp and in favor of rising powers. According to Ahmadinejad,

> Suddenly the alignments prevalent in the world today altered. Brazil and Turkey realised the true extent of their powers. They saw that if

they stand side by side and alongside Iran and they can change the rules of the game.[84]

The Tehran Declaration enabled Iranian officials to act as if international relations were changing, and by acting as such they aided the actualization of this scenario. It was particularly successful, as the Iranian regime's goals converged with those of other developing countries seeking nuclear development, as well as rising powers such as Brazil and Turkey seeking global influence. As two Washington Post correspondents described it:

> Countries such as Brazil and Turkey, but also Egypt and Indonesia, increasingly view the Western-led debate over Iran's nuclear program as an important test case for their own nuclear ambitions. Though the United States and its allies say they fear nuclear proliferation, some developing nations say that world powers are determined to control nuclear technology and want to prevent the development of independent nuclear energy programs.[85]

Effectively, through the Tehran Declaration, the Iranian regime was actualizing its discourse of change from a unipolar to a multipolar world. New powers entered the stage, and the willingness of Turkey and Brazil to negotiate with Iran was supportive of the view central to the Iranian regime's discourse that the days of the imperialist powers are numbered, and that a world is emerging on the basis of equality among nations, replacing that of bullying and imposition.

Conclusion

Foreign policy ideology makes possible, desirable even, certain foreign policy options, while precluding others.[86] This is reflected in Iran's foreign policy behavior with regard to the nuclear issue. From a discursive point of view, Iran's options to reach a constructive dialogue with the West were limited. Negotiations for Iran would have to take place on an equal basis, without preconditions, to ensure that Iran retains its independence. Moreover, it would have been hard for the regime to justify contributing to US power by brokering a nuclear deal with this adversary, and preferably Iran would have framed any deal with the West as a victory of justice over the bullying powers. This stance was a particularly bad match with the goals of the US government, which aimed at achieving the exact opposite: forcing Iran to give up enrichment.

The deal with Turkey and Brazil in 2010 may have been the regime's only option to move forward at that point in time. However, what is relevant here is that negotiations with these countries also proved the best option in terms of the regime's foreign policy discourse. First, Iran's foreign policy discourse made negotiations with Turkey and Brazil not only possible in the sense that it did not have anything against it, but also even favorable, as Brazil and Turkey are regarded more or less as equals to Iran, much different from the aforementioned imposing powers. Secondly, as Iran's discourse during Ahmadinejad conveyed a view of new rising powers, negotiations with Brazil and Turkey were particularly favorable. Ahmadinejad and Khamenei describe how developing countries and the Muslim world are now realizing their potential, while the power of the United States is shrinking. In this context, the talks with Turkey and Brazil were an ideal opportunity for the regime to actualize its discourse. Particularly, as Brazilian and Turkish leaders have expressed views converging with those of Iran, contributing to what can be seen as an emerging global counter-hegemonic discourse.

The case of the Tehran declaration shows how the Iranian regime was able to contribute to the actualization of its discourse. Instead of a one-way direction in which discourse forms the context of foreign policy, the nuclear issue shows a two-way relationship in which foreign policy, through the enactment of the discourse, actualizes and reinforces it. This means that the Tehran Declaration was a huge success for the regime, not only because it was an available option that helped it to move forward at a time when negotiations were otherwise stalled, but particularly also because it enabled the Iranian regime to "act as if" the international power balance was changing from a unipolar to a multipolar world. In this way, the Tehran Declaration and subsequent international response fed back into Iran's political discourse, reinforcing it, aiding the Islamic Republic's legitimacy both domestically and internationally.

Chapter 7

Foreign Threat and Political Repression*

The demonstrations in the summer of 2009 against the presidential election outcome were an unprecedented challenge to the legitimacy of the Iranian regime. Green Movement protestors questioned the election outcome and demanded a recount. The initially peaceful, even silent protests by millions of people who had "lost their voice" (*seda*, also vote) turned violent a week after the elections, when security forces interfered. The regime succeeded in repressing the protests, and the opposition lost its 2009 momentum. The regime did not only use repression alone, but also sought to defend its self-proclaimed identity of democracy and populism. Iran's official narrative on the 2009 elections and subsequent events aimed at defusing accusations of deceit by reversing them, justifying repression against protestors and activists. It discursively tied the opposition movement to outside interference, branded it alien, and it restated the democratic character of the Iranian state and the support of the Iranian people for the Islamic system.

This chapter aims at showing how Iran's hardliners use an inherently consistent and internally plausible account, which derives from both the broader ideological context that is supportive of Iran's regime as well as historical and contemporary developments. It describes the discursive tools the regime used as a part of their defense mechanism against this specific threat to their political survival, aimed at defusing the opposition and mobilizing support for the regime. Central in this hardline narrative is the juxtaposition between the Iranian people and their revolutionary ideals, on the one side, and the West and their deceived agents inside Iran, on the other side.

Inside Threat, Outside Threat

The discourse discussed in this chapter relies for a large part on the reports of *Keyhan*, a hardline conservative Iranian daily newspaper and website affiliated with the Office of the Supreme Leader and seen as the mouthpiece of the Iranian regime. Their reports are not representative of the broader views shared among Iranian media, but they do show the discursive mechanisms used by Iran's most conservative hardliners more so than other reports. The views expressed were in line with and echoed by Iran's leadership, and were consistent with the regime's broader foreign policy discourse. It was important for the regime to provide an analysis of the 2009 events, question the intentions of the Green Movement, and, in an as convincing manner as possible, restate their legitimacy. As Schlumberger[1] pointed out, "while the repression of political rights and civil liberties routinely is depicted as the distinctive feature of authoritarianism, this view neglects the fact that any political regime also needs to create and maintain legitimacy in order to survive over time." Moreover, it would be hard to imagine a repressive apparatus functioning without shared ideas about the legitimacy of the state among the group responsible for repression, such as the basij.

Taking as a starting point that for regime survival, some level of regime legitimacy is needed; this chapter draws attention to the mechanisms with which the regime was trying to create legitimacy. Iranian leaders' attempts at this did not become less important when the regime's message was contested by the opposition, but more important as the regime's success to counter domestic dissent depended on their strategies to convince their constituency to stand up against this challenge. Central in this endeavor was the regime's attempt to frame issues, to assign meaning, and manipulate information to construct a narrative supportive of their rule. A tight control of the public discourse and the media makes sure that for many Iranians this was the only narrative widely available. Its main elements were the focus on an outside threat, which with the help of domestic agents (the reformists) sought to stage a "velvet coup."

Both President Ahmadinejad and Supreme Leader Khamenei emphasized Western interference in the weeks following the elections:

[The West] tried to interfere in our election, made irrelevant plans, acted rudely, insulted the nation and supported sedition and attacks on public property (Ahmadinejad, 16 July 2009).[2]
...foreign elements triggered a line of destruction, arson, pillage of public wealth and unrest; they have no link to people or supporters

of candidates rather they are related to ill wishers of the Iranian nation and mercenaries of Western and Zionist services (Khamenei, 20 June 2009).[3]

In his speech on June 20, 2009, Khamenei also emphasized that "the British government proved more wicked than others in this regard," and media reports also emphasized the exceptional role of the BBC[4] and the British embassy during the unrest.[5] That hardliners identify the British as the main culprit (and not the Americans—in foreign policy discourse Iran's most prominent enemy) is probably because the United States broke off diplomatic ties with Iran after the hostage crisis of 1979 until 1981. Since then, hardliners argued, the United States relied on the British to take on the unfinished mission of the Americans. In addition, the United States had tried to open an interest section in Tehran for the purpose of coordinating the postelection unrest, but had been unsuccessful.[6]

The idea that the West had planned a velvet coup for Iran was made plausible in three ways. First, the 2009 events were framed as a continuation of the West's historical policies with regard to Iran. As discussed in chapter 4, Iran's foreign policy discourse is replete with references to Iran's contemporary history. According to the regime's narrative of the 2009 events, Iran's twentieth century history was shaped by its interactions with colonial powers, particularly Britain and the United States. Most recently during the reign of Iran's last shah, these countries were allowed a free hand in Iranian affairs to secure their own interests. Epic, in this regard, was the 1953 coup to restore Britain's oil interests in Iran. As discussed in chapter 3, when Prime Minister Mosaddeq nationalized Iran's oil, MI6 and CIA together with domestic opposition overthrew Mosaddeq's government and put the shah back in power. The 1979 revolution was directed toward this increasingly despotic shah, but was by extension a revolution against foreign interference in Iranian affairs. The "British government's dualistic approach is known from the past. It interferes in all countries' affairs by the slogan of 'divide and conquer,'" one source recounted. For example, it mentioned the UK's efforts during the constitutional movement by sowing discord among clerical leaders.[7] *Keyhan*[8] also mentions the British and American's hiring agents in Iran to conduct the 1953 coup, and BBC's special role in that coup. "It seems they are looking for another Sha'ban Bimokh,"[9] it writes.

Secondly, hardliners added credibility to the notion of foreign interference by emphasizing that the West is known for its strategy of velvet coup d'états and color revolutions.[10] In providing its own definition of color revolutions, *Keyhan* makes a clear statement about the nature of these coups. A velvet revolution, *Keyhan* argues, is the

> overthrowing of a system or a government in a non-military way, by provoking the people to riot and by using psychological, destructive propaganda and deceptive methods using the media and information and communication tools. A velvet revolution takes place by coordinating domestic and foreign assistance.[11]

Keyhan refers to the coup d'états in the Ukraine, Kirgizstan, Georgia, and Serbia,[12] and emphasized the similarities with the 2009 events.[13] The fact that the reformists used the color[14] for their movement is seen as another sign that the 2009 events were another Western attempt at a color revolution. Forced confessions by reformist in August confirmed this suspicion.[15]

Third, hardliners argue that the attempted coup of 2009 is much in line with the West's Iran policy since the 1979 revolution, and is merely a continuation of previous policies:

> Since the first day of the victory of the Islamic Revolution, Western powers, led by America, launched a project to abolish the revolution, or at least suppress it.[16]

To this purpose, the West is using not only its military might and a tight grip on the UN, but also an "evil chain of propagandas and a myriad of lie-spreading and rumour-mongering media centres," particularly aimed at "provocation of sectarian snobbery, prejudice and enmity among brothers."[17] The West's use of propaganda to create doubt and discord among Iranians is a recurrent theme in official foreign policy discourse,[18] and as seen in history "they usually try to achieve their goals through their agents."[19] The 2009 events are framed as a continuation to these Western policies of divide and rule. To be sure, perspectives on the events of 2009 differ among conservatives. However, among hardliners there seems to be consensus on the preplanned nature of those events by a coalition between reformists and outside enemies. Whether the initiative was the reformists' and outsiders merely took advantage of these events, or whether the events were preplanned by outsiders and the reformists only acted as their agents seems to be a matter of perspective among hardliners. Most hardline sources, however, imply the latter scenario, where the West created discord and deceived local agents to trigger a "velvet coup" in Iran. The foreign governments that hardline conservatives identified as the main perpetrators are without exception Western, with a special role played by the United Kingdom. In addition, Israel is mentioned as one of the designers of the postelection unrest. Most other Western countries are considered complicit, but play minor roles.

In all its planned scenarios to undermine the Iranian regime, the West depends on "aligned or hired individuals or groups within Iran," hardliners emphasize.[20] In the 2009 scenario, the West found lackeys among Iran's reformist elite. Confessions made by detained reformists uncovered, for example, the systematic relations between reformists and the CIA,[21] including guidance and training of reformist leaders by this organization.[22] In addition, purportedly the US administration in 2007 allocated large sums of money toward the goal of destabilizing Iran after the 2009 elections, and there was evidence of direct financial assistance from American sources toward Mousavi supporters.[23]

The Enemy Inside

The portrayal of reformists as foreign agents was not new for Iran's hardliners. During Khatami's term (1997 until 2005), hardliners described the reformist foreign policy of détente at best as "an acceptance of weakness and surrender to the enemy."[24] At worst, reformists were considered the enemy's "fifth column inside the country."[25] This view of reformists as representatives of outside enemies' hardliners maintained and even reinforced throughout Ahmadinejad's presidency. Toward the end of Ahmadinejad's first term, the two reformist candidates running for president[26] were targets of similar accusations of cooperation with the enemy.[27] These allegations intensified after Ahmadinejad's 2009 victory and subsequent opposition. Since then, reformism has been effectively targeted as a subversive activity directly linked to Western meddling in Iran's domestic affairs.

While some hardline sources refer to reformist elites as deceived people "who were under an illusion—and still continue to suffer from the same illusion,"[28] it is also suggested that the reformists deliberately sought to cooperate with the foreign enemy. "The unorganized situation of the candidates...forced them to do so," one news report argues.[29] Other sources concur that reformists knew they would not stand a chance against Ahmadinejad in the elections, as they were lacking domestic support[30] and, therefore, had to resort to the drastic measure of cooperating with the West.[31] Furthermore, shared ideas between the reformists and the West made this coalition possible: *Keyhan* repeatedly emphasized what it considers the Western leaning of reformists,[32] as well as the convergence in interests and goals between reformists and the West.[33] This is further supported by claims that reformists had taken advice from the American neoconservative specialist Michael Ledeen and philosopher Richard Rorty.[34] The support expressed by Western leaders toward the reformists before and after the elections is taken as another indication of their good relations.[35]

The main link between Iran's reformists and the West, hardline sources show, is through reformists' affiliation with Iranian dissident groups and individuals living abroad. The supposition of reformist ties with the West through exiled dissidents provides a strong back-up to the perception of the reform movement as being merely a lackey of outside forces. Moreover, it reinforces the connection that can be made between the current "seditionists" and those of the early days of the Islamic Republic—a powerful ideological tool. *Keyhan*, for example, emphasizes similarities between the Green Movement and the political left, the Freedom movement, and the *Mujahedin-e Khalq* (MEK or MKO) that were critical of the regime in the early 1980s.[36] Other *Keyhan* articles make the comparison between the Green Movement and the Baha'i, monarchists, the *Fedayin-e Khalq*, and the National Front as comparable antirevolutionary groups.[37]

However, the Green Movement was not only framed as yet another foreign-inspired counter-revolutionary movement comparable to the early enemies of the Islamic Republic. According to hardline sources, the Green Movement was also directly *cooperating* with the aforementioned groups. The following quote is an illustration of the ease with which Iran's Green Movement, Iranian dissident groups, Western intelligence agencies, and the Pahlavi[38] regime are connected in the hardline discourse:

> It should be noted that . . . persons of this type, who are the key members of such grouplets such as Fedayin-e Khalq, Tudeh Party and . . . [ellipses as published] other groups, have been working for the British and American intelligence agencies for a long time now and serving media organizations such as VOA, Radio Farda, BBC and . . . [ellipses as published] CIA and MI6 even encouraged the Sawak Pahlavi to hire the services of Marxists and leftists during the Pahlavi regime in order to sabotage the revolution of our people.[39]

Some sources claim that the 2009 events were a preplanned scenario by a coalition between the Reformist and the Freedom Movement,[40] while others emphasize a coalition between reformists and antirevolutionary organizations including the "imperialist powers."[41] In that last scenario, it is emphasized that dissidents are used by the enemy,[42] and that they may not like to cooperate with the enemy but do not have a choice.[43] It is emphasized that most dissidents associated with the aforementioned political groups, including many reformists or their families,[44] live in the West, and find support among Western organizations, such as Human Rights Watch,[45] and the intelligence agencies.[46] Here also the historical link is important: cooperation with, for example, the Freedom Movement, means cooperation with traitors, whose ties with the United States were revealed in documents found in the US Embassy during what is called the epic occupation of "the den of spies" (the hostage crisis). This connection is also an illustration of the claim that the reform movement is disregarding (not to say insulting towards) Iran's historical struggles against the enemy. When Green Movement's spokesperson Mohsen Makhmalbaf in a letter to Obama apologized for the occupation of the US Embassy, this served as an illustration of that accusation.[47]

The coup, according to Iran's hardliners, was based on an extensive propaganda campaign that started months before the elections. This propaganda campaign is also referred to as a media war or psychological coup. The soft overthrow that the enemy had planned for the 2009 elections, hardliners argue, had several stages.[48] According to them, the first stage took place in the months before the elections, when the foreign-based media in cooperation with domestic reformist media tried to discourage Iranians from voting for Ahmadinejad,[49] for example, by discrediting him and his administration,[50] as well as discouraging Iranians from participating in the elections all together.[51] At the same time, propaganda efforts were geared toward creating an atmosphere of doubt about the elections:

> Announcements that the election has been rigged are made very early and this allegation is continuously repeated by domestic movements and is followed up by the foreign media who support these movements inside the country[52] and especially by the U.S.[53]

For this purpose, hardliners argue, the BBC sent 55 journalists to Iran to cover the elections[54] and started a Persian service three months before the elections, and the CIA set up media centers in Dubai.[55] In addition, various news media "in order to make the claims of vote rigging seem natural (!) released false opinion polls and acceptable (!)," Shari'atmadari wrote.[56] Claims were made that Mousavi was on the winning side,[57] and efforts were made to convince even Mousavi himself of his imminent victory, hardline media wrote.[58] In a coordinated effort, reformists started a "committee to safeguard the votes" two months before the elections, also suggesting that the elections would be unhealthy.[59] Furthermore, to make sure people would take part in the antigovernment protests after the elections, arrangements were said to have been made during the months before the elections to mobilize people.[60]

On June 12, 2009, *Keyhan* writes, the propaganda campaign entered its second stage, which was to spread false information about the result of the elections. It considered it a well-known strategy for velvet coups: "They make claims about their victory, hours before the end of the voting to prepare the grounds for alleging that the election is rigged after the election outcome is officially announced!"[61] In one report, the English- and Persian-language services of the BBC are accused of taking charge of spreading the false news of unsound elections, which they had prepared months before.[62] The BBC's "55-strong media group," it is said, facilitated the flow of information and provided the Green Movement with means of communication.[63] Another source points at "America and its allies" who "used all their political and media capabilities and their financial resources to get this false message [of fraud] across."[64]

The third and possibly the most important stage, the coup itself, according to the hardline narrative, was planned to take place after the elections through street demonstrations. The fact that the demonstrations were not spontaneous but a preplanned attempt at a soft coup by reformists and outsiders was supported by the following evidence: it was argued that reformists figures, who were said to direct these events, were present at these demonstrations, and they had received US financial and political support.[65] Another source reports the extensive role played by the British Embassy (particularly its Iranian staff) in fomenting riots "even to the extent of being present in the riots and provoking others."[66] Two weeks after the 2009 elections, *Keyhan*[67] wrote, "[...] almost all Western embassies in Tehran have during the past few weeks turned into headquarters for plotting against the Islamic Republic system." When it comes to the velvet coup, major roles are attributed again to the BBC and the foreign counterrevolutionary media (often mentioned are *Radio Farda*, *Radio Zamaneh*, *VOA*, and *Gooya News*). In addition, at this stage in the velvet coup websites such as *Facebook*, *YouTube*, and *Twitter* are mentioned as particularly relevant. One Iranian political scientist is quoted emphasizing "our enemies have well understood the importance of cyberspace in the war with Islamic Iran and with the development of filter-breaking software they are trying to bring the public opinion of the people of Iran to their side."[68] The digital media proved their worth particularly in the spreading of false information, hardliners said, such as the presence of Mousavi during demonstrations when he was not,[69] and the dispersion of a manipulated account of what happened to Neda Aqa Soltan.[70] "At that juncture the BBC Persian made use of non-professional camera pictures of the rioters and thus spread their propaganda to international domains," a *Keyhan* analytical news report recounts.[71]

Soon, it is argued, the Western propaganda campaign after the election started to live a life of its own. "The Western leaders were then deceived by the psychological warfare of their own intelligence services that also fed the Western media and they started to express their stances against Iran on this basis."[72] This self-deception is blamed on the West's lack of understanding the truth of what happens in Iran, and its tendency for wishful thinking,[73] which made them miscalculate the events, put aside diplomacy, and support the rioters.[74] That the West made a big mistake here was emphasized in a later article,[75] which argued that if it was not for the 2009 events, the "massive number of networks" of the Western intelligence agencies in Iran would have been much harder to expose and neutralize. The self-deception of Western leaders and policy makers was rooted for a large part in misinformation, hardliners argue. According to them, the demonstrations that took place after the elections of 2009 were a sign of deception among a small number of Iranians. The majority meanwhile stood strong behind the elected president. It is the unawareness of this domestic situation that made the enemy miscalculate grossly:

> A big mistake of the American officials and officials of a number of European countries and their media and broadcasting agencies is that in their discourse and propaganda, they have failed to differentiate between their own lackeys, elements and rioters and millions of Iranians who have chosen to vote for a different candidate other than Dr Ahmadinezhad; they think that these people are unaware of foreign interference in Iran's affairs.[76]

When discussing the victory of the status quo, hardliners praised the efforts of the Iranian people. The 2009 events provided a challenge to Iranians, hardliners admit, and some may have been confused by it, but by their strength they were able to overcome their external enemy, as they had done many times before in Iran's long history:

> Although the water may be muddied and the atmosphere murky and some people, for a short time, are not able to see clearly, our people carried 14 centuries of experience on their shoulders.[77]

Internal Plausibility and Consistency

Discourse does not exist outside of reality; it provides views and interpretations of facts and current developments and ties in with existing understanding. The discourse on the Green Movement equally ties in with both facts as well as the Iranian regime's broader political discourse. As such, it has a high level of plausibility. First, the discourse refers to actual events that indicate Western meddling in Iranian affairs. The historical context is particularly relevant here. As mentioned the United States, and particularly the United Kingdom, is notorious for its long history of meddling in Iranian (political) affairs, particularly of exploiting its oil reserves for its own gain. The 1953 Coup against Mosaddeq is a textbook example of this meddling. But current Western policies also add to the regime's message. Since the 1979 Revolution, the US government, in particular, has made no secret of its wish for regime change in Iran, and has in this way also contributed to the credibility of the neoconservatives' accusations. Not only has the United States supported initiatives for democracy promotion in Iran,[78] hardliners claim there is evidence that the United States supports the terrorist Jundallah, who fight for Sunni rights in Iran. Moreover, the United States is at least sympathetic to the Mujahedin-e Khalq, which has been fighting the Iranian regime from abroad. Keeping this in mind, the notion of the US government initiating a coup in Iran after the 2009 elections seems a possible or even, as hardliners argue, a predictable strategy.[79] In this regard, emphasis is also put on the similarities and links between the 2009 and 1999 street riots.[80]

Secondly, the discourse on Iran's Green Movement made sense in the context of the regime's broader discourse and directly corresponded with it. Iran's identity of popularity and democracy is central here, as this identity is most affected by the opposition's accusations of vote rigging. This identity was important to the regime not only in terms of their popular legitimacy but also in its juxtaposition with the United States (which is regarded as unpopular and using democratization as a ploy) and to the days of the despotic shah. The regime sought to undermine the Green Movement's attack on this identity by reversing the claims, and accusing the Green Movement of going against public opinion and disregarding the vote of the people. There is no doubt among hardliners that the elections were free and fair, and that Ahmadinejad was therefore the rightful president of the Islamic Republic. Moreover, the "historical" election turnout showed that Iranians continue to support the Islamic Republic and have trust in the system.[81] In addition, the people who voted for candidates other than Ahmadinejad should not be mistaken for people who are against the system, hardliners argue.[82] Those protesting against the election result belong to a minority that does not only disregard the will of the Iranian people, they say. Hardliners emphasize that reformists are not serving the interest of the Islamic Republic and rather seek to undermine it. This is not only a matter of having a different opinion: "It is an issue of opposition, confrontation, dealing a blow to the system and drawing swords against the system and the revolution," Khamenei warns.[83] The West and their reformist "agents" are as such juxtaposed with the Iranian people and their popular government. These put up resistance against foreign meddling, and defend their interest and their revolution. As such, by tying the 2009 events to a foreign threat, hardliners mobilize Iranians not just against the West but also against their fellow countrymen and women. After all, it is easier to justify fighting against "agents of the West" than ones friends, family, and neighbors.

Third, plausibility is added to the discourse through enactment. The discourse first and foremost serves a domestic audience and legitimizes domestic policies. It legitimizes the treatment that Iran's Green Movement has received since the start of the demonstrations in 2009. As said, Khamenei told the "rioters" that their actions would be confronted a week after the elections. The following Friday, prayer leader Hojjat-ol Eslam Ahmad Khatami suggested to the authorities "to deal severely and ruthlessly with the leaders of the agitations whose fodder comes from America and Israel so that everyone learns a lesson from it."[84] This is but an example of how by linking domestic dissent to foreign intervention, the Iranian regime justified the use of violence against protestors as well as harsh sentences against activists. Reformist activists' status as traitors of the Islamic Republic has equated them with enemies such as Abdolmalek Rigi, commander-in-chief of Jundallah until his capture in 2010. Jundallah, an organization based in Iran's Baluchistan (an area dominated by Sunnis) that claims to fight for Sunni rights, has claimed responsibility for several bombings in Iran. Hardline discourse points at similarities between Jundallah and the Green Movement (both implicitly and explicitly): both are used by foreigners to destabilize the country[85]—something to which representatives from both groups confessed[86]—and both received training and consultation from outsiders.[87] Some sources even suggest direct cooperation between the two groups: "Normally the groups that receive the honour of acting as servants of the superpowers very fast manage to find others of the same inclinations as themselves,"

Sarayani[88] notices. Mousavi's silence after the arrest of Rigi is taken as an illustration of his shared fate as "lackey of imperialism." It seems, *Keyhan* suggests, Rigi's arrest made Mousavi nervous.[89]

To be sure, the plausibility of the hardline discourse may be aided by the aforementioned discursive mechanisms, but whether it was accepted as plausible is an entirely different matter, which depended to a large extent on the availability and content of other discourses, particularly the discourse(s) of the Green Movement itself. An investigation into the possible success of the regime's discourse would have to inquire into the narratives provided by alternative discourses and the degree to which they resonate among the populace. A discourse analysis of the Green Movement's own narratives then provides the context against which the plausibility and possible effectiveness of the regime's discourse gets shape. What matters here, however, is not so much whether the regime succeeded in selling their message, but rather what the regime's message was and how this formed the context for and rationale behind their domestic and international policies.

Foreign Policy Implications

Although the hardline discourse on the Green Movement targeted a domestic audience, it had immediate international repercussions. After Khamenei called the United Kingdom "evil" a week after the elections, the UK foreign office summoned Iranian Ambassador Rasul Movaheddian to let him know this was unacceptable.[90] Soon after, Iran expelled two British diplomats, claiming they had traveled to Iran before the elections to prepare the protests. The United Kingdom responded by expelling two Iranian diplomats in return.[91] A few days later, Iranian staff at the British Embassy was arrested for their "considerable role" in the protests—something that the United Kingdom strongly denied.[92] Diplomatic trouble rose again when civil protests in Iran flared up in December 2009: Iran accused the United Kingdom of supporting the Ashura protests, and Iran's foreign ministry summoned British Ambassador Simon Gass.[93] Gass used the opportunity to deny any Western meddling and repeated his calls for Iran to respect the rights of its people.[94] When at the end of 2010 Gass stated that civil society activists in Iran are under greater threat than anywhere else in the world, Iranian politicians called for his expulsion and Iran's Parliament's national security commission voted in favor of a draft bill to cut ties with Britain.[95] Gass resigned in March 2011, much to the satisfaction of the Iranian establishment, to start a job with NATO in Afghanistan[96] and was replaced with Dominick Chilcott in the fall of

2011.⁹⁷ Iran did not replace Ambassador Movaheddian who left his position in September 2010.⁹⁸

The recent developments in the diplomatic relations between Iran and the United Kingdom may have been catalyzed by the 2009 events, but the downward trend in their relations started a while before the 2009 elections. In fact, aside from a period of improvement under president Khatami, relations between the Islamic Republic and the United Kingdom have characteristically been unstable. After the 1979 Revolution, the British Embassy closed until the end of the Iran–Iraq War in 1988. It was closed again after the fatwa against British national and writer Salman Rushdie in that same year. Iran and the United Kingdom were able to restore ties under President Khatami and successfully work together in regional issues such as drug trafficking.⁹⁹ The deterioration in United Kingdom –Iranian relations coincides with the rise of the neoconservatives in Iran, with the seizure of British Navy personnel in March 2007 as a new low. Close to the 2009 elections, relations reached another low when the British Council suspended its activities in Tehran.¹⁰⁰ They had started their activities in 2001 at the invitation of Iran's reformist government.¹⁰¹ In their official statement, the Council said that the Office of the President of Iran had summoned their staff and suggested them to resign from their posts.¹⁰² British staff had already stopped working at the British Council, as Tehran stopped granting them visas in 2007.¹⁰³

Despite the regime's anti-UK message, both the Iranian and British governments first tried not to escalate the conflict. The Iranian government, for example, did not prioritize the longstanding Qolhak issue. The lush Qolhak compound in the north of Tehran was granted to the British by Nasr Eddin Shah in the nineteenth century and has since remained in British hands. For many years, hardliners have argued that this property should be returned to the Iranian nation and since the 2009 elections there were renewed efforts at putting this issue on the political agenda.¹⁰⁴ However, when Ahmadinejad was asked the issue at a press conference in early 2010, he stated: "Such issues are not on the priority list of the government's foreign policy. The government does not intend to follow up the evacuation of a garden."¹⁰⁵ That the government was not seeking confrontation with the United Kingdom also became clear when five British sailors were detained who had strayed into Iranian waters. Ahmadinejad's head of staff Rahim Mashaei first warned that serious measures would be taken if they had evil intentions.¹⁰⁶ After a week, however, Iran released the men without further ado. In addition, Ambassador Gass took a pragmatic approach when he was present at Ahmadinejad's inaugural ceremony in August 2009, despite the disputed elections and the absence of many prominent reformists.[107]

Despite these efforts, both on the British and Iranian side, not to aggravate tensions, the conflict between Iran and the United Kingdom worsened over the following years. The anti-UK atmosphere induced by the hardline media made such a worsening almost inevitable. Suspicion of the United Kingdom continued to run high,[108] particularly as the United Kingdom persistently criticized the human rights situation in Iran as well as the regime's nuclear ambitions.[109] From within the Iranian majles, calls to downgrade ties with the United Kingdom continued.[110] Finally, when the United Kingdom in November 2011 prohibited all financial dealings with Iranian banks, a majles majority voted in favor of reducing diplomatic relations with Britain to the level of *charge d'affaires*. The bill, effectively expelling British Ambassador Dominick Chilcott, was ratified by the Guardian Council on November 28. The same day, Khamenei reminded Iranians that Britain "has a history of humiliating nations, destroying cultural and civilization heritage and taking control of their resources."[111] The following day, students affiliated with the Basij stormed the British Embassy in Tehran, confiscated documents, and vandalized the premises. The Iranian government expressed its regret over the storming, but Western media reported that the riot police had "simply stood by" as the protestors broke into the Embassy buildings.[112] Foreign Secretary William Hague held the Iranian government accountable, closed the Iranian Embassy in Tehran, and expelled Iranian diplomats from the United Kingdom. Only in 2012, the United Kingdom opened an interest section at the Swedish embassy in Tehran. In London, Iran had opened an interest section at the Embassy of Oman.[113]

The escalation of the conflict between the United Kingdom and Iran cannot be understood outside of the hardline discourse around the 2009 events. This discourse was a continuation of the hostilities that started before the 2009 elections and originated in the 1979 Revolution. The employment of anti-British discourse for domestic political reasons made it difficult for Iran's government to keep a low profile with regard to existing ties with the United Kingdom. Despite this, relations between the United Kingdom and Iran greatly improved under Khatami. However, when the ready available discourse was employed to finger-point at the United Kingdom during the 2009 events, relations rapidly deteriorate. As age-old sentiments were revived and politicians started to call for the severing of ties, the Iranian regime could not escape the political repercussions of the hardline discourse.

Conclusion

The hardline discourse on the Green Movement is an inherently consistent account that gains internal plausibility from its references to historical events and current international developments. This foreign policy discourse is not mere paranoia, as it has a high level of inherent consistency, and a vital link to existing understanding of foreign policy meddling, which gives this narrative certain plausibility on its own premises. Echoed among hardliners in the leadership, government, and media, it ties in with popular narratives of Western interference in Iran, which are broadly shared among the Iranian public and characterize Iranian broader foreign policy discourse. State control over the media ensured that this narrative reached the Iranian public, and that no counter narrative was directly available. Whether the regime succeeded in convincing Iranians of their version of the truth is questionable. Estimates of the number of people who took part in the June 2009 postelection demonstrations suggest many Iranians no longer accepted the official narrative and that there was considerable space for a counter-narrative through word of mouth and the new media. However, whether challenged or not, the narrative described in this chapter functioned at the level of ruling elite as the official narrative, and serves to justify its repressive policies among this elite. It also had consequences for foreign policy, however, as continued reference to the United Kingdom as the imperialist culprit was made possible, inevitable even, the escalation of the diplomatic row between the United Kingdom and Iran in 2011.

Conclusion

This book makes the case that one needs to take ideology seriously when studying foreign policy. Ideology, not in the sense of a false consciousness or a tool for domination, but rather a set of shared ideas among foreign policy makers. Iranian foreign policy behavior under Ahmadinejad, the topic of this book, can only be properly understood when placed in the context of regime ideology. Iranian foreign policy makers under Ahmadinejad shared the general notion that the Islamic Republic was operating in a global space in which its goals were continuously undermined by Western powers. This worldview required resistance and independence on the part of Iran, and precluded cooperation with the West on a less than equal basis. Moreover, the dominant discourse of resistance and independence facilitated the Iranian regime's reaching out to non-Western rising and aspiring powers. Increased Western pressure on Iran during Ahmadinejad's presidency increased and confirmed the regime's perspective on international developments. Through its foreign policy of resistance and its efforts to increase South–South cooperation, the Iranian regime tried to use its marginalization at the hands of the West to its advantage among the non-West. Acting on the assumption that the days of United States dominance were numbered, and a multipolar system was on the horizon, the Iranian regime in a mutual effort with rising powers aimed at contributing to the very change it anticipated.

Foreign Policy under Ahmadinejad

Iranian foreign policy behavior under Ahmadinejad was marked by considerable consistency, which was visible in two main trends in particular. On the one hand, the Islamic Republic showed little to no effort to improve its ties with the West. In fact, in its foreign policies, it explicitly defied Western criticism and pressures. This was particularly visible in the continuation and intensification of Iran's nuclear program. Furthermore, the continued support for Hamas and Hezbollah, Iran's support for Assad's regime, and the developments leading up to the cutting of diplomatic ties with the United Kingdom did not merely underline the problematic relations between Iran and the West, but also showed their worsening. The utter unwillingness on the Iranian side to give in to any Western demands was the central element in the foreign policies of the Ahmadinejad administration. This contributed to an intensification of animosity between Iran and the West. Toward the end of Ahmadinejad's presidency, Western concerns over the Iranian regime's intentions translated more and more into restrictive sanctions that limited Iran's international options.

On the other hand, Iranian foreign policy during Ahmadinejad was characterized by cooperation. Regionally Ahmadinejad and his cabinet sought to improve ties with Arab states. Although their success at this was limited, the efforts to improve these ties were central to Iranian foreign policy, in particular, during the earlier years of Ahmadinejad's presidency. Iranian leaders watched the Arab Spring with both high expectations and uncertainty, and tried to improve regional ties in the aftermath of regime change, particularly with Egypt. However, continued suspicion of Iran's intentions eliminated the prospect of improved ties with Arab states. Relations between Iran and the Arab world further complicated as the Syrian conflict was increasingly perceived in terms of a Sunni–Shi'a divide. The Iranian regime's efforts to come to cooperation were, however, not limited to the Middle East region. In Africa, Asia, and Latin America, the Ahmadinejad administration was more successful. Particularly, so it seemed, as rising and aspiring powers were seeking to assert their independence from the United States through expressing their support for Iran. This was not exclusive to the leftists governments of Latin America, which to some extent not only shared Iran's anti-Western discourse, but also for rising powers such as South Africa, Turkey, and Brazil.

These two trends—resistance to the West and cooperation among the "rest"—were the pillars of Iranian foreign policy under Ahmadinejad. It was made possible in the context of a revolutionary ideology that can be traced back to 1979, but gained new impetus under the neo-conservative government. Consistent constructivism shows us that foreign policy behavior is not merely a response to international developments, or a trade-off between objectively defined national interests. Which policies are possible, let alone desirable, depends on the way international developments are made sense of by foreign policy makers. Foreign policy as such cannot be understood outside of the discursive context in which policy makers interpret their international environment and their country's role in international developments. The question that is of crucial importance in understanding Iranian foreign policy behavior during the Ahmadinejad presidency is then: how was this behavior made possible in the context of the regime's foreign policy ideology?

In the Western world, the Iranian regime's remarks on Israel and Ahmadinejad's questioning of the holocaust are the most well-known aspects of its political discourse. Chapter 4 has shown that these elements were rather marginal to Iran's broader foreign policy ideology. Rather, these remarks should be seen in the context of an elaborate discourse that questions the legitimacy of the so-called arrogant powers. This shared discourse among Iranian conservative elites is principally a discourse of change. The Iranian Revolution of 1979 is of central relevance in this regard. Through this revolution, according to the regime, the Iranian nation changed itself from oppressed by the arrogant powers to resistant, and from helpless to independent. According to the views expressed in this discourse, a similar change is happening internationally. People around the world are described as "awakening," and as standing up against their oppressors. Iranian leaders see evidence for this change in increased assertiveness not only among African, Latin American, and Asian nations, but also in the region since the start of the Arab Spring. This awakening meant to the regime that the world was going from a past of oppression at the hand of a small group to a future of justice and multipolarity. The regime saw the Iranian nation as a flag bearer in this development: an example for other nations. In line with this, the Iranian regime saw important moral responsibilities for Iran in defending the rights of the oppressed. Therefore, its international goals were not framed merely in terms of Iran's self-interest, but rather as an effort on the Iranian side to establish global justice for all.

The Iranian regime's foreign policy ideology is not an invention. Ideologies are social and historical constructs. Chapter 3 showed the importance of Iran's past interactions with the West in the historical construction and cultivation of a Western threat. This threat perception is not delusional: it corresponds to observable fact. In particular, it refers to real instances in which the United States and other Western countries interfered negatively in Iranian affairs. Since the Islamic Republic's establishment in 1979, this historically grown perception of the West, and particularly the United States, was confirmed in Western foreign policies toward Iran. During the Ahmadinejad administration, not only the memory of the Iran–Iraq War in which the West had supported Saddam was omnipresent. The disproportional preoccupation of Western governments and media with an Iranian threat, their support for the Iranian opposition, the US and UK invasion of Iraq and Afghanistan, and the systematically intensified sanctions against Iran were all examples of Western foreign policies that confirm the perception of a continuous threat emanating from the West. However, even though this threat was not imagined, it *was* purposefully cultivated by the regime, and is in many ways instrumental to its domestic and foreign policy goals. This cultivation is a mutual effort: In the same way, the Western threat is cultivated in Iran, and the Iranian threat is cultivated in the West. In their policies toward one another, the United States and Iran confirm each other's suspicions.

However, the Iranian regime's overconcern with outside threats cannot be explained solely in terms of international developments. In addition, domestically, the Iranian regime is facing increased challenges to its legitimacy, and the perception of foreign threat plays a crucial role in the regime's coping mechanism. The ready available discourse of foreign threat facilitates the identification of domestic dissent as "foreign meddling." By interpreting indigenous calls for change as instances of outside interference, the regime aims to neutralize these challenges and to mobilize its constituency against "agents of the West" among their own people. Particularly since the 2009 presidential elections, in an increasingly securitized Iranian sociopolitical system, the focus on external threat received new impetus. It implicated the regime's international efforts to challenge the West in a domestic struggle for the survival of the Islamic Republic. This had consequences for foreign policy, as the regime's preoccupation with foreign meddling, particularly by the United Kingdom, made inevitable the diplomatic crisis between the United Kingdom and Iran.

What is evident then is the central relevance of foreign policy issues for Iran's domestic politics. Chapter 4 analyzed many texts directed at a domestic audience, which fervently discussed international developments. The Iranian case seems a textbook example of what Hudson calls foreign policy as the continuation of domestic politics by other means.[1] The foreign policy effects of the anti-UK atmosphere that was revived after the 2009 elections illustrate this: the cutting of ties with the United Kingdom would not have been necessary in terms of Iran's international goals, but became inevitable as a consequence of domestic developments. However, the Iranian regime's foreign policy behavior cannot be understood as merely domestic politics by other means. There is, in fact, a high level of convergence between the regime's domestic and international goals in terms of its identification of good and evil, and its resistance and independence. Foreign policy tended to simultaneously contribute to the regime's legitimacy at home and abroad. At home, by reinforcing perceptions of Western interference and enactment of revolutionary principles, abroad as it increased Iran's options among states that shared its grievances—which is likely to have fed back into domestic legitimacy among the regime's constituency. The Iranian regime was able to point at international policies on Iran to confirm that the United States and other Western countries were seeking to undermine Iran, reinforcing the discourse, calling for unity among Iranians, and legitimizing repression.

The Mutual Constitution of Ideology and Foreign Policy

This book has identified three interrelated mechanisms through which ideology and foreign policy constitute each other, which are elaborated below but can be summarized as follows. Ideology is, first, constitutive of foreign policy, in that it forms the context of the foreign policy behavior of the Islamic Republic, reproducing the dominant ideology and, through that, contributing to the legitimacy of the sociopolitical order. Second, ideology is reproduced through foreign policy. Enacting ideology confirms it in its role as providing the context in which decisions are made. Moreover, enactment of ideology also contributes to its actualization: the social world comes to resemble the foreign policy views. This can be both a subconscious effect of ideology, such as not only when behavior resulting from paranoia contributes to the sustenance of an intimidating environment, but also a conscious effort by rulers to contribute to international change by acting as if this change was happening.[2] Third, foreign policy ideology is also actively instrumental in achieving both domestic and international goals: domestically, state ideology is instrumental for repression; internationally, Iran's ideology is used to increase international legitimacy by emphasizing Iran's resistance to what the regime frames as an unjust international order.

Foreign policy ideology comprises the shared ideas that constitute foreign policy behavior: it is in this context that foreign policy makers identify challenges and opportunities, as well as the possible responses. This means that ideology is not one factor among other (material) factors in the determination of foreign policy: it is the context in which challenges and opportunities, as well as the possible responses to these, are identified. Iranian foreign policy is not an ad hoc response to international developments: foreign policy is made within an ideological context with high levels of continuity and consistency. This ideology is not a posthoc justification of foreign policies, but is rooted

in historically developed understandings of the world. These understandings make possible some foreign policy options, while precluding
others. The regime's foreign policy discourse precluded the possibility
to come to a settlement with the United States on the nuclear and
other issues. This despite the fact that the animosity with the United
States in many ways limited the regime's international options. The
main disadvantage to Iran is the international consensus the United
States has been trying to create against it, particularly by suggesting the
prospect of an Iranian nuclear weapon. Although the effect of international sanctions on Iran's international options is debatable, US efforts
were relatively successful in discouraging third parties from coming
to cooperation with the Islamic Republic. Iran was having trouble, in
particular, with coming to cooperation with countries that are on good
terms with the United States and are afraid to risk their good relations.
The question that needs to be asked, therefore, is why the Islamic
Republic did not try to improve its relations with the United States, at
least to such an extent that sanctions would be lifted. In the context
of Iran's political discourse under Ahmadinejad, such a unilateral rapprochement is however unthinkable. Not because the Iranian regime
benefits from animosity with the West. Of course, the discourse on the
United States and United Kingdom has been useful in the legitimization of confronting domestic opposition. However, if rapprochement
with the United States could be framed in terms of change that finally
came or in some way as a victory for the Islamic Republic, this would
be very possible—even favorable—in terms of regime ideology during
Ahmadinejad. However, settlement with the United States was precluded in the sense that the latter demanded of Iran full suspension of
nuclear enrichment and is likely to make other demands if further talks
on the restoration of ties were to take place. Giving in to such demands
on the Iranian side would be to compromise the elements central to
Iran's identity under Ahmadinejad—its resistance and independence.

There were, however, within the context of the Iranian regime's discourse between 2005 and 2013, no limits to cooperation with nations
that were not imposing on Iran. Particularly interesting in this regard
is the case of Russia, as anti-Russian sentiments continue to run deep
in Iranian society. The Iranian regime chose not to tap into these sentiments, but rather expressed understanding for the predicaments Russia
was facing with regard to cooperation with Iran. Here the regime was
actively making possible cooperation with Russia. In addition, China was
generally discussed in neutral terms, which facilitated cooperation. When
the Iranian regime's reaching out to these powers was not reciprocated,
most noticeable in 2010 when the UN Security Council adopted new

sanctions, the Iranian regime expressed criticisms that ridiculed the great power pretentions of China and Russia. Nevertheless, the Iranian regime continued to welcome cooperation with these powers.

While the regime's discourse on China and Russia did not preclude cooperation, it was particularly favorable toward countries that shared Iran's victimized status. The Iranian self-identification of a leader among states that challenge Western dominance made cooperation with like-minded status such as Cuba and Venezuela most likely. While these countries had little to offer for Iran in material terms, the symbolism of these ties was important. However, in terms of its own discourse, the regime's most important successes were without doubt in the field of nuclear development, where it received support from several rising and aspiring powers. The resistance of these powers to Western attempts to isolate Iran underlined the perception among Iranian policy makers that the world was changing from an American dominated to a multipolar system. In line with this discourse, negotiations in the nuclear field with Brazil and Turkey were both possible and desirable for the Iranian regime. The May 2010 Tehran Declaration can be seen as the peak of the Ahmadinejad administration's international success.

Foreign policy is not only made possible in the context of ideology, but foreign policy itself also shapes and reproduces ideology. Ideology is confirmed (made true, so to speak) when foreign policy is given shape in its context. A message is more than empty words when a regime acts according to what it says. Conversely, if a regime would consistently give off one message, and do something that is entirely different, its message would lose its meaning, and the regime's legitimacy could be questioned on its own terms. Hence, the Iranian regime confirmed its own legitimacy, by acting on the premises of its own discourse. By behaving according to its own ideas, it confirmed these ideas and legitimized its actions among its constituency. What is more, the Iranian regime, through the actualization of foreign policy, was shaping the international order in line with its discourse. Of particular interest to Iran in this regard was the mutual efforts of international actors in challenging the existing order and the creation of a new one. The Iranian regime was challenging the international order in a mutual effort with other marginalized states and rising powers, criticizing the dominance of the United States, and acting in favor of a multipolar world order. Thus, in finding international allies, the Iranian regime was not merely trying to increase its international options, but was "acting as if" international change was happening. In particular, in a mutual effort that other states that dispute the rules set by the dominant powers, the Iranian regime aimed to increase its international legitimacy. From this perspective, Iranian foreign policy behavior in the nuclear issue is not a counter-productive strategy that contributes only to Iran's isolation, but an example of resistance to the West and a claim to moral superiority. This moral dimension is particularly important to Iran's international goals as more and more countries criticize the double standards in the nonproliferation regime and speak out against (unilateral) sanctions against Iran.

Iranian foreign policy discourse during Ahmadinejad precluded a rapprochement with the United States on a less than equal basis. However, it made possible other options, and made desirable the option of reaching out to non-Western nations, particularly those that share Iran's grievances against the West. However, ideology is not something static: the content and boundaries of ideology are continuously renegotiated and reshaped. This means that ideology cannot be seen as a "straightjacket": ideology evolves over time and it is malleable to certain extent. The regime was able to shape its ideology, and redirect it, even if limitedly. This implies an element of instrumentality to ideology. Under Ahmadinejad, a purposeful cultivation of Western animosity was visible, both in the regime's discourse and the hardline media. Internationally, this served the purpose of highlighting the failure of the West, and the moral superiority of Iran as a resistant nation. It aided the identification of Iran as a victim of the bullying tactics of Western powers. Domestically, the overconcern with foreign interference facilitated the exclusion of reformists from the political landscape and the repression of proreform activism. This has resulted in a society of fear and suspicion. "Today, everyday actions such as taking a picture on the street can be seen as an act of resistance," one Iranian scholar said on a visit to Amsterdam in 2011. "The obsession with Western interference has become pathological."[3] The regime's obsession with its security highlights the most apparent contradiction in the Iranian regime's discourse under Ahmadinejad: the international advocacy of equality and human rights, on the one hand, and the repression of Iranian citizens, on the other.

Conclusion

Foreign policy ideology was not keeping the Iranian regime from pursuing a rational foreign policy: it is the context within which certain options were rational and others not. Iranian foreign policy makers during Ahmadinejad's presidency acted within this context, and were not concerned with what it precluded, but acted according to what was made possible. In the international environment in which Ahmadinejad became president, the regime's options had increased with the fall of Saddam and the Taliban, with the rise of leftism in Latin American politics and the increasing assertiveness of countries such as Brazil, South Africa, and Turkey. Iran's foreign policy ideology enabled the regime to take advantage of these international developments. Within the regime's foreign policy discourse, engagement with these countries was not only possible, but even desirable. In particular, as through engagement with these countries, the Iranian regime was actively challenging and contributing to the diminishing power of the United States in favor of rising middle powers. Iranian foreign policy makers were *acting as if* the days of US hegemony were over, by simultaneously challenging US power, and acting in the space of a "new game" in which not the United States, but developing countries and rising middle powers make the rules. This foreign policy behavior then fed back into the domestic context, where the regime struggled for legitimacy. On the one hand, challenging the United States internationally and as such building foreign policy on the premises of the 1979 Revolution may have helped yield legitimacy among the regime's constituency. On the other hand, the focus on the perceived threat coming from the West was used as a tool in repressing opposition, denying the indigenous nature of the calls for change.

Its foreign policies of resistance and cooperation may not have taken the Ahmadinejad administration very far. Regional and international developments during his two terms in office did not play out in Iran's favor. Taking United States international dominance as a given fact, one may call Iranian foreign policy counterproductive and irrational. The international system, however, is not static, and the Islamic Republic was demanding its share in international change. There is no way of knowing if United States power is indeed going to be replaced by smaller rising powers any time soon. There are, however, indications that the international discourse of rising and aspiring power is focusing less on the Unites States and more on alternative partnerships, creating more assertiveness among aspiring powers.[4] What matters here is not whether actual change is on its way, but rather the confidence among aspiring powers, and particularly the Islamic Republic, that this change is imminent. It is this anticipation of global change that inspired Iran's foreign policy of resistance and cooperation under Mahmoud Ahmadinejad.

Notes

Introduction

1. Thomas Erdbrink, "Iran Enters Nuclear Talks in a Defiant Mood," *The New York Times* February 25, 2013. http://www.nytimes.com/2013/02/26/world/middleeast/iran-enters-nuclear-talks-in-a-defiant-mood.html;Rick Gladstone, "Iran's Double-Digit Inflation Worsens," *The New York Times* April 1, 2013. http://www.nytimes.com/2013/04/02/world/middleeast/irans-double-digit-inflation-worsens.html; Rick Gladstone, "Iran's Oil Exports and Sales Down 40 Percent, Official Admits," *The New York Times* January 7, 2013. http://www.nytimes.com/2013/01/08/world/middleeast/irans-oil-exports-and-sales-down-40-percent-official-admits.html; Rick Gladstone, "U.S. Imposes Sanctions on Those Aiding Iran," *The New York Times* May 9, 2013. http://www.nytimes.com/2013/05/10/world/middleeast/us-imposes-sanctions-on-those-aiding-iran.html; David M. Herszenhorn and Rick Gladstone, "Iran Expands Nuclear Fuel Production After Talks," *The New York Times* April 9, 2013. http://www.nytimes.com/2013/04/10/world/middleeast/iran-expands-nuclear-fuel-production-after-talks.html; Jodi Rudoren, "Netanyahu Strikes Tough Tone on Possible Iran Strike," *The New York Times* November 5, 2012. http://www.nytimes.com/2012/11/06/world/middleeast/netanyahu-uses-tough-tone-on-possible-iran-strike.html; Thom Schmitt, Eric Shanker, and David E. Sanger. "U.S. Adds Forces in Persian Gulf, a Signal to Iran," *The New York Times* July 3, 2012. http://www.nytimes.com/2012/07/03/world/middleeast/us-adds-forces-in-persian-gulf-a-signal-to-iran.html.
2. Shireen Hunter, *Iran's Foreign Policy in the Post-Soviet Era: Resisting the New International Order* (Santa Barbara, California: Praeger, 2010).
3. Nicholas Burns, "India's Support for Iran Threatens Its US Relationship and Global Leadership Role," *Christian Science Monitor* February 14, 2012. http://www.csmonitor.com/Commentary/Opinion/2012/0214/India-s-support-for-Iran-threatens-its-US-relationship-and-global-leadership-role;ThomasErdbrink,"Nonaligned Nations Back Iran on Nuclear Bid, but not on Syria," *The New York*

Times August 31, 2012. http://www.nytimes.com/2012/09/01
/world/middleeast/iran-criticizes-egypts-mohamed-morsi-over
-syria-comments.html; "Russia Criticizes EU Iran Sanctions, Urges
Talks," Reuters. http://www.reuters.nl/article/2012/10/17/us
-iran-nuclear-russia-idUSBRE89G1FM20121017; Sabrina Tavernise,
"Russia, Turkey and Iran Meet, Posing Test for U.S.," *The New
York Times* June 8, 2010. http://www.nytimes.com/2010/06/09
/world/09iran.html.
   4. Manouchehr Mottaki, "Iran's Foreign Policy under President
      Ahmadinejad," *Discourse: An Iranian Quarterly* 8, no. 2 (2009):
      1–15.
   5. Roxanne L. Doty, "Foreign Policy as Social Construction: A Post-
      positivist Analysis of U.S. Counterinsurgency Policy in the Philippines,"
      International Studies Quarterly 37 no. 3 (1993): 297–320.
   6. Ibid.
   7. According to Article 176, the Supreme Council for National Security
      has the following responsibilities: "1. Determining the defence and
      national security policies within the framework of general policies
      determined by the Leader; 2. Coordination of activities in the areas
      relating to politics, intelligence, social, cultural and economic fields
      in regard to general defence and security policies; 3. Exploitation of
      materialistic and intellectual resources of the country to cope with
      internal and external threats." *The Constitution of the Islamic Republic
      of Iran* (1979/1989). http://www.iranchamber.com/government
      /laws/constitution.php, Accessed May 13, 2013.
   8. Arshin Adib-Moghaddam, *Iran in World Politics: The Question of the
      Islamic Republic* (London: Hurst, 2007), 70–71.
   9. Doty, "Foreign Policy as Social Construction."
  10. Lene Hansen, *Security as Practice: Discourse analysis and the Bosnian
      War* (London: Routledge, 2006).
  11. Jean Carabine, "Unmarried Motherhood: 1830–1990: A Genealogical
      analysis," in *Discourse as Data*, ed. Margaret Wetherell, Simeon Yates,
      and Stephanie Taylor (London: Sage, 2001), 268.
  12. Doty, "Foreign Policy as Social Construction," 302.
  13. Carabine, "Unmarried Motherhood," 269.

1   Studying Iranian Foreign Policy: A Constructivist Approach

   1. For example, Trita Parsi, *Treacherous Alliance: The Secret Dealings of Israel,
      Iran, and the United States* (New Haven: Yale University Press, 2008);
      Shireen Hunter, *Iran's Foreign Policy in the Post-Soviet Era: Resisting the
      New International Order* (Santa Barbara, California: Praeger, 2010); Ray
      Takeyh, *Guardians of the Revolution: Iran and the World in the Age of the
      Ayatollahs* (Oxford: Oxford University Press, 2009).
   2. Mehdi Khalaji, "Apocalyptic politics: On the Rationality of Iranian
      Policy," *Policy Focus* no. 79, The Washington Institute for Near East
      Policy, 2008.

3. Homeira Moshirzadeh, "Discursive Foundations of Iran's Nuclear Policy," *Security Dialogue* 38, no. 4 (2007): 521–543; S. J. Dehghani Firouz Abadi, "Emancipating Foreign Policy: Critical Theory and Islamic Republic of Iran's Foreign Policy," *The Iranian Journal of International Affairs* XX, no. 3 (Summer 2008): 1–26; M. M. Nia, "Discourse and Identity in Iran's Foreign Policy, " *Iranian Review of Foreign Affairs* 3, no. 3 (Fall 2012): 29–64; V. Noori, "Status-seeking and Iranian Foreign Policy: The Speeches of the President at the United Nations," *Iranian Review of Foreign Affairs* 3, no. 1 (Spring 2012): 157–152; F. Sharifian, "Figurative Language in International Political Discourse: The Case of Iran," *Journal of Language and Politics* 8, no. 3 (December 2009) 416–432; Arshin Adib-Moghaddam, *Iran in World Politics: The Question of the Islamic Republic* (London: Hurst, 2007); William O. Beeman, *The Great Satan Vs. the Mad Mullahs: How the United States and Iran Demonize Each Other* (Chicago: University of Chicago Press, 2008).

4. Suzanne Maloney, "Identity and Change in Iran's foreign Policy," in *Identity and Foreign Policy in the Middle East*, ed. Shibley Telhami and Michael Barnett (New York: Cornell University Press, 2002), 88–116; Raymond A. Hinnebusch and Anoushiravan Ehteshami, eds, *The Foreign Policies of Middle East States* (Boulder, Colorado: Lynne Rienner Publishers, 2002); Raymond A. Hinnebusch, *The International Politics of the Middle East* (Manchester: Manchester University Press, 2003); Fred Halliday, *The Middle East in International Relations: Power, Politics and Ideology* (Cambridge: Cambridge University Press, 2005); Bahgat Korany and Hillal Dessouki, *The Foreign Policies of Arab States: The Challenge of Globalization* (Cairo: American University in Cairo Press, 2008).

5. Regime here is defined as a system of government, particularly the administration and state institutions. The Iranian regime includes both the government and other state institutions.

6. Another advantage of the use of constructivism is that it can serve as a bridge between area studies and the discipline of IR. Andrea Teti, "Bridging the Gap: IR, Middle East Studies and the Disciplinary Politics of the Area Studies Controversy," *European Journal of International Relations* 13, no. 1 (2007): 117–145.

7. Shibley Telhami and Michael Barnett, *Identity and Foreign Policy in the Middle East* (New York: Cornell University Press, 2002), 22.

8. Stephen M. Walt, *The Origins of Alliances* (Ithaca, New York: Cornell University Press, 1987). For realism as a theory of foreign policy, consult: Colin Elman, "Horses for Courses: Why Not Neorealist Theories of foreign Policy?" *Security Studies* 6, no. 1 (1996): 7–53.

9. Hinnebusch, *The International Politics*, 1.

10. Halliday, *The Middle East*, 25.

11. Hinnebusch and Ehteshami, *The Foreign Policies*, 1. Similarly, Telhami and Barnett, *Identity and Foreign Policy in the Middle East*; Halliday, *The Middle East*; Hinnebusch, *The International Politics*.

12. Korany and Dessouki, *The Foreign Policies*, 21.
13. Steven R. David, "Explaining Third World Alignment," *World Politics* 43, no. 2 (1991): 233–256.
14. Raymond A. Hinnebusch, "Omni-balancing Revisited; Syrian foreign Policy between Rational Actor and Regime Legitimacy," Unpublished article, n.d.; Raymond A. Hinnebusch, "Syria: The Politics of Peace and Regime Survival," *Middle East Policy* 3, no. 4 (1995): 74–87; Raymond A. Hinnebusch, "Does Syria Want Peace?" *Journal of Palestine Studies* 26, no. 1 (1996): 42–57.
15. Hinnebusch and Ehteshami, *The Foreign Policies*, 15.
16. It has been suggested, for example, that when applying the concept of omni-balancing one should not only include threat, but also opportunities such as economic resources. **Lawrence Katzenstein and Jason Strakes, "Omnibalancing and Substitutability in Analyzing Middle East Foreign Policies: Applications to post-2005 Iraq,"** Paper presented at the annual meeting of the International Studies Association Annual Conference "Global Governance: Political Authority in Transition", Le Centre Sheraton Montreal Hotel, Montreal, Quebec, Canada, Mar 16, 2011.
17. Ibid.
18. Hinnebusch and Ehteshami, *The Foreign Policies*, 7–9.
19. Telhami and Barnett, *Identity and Foreign Policy in the Middle East.*
20. Hinnebusch and Ehteshami, *The Foreign Policies*, 15.
21. Korany and Dessouki *The Foreign Policies.*
22. Halliday, *The Middle East.*
23. Telhami and Barnett, *Identity and Foreign Policy in the Middle East*, 16.
24. Raymond A. Hinnebusch, "Identity in International Relations: Constructivism versus Materialism and the Case of the Middle East," *Review of International Affairs* 3, no. 2 (2003): 362.
25. Halliday, *The Middle East*, 33.
26. Doty, "Foreign Policy as Social Construction."
27. For a discussion of the ontological inconsistencies in constructivism, see Karin M. Fierke, "Constructivism," in *International Relations Theories: Discipline and Diversity*, ed. Timothy Dunne, Milja Kurki and Steve Smith (Oxford: Oxford University Press, 2007), 166–184.
28. Doty, "Foreign Policy as Social Construction."
29. Rachel Bronson, *Thicker than Oil: America's Uneasy Partnership with Saudi Arabia* (New York: Oxford University Press, 2008); Paul Aarts and Gerd Nonneman, *Saudi Arabia in the Balance: Political Economy, Society, Foreign Affairs* (London: Hurst, 2005).
30. Stephen M. Walt, *Revolution and War* (Ithaca, New York: Cornell University Press, 1996).
31. Parsi, *Treacherous Alliance.*
32. Walt, *Revolution and War*, 337.
33. Ibid., 264.

34. Ibid., 333.
35. Ibid., 4.
36. Ibid., 43.
37. Ibid., 239.
38. Ibid., 240.
39. Ibid., 241.
40. Ibid., 340.
41. Michael Barnett, "Identity and Alliances in the Middle East," in *The Culture of National Security*, ed. Peter J. Katzenstein (New York: Columbia University Press, 1996), 403.
42. Arshin Adib-Moghaddam, *The International Politics of the Persian Gulf: A Cultural Genealogy* (London: Routledge, 2006).
43. Ibid., 1.
44. Ibid., 32.
45. Ibid., 32–33.
46. Walt, *Revolution and War*, 239.
47. Adib-Moghaddam, *The International Politics of the Persian Gulf*, 34.
48. Ibid., 38.
49. Adib-Moghaddam, *The International Politics of the Persian Gulf*, 35.
50. Ibid., 36–37.
51. Ibid., 40.
52. Ibid.
53. Maloney, "Identity and Change."
54. Ibid., 91.
55. Ibid., 106.
56. Walt, *Revolution and War*, 243.
57. Maloney, "Identity and Change," 91.
58. Ibid., 108.
59. Ibid., 90.
60. Adib-Moghaddam, *The International Politics of the Persian Gulf*, 7–9.
61. Parsi, *Treacherous Alliance*.
62. Ibid., 4.
63. Ibid., xvi.
64. Ibid., 89.
65. Ibid., 93.
66. Are the secret dealings between Iran and Israel, known as the Iran Contra Affair, which came to light in 1986 not an example of rationalism over ideology? To be sure, ideology should not be mistaken for irrationality, let alone a death wish. Tired and broken after months of revolution, the revolutionary regime needed to adequately respond to security challenges, most urgently when Iraq invaded Iran in September 1980. The Iranian regime was now in dire need of any support they were able to get, and Israel, at the time still eager to improve relations with the new Iranian regime, was offering. What matters here is the fact that cooperation was kept secret and did not

spin off toward other, nonsecurity fields, as that shows that ideological considerations remained prevalent.

67. Ibid., 5.
68. Parsi, *Treacherous Alliance*, 3.
69. Ibid., 2.
70. Kal J. Holsti, "National Role Conceptions in the Study of foreign Policy," *International Studies Quarterly* 14, no. 3 (1970): 233–309; Liesbeth Aggestam, "Role Conceptions and the Politics of Identity in foreign Policy," ARENA Working Papers (1999). http://www.deutsche-aussenpolitik.de/resources/seminars/gb/approach/document/wp99_8.htm.
71. Peter J. Katzenstein, ed., *The Culture of National Security* (New York: Columbia University Press, 1996).
72. Judith Goldstein and Robert O. Keohane, *Ideas and Foreign Policy: Beliefs, Institutions, and Political Change* (Ithaca, New York: Cornell University Press, 1993).
73. Martha L. Cottam, Beth Dietz-Uhle, Elena Mastors, and Thomas Preston, *Introduction to Political Psychology* (Mahwah, New Jersey: Lawrence Erlbaum Associates, 2004) for an overview of the contributions of political psychology.
74. Doty, "Foreign Policy as Social Construction"; Fierke, Critical Approaches; Hansen, *Security as Practice*.
75. Fierke, *Critical Approaches*, 76.
76. David Campbell, *Writing Security: United States Foreign Policy and the Politics of Identity* (Minneapolis: University of Minnesota Press, 1998), 12–13.
77. Hansen, *Security as Practice*, 39.
78. Fierke, *Critical Approaches*, 78.
79. Hansen, *Security as Practice*, 47.
80. Ibid., 48–50.
81. Ibid., 50.
82. Telhami and Barnett, *Identity and Foreign Policy in the Middle East*, 11.
83. Hinnebusch, *The International Politics*, 94.
84. Judith Goldstein and Robert O. Keohane, *Ideas and Foreign Policy*.
85. Ibid., 13.
86. Doty, "Foreign Policy as Social Construction," 297–298.
87. Ibid., 301.
88. Fierke, *Critical Approaches*.
89. Mark Sedgwick, "Measuring Egyptian Regime Legitimacy," *Middle East Critique* 19, no. 3 (2010): 251–267.
90. J. Samuel Barkin, "Realist Constructivism and Realist-constructivisms," *International Studies Review* 6, no. 2 (2004): 348–352; J. Samuel Barkin, "Realist Constructivism," *International Studies Review* 5, no. 3 (2003): 325–342; Jennifer Sterling-Folker, "Realism and the Constructivist Challenge: Rejecting, Reconstructing, or

Rereading," *International Studies Review* 4, no. 1 (2002): 73–97; Jennifer Sterling-Folker, "Realist-Constructivism and Morality," *International Studies Review* 6, no. 2 (2004): 341–343l; Janice B. Mattern, "Power in Realist-constructivist Research," *International Studies Review* 6 no. 2 (2004): 343–346.

91. Patrick Thaddeus Jackson and Daniel H. Nexon, eds, "Constructivist Realism or Realist-constructivism?" *International Studies Review* 6, no. 2 (2004): 337–341.
92. Fierke, "Contructivism."
93. Other studies have pointed toward the advantages of an eclectic approach; see, for example, Adib-Moghaddam 2008; Hansen 2006.
94. For exceptions, see footnote 3.
95. Academic visits within the framework of the exchange programmes of the University of Amsterdam with respectively the School of International Relations in Tehran and the University of Tehran show that much of the Iranian debate on Iranian foreign policy is about whether Iran fits within a realist understanding of the world and as such can be treated as any other country, or is exceptional in that in Iran the ideals of the revolution shape its foreign policies.
96. Hunter, *Iran's Foreign Policy*.
97. Ibid., 116.
98. The concept of foreign policy elites is used in this book to denote the officials dealing with foreign policy affiliated with the Supreme National Security Council, the Office of the Supreme Leader, and the Foreign Ministry.
99. Hunter, *Iran's Foreign Policy*, 96.
100. Mahjoob Zweiri and Anoushiravan Ehteshami, eds, *Arab-Iranian Relations: New Realities? Iran's foreign Policy from Khatami to Ahmadinejad*, (Reading: Ithaca Press, 2008, xiii-xiv).
101. Arshin Adib-Moghaddam, *Iran in World Politics: The Question of the Islamic Republic* (London: Hurst, 2007), 67.
102. Ibid.
103. R. K. Ramazani, "Iran's Foreign Policy: Independence, Freedom and the Islamic Republic," in *Iran's foreign Policy from Khatami to Ahmadinejad*, ed. M. Zweiri and A. Ehteshami (Reading: Ithaca Press, 2008), 2–10.
104. Maloney, "Identity and Change."
105. Ali M. Ansari, "Civilizational Identity and foreign Policy: The Case of Iran," in *The Limits of Culture: Islam and Foreign Policy*, ed. Brenda Shaffer (Cambridge, Massachusetts: MIT Press, 2006), 241–262.
106. Hunter, *Iran's Foreign Policy*, 25–28.
107. Ansari, "Civilizational Identity"; Maloney, "Identity and Change"; Hunter, *Iran's Foreign Policy*. Exceptions, Adib-Moghaddam, *Iran in World Politics*; Moshirzadeh, "Discursive Foundations."
108. Hunter, *Iran's Foreign Policy*, 24.
109. Brenda Shaffer, ed., *The Limits of Culture: Islam and foreign Policy* (Cambridge, Massachusetts: MIT Press, 2006), 229–234.

110. Interview of the author with an anonymous IR scholar at an Iranian university in June 2008.

111. Adib-Moghaddam, *Iran in World Politics*; Adib-Moghaddam, *The International Politics of the Persian Gulf.*

112. Ibid., 53–54.

113. Fierke, *Critical Approaches*; Doty, "Foreign Policy as Social Construction"; Hansen, *Security as Practice.*

114. Hunter, *Iran's Foreign Policy*, 29.

115. James Devine, "Understanding Iranian foreign Policy: Combining Ideological and Realist Explanations," paper prepared for the International Studies Association annual Conference 2011, March 16–19, 2011, Montreal.

116. Takeyh, *Guardians of the Revolution.*

2   Ideology and Legitimacy during Ahmadinejad's Presidency

1. John Gerring, "Ideology: A Definitional Analysis," *Political Research Quarterly* 50, no. 4 (1997): 957–994.

2. Robert W. Cox, "Gramsci, Hegemony and International Relations: An Essay in Method," *Millennium Journal of International Studies* 12, no. 2 (1983): 162–175, 163.

3. This conceptualization is based on Thompson but parts with its critical dimension and adds the element of mutual constitution between ideology and sociopolitical order. John B. Thompson, *Ideology and Modern Culture: Critical Social Theory in the Era of Mass Communication* (Cambridge: Polity, 1990), 58.

4. Ibid., 5.

5. David Mclellan, *Ideology* (Buckingham: Open University Press, 1995), 1.

6. Terry Eagleton, *Ideology* (London: Verso, 1991), 45.

7. Ibid.

8. Chantal Mouffe, *Gramsci and Marxist Theory* (London: Routledge and Kegan Paul, 1979), 186.

9. Ibid.,193.

10. Ibid.

11. Eagleton, *Ideology*, 14.

12. John B. Thompson, *Ideology* (Cambridge: Polity, 1990), 10.

13. Eagleton, *Ideology*, 58.

14. Robert W. Cox, "Social Forces, States and World Orders: Beyond International Relations Theory," *Millennium Journal of International Studies* 10, no. 2 (1981): 126–155, 137.

15. Thompson, *Ideology*, 69.

16. Stuart Hall, "The Spectacle of the Other," in *Discourse Theory and Practice: A Reader*, ed. Margaret Wetherell, Simeon Yates, and Stephanie Taylor, (London: Sage, 2001), 324–344, 340, original emphasis.

17. Ibid., 339.

18. Structuration is generally associated with Anthony Giddens (*The Constitution of Society: Outline of the Theory of Structuration,* Cambridge: Polity Press, 1984). This paper follows the neo-Gramscian understanding of structure as "persistent social practices, made by collective human activity and transformed through collective human activity." (Robert Cox quoted in Andreas Bieler and Adam D. Morton, "The Gordian Knot of Agency—Structure in International Relations," *European Journal of International Relations 7*, no. 1 [2001]: 5–35.)

19. Mouffe, *Gramsci and Marxist Theory*, 187.

20. Norman Fairclough, "The Discourse of New Labour: Critical Discourse analysis," in *Discourse as Data*, ed. Margaret Wetherell, Simeon Yates, and Stephanie Taylor (London: Sage, 2001), 229–266.

21. David Campbell, *Writing Security: United States foreign Policy and the Politics of Identity* (Minneapolis: University of Minnesota Press, 1998), 6.

22. See Mansoor Moaddel, *Class, Politics, and Ideology in the Iranian Revolution* (New York: Columbia University Press, 1992).

23. Eagleton, *Ideology*, 39.

24. Marlies Glasius, "Dissident Writings as Political Theory on Civil Society and Democracy," *Review of International Studies 37*, no. 1 (2011): 1–22, 6.

25. Ibid.

26. Orlando Figes, *The Whisperers: Private Life in Stalin's Russia* (New York: Metropolitan Books, 2007).

27. Eagleton, *Ideology*, 34.

28. Lisa Wedeen, *Ambiguities of Domination: Politics, Rhetoric, and Symbols in Contemporary Syria* (Chicago: University of Chicago Press, 1999), 6.

29. James C. Scott, *Weapons of the Weak: Everyday forms of Peasant Resistance* (New Haven, London: Yale University Press, 1985).

30. Timothy Mitchell, "Everyday Metaphors of Power," *Theory and Society 19*, no. 5 (1990): 545–577.

31. Wedeen, *Ambiguities of Domination*, 5 (emphasis added).

32. Fairclough, "The Discourse of New Labour," 234.

33. Holger Albrecht and Oliver Schlumberger, "'Waiting for Godot': Regime Change Without Democratization in the Middle East," *International Political Science Review 25*, no. 4 (2004): 371–392; Sedgwick, "Measuring Egyptian Regime Legitimacy."

34. Sedgwick, "Measuring Egyptian Regime Legitimacy," 251.

35. Louis Althusser "Ideology and Ideological State Apparatuses," 1970. http://www.marxists.org/reference/archive/althusser/1970/ideology.htm.

36. Ibid., 145–146.

37. Albrecht and Schlumberger, "'Waiting for Godot.'"

38. Ibid., 373 (original emphasis).

39. Julie E. Pruzan-Jørgensen, "Analyzing Authoritarian Regime Legitimation: Findings from Morocco," *Middle East Critique* 19, no. 3 (2010): 269–286, 272.

40. Polls, where available, are highly unreliable.

41. The most accurate definition of authoritarianism as it is described in this chapter I found in the Oxford American Dictionary for Apple: "favoring or enforcing strict obedience to authority, esp. that of the government, at the expense of personal freedom."

42. Albrecht and Schlumberger, "'Waiting for Godot,'" 378–379.

43. Ali Khamenei, "Leader Urges End to Protests, Says Poll Results Can Be Investigated Legally. Second Friday Sermon Delivered by Ayatollah Ali Khamenei, Leader of Iran's Islamic revolution, at Tehran University—Live," Islamic Republic of Iran News Network Television (IRINN), June 19, 2009. http://www.juancole.com/2009/06/supreme-leader-khameneis-friday-address.html.

44. Ali Hashemi Rafsanjani, "Iran's Rafsanjani Offers Suggestions for Resolving Post-election 'Crisis'—More," Trans. BBC Worldwide Monitoring, VIRIN, July 17, 2009, LexisNexis Academic.

45. The original constitution was adopted by referendum in late 1979. After the death of Khomeini, this constitution was amended. The amendments were meant to help to prevent stalemates that had often occurred in politics particularly between the prime minister and the president, by abolishing the post of the prime minister and installing an Expediency Council to resolve conflicts between the majles and the Guardian Council.

46. Wilfred Buchta, et al. *Who Rules Iran? The Structure of Power in the Islamic Republic* (Washington: Institute for Near East Policy and the Konrad Adenauer Stiftung, 2000); David E. Thaler and Rand Corporation. *Mullahs, Guards, and Bonyads : An Exploration of Iranian Leadership Dynamics* (Santa Monica, California: RAND, 2010). On the role of the Supreme Leader in Iranian politics, also consult Akbar Ganji, "The Latter-day Sultan," *Foreign Affairs* 87, no. 6 (2008): 45–65.

47. Eva P. Rakel, "The Political Elite in the Islamic Republic of Iran: From Khomeini to Ahmadinejad," *Comparative Studies of South Asia, Africa and the Middle East* 29, no. 1 (2009a), 124.

48. Sahar Namazikhah, "Khamenei Challenged by Senior Cleric," *Mianeh* October 29, 2010. http://mianeh.net/article/khamenei-challenged-senior-cleric.

49. Examples are the 2004 Grand Bargain and the decision to allow foreign aid after the Bam earthquake in 2004. In addition, Khamenei is said to have kept lines of communication open to reformist camps. He is on good personal terms with Khatami, and one of his sons is married to the sister of an influential reformist diplomat.

50. Buchta, *Who Rules Iran?*, 4.

51. International Crisis Group (ICG), "Iran: Ahmadi-Nejad's Tumultuous Presidency," 2007. http://www.crisisgroup.org/home/index.cfm?id=4647&l=1, 19.
52. International Crisis Group (ICG), "What Does Ahmadi-Nejad's Victory Mean?," 2005. http://www.crisisgroup.org/home/index.cfm?id=3604&l=1, 8.
53. Omid Memarian, "Ahmadinejad Alienates Key Protector," *Mianeh* January 28, 2011. http://mianeh.net/article/ahmadinejad-alienates-key-protector.
54. Mehdi Jedinia, "Iran's Hardliners Fall Out," *Mianeh* September 22, 2010b. http://mianeh.net/article/iran%E2%80%99s-hardliners-fall-out; Mehdi Jedinia, "Iranian President Gunning for foreign Minister," *Mianeh*, September 22, 2010a. http://mianeh.net/article/iranian-president-gunning-foreign-minister.
55. Mashaei is particularly controversial among senior clerics in Qom, because of his downplaying of the role of the clergy in Islam (Memarian 2010). Memarian, "Ahmadinejad Alienates."
56. Memarian, "Ahmadinejad Alienates."
57. Buchta. *Who Rules Iran?*, 59; Farhad Khosrokhavar, "The New Conservatives Take a Turn," *Middle East Report* 233 (2004): 24–27.
58. Kaveh-Cyrus Sanandaji, "The Eighth Majles Elections in the Islamic Republic of Iran: A Division in Conservative Ranks and the Politics of Moderation," *Iranian Studies* 42, no. 4 (2009): 621–648, 622–623.
59. Eva P. Rakel, *Power, Islam, and Political Elite in Iran: A Study on the Iranian Political Elite from Khomeini to Ahmadinejad* (Leiden: Brill, 2009); Mehdi Moslem, *Factional politics in Post-Khomeini Iran* (Syracuse: Syracuse University Press, 2002).
60. Buchta, *Who Rules Iran?*, 7. For example, Khamenei is through marriage of his son Masud connected to the reformist Kharazi family, as well as to the families Haddad 'Adel, Golpayangani, and ayatollah Khosvagt. Khamenei's younger brother ran a liberal newspaper and was a press advisor to Khatami. Although it does not seem that family relations constitute Iranian politics in a primary way, reformist candidates seem to find themselves protected at least to some degree by family relations.
61. The fact that Khomeini himself did not have clear views on this meant that he did not "provide specific guidelines about what this Islamicity meant in terms of governing principles or particular polities in different spheres of government," and that he changed his views on things repeatedly, fuelled competition among different factions. Moslem, *Factional Politics*, 4–5.
62. One graduate student in Iran described the categories used in table 2.1 to me as "meaningless categorization that mislead Western analysts in relation to Iranian politics."
63. Moslem, *Factional Politics*, 266.
64. Buchta, *Who Rules Iran?*, 3.

65. Mahjoob Zweiri, "Arab-Iranian Relations: New Realities?" Ed. Mahjoob Zweiri and Anoushiravan Ehteshami, *Iran's foreign Policy from Khatami to Ahmadinejad*. Reading: Ithaca Press, 2008.; Ervand Abrahamian, *A History of Modern Iran* (Cambridge, UK: Cambridge University Press, 2008); Anoushiravan Ehteshami, "Failure of Khatami Reformers, not Reform Movement," *Journal of Iranian Research and analysis* 18, no. 2 (2002): 69–72; Mehrdad Mashayekhi, "The Rise and Fall of the Really-existing Reform Movement in Iran," *Journal of Iranian Research and analysis* 18, no. 2 (2002): 79–83.

66. ICG, "What Does Ahmadi-Nejad's Victory Mean?," 8–9.

67. Anoushiravan Ehteshami and Mahjoob Zweiri, *Iran and the Rise of its Neoconservatives: The Politics of Tehran's Silent Revolution* (London: I.B. Tauris, 2007), 67.

68. "In order to finance his additional public expenditure, Ahmadinejad demanded a much larger budget from the parliament. Thus, whereas Khatami's 2005–2006 budget allocated $14.2 billion from oil revenues, Ahmadinejad received an astonishing $40 billion from the conservative-dominated parliament"; Manouchehr Dorraj, "Neo-populism in Comparative Perspective: Iran and Venezuela," *Comparative Studies of South Asia, Africa and the Middle East* 29, no. 1 (2009): 137–151, 142.

69. ICG, "Iran," 11.

70. Sanandaji, "The Eighth Majles Elections in the Islamic Republic of Iran," 635; The oil stabilization fund was created under Khatami as a buffer against oil booms and busts.

71. Ibid.

72. Khosrokhavar, "The New Conservatives," 27.

73. As one source put it, "Never before was there a time when all the media networks, political figures and political parties in the country had expressed protest at him [Ahmadinejad], though in different issues, in such a simultaneous manner"; Sajjad Salek, "Ahmadinezhad's Purgatorial Week," trans. BBC Worldwide Monitoring, *E'temad*, July 28, 2009, LexisNexis Academic.

74. "A Number of Principlist Representatives Warned Ahmadinezhad: Warnings and Limitations over the 10th Cabinet; Real Warning or Continuation of a Scenario," Aftab-e Yazd, July 7, 2009, LexisNexis Academic.

75. Ibid.

76. Mehdi Jedinia, "Iranian President Gunning for foreign Minister," *Mianeh* September 22, 2010a, http://mianeh.net/article/iranian-president-gunning-foreign-minister.

77. Anoushiravan Ehteshami. "Iran's New Order: Domestic Developments and foreign Policy Outcomes". *Global Dialogue* 3(2–3), 2001. http://www.worlddialogue.org/print.php?id=1460.

78. Adib-Moghaddam, *Iran in World Politics*, 155–184.

79. Ahmadinejad received much criticism from students around the country. When he visited Amir Kabir University, angry students burned the president's picture. While the student movement was but a shadow of its previous self, with about half of Iran's electorate under the age of 30, and many highly educated, students remained a force to reckon with. This was increasingly the case as Ahmadinejad's term progressed and criticism mounted. Indeed in May 2009, "fifty-four established student groups in an open letter have called for a stand against Ahmadinejad's 'persistent onslaught on civil society' and his 'reckless' economic and foreign policies that have 'endangered national interest'"; Nasrin Alavi "Iran: A Blind Leap of Faith," *Open Democracy* September 19, 2009. http://www.opendemocracy.net/article/iran-a-blind-leap-of-faith.

80. A report by the Chatham House observed that (1) a turn-out of more than 100 percent was recorded in two conservative provinces; (2) the greatest increase in voter turn-out did not translate to the greatest swing in support toward Ahmadinejad; (3) in a third of the provinces, Ahmadinejad took up to an unlikely 44 percent of the former reformist votes; and (4) Ahmadinejad was particularly successful in rural areas, despite his unpopularity in these areas in 2005, 2001, and 1997. Ali M. Ansari, ed., *Preliminary Analysis of the Voting Figures in Iran's 2009 Presidential Election* (London: Chatham House, 2009). http://www.chathamhouse.org/publications/papers/view/109081/.

81. The lower voter turnout in 2004 and 2005 is often seen as a sign of the public's disillusion with politics, and Ahmadinejad's 2005 victory was partly accredited to reformist voters staying at home.

82. Sadjadpour (2009) summarizes Mousavi's merits: "Mir-Hossein Mousavi is considered Ahmadinejad's strongest challenger, thanks in part to the endorsement of popular former President Mohammed Khatami. One of the few politicians in Iran with a reputation for being a competent manager, Mousavi is credited with keeping the economy stable during the 1980–1988 Iran-Iraq war." Also, "Mousavi's wife, former university chancellor Zahra Rahnavard, has proven an effective asset in helping to attract female voters." She is "the first-ever post-revolution political spouse to campaign alongside her husband" (Alavi 2009). "And as the only ethnic Azeri candidate (Azeri's constitute around a quarter of Iran's population), the backing of north-western province of Azerbaijan could play a decisive role" (Sadjadpour 2009). Moreover, "Mousavi in particular may receive many votes driven by fear of an Ahmadinejad re-election, rather than a great desire to see a Mousavi presidency." Alavi (2009) further mentions that Mousavi was popular among young people, that the renowned Iranian filmmaker Mohsen Makhmalbaf endorsed him, and that Shariati mentioned him in his speeches, who recommended his work and that of his wife Zahra Rahnavard. (Both were artists at the time.) Karim Sadjadpour,

"Setting the Scene: Iran's Presidential Elections," 2009. http://www
.carnegieendowment.org/publications/?fa=view&id=23210; Alavi,
"Iran: A Blind Leap of Faith."

83. VIRIN "Iran TV Airs 'Press Conference' of Reformist Detainees," trans.
BBC Worldwide Monitoring, August 1, 2009, LexisNexis Academic.

84. Yahya-Kian Tajbakhsh quoted by Ali Alfoneh, "Iran News Round-up
August 2–3, 2009"' Michael Rubin and A. Majidyar, ed., *Iran News
Round-up* (Washington: American Enterprise Institute, 2009).

85. "Iran Intelligence Minister Sacked," BBC, July 27, 2009, sec. Middle
East. http://news.bbc.co.uk/2/hi/middle_east/8169839.stm.

86. "Iran's Standoff: Khamenei vs Ahmadinejad," *Al Jazeera* May 12, 2011.
http://www.aljazeera.com/indepth/opinion/2011/05/201151210
1644247806.html; "Ahmadinejad Row with Khamenei Intensifies—
Middle East," *Al Jazeera* May 6, 2011. http://www.aljazeera.com
/news/middleeast/2011/05/201156113955925329.html.

87. Robert F. Worth, "In Iran Rivalry, Khamenei Takes on Presidency
Itself," *The New York Times* October 26, 2011. http://www.nytimes
.com/2011/10/27/world/middleeast/in-iran-rivalry-khamenei
-takes-on-presidency-itself.html?_r=0.

88. Albrecht And Schlumberger, "'Waiting for Godot,'" 377.

89. Ibid., 384.

90. Interview with an anonymous IR Scholar in Tehran, 2008.

91. Elliot Hen-Tov, "Understanding Iran's New Authoritarianism," *The
Washington Quarterly* 30, no. 1 (2006): 163–179, 174.

92. Ali A. Saeidi, "The Accountability of Para-governmental Organisations
(Bonyads): The Case of Iranian Foundations," *Iranian Studies* 37,
no. 3 (2004): 479–498, 486.

93. Ibid., 487.

94. Some argue that the election of Khatami in 1997 proves that the elections do not always produce the outcome the establishment desires,
suggesting an albeit relative degree of free-and-fairness (see Sanandaji
2009, 622). This argument could easily be turned around, however:
Perhaps the experience of Khatami's election in 1997 simply showed
the establishment the risk of having fair elections. They may not have
wanted to take this risk again; Sanandaji, "The Eighth Majles Elections
in the Islamic Republic of Iran."

95. "Highly subsidised, inefficient and overstaffed [they] account for a
major share of the economy's output…Available data suggests that a
large number of SOEs are loss making and highly dependent on substantial government subsidies." Parvin Alizadeh, "Iran's Quandary:
Economic Reforms and the Structural Trap," *Brown Journal of
International Affairs* 9 no. 2 (2003): 267–281, 274.

96. Kazem Alamdari, "The Power Structure of the Islamic Republic of
Iran: Transition from Populism to Clientelism, and Militarisation of the
Government," *Third World Quarterly* 26, no. 8 (2005): 1285–1301.

97. Ibid., 1296.

98. This had led some to conclude that "only a severe economic downturn, such as a total collapse in oil revenues if process crash or an international embargo is imposed, could hasten the creation of serious opposition"; Hen-Tov, "Understanding Iran's New Authoritarianism," 169.

99. "If this is the case, U.S. and international sanctions may not weaken the Revolutionary Guards, but instead enhance its formal and illicit economic capabilities" Frederic Wehrey, et al., *The Rise of the Pasdaran Assessing the Domestic Roles of Iran's Islamic Revolutionary Guards Corps,* (RAND National Defense Research Institute, 2009), 71.

100. Saeidi, "The Accountability."

101. In this chapter, the term hardline is used to denote conservatives in Iran who take a fundamentalist view of the original ideals of the revolution, and who staunchly support the structure of power as it came into being after the revolution, including the leadership of Khamenei. These hardliners still make up the core of the power structure in Iran, particularly through the Expert Assembly, the Guardian Council, among Friday Prayer imams, and the state media. They are not only weary of reformist and pragmatist calls for reforms, but also of some more controversial neoconservative initiatives.

102. Ali M. Ansari, *Iran under Ahmadinejad* (Abingdon, Oxon: Routledge, 2007), 36.

103. Alamdari, "The Power Structure of the Islamic Republic of Iran," 1297.

104. Ehteshami and Zweiri, *Iran and the Rise of Its Neoconservatives,* 63.

105. Ansari, *Iran under Ahmadinejad,* 36.

106. Alizadeh, "Iran's Quandary," 273.

107. Ahmad R. Jalali-Naini, "Capital Accumulation and Economic Growth in Iran: Past Experience and Future Prospects," *Iranian Studies* 38, no. 1 (2005): 91–116, 91; International Bank for Reconstruction and Devolopment (IBRD), *Iran Country Brief* 2009. http://siteresources.worldbank.org/INTIRAN/Resources/IRAN-web-brief-June2009.pdf, 2.

108. "Crude oil Latest Data," *Trading Economics.* Accessed May 13, 2013. http://www.tradingeconomics.com/commodity/crude-oil. Checked against World Bank data at http://data.worldbank.org/.

109. "Official figures put inflation at around 20 percent, but it appears that the figure was substantially higher"; Ansari, *Iran under Ahmadinejad,* 84.

110. Dorraj, "Neo-populism"; International Crisis Group (ICG), "What Does Ahmadi-Nejad's Victory Mean?," 2005. http://www.crisisgroup .org/home/index.cfm?id=3604&l=1, 1.

111. Hen-Tov, "Understanding Iran's New Authoritarianism," 167.

112. Ibid.

113. Ibid.

114. In the words of Anoush Ehteshami, "The way he presented himself to
the public was comprehensively different to the flashy and expensive
electoral campaigns of Bagher Qalibaf and Rafsanjani. Ahmadinejad
used black and white posters, he showed pride in his Spartan home
and frugal lifestyle and came across as a man of the people, in touch
with their everyday concerns." Ehteshami and Zweiri, *Iran and the
Rise of Its Neoconservatives*, 61.

115. Hen-Tov, "Understanding Iran's New Authoritarianism," 167.

116. See International Montary Fund (IMF), "Islamic Republic of Iran:
Selected Issues," *IMF Country Report* No. 08/285, 2008. http://
www.imf.org/external/pubs/cat/longres.aspx?sk=22282.0, 5.

117. Karshenas and Hakimian, "Oil, Economic Diversification." One
should forget neither the economic impact that the Iran–Iraq war
had on the Iranian economy, nor the negative impact of the economic boycott imposed on Iran by the United States and the UN
Security Council.

118. Ansari, *Iran under Ahmadinejad*, 81.

119. Most analysts argue that high government involvement in the economy (including SOEs), coupled with high oil dependency, formed
the main obstruction to economic development. According to the
World Bank, the challenge Iran had to face was "a broader participation of the private sector in the economy, particularly in non-oil and
export sectors," IBRD, 2009, 2; "Policy makers need to implement
macro-economic policies friendly to growth and to greater private
sector participation," Jalali-Naini concurred; IBRD *Iran Country
Brief*, 2; Jalali-Naini, "Capital Accumulation," 115.

120. Karshenas and Hakimian, "Oil, Economic Diversification," 77.

121. IBRD, *Iran Country Brief*, 2.

122. http://data.worldbank.org/.

123. "Q&A: Petrol Rationing in Iran," BBC News, June 27, 2007,
sec. Middle East. http://news.bbc.co.uk/1/hi/world/middle
_east/6244574.stm.

124. "Police Oversee Iran Subsidy Cuts," BBC News, November 9, 2010,
sec. Middle East. http://www.bbc.co.uk/news/world-middle-east
-11685293.

125. Ibid.

126. Robert F. Worth, "As Iran Gets Ready to Vote, Economy
Dominates," *The New York Times*, June 10, 2009, sec. International
/Middle East. http://www.nytimes.com/2009/06/10/world
/middleeast/10iran.html.

127. Ansari, *Iran under Ahmadinejad*, 87–88.

128. Among whom Ali Eshraqi, grandson of Khomeini. Sanandaji, "The
Eighth Majles Elections in the Islamic Republic of Iran," 628.

129. The United Principalist Front (UPF), at the time under the leadership of then parliamentary speaker Gholam-'Ali Haddad 'Adel,
represents a neoconservative outlook, while the Broad Principalist

Coalition (BPC) holds a pragmatic conservative position. The official election results were interpreted by the UPF as their victory with a 70 percent majority. (E.g., the report by PressTV, "Principalists Win Majority of Seats," PressTV, March 15, 2008. http://edition.presstv.ir/detail/47596.html), but as MPs political affiliation is not always clear, this number is questionable. A study based on different party lists and Ministry of Interior reports in 2009 gave a different, detailed analysis: the UPF had won most seats (28 percent), followed by independents (21 percent), and the BPC (17 percent). Another 17 percent of MPs was endorsed by both the BPC and the UPF, and 4 percent by both the BPC and reformists; Ibid., 622.

130. "75% Principalists Win Majlis Vote," PressTV, March 3, 2013. http://www.presstv.ir/detail/229714.html; Neil Macfarquhar, "Elections in Iran Favor Ayatollah's Allies, Dealing Blow to President and His Office," *The New York Times* March 4, 2012. http://www.nytimes.com/2012/03/05/world/middleeast/iran-elections-deal-blow-to-ahmadinejad-and-the-presidency.html?pagewanted=all&_r=1&.

131. Ervand Abrahamian, *Khomeinism: Essays on the Islamic Republic* (London: I.B.Tauris, 1993), 2.

132. Ibid., 31.

133. Misagh Parsa, *Social Origins of the Iranian Revolution* (New Brunswick, London: Rutgers University Press, 1989), 217.

134. Abrahamian, *Khomeinism*, 32.

135. Asef Bayat, *Making Islam Democratic: Social Movements and the Post-Islamist Turn* (Stanford, California: Stanford University Press, 2007), 24.

136. Richard Cottam, "Inside Revolutionary Iran," in *Iran's Revolution: The Search for Consensus,* ed. R. K. Ramazani and Middle East Institute (Bloomington, Indiana: Indiana University Press, 1990), 3.

137. Vanessa Martin, *Creating an Islamic State: Khomeini and the Making of a New Iran* (London: I.B. Tauris, 2000), 167.

138. Ibid., 168–169.

139. Shabnam J. Holliday, *Defining Iran* (Farnham: Ashgate, 2011).

140. Abrahamian, *Khomeinism*, 17.

3 International Legitimacy: Constraints and Opportunities

1. Ian Clark, *Legitimacy in International Society* (Oxford: Oxford University Press, 2005), 29.

2. Paraphrasing Alexander Wendt, "Anarchy is What States Make of It: The Social Construction of Power Politics," *International Organization* 46, no. 2 (1992): 391–425.

3. Clark, *Legitimacy in International Society*, 30.

4. Ibid., 2.

5. Holger Albrecht and Oliver Schlumberger, "Waiting for Godot," *International Political Science Review* 25, no. 4 (2004): 371–392.

6. Ibid., 376.
7. Clark, *Legitimacy in International Society*, 188.
8. Karin M. Fierke, *Critical Approaches* (Cambridge: Polity, 2007).
9. Karin M. Fierke, "Besting the West: Russia's Machiavella Strategy," *International Feminist Journal of Politics* 1, no. 3 (2001): 403–434.
10. Ibid., 413.
11. Fierke, *Critical Approaches*, 62–64.
12. See chapter 2.
13. Ervand Abrahamian, *Khomeinism* (London: I.B.Tauris, 1993).
14. Ibid.
15. Ibid., 113.
16. Ibid., 119–120.
17. Robert S. Robins and Jerrold M. Post, "The Paranoid Political Actor," *Biography* 10, no. 1 (1987): 1–19. 2.
18. The Copenhagen School has developed the concept of securitization and applied it to international relations. See Barry Buzan, Ole Wæver, and Jaap de Wilde, *Security: A New Framework for Analysis* (London: Lynne Rienner Publishers, 1998).
19. Robins and Post, "The Paranoid Political Actor."
20. This account is disputed. Cf. Darioush Bayandor, *Iran and the CIA: The Fall of Mosaddeq Revisited* (New York: Palgrave Macmillan, 2010.)
21. Nikki R. Keddie and Yann Richard, *Roots of Revolution: An Interpretive History of Modern Iran* (New Haven: Yale University Press, 1981), 144.
22. R. K. Ramazani, *Revolutionary Iran: Challenge and Response in the Middle East* (Baltimore, Maryland: Johns Hopkins University Press, 1987), 204.
23. Mohsen M Milani, *The Making of Iran's Islamic Revolution: From Monarchy To Islamic Republic* (Boulder, Colorado: Westview Press, 1994), 72.
24. Abrahamian, *Khomeinism*, 130–131.
25. Milani, *The making of Iran's Islamic Revolution*, 163–165.
26. Milani, *The making of Iran's Islamic Revolution*, 173.
27. Mansoor Moaddel, *Class, Politics, and Ideology in the Iranian Revolution* (New York: Columbia University Press, 1992), 210.
28. Milani, *The making of Iran's Islamic Revolution*, 183–184.
29. R. K. Ramazani and Middle East Institute (Washington, DC). *Iran's Revolution: The Search for Consensus* (Bloomington, Indiana: Indiana University Press, 1990), 57.
30. Milani, *The making of Iran's Islamic Revolution*, 180.
31. Moaddel, *Class*, 219.
32. Ervand Abrahamian, *A History of Modern Iran* (Cambridge, UK: Cambridge University Press, 2008), 176.
33. Milani, *The making of Iran's Islamic Revolution*, 181.
34. See chapter 7.

35. William O. Beeman, *The Great Satan Vs. the Mad Mullahs: How the United States and Iran Demonize Each Other* (Chicago: University of Chicago Press, 2008).
36. Trita Parsi, *Threacherous Alliance*.
37. This was under the consolidated Appropriation Act 2008. Stephan de Vries discusses this in his comprehensive overview of US democracy promotion in Iran. (Stephan de Vries, *Dynamics and Dilemmas of "Democratization": Non-democratic Rule, Democratization and U.S. Efforts to 'Democratize' Iran*, Master thesis, University of Amsterdam, 2010. Also see Anthony H. Cordesman, et al., "U.S. and Iran Strategic Competition; Sanctions, Energy, Arms Control, and Regime Change," Centre for Strategic and International Studies, January 22, 2013. http://csis.org/files/publication/130122_IranVSanctions _Final_AHC_1_22_13.pdf.)
38. Moreover, the United States 111th Congress (January 3, 2009, until January 3, 2011) passed the following legislation on Iranian human rights: H.Res.175/S.Res.71 on Bahai persecution, H.Res.560/S .Res.193 that expressed support for the Iranian protestors following the disputed 2009 elections, S.3022/H.R.4647 Iranian Human Rights Sanctions Act, S.Res.415 on Iran's violation of human rights, S.Res.386 on freedom of speech in Iran, and S.Res. 355 also on Iran's violations of human rights. (National Iranian American Council, "Summary of Iran Human Rights Legislation in 111th Congress." http://www.niacouncil.org/site/DocServer/Guide_to_Iran _Human_Rights_Legislation.pdf?docID=302.)
39. US sanctions in the period 1979–2012 comprised the following US executive orders: E12170 (1979), EO 12205 (1980), EO 12211 (1980), EO12613 (1987), EO 12957 (1995), EO 12959 (1995), EO 13059 (1997), EO 13224 (2001, EO 13382 (2005), EO 13553 (2010), EO 13527 (2011), 13574 (2011), EO13590 (2011), EO 13599 (2012), 13606 (2012), EO 13608 (2012), EO 13622 (2012), and EO 13628 (2012), and the following US Acts of congress: National Defence Authorization Act of 1993 (1992), Iran Sanctions Act (1996), Iran Nonproliferation Act (2000), Iran Freedom Support Act (2006), Comprehensive Iran Sanctions, Accountability, and Divestment Act of 2010 (2010), Iran-Syria-North Korea Nonproliferation Act (2011), Section 311 of the USA Patriot Act (2011), National Defense Authorization Act of 2012, Sec 1245 (2011), Iran Threat Reduction and Syrian Human Rights Act of 2012 (2012), and the National Defense Authorization Act of 2013, Subtitle D (2012). (International Crisis Group (ICG), "Spider Web: The Making and Unmaking of Iran Sanctions," February 25, 2013. http://www.crisisgroup.org /en/regions/middle-east-north-africa/iraq-iran-gulf/iran/138 -spider-web-the-making-and-unmaking-of-iran-sanctions.aspx, Appendices 2 and 3.)

40. EU Restrictive Measures on Iran during the Ahmadinejad Presidency: Council Common Position 2007/140/CFSP, Council regulation 423/2007; Council Common Position 2010/413/CFSP, Council Regulation 961/2010; Council Decision 2011/235/CSFP, Council Regulation 359/201; and Council Decision 2012/235/CFSP, amending 2010/413/CSFP, Council Regulation 267/2012. (ICG, "Spider Web." Also see, "EU Imposes New Sanctions on Iran," BBC News, October 15, 2012, sec. Middle East. http://www.bbc.co.uk /news/world-middle-east-19947507; "Q&A: Iran Sanctions," BBC News, October 16, 2012, sec. Middle East. http://www.bbc.co.uk /news/world-middle-east-15983302.)

41. "Shell Reveals Iranian Oil Trade Loss, $2.3 Bln Iran Debt," Reuters, March 20, 2013. http://www.reuters.com/article/2013/03/20 /shell-iran-idUSL6N0CCCL220130320.

42. DG Trade Statistics, "Iran: EU Bilateral Trade and Trade with the World," April 26, 2013. http://trade.ec.europa.eu/doclib /docs/2006/september/tradoc_113392.pdf.

43. In 2011, Italy with 5.3 percent was the only European country in Iran's export top-five, and Germany (9.66 percent) and Italy (5.27 percent) were important import partners to Iran (CIA World Factbook 2011). According to the IMF, the EU27 accounted for 15.8 percent of imports to Iran and for 16.5 percent of exports. (DG trade statistics, "Iran.") The United States accounted for 0.3 percent and 0.0 percent, respectively. The Iranian government reported in 2007 that from 1992 onward more than 20 European countries made investments in Iran, with a total value of 10.1 billion US dollars. Germany, the Netherlands, Spain, Turkey, Italy, and France were the main investors. In addition, Canada made 1 billion U.S. dollar of investments in Iran and Australia 682 million ("Iran Absorbed $34bln of FDI," Moj News Agency, December 7, 2008, LexisNexis Academic.)

44. Benjamin Weinthal, "Deutsche Firmen Weiter Im Iran Aktiv," *Welt Online* October 3, 2010, sec. Home. http://www.welt.de/welt _print/wirtschaft/article6711136/Deutsche-Firmen-weiter-im -Iran-aktiv.html.

45. "'Italy to be Iran's Top EU Trade Partner,'" PressTV January 30, 2013. http://www.presstv.ir/detail/2013/01/30/286279/italy -to-be-irans-top-eu-trade-partner/.

46. United Nations Security Council Resolutions 1737, 1747, 1803 and 1929. (ICG, "What Does Ahmadi-Nejad's Victory Mean?," Appendix 5.)

47. Particularly in the energy sector, the impact of sanctions was felt; however, high energy prices meant that Iran still generated record oil and gas revenues during most of Ahmadinejad's presidency. (ICG, 2013, 21). Only when US sanctions started targeting oil payment transactions and transportation did oil revenues drop significantly. (International Crisis Group (ICG), "Spider Web: The Making and

Unmaking of Iran Sanctions," February 25, 2013. http://www
.crisisgroup.org/en/regions/middle-east-north-africa/iraq-iran
-gulf/iran/138-spider-web-the-making-and-unmaking-of-iran
-sanctions.aspx.) Also see, "Iran Rial Drop Dents Border Trade," BBC
October 3, 2012, sec. Middle East, http://www.bbc.co.uk/news
/world-middle-east-19815103; "Iran Rial Hits Record Dollar Low,"
BBC October 1, 2012, sec. Business, http://www.bbc.co.uk/news
/business-19786662; "Iranian Oil Revenues 'Plunge 45%,'" BBC
January 8, 2013, sec. Middle East, http://www.bbc.co.uk/news
/world-middle-east-20942138; "Sanctions Detonate Iran Currency,"
BBC October 2, 2012, sec. Business, http://www.bbc.co.uk/news
/business-19800532.
48. Suzanne Maloney, "Sanctioning Iran: If Only It Were So Simple,"
    Washington Quarterly 33, no. 1 (2010): 131–147.
49. ICG, "Spider Web," 20.
50. ICG, "Spider Web," 32.
51. Opposition leader Karubi expressed concerns that sanctions are only
    contributing to the power of the revolutionary organizations that
    are mandated to operate in Iran's clandestine economy. "Opposition
    Leader Says Revolutionary Guards Will Benefit from Iran Sanctions,"
    Payvand July 10, 2010. http://www.payvand.com/news/10
    /jul/1092.html. It has also been argued that sanctions undermine the
    opposition by limiting the access to alternative news sources. Mania
    Tehrani, "Sanctions Help Iran Limit Internet Use," *Mianeh* February
    16, 2010. http://mianeh.net/article/sanctions-help-iran-limit-inter-
    net-use.Last, the ICG argues that "members of the elites with greatest
    access to the regime and state privileges are best positioned to survive
    and even thrive in the new environment." (ICG, "Spider Web," 33.)
52. When Ahmadinejad started his presidency in 2005, the United States
    was becoming less popular in world opinion, as a PEW poll in showed
    June 2006: "support for the war on terrorism has declined even among
    close U.S. allies like Japan. The war in Iraq is a continuing drag on opin-
    ions of the United States, not only in predominantly Muslim countries
    but in Europe and Asia as well." (PEW Research Center, "America's
    Image Slips, But Allies Share U.S. Concerns over Iran, Hamas,"
    2006. http://pewglobal.org/2006/06/13/americas-image-slips
    -but-allies-share-us-concerns-over-iran-hamas/.) PEW reported that
    even though anti-Americanism that had been extensive for five years
    had not widened is had deepened: "The U.S. image remains abysmal
    in most Muslim countries in the Middle East and Asia, and contin-
    ues to decline among the publics of many of America's oldest allies.
    Favourable views of the U.S. are in single digits in Turkey (9 percent)
    and have decline to 15 percent in Pakistan." Also in Latin America,
    US popularity continued to fall, but the majority still held a favorable
    opinion of America (PEW Research Center, "Global Unease with
    Major World Powers," *Pew Global Attitudes Project*, June 27, 2006.

http://www.pewglobal.org/2007/06/27/global-unease-with
-major-world-powers/), though a majority in Venezuela and
Argentina also viewed the United States as a potential threat (PEW
Research Center, "A Rising Tide Lifts Mood in the Developing
World," *Pew Global Attitudes Project*, July 24 2007. http://www
.pewglobal.org/2007/07/24/a-rising-tide-lifts-mood-in-the-devel-
oping-world/). At the end of Ahmadinejad's presidency, views of the
United States improved a little in Turkey, to 15 percent of Turks
viewing the United States as favourable. However, in Egypt the percentage went down from 30 percent in 2006 to 19 percent in 2012.
Also in Jordan (from 15 percent to 12 percent) and Pakistan (from
27 percent to 12 percent), views of the United States had become
less favourable.

53. A term used by Nau and Ollapally in their edited volume *Worldviews of Aspiring powers* to denote both rising powers, "prospective" powers and "conflicted" powers. Henry R. Nau and Deepa M. Ollapally,
eds, *Worldviews of Aspiring Powers: Domestic Foreign Policy Debates in China, India, Iran, Japan, and Russia* (New York: Oxford University Press, 2012).

54. Fierke, "Constructivism."

55. Fierke, *Critical Approaches.*

56. For a comprehensive discussion on the concept of Peaceful Rise and its
chance to Peaceful Development, consult Bonnie S. Glaser and Evan
S Medeiros, "The Changing Ecology of Foreign Policy-Making in
China: The Ascension and Demise of the Theory of 'Peaceful Rise,'"
The China Quarterly 190 (2007): 291–310.

57. Ibid., 295.

58. David Shambaugh and Ren Xiao, "China: The Conflicted Rising
Power," in *Worldviews of Aspiring Powers: Domestic Foreign Policy
Debates in China, India, Iran, Japan, and Russia*, ed. Henry R. Nau
and Deepa M. Ollapally (New York: Oxford University Press, 2012),
43.

59. Shambaugh and Xiao, "China," 43–44.

60. Andrew C. Kuchins and Igor Zevelev, "Russia's Contested National
Identity and Foreign Policy," in *Worldviews of Aspiring Powers:
Domestic Foreign Policy Debates in China, India, Iran, Japan, and
Russia*, ed. Henry R. Nau and Deepa M. Ollapally (New York: Oxford
University Press, 2012), 190.

61. Kuchins and Zevelev "Russia's identity," 198.

62. Deepa M. Ollapally and Rajesh Rajagopalan, "India: Foreign Policy
Perspectives of an Ambiguous Power," in *Worldviews of Aspiring
Powers: Domestic Foreign Policy Debates in China, India, Iran, Japan,
and Russia*, ed. Henry R. Nau and Deepa M. Ollapally (New York:
Oxford University Press, 2012), 101–105.

63. Ollapally and Rajagopalan, "India: Foreign Policy," 106.

64. Evan A. Feigenbaum, "India's Rise, America's Interest," *Foreign Affairs* March 1, 2010. http://www.foreignaffairs.com/articles/65995/evan-a-feigenbaum/indias-rise-americas-interest.

65. Ollapally and Rajagopalan, "India: Foreign Policy," 107.

66. Kuchins and Zevelev, "Russia's Identity," 200.

67. Xinhua General News Service, "China Urges Conditions for Resolving Iran Nuclear Issue," April 10, 2013. http://news.xinhuanet.com/english/china/2013-04/10/c_124564922.htm.

68. Foreign Ministry of the People's Republic of China, "Foreign Ministry Spokesperson Ma Zhaoxu's Remarks on Iran Building a Uranium Enrichment Factory," September 27, 2009. http://www.fmprc.gov.cn/eng/xwfw/s2510/t607387.htm; Foreign Ministry of the People's Republic of China, "Foreign Ministry Spokesperson Hong Lei's Regular Press Conference on December 14, 2012," December 14, 2012. http://www.fmprc.gov.cn/eng/xwfw/s2510/2511/t998567.htm.

69. Foreign Ministry of the People's Republic of China, "Foreign Ministry Spokesperson Hong Lei's Regular Press Conference on November 6, 2012," November 6, 2012. http://www.fmprc.gov.cn/eng/xwfw/s2510/2511/t986346.htm; Foreign Ministry of the People's Republic of China, "Foreign Ministry Spokesperson Hong Lei's Regular Press Conference on November 13, 2012," November 13, 2012. http://www.fmprc.gov.cn/eng/xwfw/s2510/2511/t988806.htm.

70. "Russia Stresses Iran's Right to Peaceful Nuclear Energy," PressTV December 28, 2012. http://www.presstv.com/detail/2012/12/28/280565/russia-stresses-iran-right-to-nenergy/.

71. "Russia Resists U.S. Position on Sanctions for Iran," *The New York Times* October 14, 2009. http://www.nytimes.com/2009/10/14/world/europe/14diplo.html?_r=1&.

72. Mariya Y. Omelicheva, "Russia's Foreign Policy Toward Iran: A Critical Geopolitics Perspective," *Journal of Balkan and Near Eastern Studies* 14, no. 3 (2012): 331–344.

73. Ollapally and Rajagopalan, "India: Foreign Policy," 101.

74. Ministry of External Affairs, Government of India, "External Affairs Minister's Speech at Global India Foundation Conference on 'Iran's Eurasian Dynamic: Mapping Regional and Extra-Regional Interests,'" February 13, 2013. http://www.mea.gov.in/Speeches-Statements.htm?dtl/21246/External+Affairs+Ministers+speech+at+Global+India+Foundation+Conference+on+Irans+Eurasian+Dynamic+Mapping+Regional+and+ExtraRegional+Interests.

75. Ministry of External Affairs, Government of India, "Joint Statement on the 13th India-Russia annual Summit: 'Partnership for Mutual Benefit and a Better World,'" December 24, 2012. http://mea.gov.in/bilateral-documents.htm?dtl/20993/Joint+Statement+on+the+

13th+IndiaRussia+annual+Summit+Partnership+for+mutual+benefit +and+a+better+world.

76. While the Russian Federation was the first to advance the idea of a multipolar international system, it also found some resonance in China and France that called for the creation of a multipolar world in a joint statement in 1998 (Hunter, *Iran's Foreign Policy*, 12).

77. Par Engstrom, "Brazilian Foreign Policy and Human Rights: Change and Continuity under Dilma," *Critical Sociology* June 26, 2012, 840.

78. Alexei Barrionuevo, "Brazil Defends Iran President's Visit," *International Herald Tribune* November 24, 2009, LexisNexis Academic.

79. Rory Carroll, "Brazil Stands up to U.S. over Iran Sanctions," *The Guardian Unlimited* March 4, 2010, LexisNexis Academic.

80. Ibid.

81. "Israeli FM 'Boycotts Brazil Head,'" BBC News March 16, 2010, sec. Middle East. http://news.co.uk/2/hi/middle_east/8569471.stm.

82. Engstrom, "Brazilian Foreign Policy," 839–840.

83. In March 2007, for example, in response to a proposed UNSC resolution, South Africa, at the time chair of the UNSC, called for the suspension of sanctions against Iran for 90 days "to allow for political negotiation to find a long-term solution,", as well as for the deletion of substantive measures in the proposal that would have had as an effect, among other things, the lifting of the arms embargo on Iran. Although South Africa was not able to stop the new resolution being agreed, the symbolism of this move was important (Mark Turner, "Pretoria Jeopardises New UN Deal on Iran Sanctions Security Council," *The Financial Times* March 20, 2007, LexisNexis Academic). It was one of the many ways in which South Africa was trying to undermine the United States at the UNSC, objecting to US unilateralism and positioning themselves as a global power and voice of the developing world (Janine Zacharia, "U.S. Finds an antagonist in a Country on the Rise; Letter from South Africa," *International Herald Tribune* June 27, 2007, LexisNexis Academic.).

84. Michal Onderco, "South Africa's Iran Policy: 'Poster Child' Meets Renegade," *South African Journal of International Affairs* 19, no. 3 (2012): 299–318.

85. Ibid.

86. Tanya Ogilvie-White, "The Non-proliferation Diplomacy of the Non-nuclear-weapon States: Understanding International Responses to Iran's Nuclear Defiance," *European Journal of International Law* 18, no. 3 (2007): 464.

87. "Nonaligned Nations Back Iran on Nuclear Bid, But not on Syria," *The New York Times* September 1, 2012. http://www.nytimes .com/2012/09/01/world/middleeast/iran-criticizes-egypts -mohamed-morsi-over-syria-comments.html?_r=0.

88. "Non-aligned Movement: A Two-edged Summit in Tehran," *The Guardian*, August 29, 2012, sec. Comment is free. http://www.guardian.co.uk/commentisfree/2012/aug/29/non-aligned-movement-two-edged-summit-tehran.

89. See Simon Tisdall, "Can the BRICS Create a New World Order?" *The Guardian*, March 29, 2012, sec. Comment is free. http://www.guardian.co.uk/commentisfree/2012/mar/29/brics-new-world-order?INTCMP=SRCH.

90. Even if this was mainly to their own economic interest.

91. Min-Jeong Lee, "South Korea's Iran Imports Fall While China's Increase," *Wall Street Journal* March 22, 2013; "Chinese Supertanker Gets Oil at Iran Port," Press TV April 7, 2013. http://www.presstv.ir/detail/2013/03/28/295493/chinese-supertanker-gets-oil-at-iran-port/; Reuters, "India Asks EU to Clarify Stance on Iran Oil Insurance," March 22, 2013. http://www.reuters.com/article/2013/03/22/india-iran-idUSL3N0CE0PE20130322; Nicholas Burns, "India's Support for Iran Threatens Its US Relationship and Global Leadership Role," *Christian Science Monitor* February 14, 2012. http://www.csmonitor.com/Commentary/Opinion/2012/0214/India-s-support-for-Iran-threatens-its-US-relationship-and-global-leadership-role; "U.S. Extends Waivers on Iran Sanctions to China and India," Reuters. http://www.reuters.nl/article/2012/12/07/us-usa-iran-sanctons-idUSBRE8B615M20121207.

92. Iran Pulse, "Chinese Investment in Iran Said to Drop from $3 Billion to $400 Million," March 15, 2013. http://iranpulse.al-monitor.com/index.php/2013/03/1555/chinese-investment-in-iran-said-to-drop-from-3-billion-to-400-million/.

93. Min-Jeong Lee, "South Korea"; Rick Gladstone, "Iran: Oil Exports Rose, Report Says," *The New York Times* March 13, 2013, sec. World/Middle East. http://www.nytimes.com/2013/03/14/world/middleeast/iran-oil-exports-rose-report-says.html.

4 A Foreign Policy Ideology of Change

1. Mahmoud Ahmadinejad, "A Reply to an American Mother's Message," Presidency of the Islamic Republic of Iran News Service, March 18, 2007; "Dr Ahmadinejad in Reply to Imam Al Haj Talib Abd Al Rashid's Letter Today All Nations of the World Are Seeking Justice," Presidency of the Islamic Republic of Iran News Service, April 4, 2007. http://www.president.ir/en/print.php?ArtID=3626&noimage; "Iran President Defends Right to Nuclear Fuel, Re-asserts Statement on Holocaust," IRNA, September 25, 2007, LexisNexis Academic; "President Ahmadinejad Addressing 62nd UN General Assembly—Full Text," Presidency of the Islamic Republic of Iran News Service, September 26, 2007. http://www.president.ir/en/print.php?ArtID=6781&noimage; "Full Text of President's Address

to APA General Assembly," Presidency of the Islamic Republic of Iran News Service, November 19, 2007. http://www.president.ir/en /print.php?ArtID=7376&noimage; "President Ahmadinejad Addressing the 11th Summit of the Organization of the Islamic Conference in Senegal," Presidency of the Islamic Republic of Iran News Service, March 14, 2008. http://www.president.ir/en/print .php?ArtID=9261&noimage; "President: Unilateral, Oppressive Ties Must be Replaced by Just Mechanisms," Presidency of the Islamic Republic of Iran News Service, June 3, 2008. http://www.president .ir/en/print.php?ArtID=10102&noimage; "President: D-8 Can be Pioneer of Peace, Justice in World," Presidency of the Islamic Republic of Iran News Service, July 8, 2008. http://www.president.ir/en /print.php?ArtID=10647&noimage; "Text of the President's Speech, Addressing African Nations," Presidency of the Islamic Republic of Iran News Service, September 23, 2008. http://www.president.ir /en/print.php?ArtID=12175&noimage; "President Ahmadinejad's Speech Addressing the UN General Assembly," Presidency of the Islamic Republic of Iran News Service, September 24, 2008. http://www.president.ir/en/print.php?ArtID=12188&noimage; "Honourable Barack Obama President Elect of the United States of America," Presidency of the Islamic Republic of Iran News Service,   November 8, 2008. http://www.president.ir/en/print. php?ArtID=13116&noimage; "Message for the Birth of Jesus Son of Mary Word of God the Messenger of Mercy," Presidency of the Islamic Republic of Iran News Service, December 25, 2008. http://www.president.ir/en/print.php?ArtID=14056&noimage; "President Congratulates Pope Catholics on Christmas," Presidency of the Islamic Republic of Iran News Service, December 25, 2008. http://www.president.ir/en/print.php?ArtID=14066&noimage; "Ahmadinejad: Gaza, Sight for Independent Nations and Govt's Victory over Oppressor Powers' Will," Presidency of the Islamic Republic of Iran News Service, January 20, 2009. http://www. president.ir/en/print.php?ArtID=14505&noimage;   "President Speech in Durban II," Presidency of the Islamic Republic of Iran News   Service,   April 21, 2009. http://www.president.ir/en/print .php?ArtID=16845&noimage; "President Ahmadinejad Addressed the U.N. 64rd General Assembly," Presidency of the Islamic Republic of Iran News Service, September 25, 2009. http://www.president.ir /en/print.php?ArtID=17937&noimage; "Ahmadinejad   Proposed Designation   of   2011   as   Year   of   Rectifying   Consumption Pattern,   Reducing   Pollution,"   Presidency   of   the   Islamic Republic of Iran News Service, December 17, 2009. http:// www.president.ir/en/print.php?ArtID=19320&noimage; Ali Khamenei, "Leader's Speech on Feast of Mab'ath," The Office of the Supreme Leader, September 2, 2005. http://www.leader.ir /langs/en/print.php?sec=content&id=3467; "Leader's Message in

Commemoration of Martyrs and Devotees of the Sacred Defense Era," the Office of the Supreme Leader, September 22, 2005. http://www.leader.ir/langs/en/print.php?sec=content&id=3468; "Leader Appoints CSDS Director and Deputy Chief of General Staff of the Armed forces for Inspection Affairs," The Office of the Supreme Leader, September 26, 2005. http://www.leader.ir/langs/en/print.php?sec=content&id=3469; "Leader's Statements at the Graduation Ceremony of Army Cadets," The Office of the Supreme Leader, September 28, 2005. http://www.leader.ir/langs/en/print.php?sec=bayanat&id=347; "Leader's Message of Condolence on Tragic Pakistan Earthquake," The Office of the Supreme Leader, October 10, 2005. http://www.leader.ir/langs/en/print.php?sec=content&id=3471; "Leader's Address to University Professors and Elite Academics," The Office of the Supreme Leader, October 13, 2005. http://www.leader.ir/langs/en/print.php?sec=bayanat&id=3472; "Leader's Statements at the Tehran Friday Prayers," Office of the Supreme Leader Website, October 21, 2005. http://www.leader.ir/langs/en/print.php?sec=content&id=3473; "Leader's Address to War-disabled Veterans," The Office of the Supreme Leader, October 26, 2005. http://www.leader.ir/langs/en/print.php?sec=bayanat&id=3474; "Leader's Speech to Government Officials on the Eid-al-Fitr," The Office of the Supreme Leader, November 4, 2005. http://www.leader.ir/langs/en/print.php?sec=bayanat&id=3477; "Leader Appreciates Armed Forces," The Office of the Supreme Leader, December 21, 2005. http://www.leader.ir/langs/en/print.php?sec=content&id=3488; "The Message of H. E. Ayatullah Khamenei to the Hajj Pilgrims from the Whole World," The Office of the Supreme Leader Website, January 9, 2006. http://www.leader.ir/langs/en/print.php?sec=content&id=349; "Leader's Speech to Residents of the Holy City of Qom," The Office of the Supreme Leader, January 9, 2006. http://www.leader.ir/langs/en/print.php?sec=bayanat&id=3492; "Leader's Statements at the Funeral of Major General Kazemi and his Colleagues," The Office of the Supreme Leader, January 11, 2006. http://www.leader.ir/langs/en/print.php?sec=content&id=3493; "Leader Receives Air force Servicemen," The Office of the Supreme Leader, February 7, 2006. http://www.leader.ir/langs/en/print.php?sec=content&id=3500; "Leader's Message on Sammara Tragedy," The Office of the Supreme Leader, February 22, 2006. http://www.leader.ir/langs/en/print.php?sec=content&id=3505; "Leader's Speech to Governor-Generals," The Office of the Supreme Leade, February 27, 2006. http://www.leader.ir/langs/en/print.php?sec=bayanat&id=3506; "IR Leader's New Year's Day Message," The Office of the Supreme Leader, March 20, 2006. http://www.leader.ir/langs/en/print.php?sec=content&id=3511; "Leader's Statements in a Meeting with

Residents of Dasht-e-Azadegan, Sousangerd, Bostan, Hamidiyeh and Hovayzeh," The Office of the Supreme Leader, March 25, 2006. http://www.leader.ir/langs/en/print.php?sec=bayanat&id=3513; "Palestinian Issue, at Focal Point," The Office of the Supreme Leader, April 14, 2006. http://www.leader.ir/langs/en/print .php?sec=content&id=3515; "IR Leader Receives Cinema Directors," The Office of the Supreme Leader, June 13, 2006. http://www .leader.ir/langs/en/print.php?sec=content&id=3531; "Ayatollah Khamenei Condemns Qana Tragedy," The Office of the Supreme Leader, August 2, 2006. http://www.leader.ir/langs/en/print .php?sec=content&id=3541; "IR Leader Sends Congrats Message to Nasrallah," The Office of the Supreme Leader, August 17, 2006. http://www.leader.ir/langs/en/print.php?sec=content&id=3545; "IR Leader Salutes Basiji Students," The Office of the Supreme Leader, August 23, 2006. http://www.leader.ir/langs/en/print .php?sec=content&id=3549; "Message to the General Meeting of the United Islamic Students Association in Europe," The Office of the Supreme Leader, September 23, 2006. http://www.leader.ir/langs /en/print.php?sec=content&id=3557; "Leader's Address at the Graduation and Oath-taking Ceremony of IRGC Cadets," The Office of the Supreme Leader, November 25, 2006. http://www.leader.ir /langs/en/print.php?sec=bayanat&id=3578; "Leader's Address to the Iranian People from Various Social Strata," The Office of the Supreme Leader, December 13, 2006, http://www.leader.ir/langs /en/print.php?sec=bayanat&id=3583; "Leader's Statements on the Day of Elections for the Experts Assembly and Islamic Councils," The Office of the Supreme Leader, December 15, 2006. http://www .leader.ir/langs/en/print.php?sec=bayanat&id=3584;   "Ayatollah Khamenei Thanks Nation," The Office of the Supreme Leader, December 23, 2006. http://www.leader.ir/langs/en/print .php?sec=content&id=3585; "Ayatollah Khamenei: The Cardinal Purpose of Hajj is to Show the United Identity of the Muslim Ummah," The Office of the Supreme Leader, December 29, 2006. http://www.leader.ir/langs/en/print.php?sec=content&id=3586; "Leader's Speech to the Residents of Qom," The Office of the Supreme Leader, January 8, 2007. http://www.leader.ir/langs/en /print.php?sec=bayanat&id=3587; "Leader's Address to the Participants in the 2nd Congress in Commemoration of Ibn Maytham Bahrani," The Office of the Supreme Leader, January 15, 2007. http://www.leader.ir/langs/en/print.php?sec=bayanat&id=3588; "Leader's Speech to the Residents of the Eastern Azarbaijan Province," The Office of the Supreme Leader, February 17, 2007. http://www .leader.ir/langs/en/print.php?sec=bayanat&id=3595;   "Islamic Republic, Modern Example of Religious Democracy," The Office of the Supreme Leader, February 20, 2007. http:// www.leader.ir/langs/en/print.php?sec=content&id=3598;

"Leader's Address to the Officials and Executives of the Islamic Republic," Office of the Supreme Leader Website, April 6, 2007. http://www.leader.ir/langs/en/print.php?sec=bayanat&id=3603; "Leader's Address to Executive Officials," The Office of the Supreme Leader, June 30, 2007. http://www.leader.ir/langs/en/print.php?sec=bayanat&id=3617; "Leadership Assembly of Experts Stands Essential Beacon of the System," The Office of the Supreme Leader, September 6, 2007. http://www.leader.ir/langs/en/print.php?sec=content&id=3634; "The Message of H.E. Ayatullah Khamenei to the Hajj Pilgrims from the Whole World," The Office of the Supreme Leader, December 18, 2007. http://www.leader.ir/langs/en/print.php?sec=content&id=3657; "Supreme Leader's Speech to Air force Staff," The Office of the Supreme Leader, February 8, 2008. http://www.leader.ir/langs/en/print.php?sec=bayanat&id=3703; "Mughniyeh's Blood Would Double the Resistance," The Office of the Supreme Leader, February 14, 2008. http://www.leader.ir/langs/en/print.php?sec=content&id=3707; "Islamic Umma Must Generate Waves of Wrath," The Office of the Supreme Leader, March 2, 2008. http://www.leader.ir/langs/en/print.php?sec=content&id=3716; "Your Islamic Republic Threw Challenge to All Anti-religion or Anti-people Models of Government," The Office of the Supreme Leader, March 15, 2008. http://www.leader.ir/langs/en/print.php?sec=content&id=3739; "IR Leader Condoles Shiraz Mishap," The Office of the Supreme Leader, April 14, 2008. http://www.leader.ir/langs/en/print.php?sec=content&id=3770; "Scientific Progress Vital for Country," The Office of the Supreme Leader, September 24, 2008. http://www.leader.ir/langs/en/print.php?sec=content&id=4058; "Supreme Leader's Public Address on Eid Ul-Fitr," The Office of the Supreme Leader, October 1, 2008. http://www.leader.ir/langs/en/print.php?sec=bayanat&id=4074; "Supreme Leader's Speech to Government Officials on Eid Ul-Fitr," The Office of the Supreme Leader, October 1, 2008. http://www.leader.ir/langs/en/print.php?sec=bayanat&id=4079; "The Message of H. E. Ayatullah Khamenei to the Hajj Pilgrims from the Whole World," The Office of the Supreme Leader, "Islamic Revolution Leader Issued a Statement Sunday on the Horrendous Tragedy of Gaza Bloodbath in the Hand of the Zionists," The Office of the Supreme Leader, December 28, 2008. http://www.leader.ir/langs/en/print.php?sec=content&id=4603; "Islamic Revolution Leader Issued a Statement Sunday on the Horrendous Tragedy of Gaza Bloodbath in the Hand of the Zionists," The Office of the Supreme Leader, December 28, 2008. http://www.leader.ir/langs/en/print.php?sec=content&id=4603; Sabrina Tavernise, "Turkey Offers to Mediate Between U.S. and Iran," *International Herald Tribune* November 12, 2008, LexisNexis Academic; "A Message Friday to Ismail Haniya," The Office of the Supreme Leader, January 17, 2009.

http://www.leader.ir/langs/en/print.php?sec=content&id=4688; "Islamic Revolution Leader in Response to President 's Letter," The Office of the Supreme Leader, February 4, 2009. http://www.leader.ir/langs/en/print.php?sec=content&id=4746. "Fourth International Conference for Support of Palestine, the Model of Resistance, and Ghaza, the Victim of war crimes," The Office of the Supreme Leader, March 4, 2009. http://www.leader.ir/langs/en/print.php?sec=content&id=4858; "US forces, Prime Suspect in Iraqi Bombings," The Office of the Supreme Leader, April 25, 2009. http://www.leader.ir/langs/en/print.php?sec=content&id=5193; "President Elect is President of All Iranians," The Office of the Supreme Leader, June 13, 2009. http://www.leader.ir/langs/en/print.php?sec=content&id=5566; "IR Leader Endorses Vote to President-elect Mahmoud Ahmadinejad," The Office of the Supreme Leader, August 3, 2009. http://www.leader.ir/langs/en/print.php?sec=content&id=5723; "The Message of H. E. Ayatullah Khamenei to The Hajj Pilgrims," The Office of the Supreme Leader, November 2, 2009. http://www.leader.ir/langs/en/print.php?sec=content&id=6135; "The Message of H. E. Ayatullah Khamenei to the Hajj pilgrims," Office of the Supreme Leader Website, November 26, 2009. http://www.leader.ir/langs/en/print.php?sec=content&id=6135; "IR Leader Condoles with Ayatollah Montazeri's Demise," The Office of the Supreme Leader, December 20, 2009. http://www.leader.ir/langs/en/print.php?sec=content&id=6238; "Supreme Leader Thanks Iranian Nation for Impressive Bahman 22 Rallies," The Office of the Supreme Leader, February 12, 2010. http://www.leader.ir/langs/en/print.php?sec=content&id=6459.

2. As discussed in the introduction, Ahmadinejad and Khamenei as the main leaders of the Islamic Republic are also the main individuals responsible for communicating Iran's official ideology. Despite some differences in their orientation, stemming both from their respective positions in the government as well as a certain level of divergence in their political views, their expressed views build on the revolutionary ideology of Khomeini, converge to a large extent and where they do not, generally complement, and rarely contradict each other. Their respective discourses have more than enough in common to create and recreate a coherent foreign policy discourse within which foreign policy is made. As their discourses do not only overlap but also complement each other, these leaders together present the audience at home and abroad with an integrated and coherent foreign policy ideology. This chapter will focus on this overlap and complementarily and aims to give an integrated overview.

3. This research uses the concept "worldview" as the conception of the world (not a philosophy of life). For the double meaning of worldview, consult the Oxford English Dictionary online.

4. To be sure, the worldview leaders put forward in their discourse is not necessarily a representation of their personal conception of the world; rather, it is a representation of the world, as they want their audience to look at it.

5. The following entities are most recurrent in the combined discourse of Ahmadinejad and Khamenei (in order of salience high-low): The West (also bullying powers, colonial powers, domineering powers, hegemonic powers, and Western countries), Iran/the Iranian people, humanity, the United States, the Islamic world (Ummah), Israel, Palestine/Palestinians, Iraq, Lebanon, the Middle East, Europe, Afghanistan, Asia, the United Kingdom, Arabs/Arab World, Africa, Latin America, Soviet Union, Syria, Pakistan, and Egypt. The top-3 most discussed entities for Ahmadinejad are the West, humanity, and Iran/the Iranian people, and for Khamenei Iran/the Iranian people, the Islamic world, and the West. The Islamic World is in 13th place on Ahmadinejad's list, and humanity in the 11th place on Khamenei's list. For both men, the United States, Israel, Iraq, and Palestine /Palestinians are numbers 4–7, with Iraq and Palestine in reverse order for Khamenei.

6. The discourse analysis presented in this chapter is based on the assumption that the more often a certain subject appears in the discourse, the more relevant it is to the discourse. A similar premise underlies content analysis, which focuses on the recurrence of individual words. This study, however, does not focus on individual words, but on paragraphs discussing subjects, which were inductively identified within the context in which they appear. Words after all can have different meanings depending on their context. The amount of times these subjects appear, moreover, are the first, and not the final step, in the process of data gathering, as these subjects and their predicates are then used to identify patterns in which social meanings "constitute the parameters of a particular world" (Fierke 2007, 85). The focus on subject position, as well as the relatively large amount of texts used, also minimizes the limitations of using translated texts instead of the original Persian.

7. Khamenei, "Leader's Speech to the Residents of the Eastern Azarbaijan."

8. For example, Khamenei, "Ayatollah Khamenei: The Cardinal Purpose"; "Leader Receives Air Force Servicemen"; "Fourth International Conference."

9. Ahmadinejad, "President Ahmadinejad Addressing 62nd UN General Assembly."

10. Ahmadinejad, "President Congratulates Pope."

11. Ibid. Similarly, Khamenei, "Leader's Address to the Iranian People from Various Social Strata."

12. Khamenei, "Leader's Address to the Officials and Executives of The Islamic Republic."

13. Norman Fairclough, "The Discourse of New Labour," in *Discourse as Data*, ed. M. Wetherell, S. Yates, and S. Taylor (London: Sage, 2001), 234–239.

14. Ahmadinejad, "President Ahmadinejad Addressing 62nd UN General Assembly"; "Text of the President's Speech, Addressing African Nations"; "President Ahmadinejad Addressed the U.N. 64rd General Assembly."

15. Ahmadinejad, "President Ahmadinejad Addressing 62nd UN General Assembly"; "Full Text of President's Address to APA General Assembly"; "President Speech in Durban II."

16. Ahmadinejad, "President Ahmadinejad Addressing 62nd UN General Assembly"; "President Ahmadinejad Addressing the 11th Summit of the Organization of the Islamic Conference in Senegal"; Khamenei, "Leader Receives Air Force Servicemen."

17. For example, Ahmadinejad, "President Ahmadinejad's Speech Addressing the UN General Assembly." http://www.president.ir/en/print.php?ArtID=12188&noimage; Khamenei, "Leader's Speech on Feast of Mab'ath"; "Leader's Address to the Officials and Executives of the Islamic Republic."

18. Khamenei, "Fourth International Conference for Support."

19. Ahmadinejad, "President Ahmadinejad Addressing 62nd UN General Assembly."

20. For example, Ahmadinejad, "President Ahmadinejad Addressing the 11th Summit"; Khamenei, "Fourth International Conference for Support."

21. Ahmadinejad, "President Ahmadinejad Addressing the 11th Summit."

22. Ahmadinejad, "President Ahmadinejad's Speech Addressing the UN General Assembly"; Khamenei in this regard talks mainly about Israel escaping punishment: for example, Khamenei, "Fourth International Conference for Support."

23. Ahmadinejad, "President: D-8 Can Be Pioneer of Peace."

24. Khamenei, "Leader Appreciates Armed forces."

25. Two examples: During a speech to government officials on the event of Eid al-Fitr, Khamenei recounted how the arrogant powers with all their technological development nevertheless felt subjugated to the Muslim world, and said: "If there are any people who think otherwise, they should know that they are denying the realities." (Khamenei, "Supreme Leader's Public Address on Eid Ul-Fitr.") Another example is Ahmadinejad addressing the United Nations General Assembly: "Of course, you are already aware of what I am talking about, but I think it is necessary to remind ourselves." (Ahmadinejad, "President Ahmadinejad's Speech Addressing the UN General Assembly).

26. Khamenei, "Supreme Leader's Speech to Air force Staff."

27. For example, Khamenei, "IR Leader Sends Congrats Message to Nasrallah"; "Ayatollah Khamenei: The Cardinal Purpose of Hajj";

Ahmadinejad, "President Ahmadinejad Addressed the U.N. 64rd General Assembly."

28. Ali Khamenei, "The Message of H. E. Ayatullah Khamenei to the Hajj Pilgrims from the Whole World."
29. Khamenei, "Leader's Address to the Officials."
30. See Ahmadinejad, "President Ahmadinejad's Speech Addressing the UN General Assembly"; "Text of the President's Speech, Addressing African Nations; "Full Text of President's Address to APA."
31. Ibid.
32. Ahmadinejad, "Full Text of President's Address to APA."
33. Ahmadinejad, "President Congratulates Pope"; "Message for the Birth of Jesus."
34. See Ahmadinejad, "President Ahmadinejad Addressing 62nd UN General Assembly."
35. Ahmadinejad, "President Congratulates Pope"; "Message for the Birth of Jesus."
36. Fierke, *Critical Approaches.*
37. Ahmadinejad, "President Ahmadinejad Addressing 62nd UN General Assembly."
38. Khamenei, "Supreme Leader's Public Address on Eid Ul-Fitr."
39. Fierke, "Besting the West."
40. Ahmadinejad, "President Ahmadinejad Addressed the U.N. 64rd General Assembly."
41. Ahmadinejad, "President Ahmadinejad Addressing 62nd UN General Assembly."
42. Hansen, *Security as Practice,* 39.
43. See, for example, Khamenei's remarks about the constitutional revolution, Khamenei, "Leader's Speech to the Residents of the Eastern Azarbaijan Province."
44. Khamenei, "IR Leader Receives Cinema Directors."
45. Khamenei, "Message to the Hajj Pilgrims from the Whole World," 2006.
46. Khamenei, "Supreme Leader's Speech to Air Force Staff."
47. The word popular in the context of this chapter is used in its meaning "of the people," following the OED definition: "Of, relating to, deriving from, or consisting of ordinary people or the people as a whole; generated by the general public; democratic." The concept is close to but should not be confused with populism, which means "seeking to represent the interests of ordinary people." (Oxford English Dictionary, 2011). Although in particular Ahmadinejad can be labeled as a populist, what is particularly present in the discourse used by both leaders is an emphasis on Iran's identity as a nation of the people, as a whole, particularly (but not exclusively) through its democratic character.
48. Khamenei, "Leader Receives Air Force Servicemen."
49. Khamenei, "Leader's Address to the Iranian People from Various Social Strata."

50. Khamenei, "Supreme Leader's Speech to Air Force Staff."
51. Khamenei, "Leader's Message in Commemoration of Martyrs."
52. Khamenei, "Leader's Speech to Governor-Generals."
53. Khamenei "Leader's Statements in a Meeting with Residents of Dasht-e-Azadegan"; "Leader's Address to University Professors"; "President Ahmadinejad Addressing 62nd UN General Assembly."
54. Khamenei, "Leader's Statements at the Tehran Friday Prayers"; "The Message of H. E. Ayatullah Khamenei to the Hajj Pilgrims from the Whole World"; "Leader Receives Air force Servicemen"; "Ayatollah Khamenei Thanks Nation"; "Leader's Speech to the Residents of Qom"; "Supreme Leader's Speech to Air force Staff"; "Your Islamic Republic Threw Challenge to All anti-Religion or anti-People Models of Government"; "Supreme Leader's Speech to Government Officials on Eid Ul-Fitr"; "President Elect is President of All Iranians"; "The Message of H. E. Ayatullah Khamenei to the Hajj pilgrims"; "Leader's Statements at the Tehran Friday Prayers"; Ahmadinejad, "A Reply to an American Mother's Message."
55. Khamenei "Leader's Address to Executive Officials"; Ahmadinejad "President Ahmadinejad Addressing 62nd UN General Assembly".
56. Khamenei "The Message of H. E. Ayatullah Khamenei to the Hajj Pilgrims from the Whole World," 2006; "The Message of H. E. Ayatullah Khamenei to the Hajj pilgrims," 2009;"Leader's Speech to Residents of the Holy City of Qom"; Ahmadinejad "President Ahmadinejad's Speech Addressing the UN General Assembly."
57. Khamenei "Leader's Address to War-Disabled Veterans"; Ahmadinejad "President Ahmadinejad Addressed the U.N. 64rd General Assembly."
58. Ahmadinejad "President Ahmadinejad Addressing 62nd UN General Assembly," Iran defends its rights: "President Ahmadinejad Addressed the U.N. 64rd General Assembly,"Khamenei "Leader's Statements at the Tehran Friday Prayers"; "Leader's Speech to Residents of the Holy City of Qom";"Leader's Address to the Iranian People from Various Social Strata"; "Ayatollah Khamenei Thanks Nation";"Leader's Speech to the Residents of Qom"; "Leader's Speech to the Residents of the Eastern Azarbaijan Province"; is a victim of terrorism: "President Ahmadinejad Addressed the U.N. 64rd General Assembly."
59. Khamenei, "Leader's Address to the Iranian People from Various Social Strata"; "Leader's Speech to the Residents of Qom";"Leader's Address to the Participants in the 2nd Congress in Commemoration of Ibn Maytham Bahrani."
60. Ahmadinejad, "President Ahmadinejad Addressing 62nd UN General Assembly"; Khamenei "Leader Appreciates Armed forces"; "Leader Receives Air force Servicemen"; "Leader's Statements in a Meeting with Residents of Dasht-e-Azadegan, Sousangerd, Bostan, Hamidiyeh and Hovayzeh";"Ayatollah Khamenei: The Cardinal Purpose of Hajj

is to Show the United Identity of the Muslim Ummah"; "Leader's Speech to the Residents of the Eastern Azarbaijan Province."

61. Khamenei "President Elect is President of All Iranians"; "The Message of H. E. Ayatullah Khamenei to the Hajj pilgrims," 2009.
62. Khamenei, "Leader's Speech to the Residents of the Eastern Azarbaijan"; "The Message of H. E. Ayatullah Khamenei to the Hajj pilgrims," (2009).
63. Khamenei, "Supreme Leader's Speech to Air Force Staff."
64. Khamenei, "Message to the Hajj Pilgrims from the Whole World," 2006.
65. Khamenei, "Leader's Address to University Professors and Elite Academics."
66. Ibid.
67. Khamenei, "Supreme Leader's Speech to Air Force Staff."
68. Khamenei, "Supreme Leader's Public Address on Eid Ul-Fitr."
69. Ahmadinejad, "President Ahmadinejad Addressed the U.N. 64rd General Assembly."
70. Khamenei, "Ayatollah Khamenei Thanks Nation."
71. Khamenei, "IR Leader Receives Cinema Directors."
72. Khamenei, "Leader's Address to the Iranian People."
73. Ibid.
74. Khamenei, "Leader's Statements at the Tehran Friday Prayers."
75. Khamenei, "Leader's Statements in a Meeting with Residents of Dasht-e-Azadegan."
76. Khamenei, "Leader's Statements at the Tehran Friday Prayers."
77. Ali Khamenei, "The Message of H. E. Ayatullah Khamenei to the Hajj Pilgrims from the Whole World," (2008)
78. Abrahamian, *A History of Modern Iran.*
79. Khamenei, "Leader Receives Air Force Servicemen."
80. When not made explicit, Hezbollah is implied in the term "Lebanon."
81. All three countries are a victim of aggression and bombings, discord (usually caused by the enemy), martyrdom, and violation of their rights. Iran, Palestine, Iraq, and Afghanistan are all described as experiencing sorrow and grief, insecurity and threat, and domination (for Iran in the past). Iran, Palestine, and Lebanon are victims of plotting; Iran, Palestine, and Iraq of propaganda and terrorism and Iran and Palestine of false accusations. Palestine, Iraq, Afghanistan, and Lebanon all share the following attributes: victims of homelessness, massacre, suffering, oppression, occupation, assassination, and criminal acts. With the exception of Afghanistan, these countries also share with Iran the following positive attributes: victory, awakening, changed nature, determination, hatred (toward the West, presumably), resistance, courage, dignity, faith, God, honour, struggle, future success, former tyranny, power, awareness, steadfastness, brotherhood, development, glory,

hope, independence, Islam, having resources, nobleness, confrontation of oppression, democracy, pride, willpower, and defeat of the arrogant powers. Iran, Palestine, and Lebanon are most alike in these predicates, whereas Iraq has the least in common with the other three.

82. Khamenei, "Leader Receives Air Force Servicemen."

83. Khamenei, "Ayatollah Khamenei: The Cardinal Purpose."

84. The Ummah is accused of (in order of salience from high to low) silence and indifference, humiliation, betrayal/treachery, cooperation with the West, blackmail, ignorance, evil, bullying, excommunication of Muslims, indolence, inferiority, irresponsibility, laziness, irrational, yielding to temptations, fabricating threats, and weakness. The Arab world is criticized for their silence and indifference, betrayal/treachery, being used by the enemy, blackmail, bullying, (false) claims to be Muslims, opposing Iran, lack of honor, and bad reputation.

85. Khamenei, "Ayatollah Khamenei: The Cardinal Purpose"; Ali Khamenei, "Leader's Address to the Participants in the 2nd Congress"; Ali Khamenei, "Palestinian Issue, at Focal Point"; Khamenei, "Message to the Hajj Pilgrims From the Whole World," 2006.

86. Suggested change for the Ummah (in order of salience from high to low): The Ummah should be united, have solidarity, be dutiful, be vigilant, support the Palestinians, support the oppressed, have dignity, solve problems, be resistant, be aware, have compassion or empathy, be powerful, have piety, have hope, be an example, defend themselves, turn to Islam, not be silent, fight humiliation, awaken, be principled, oppose the Zionists, have faith, and be independent.

87. Khamenei, "Leader's Speech to the Residents of Qom."

88. Ahmadinejad, "Text of the President's Speech, Addressing African Nations."

89. Ahmadinejad, "Full Text of President's Address to APA."

90. Ahmadinejad, "President Ahmadinejad's Speech Addressing the UN General Assembly."

91. Ahmadinejad, "President Ahmadinejad Addressing 62nd UN General Assembly."

92. Ahmadinejad, "President Ahmadinejad Addressed the U.N. 64rd General Assembly."

93. Predicates arrogant powers (the West, bullying powers, domineering powers, etc.) in order of salience (high-low): domination, sowing discord, hegemony, psychological warfare, threats, militarism, deliberately causing insecurity, greed, plundering, plotting, imposition, enmity, bullying, aggression, immorality, hindering progress of other nations, oppression, colonialism, making instrumental use of the security council, lying, human rights violation (domestic), weapons, supporting the zionists, poverty, murder, monopolizing science, evilness, drafting international law, double standards, preventing the security council from operating properly, occupation, materialism, consumerism, destruction, falsely defining democracy, and war.

94. For the identification of a threat, this may be less relevant, as having a common threat in itself is usually enough to create a sense togetherness among people. This threat does not even need be human—it could be a natural disaster. Undoubtedly, this common threat shapes the identity of the group that shares this threat.

95. See Mahmoud Ahmadinejad, "A Reply to an American Mother's Message"; "President Ahmadinejad Addressing the 11th Summit"; "Ahmadinejad: Gaza, Sight for Independent Nations and Govt's Victory over Oppressor Powers' Will"; "President Ahmadinejad Addressed the U.N. 64rd General Assembly"; Khamenei, "Palestinian Issue, at Focal Point"; "Ayatollah Khamenei Condemns Qana Tragedy"; "IR Leader Sends Congrats Message to Nasrallah"; "Ayatollah Khamenei: The Cardinal Purpose"; "Mughniyeh's Blood Would Double the Resistance"; "Islamic Umma Must Generate Waves of Wrath"; "The Message of H. E. Ayatullah Khamenei to the Hajj Pilgrims from the Whole World"; Ali Khamenei, "Islamic Revolution Leader Issued a Statement Sunday on the Horrendous Tragedy of Gaza Bloodbath in the Hand of the Zionists"; "Fourth International Conference for Support.".

96. Khamenei, "Fourth International Conference for Support."

97. Khamenei, "Leader's Statements at the Graduation Ceremony of Army Cadets"; "Supreme Leader's Public Address on Eid Ul-Fitr."

98. Ahmadinejad, "President Ahmadinejad Addressed the U.N. 64rd General Assembly"; Khamenei, "Leader's Statements at the Tehran Friday Prayers"; "Leader's Speech to Government Officials on the Eid-al-Fitr"; "Fourth International Conference for Support."

99. Ahmadinejad was criticized for calling for the destruction of Israel in the fall of 2005. Hunter (*Iran's Foreign Policy*) writes that Ahmadinejad had, in fact, repeated Khomeini's statement that *Israel az sahneh-e rouzegar mahv shavad*: Israel will disappear from the stage of time. Another source quotes Ahmadinejad as saying *Emam goft een rezhim-e eshghalgar-e qods bayad az safheh-ye ruzegar mahv shavad*: "Imam said this occupying regime in Jerusalem must vanish from the page of times." (Sam Sedaei, "The Biggest Lie Told to the American People: Ahmadinejad's Alleged Remarks on Israel," *Huffington Post* October 29, 2007. http://www.huffingtonpost.com/sam-sedaei/the-biggest-lie-told-to-t_b_70248.html). Either way, the correct translation from the original Persian would be along the following lines: "The occupier of Jerusalem must disappear from the stage (or page) of time, "not" it should be wiped off the map," let alone "it should be made disappear."

100. Khamenei, "Leader's Speech to Government Officials on the Eid-al-Fitr."

101. Khamenei, "Leader's Address to University Professors and Elite Academics."

102. Ahmadinejad, "Ahmadinejad Proposed Designation of 2011."

103. Ahmadinejad, "President Ahmadinejad Addressed the U.N. 64rd General Assembly."
104. Khamenei, "Leader's Speech on Feast of Mab'ath"; "Supreme Leader's Public Address on Eid Ul-Fitr."
105. Ahmadinejad, "President Ahmadinejad Addressing 62nd UN General Assembly."
106. Ahmadinejad, "President Ahmadinejad Addressing the 11th Summit."
107. Khamenei, "Leader Receives Air Force Servicemen."
108. Khamenei, "The Message of H.E. Ayatullah Khamenei to the Hajj Pilgrims From the Whole World," (2007).
109. The Arab World is implied in the Ummah, as Islam is the dominant religion in the Arab world.
110. Khamenei, "Leader's Speech to Residents of the Holy City of Qom."
111. See footnote 86.
112. Khamenei, "Leader Receives Air Force Servicemen."
113. Khamenei, "Leader's Address to Executive Officials."
114. Khamenei, "Leader's Statements at the Tehran Friday Prayers."
115. See chapter 6.
116. Ahmadinejad, "President Ahmadinejad Addressed the U.N. 64rd General Assembly"; "Reply to American Mother"; "President Ahmadinejad's Speech Addressing the UN General Assembly"; Khamenei, "Leader's Statements at the Graduation Ceremony of Army Cadets"; "Leader's Statements at the Tehran Friday Prayers"; "Leader Appreciates Armed Forces"; "Leader Receives Air Force Servicemen"; "Leader's Speech to the Residents of Qom"; "Leader's Speech to the Residents of the Eastern Azarbaijan Province"; "Supreme Leader's Public Address on Eid Ul-Fitr."
117. Khamenei, "US Forces."
118. Ahmadinejad, "Reply to American Mother."
119. Ahmadinejad, "President Ahmadinejad Addressing 62nd UN General Assembly"; Khamenei, "Leader Receives Air Force Servicemen"; Khamenei, "Ayatollah Khamenei: The Cardinal Purpose" Khamenei, "Fourth International Conference for Support."
120. Ahmadinejad, "President Ahmadinejad Addressed the U.N. 64rd General Assembly"; Khamenei, "Leader's Speech on Feast of Mab'ath"; Khamenei, "Leader Receives Air Force Servicemen."
121. Khamenei, "Ayatollah Khamenei: The Cardinal Purpose."
122. Iran's moral identity as described by both by Khamenei and Ahmadinejad (in order of salience, high-low): Iran promotes justice, is resistant, defends its rights, supports the Palestinians, promotes friendship, is dutiful, has proposals (take initiative), offers its assistance, is not aggressive, takes constructive measures, values human dignity, is not seeking nuclear weapons, observes international law, and stands by the oppressed.

123. Khamenei, "Leader's Speech to Governor-Generals."
124. Hansen, *Security as Practice*, 50.
125. Khamenei, "Leader's Address to the Iranian People."
126. Ahmadinejad, "President Ahmadinejad Addressed the U.N. 64rd General Assembly."
127. Khamenei, "Leader's Address to the Iranian People."
128. Khamenei, "Leader's Address to the Participants in the 2nd Congress."
129. Khamenei, "Fourth International Conference for Support."
130. Khamenei, "IR Leader Receives Cinema Directors."
131. Khamenei, "IR Leader Receives Cinema Directors"; Khamenei, "Leader's Address to the Iranian People"; Khamenei, "Islamic Republic, Modern Example"; Khamenei, "Supreme Leader's Public Address on Eid Ul-Fitr."
132. Ahmadinejad, "Reply to American Mother"; Ahmadinejad, "President Ahmadinejad Addressing 62nd UN General Assembly."
133. Hansen, *Security as Practice*, 19–20.

5 Iranian Foreign Policy Behavior 2005–2013

1. Manouchehr Mottaki, "Iran's foreign Policy Under President Ahmadinejad," *Discourse: An Iranian Quarterly* 8, no. 2 (2009): 1–15.
2. Xinhua General News Service, "Iran FM Expresses Keenness to Further Cooperate with GCC, Iraq," October 7, 2005; Agence France Presse, "Iranian FM Visits Qatar," October 6, 2005, LexisNexis Academic.
3. Jamal Halaby, "Iran foreign Minister Visits Jordan," Associated Press May 17, 2006, LexisNexis Academic.
4. IRNA, "President-Ahmad-Bahrain," March 1, 2006, LexisNexis Academic; Daniel Williams, "Tehran Courts Support of Arabs; Officials Seek Alliances, Backing for Nuclear Program," *The Washington Post* March 20, 2006, LexisNexis Academic.
5. Steven R. Hurst and Diana Elias, "Arab Distrust of Iran Gains Momentum," *Associated Press* May 3, 2006, LexisNexis Academic.
6. IRNA, "Riyadh-Visit-Iran," April 12, 2006, LexisNexis Academic.
7. Although well aware that the accepted designation for this body of water is Persian Gulf, the word Gulf will also be used in this study, both as an abbreviation of the word Persian Gulf as well as to avoid confusion about the nationality of the inhabitants of the Gulf countries or GCC member states, which are Arab.
8. Fareed Zakaria, "For Iran, a Policy of Patience," *The Washington Post* September 25, 2006, LexisNexis Academic.
9. Hurst and Elias, "Arab Distrust."
10. Roula Khalaf, "Resurgent Iran Sets Challenge for Arab Rulers in Troubled Gulf Sunni Regimes Are Struggling to Formulate a Strategy

to Deal with a Shift in the Balance of Power, Reports Roula Khalaf," *The Financial Times* January 2, 2007, LexisNexis Academic.

11. Mahjoob Zweiri, "Arab-Iranian relations: New realities?," in *Iran's Foreign Policy from Khatami to Ahmadinejad*, ed. Mahjoob Zweiri and Anoushiravan Ehteshami (Reading: Ithaca Press, 2008), 115–128.

12. Arshin Adib-Moghaddam, *The International Politics of the Persian Gulf: A Cultural Genealogy* (London: Routledge, 2006).

13. Agence France Presse, "Bahrain Fears Fallout from Iran Nuclear Crisis," June 2006, LexisNexis Academic.

14. Jim Krane, "Many Gulf Arabs Uneasy about Iran," *Associated Press* April 6, 2006, LexisNexis Academic.

15. H. M. Fattah, "Iran's Growing Power Has Saudis Worried; Riyadh Weighs How to Confront Tehran," *International Herald Tribune* December 22, 2006, LexisNexis Academic.

16. Roula Khalaf, "Iran-Saudi Talks Aim to Reduce Tensions," *The Financial Times* March 3, 2007, LexisNexis Academic.

17. "A Dodgy Dossier on Iran's Activity in Iraq: The U.S. Should Start a More Diplomatic Offensive Against Tehran," *The Financial Times* February 13, 2007, LexisNexis Academic.

18. Robin B. Wright, "As Pressure for Talks Grows, Iran and Syria Gain Leverage," *The Washington Post* November 16, 2006, LexisNexis Academic.

19. Julian Borger, "Middle East: Strategy: Surprising Partners Among Tehran's Layer of Alliances," *The Guardian* February 10, 2007, LexisNexis Academic; Mohsen M. Milani, "Tehran's Take," *Foreign Affairs* 88, no. 4 (2009): 46–62.

20. "Lots of people in the Shi'a community are happy to take Iranian money and arms but they are not willing to take Iranian orders." Patrick Clawson (quoted by Wright, "As Pressure for Talks Grows, Iran and Syria Gain Leverage") of the Washington Institute for Near East Policy.

21. IRNA, "Iraqi President Arrives in Tehran," November 21, 2005, LexisNexis Academic; "Talabani 'Trusts in Iran Support,'" BBC News November 21, 2005, LexisNexis Academic.

22. Babak Rahimi, "Iran's Declining Influence in Iraq," *The Washington Quarterly* Winter 2012, 25–40.

23. Roula Khalaf, "Sunni Arab States Wary of Role for Iran Jordan, Egypt and Saudi Arabia Are Keen to Head Off Any Move by the U.S. to Talk to Tehran, Reports Roula Khalaf," *The Financial Times* November 30, 2006, Lexisnexis Academic.

24. IRNA, "Algerian-Lebanon-Israel," August 14, 2006, LexisNexis Academic.

25. S. Al-Shibani, "A Very Important Visit," trans. BBC Monitoring, *Tishrin Website* January 22, 2006, LexisNexis Academic.

26. Lara Marlowe, "Syria and Iran Take a Stand Against U.S. and the West," *The Irish Times* January 21, 2006, LexisNexis Academic.

27. Hugh Naylor, "U.S. Sanctions Drive Iranian Businesses and Exports to Syria," *International Herald Tribune* October 4, 2007, LexisNexis Academic.
28. Hunter, *Iran's Foreign Policy*, 68.
29. Khalaf, "Sunni Arab States Wary."
30. Khalaf, "Iran-Saudi Talks."
31. Heba Saleh, "Saudi Arabia Offers Counterweight to Resurgent Iran," *The Financial Times* February 7, 2007, LexisNexis Academic.
32. Nasser Karimi, "Iran Blames U.S., Britain for Bombings," *Associated Press* January 26, 2006, LexisNexis Academic.
33. Nasser Karimi, "Iranian President Blames U.S., Israel for Destruction of Samarra Shrine's Golden Dome," *Associated Press Worldstream* February 23, 2006, LexisNexis Academic.
34. Robin B. Wright, "Iran is Critical as U.S. Unveils Arms Sales in the Middle East," *The Washington Post* July 31, 2007, LexisNexis Academic.
35. Michael Slackman and Robert F. Worth. "Arab Leaders on Edge as Iran Stretches its Sway; Welcome Mat Isn't Out for Tehran Officials at League Summit in Qatar," *International Herald Tribune* March 31, 2009. http://academic.lexisnexis.nl/uva/.
36. Slackman and Worth, "Arab Leaders on Edge."
37. Sudarsan Raghavan, "Yemen Denounces Iran's 'Interference'; Sunni Government Says Shiite Tehran Meddling in Conflict with Rebels," *The Washington Post* November 12, 2009, LexisNexis Academic.
38. Najmeh Bozorgmehr, "Iran Says Saudis Seized Atom Expert," *The Financial Times* December 9, 2009, LexisNexis Academic.
39. Ian Black, "The U.S. Embassy Cables: Reaction: Iran Dismisses Arab Worries as Psychological Warfare: Middle East Reaction," *The Guardian* November 30, 2010, LexisNexis Academic.
40. Hunter, *Iran's Foreign Policy*.
41. Mark Landler, "Tehran Casts its Shadow on Clinton Mideast Trip; Iran Is on the Agenda, If Not the Itinerary," *International Herald Tribune* March 6, 2009, LexisNexis Academic.
42. Mahmoud Ahmadinejad, "Full Text of Speech Presented by H.E. Dr. Mahmoud Ahmadinejad," August 30, 2012. http://www.president.ir/en/41317/printable.
43. "Supreme Leader Meets with Participants of International Conference on Islamic Awakening," Office of the Supreme Leader Sayyid Ali Khamenei, December 11, 2012. http://www.leader.ir/langs/en/?p=contentShow&id=10215.
44. Ahmadinejad, "Full Text of Speech"; The Office of the Supreme Leader, "Imam Khomeini, Father of Islamic Awakening," June 3, 2012. http://www.leader.ir/langs/en/?p=contentShow&id=9483.
45. Iran Diplomacy, "Iran-Egypt Relations Enters a New Phase," February 18, 2010. http://www.irdiplomacy.ir/en/page/1471/IranEgypt+Relations+Enters+a+New+Phase.html.

46. BBC News, "Iran President Ahmadinejad Begins Historic Egypt Visit," February 5, 2013. http://www.co.uk/news/world-middle-east-21336367.

47. "Egyptian Official Says Cairo May Open Embassy in Iran Soon, Reports Iranian Media," *Egypt Independent* August 28, 2012. http://www.egyptindependent.com/news/egyptian-official-says-cairo-may-open-embassy-iran-soon-reports-iranian-media; Fars News Agency, "Iran After Opening Embassy in Egypt," April 16, 2012. http://english.farsnews.com/newstext.php?nn=9101142029; Effort on Egyptian side to include Iran in solving regional problems: David D. Kirkpatrick, "Egyptian President Seeks Regional Initiative for Syria Peace," *The New York Times* August 26, 2012, sec. World / Middle East. http://www.nytimes.com/2012/08/27/world/middleeast/egyptian-president-seeks-regional-initiative-for-syria-peace.html.

48. In March 2013, the first flight in 34 years to Tehran took off from Cairo Airport. "AP Interview: Egypt's Tourism Minister Says Iranian Tourists Pose No Threat to Egypt," Text Article, *Associated Press* March 28, 2013. http://www.foxnews.com/world/2013/03/28/ap-interview-egypt-tourism-minister-says-iranian-tourists-pose-no-threat-to/. There were also initiatives in the field of economic cooperation: "Iran Plans US$5 Bln Worth of Investments in Egypt," *Egypt Independent* February 19, 2012. http://www.egyptindependent.com/news/iran-plans-us5-bln-worth-investments-egypt.

49. "Salafis Plan Tahrir Demo to Protest Iran, Shia Relations," *Egypt Independent* March 3, 2013. http://www.egyptindependent.com/news/salafis-plan-tahrir-demo-protest-iran-shia-relations; "Protests Outside Iranian Embassy," *Egypt Independent* February 2, 2013. http://www.egyptindependent.com/news/protests-outside-iranian-embassy; Reuters, "Egypt Suspends Commercial Flights from Iran After Protests," April 8, 2013. http://www.reuters.com/article/2013/04/08/egypt-iran-idUSL5N0CV0NL20130408; Shoe throwing: BBC News, "Iranian Leader Targeted with Shoe," February 6, 2013, sec. Middle East. http://www.co.uk/news/world-middle-east-21348630.

50. "Egypt's President Morsi to Visit Saudi Arabia on Wednesday," *Ahram Online* July 10, 2012. http://english.ahram.org.eg/News/47362.aspx.

51. Statements Morsi at NAM Saeed Kamali Dehghan, "Non-aligned Movement Summit: 'You'd Think Iran Was Hosting the Olympics,'" *The Guardian* August 30, 2012, sec. World News. http://www.guardian.co.uk/world/2012/aug/30/iran-non-aligned-movement-summit.

52. Maysam Behravesh, "Revolt in Syria: An Alternative View from Iran," October 3, 2011. http://www.irdiplomacy.ir/en/page/16724/Revolt+in+Syria+An+alternative+view+from+Iran.html.

53. Ibid.

54. Fares Akram, "Hamas Supports Syrian Opposition," *The New York Times* February 24, 2012, sec. World, Middle East. http://www.nytimes.com/2012/02/25/world/middleeast/hamas-leader-supports-syrian-opposition.html.

55. Fares Akram and Jodi Rudoren, "Hamas Says Egypt Will Reopen Crossing Into Gaza," *The New York Times* August 25, 2012, sec. World, Middle East. http://www.nytimes.com/2012/08/26/world/middleeast/hamas-says-egypt-will-reopen-crossing-into-gaza.html.

56. "Hamas Military Wing Denies Planning Deadly Attack on Rafah Army Camp," *Egypt Independent* March 14, 2013. http://www.egyptindependent.com/news/hamas-military-wing-denies-planning-deadly-attack-rafah-army-camp.

57. "Iran Sought Turkey's Help to Mend Links with U.S., says Erdogan," *Guardian Unlimited* February 24, 2009, LexisNexis Academic.

58. Asli Kandemir, "Exclusive: Turkey-Iran Gold Trade Wiped Out by New U.S. Sanctions," *Reuters* February 16, 2013. http://www.reuters.com/article/2013/02/16/us-iran-turkey-sanctions-idUSBRE91F01F20130216; Valentin Mândrăşescu, "Turkey Trade with Iran to Resume Despite the US Sanctions," Radio the Voice of Russia, March 31, 2013 http://english.ruvr.ru/2013_03_31/Turkey-trade-with-Iran-to-resume-despite-the-US-sanctions/; "Turkey-Iran Gold-for-Gas Hits $120 Million in a Month," *Hurriyet Daily News* April 1, 2013. http://www.hurriyetdailynews.com/turkey-iran-gold-trade-resumes-after-stopping-in-january.aspx?pageID=238&nID=43982&NewsCatID=344.

59. Semih Idiz, "Turkey-Iran Ties Strained By Iraq, Syria—Al-Monitor: The Pulse of the Middle East," *Al-Monitor* February 19, 2013. http://www.al-monitor.com/pulse/originals/2013/02/turkey-iran-tensions-rise-syria.html.

60. "Turkey to Site NATO Missile Shield Radar in its South-East," *The Guardian* September 14, 2011, sec. World news. http://www.guardian.co.uk/world/2011/sep/14/turkey-nato-missile-shield-radar.

61. "Iran Attacks Turkey's NATO Shield, If Hit," PressTV November 26, 2011, http://www.presstv.ir/detail/212321.html.

62. Robin Pomeroy, "Iran Tells Turkey: Change Tack or Face Trouble," *Reuters* October 8, 2011. http://www.reuters.com/article/2011/10/08/us-iran-turkey-khamenei-idUSTRE7970XI20111008.

63. Babak Rahimi, "Iran's Declining Influence in Iraq," *The Washington Quarterly* 5, no. 1 (Winter 2012): 35.

64. Ibid., 36.

65. See Adib-Moghaddam, *The International Politics of the Persian Gulf.*

66. Rahimi"Iran's Declining Influence in Iraq," 26.

67. BBC News, "On Board US Carrier in Strait of Hormuz," February 14, 2012, sec. Middle East. http://www.co.uk/news/world-middle

-east-17034496; Reuters, "Iran Renews Hormuz Closure Threats," July 15, 2012. http://www.reuters.com/article/2012/07/15 /us-iran-hormuz-idUSBRE86E0CN20120715.

68. BBC News, "Iran Says it Could Attack First," February 21, 2012, sec. Middle East. http://www.co.uk/news/world-middle-east -17116588.

69. Oil prices rose from around 60 U.S. dollar per barrel in 2006 to an approximate 140 dollars in the summer of 2008 after which it quickly dropped to around 40 U.S. dollars, slowly rising again to 90 dollars at the end of 2010, around which it stabilized for the rest of Ahmadinejad's presidency. Trading Economics, "Crude Oil Latest Data." http://www.tradingeconomics.com/commodity/crude-oil, Accessed May 13, 2013; Dmitry Zhdannikov and Claire Milhench, "Oil Bull Goldman Sees End to Rising Prices," *Reuters* October 18, 2012. http://www.reuters.com/article/2012/10/18/us-goldman -crude-research-idUSBRE89H0LC20121018.

70. Anna Fifield, "For Oil-rich Iran, Friends Are not Proving Hard to Find," *The Financial Times* May 28, 2008, LexisNexis Academic.

71. John Gee, "Behind Indonesia's Warm Welcome for Iranian President Ahmadinejad," *Washington Report on Middle East Affairs* August, 2006, LexisNexis Academic.

72. Ibid.

73. Mark Forbes, "Indonesia Offers Summit on Iran Crisis: Jakarta Says Muslim Nations Must be Involved in Finding Peaceful Solution to Deepening Nuclear Stand-off," *The Age* May 11, 2006, LexisNexis Academic.

74. Fifield 2008. Iran has limited oil-refining capacity partly due to international sanction, forcing it to import more than half its domestic need (Carroll 2007b).

75. Mottaki, "Iran's foreign Policy," 5.

76. Helene Cooper, "Voices of Discontent: Anti-U.S. Leaders Seek Allies," *The New York Times* September 23, 2006, LexisNexis Academic.

77. Ibid.

78. Ibid.

79. "Non-aligned Movement: A Two-edged Summit in Tehran," *The Guardian* August 29, 2012, sec. Comment is free. http://www .guardian.co.uk/commentisfree/2012/aug/29/non-aligned -movement-two-edged-summit-tehran.

80. Mahmoud Ahmadinejad, "Full Text of Speech Presented by H.E. Dr. Mahmoud Ahmadinejad," August 30, 2012. http://www.president.ir/en/41317/printable.

81. Chiponda Chimbelu, "Iran Makes Inroads in Parts of Africa," *Deutsche Welle* February 28, 2010, LexisNexis Academic.

82. Chris Mcgreal, "Zimbabwe Bans Western Observers from Ballot: Fears of Rigging as Mugabe Faces Strong Challenges: China and Iran

among Few foreign Teams Allowed In," *The Guardian* March 8, 2008, LexisNexis Academic.

83. Fifield, "For Oil-rich Iran."

84. Blessing-Miles Tendi, "Iran's Africa foray No Cause for Panic," *Guardian Unlimited* April 28, 2010, LexisNexis Academic.

85. Fars News Agency, "President Ahmadinejad to Go on Tour of Africa in Days," April 6, 2012. http://english.farsnews.com/newstext .php?nn=9107158026.

86. Fars News Agency, "President Ahmadinejad to Go on Tour."

87. In September 2006, Ahmadinejad visited Cuba for the NAM summit and Venezuela; in January 2007, he visited Venezuela, Nicaragua, and Ecuador; in September 2007, Bolivia and Venezuela; in November 2009, Venezuela, Bolivia, and Brazil; in January 2012, Venezuela, Nicaragua, Cuba, and Ecuador; and in June 2012, Venezuela, Bolivia, and Brazil.

88. "Venezuelan president Hugo Chávez visited Iran nine times, Nicaragua's Daniel Ortega has gone three times, Bolivian president Evo Morales twice, Ecuador's Rafael Correa once, Guyanese president Bharrat Jagdeo once, and Brazilian president Inacio Lula da Silva once." (Stephen Johnson, "Iran's Influence in the Americas: Full Report," March 12, 2012, Centre for Strategic and International Studies, IX.)

89. IRNA, "Day of Public Mourning announced in Iran for Hugo Chavez," March 6, 2013. http://www.irna.com/en/News/80572936/Politic /Day_of_public_mourning_announced_in_Iran_for_Hugo_Chavez.

90. Fifield, "For Oil-rich Iran."

91. S. Romero, "Iranian President Visits Venezuela to Strengthen Ties," *The New York Times* January 14, 2007, sec. International, Americas. http://www.nytimes.com/2007/01/14/world/americas/14iran .html.

92. See Andrew E. Kramer, "Despite Price Drop, Oil Cartel Keeps Production Limit," *The New York Times* June 14, 2012, sec. Business Day/Global Business. http://www.nytimes.com/2012/06/15 /business/global/opec-is-said-to-leave-production-steady.html.

93. Simon Romero, "Venezuela Says Iran Is Helping It Look for Uranium," *The New York Times* September 26, 2009, LexisNexis Academic; Johnson, "Iran's Influence in the Americas," 90–91.

94. Romero 2007a; Bozorgmehr 2007.

95. Simon Romero, "Iranian President Visits Venezuela to Strengthen Ties," *The New York Times* January 14, 2007a, LexisNexis Academic.

96. Simon Romero, "Venezuela and Iran Strengthen Ties with Caracas-to-Tehran Flight," *The New York Times* March 3, 2007b, LexisNexis Academic.

97. CNN, "Venezuela Defends Controversial Flights to Iran and Syria," August 22, 2010. http://edition.cnn.com/2010/WORLD /asiapcf/08/21/venezuela.flights.iran/index.html.

98. Johnson, "Iran's Influence in the Americas," 89–100.
99. Ibid., 64–65.
100. Ibid., 67.
101. Rory Carroll, "Venezuela Sells Petrol to Iran to Reinforce Front Against U.S.," *The Guardian* July 4, 2007a, LexisNexis Academic.
102. Anne-Marie O'Connor and Mary Beth Sheridan, "Iran's Invisible Nicaragua Embassy; Feared Stronghold Never Materialized," *The Washington Post* July 13, 2009, LexisNexis Academic.
103. O'Connor and Sheridan, "Iran's Invisible."
104. Johnson, "Iran's Influence in the Americas," 69.
105. DG Trade Statistics, "Iran: EU Bilateral Trade."
106. Johnson, "Iran's Influence in the Americas," 69.
107. DG Trade Statistics, "Iran: EU Bilateral Trade."
108. Carroll, "Venezuela Sells Petrol."
109. Najmeh Bozorgmehr, "Iran Praises Lula for His Mediator Role," *The Financial Times* May 17, 2010, LexisNexis Academic.
110. Tavernise, "Turkey Offers to Mediate Between U.S. and Iran."
111. "Iran Sought Turkey's Help," *Guardian Unlimited.*
112. "Remarks by Clinton, Treasury Secretary Geithner in Beijing; Answer Questions on North Korea, U.S.-China dialogue, Iran and more," United States State Department Documents and Publications, May 25, 2010, LexisNexis Academic.
113. IRNA, "Speaker Criticizes U.S. for Involvement in Iran's Bombing Attack," October 29, 2009, LexisNexis, Academic; Leila Fadel, "Iranian Nobel Winner Urges Obama to Stress Human Rights," *McClatchy-Tribune News Service* October 14, 2009, LexisNexis Academic.
114. Ali Akbar Salehi, "Head of Iran's Nuclear Organization on Nuclear Policy and Enrichment," trans. BBC Worldwide Monitoring, *Javan* March 18, 2010, LexisNexis Academic.
115. In fact, the 78 official transcripts and statements by Khamenei and Ahmadinejad that served as the basis of the discourse analysis in chapter 4 make mention of Russia only once, and the Soviet Union 11 times.
116. "Pursuing the Policy of Détente in the New Government," trans. BBC Worldwide Monitoring, *Mardom Salari* September 23, 2009, LexisNexis Academic.
117. Richard W. Bulliet, "Iran between the East and the West," *Journal of International Affairs* 60, no.2 (2007): 1–14.
118. Hunter, *Iran's Foreign Policy*, 140.
119. Fifield, "For Oil-rich Iran."
120. Milani, "Tehran's Take."
121. Dominic Barton and Kito De Boer, "Tread Lightly Along the New Silk Road," *The Financial Times* January 30, 2007, LexisNexis Academic; "Sinopec Signs Deal to Develop Iranian Oil; $2 Billion

Pact Firms Beijing-Tehran Links," *International Herald Tribune* December 11, 2007, LexisNexis Academic.

122. Ghoncheh Tazmini, "Russian-Iranian Relations in the Context of the Tehran Declaration," *Iranian Review of Foreign Affairs* 1, no. 3 (2010): 14.

123. Ibid., 19.

124. Glenn Kessler and Keith B. Richburg, "Russia Halts Sale of Air Defence Missiles to Iran: The Weapons Fall Under New U.N. Sanctions against Tehran," *The Washington Post* June 12, 2010, LexisNexis Academic.

125. Ibid.

126. Daniel Dombey and Jonathan Wheatley, "Brazil Ends its Role as Mediator," *The Financial Times* June 21, 2010, LexisNexis Academic.

127. Fierke, *Critical Approaches.*

128. BBC News, "Iran Leader Dismisses US Currency," November 18, 2007, sec. Americas. http://news.co.uk/2/hi/7101050.stm; Reuters, "UPDATE 1-Ahmadinejad Labels Iran Sanctions Worthless Paper," June 11, 2010. http://www.reuters.com/article/2010/06/11/nuclear-iran-china-idAFSGE65A0AY20100611.

129. Presidency of the Islamic Republic of Iran News Service (PIRINS), "Dr. Ahmadinejad Downplays Effects of Western Oil Embargos Against Iran," May 8, 2013. http://www.president.ir/en/48531.

6   "Nuclear Power Is Our Right!": The 2010 Tehran Declaration

1. Hunter, *Iran's Foreign Policy.* 63–66; David Albright and Andrea Stricker, "Iran's Nuclear Programme," in *The Iran Primer: Power, Politics, and U.S. Policy,* ed. Robin Wright (Washington, DC: United States Institute of Peace, 2010); Suzanne Maloney and United States Institute of Peace, *Iran's Long Reach: Iran as a Pivotal State in the Muslim World* (Washington, DC: United States Institute of Peace Press, 2008), 50–60; Shahram Chubin, *Iran's Nuclear Ambitions* (Washington, DC: Carnegie Endowment for International Peace, 2006).

2. Hunter, *Iran's Foreign Policy.*

3. Ibid.

4. See chapter 3.

5. BBC News, "Nuclear Fuel Declaration by Iran, Turkey and Brazil," May 17, 2010. http://news.BBCNews.co.uk/2/hi/middle_east/8686728.stm.

6. The documents used in this chapter are as follows: Mottaki, Fars News Agency, "Iran Foreign Minister-designate Says No Pre-conditions in Nuclear Talks with EU," trans. BBC Worldwide Monitoring, August 21, 2005, LexisNexis Academic; VIRIN,

"Foreign Minister Says Iran Wishes to Defuse Tension with UK," trans. BBC Worldwide Monitoring, October 19, 2005, LexisNexis Academic; VIRIN, "Iranian TV Interviews foreign Minister Mottaki on Qods Day," trans. BBC Worldwide Monitoring, October 27, 2005, LexisNexis Academic; IRINN, "Iran foreign Minister Calls for Purposeful Nuclear Talks with EU3," trans. BBC Worldwide Monitoring, December 21, 2005, LexisNexis Academic; VIRIN, "Iran foreign Minister and Russian President Discuss Tehran's Nuclear Policy," trans. BBC Worldwide Monitoring, January 11, 2006, LexisNexis Academic; VIRIN "Iranian foreign Minister Threatens to End Nuclear Cooperation If Case Referred to UN," trans. BBC Worldwide Monitoring, January 31, 2006, LexisNexis Academic; VIRIN, "Iranian Minister Says 'Essence' of Nuclear Incentive Package 'Could be Positive,'" trans. BBC Worldwide Monitoring, June 7, 2006, LexisNexis Academic; Al-Arabiya TV, Al-Arabiya TV, "Iran foreign Minister Discusses Policy on Nuclear, Iraq, Saudi, Lebanon Issues," trans. from Arabic by BBC Worldwide Monitoring, December 21, 2006, LexisNexis Academic; Al-Arabiya TV, "Iran Minister Downplays Brief US Contact on Al-Arabiya," trans. from Arabic by BBC Worldwide Monitoring, May 6, 2007, LexisNexis Academic; VIRIN, "Foreign Minister Says Iranian Diplomats to be Released in June," trans. BBC Worldwide Monitoring, May 10, 2007, LexisNexis Academic; Al-Alam TV, "Mottaki Rules Out US War on Iran, Says Iran Will Resume Cooperation with IAEA," trans. BBC Worldwide Monitoring, February 22, 2010, LexisNexis Academic; Al-Alam TV, "Iranian foreign Minister Comments on Stand-off with USA, Nuclear Fuel Swap," trans. BBC Worldwide Monitoring, February 21, 2010, LexisNexis Academic; "Head of Iran's Nuclear Organization on Nuclear Policy and Enrichment," trans. BBC Worldwide Monitoring, *Javan* March 17, 2010, LexisNexis Academic; "Iranian foreign Minister: Nuclear Disarmament an Achievable Goal," trans. BBC Worldwide Monitoring, Mehr News Agency, April 7, 2010, LexisNexis Academic; IRINN, "Iran foreign Minister Urges West to Give up on 'Biased' Views," trans. BBC Worldwide Monitoring, April 7, 2010, LexisNexis Academic; IRINN, "Iran FM Says Latest Obama Statements 'Propaganda,' Criticizes UN Security Council," trans. BBC Worldwide Monitoring, April 7, 2010, LexisNexis Academic; IRNA, "Foreign Minister: G5+1 Lack Political Will to Resolve Dispute on Iran Nuclear Programme," trans. BBC Worldwide Monitoring, April 7, 2010, LexisNexis Academic; IRINN, "Iran Minister Urges Dialogue, Trust Building—TV," trans. BBC Worldwide Monitoring, April 20, 2010, LexisNexis Academic; IRINN, "Iran's Nuclear Activities 'Transparent'—Foreign Minister," trans. BBC Worldwide Monitoring, April 20, 2010, LexisNexis Academic; IRNA, "Fuel Swap a Chance for Mutual

Trust-building—Iran Minister," trans. BBC Worldwide Monitoring, April 20, 2010, LexisNexis Academic; VIRIN, "Foreign Minister Says Iran Ready to Resume Nuclear Talks ASAP," trans. BBC Worldwide Monitoring, July 26, 2010, LexisNexis Academic; "US Admitting to Iran's Nuclear Right Positive—Foreign Minister," PressTV, December 5, 2010, LexisNexis Academic; Larijani: Ali A. Larijani, "Iranian Negotiator Gives Press Conference on Nuclear Issue," trans. BBC Worldwide Monitoring, Islamic Republic of Iran News Network, September 21, 2005, LexisNexis Academic; Ali A. Larijani, "Iran's Security Chief Explains Tehran's Nuclear Strategy in TV Interview," trans. BBC Worldwide Monitoring, Vision of the Islamic Republic of Iran (Television), January 1, 2006, LexisNexis Academic; Ali A. Larijani, "Iran's Nuclear Negotiator on Failure of Western Policy—Text of Interview," trans. BBC Worldwide Monitoring, Mehr News Agency, October 18, 2006, LexisNexis Academic; Ali A. Larijani, "Security Chief Warns West Not to Seek Adventurism on Iran's Nuclear Case," trans. BBC Worldwide Monitoring, Islamic Republic of Iran News Network, September 12, 2007, LexisNexis Academic; Jalili: Saeed Jalili, "Iran: Deputy foreign Minister Defends Nuclear Policy; Outlines foreign Policy," trans. BBC Worldwide Monitoring, Fars News Agency, March 7, 2007, LexisNexis Academic; Saeed Jalili, "Iran's Top Nuclear Negotiator Jalili Speaks of 'A Positive Climate,'" trans. BBC Worldwide Monitoring, Vision of the Islamic Republic of Iran (Television), December 1, 2007, LexisNexis Academic; VIRI, "If Some Are Unhappy About Iran's Rights That Is a 'Different Matter,'" trans. BBC Worldwide Monitoring, December 1, 2007, LexisNexis Academic; VIRI, "Top Nuclear Negotiator Defends Iran's 'Rights' in European Parliament," trans. BBC Worldwide Monitoring, January 23, 2008, LexisNexis Academic; Saeed Jalili, "Security Chief Says Nuclear Watchdog Report Confirms Iran's Truthfulness," trans. BBC Worldwide Monitoring, Islamic Republic of Iran News Network, February 22, 2008, LexisNexis Academic; IRINN, "Iranian Nuclear Negotiator Says 5+1 Talks 'Positive,'" trans. BBC Worldwide Monitoring, October 1, 2009, LexisNexis Academic; "Jalili's Bitter Chinese News for the US," trans. BBC Worldwide Monitoring, *Javan* April 3, 2010, LexisNexis Academic; Aqazadeh: ISNA, "There is No Legal Basis or UN Referral," trans. BBC Worldwide Monitoring, January 31, 2006, LexisNexis Academic; IRNA, "Installation of Nuclear Centrifuges Continues in Natanz—Iran Nuclear Official," April 17, 2007, LexisNexis Academic; Gholam Reza Aqazadeh, "Iran Willing to Continue Nuclear Talks with West," trans. BBC Worldwide Monitoring, Vision of the Islamic Republic of Iran (Television), February 16, 2006, LexisNexis Academic; Gholam Reza Aqazadeh, "Full Text of Iran's Statement to IAEA Meeting," Fars News Agency, September 17, 2007. http://

english.farsnews.com/printable.php?nn=8606260606;   Gholam
Reza Aqazadeh, "Iranian Nuclear Official Says the Country Now
Has 7,000 Centrifuges," trans. BBC Worldwide Monitoring, Islamic
Republic of Iran News Network, April 10, 2009, LexisNexis
Academic; Salehi: VIRIN, "New Head of Iran Nuclear Body Says
Committed to International Obligations," trans. BBC Worldwide
Monitoring, July 18, 2009, LexisNexis Academic; VIRIN, "Mass
Production of New Centrifuges to Start in 2011 Iran Nuclear Chief,"
BBC Worldwide Monitoring, January 9, 2010, LexisNexis Academic;
VIRIN, "Iran Ready to Stop 20-Per-Cent Enrichment If West
"Comes to its Senses," trans. BBC Worldwide Monitoring, February
8, 2010, LexisNexis Academic; Salehi, "Iran Nuclear Chief"; Salehi,
"Head of Iran's Nuclear"; "Head of Nuclear Program Says Iran
Ready to Find Way Out of Impasse," trans. BBC Worldwide
Monitoring, *Quds*, March 7, 2010, LexisNexis Academic; IRINN,
"Iran Nuclear Official Announces Production of Yellow Cake,"
trans. by BBC Worldwide Monitoring, December 5, 2010, LexisNexis
Academic; Qashqavi: VIRI, "US 'Confrontational Policy' Must Be
Changed—Iran Spokesman," trans. BBC Worldwide Monitoring,
December 8, 2008, LexisNexis Academic; VIRI, "Iran Spokesman
Dismisses US Efforts to Create Iranophobia in Region," trans. BBC
Worldwide Monitoring, December 22, 2008, LexisNexis Academic;
VIRI, "Iran Spokesman Says No Letter Received from US," trans.
BBC Worldwide Monitoring, September 2, 2009, LexisNexis
Academic; Hassan Qashqavi, "Spokesman Reacts to US Claims on
Iran's Nuclear Programme, Hollywood Films," trans. BBC
Worldwide Monitoring, Vision of the Islamic Republic of Iran
(Television). March 2, 2009, LexisNexis Academic; IRINN,
"Spokesman Hopes Obama Remarks on Iran's Nuclear Rights
Become Reality," trans. BBC Worldwide Monitoring, April 6, 2009,
LexisNexis Academic; IRINN, "Spokesman Says Iran Ready for
Talks on Its Nuclear Programme," trans. BBC Worldwide Monitoring,
June 29, 2009, LexisNexis Academic; IRINN, "Iran Foreign
Ministry Spokesman's Weekly News Conference," trans. BBC
Worldwide Monitoring, October 12, 2009, LexisNexis Academic;
"Pursuing the Policy," Mardom Salari; Soltanieh: Ali Asghar
Soltanieh, "Full Text of Statements of Iran's Representative to Board
of Governors," *Fars News Agency*, September 13, 2006. http://eng-
lish.farsnews.com/printable.php?nn=8506220617 24; Ali Asghar
Soltanieh, "Full Text of Speech Delivered by Iran's Envoy to the
International Atomic Energy Agency (IAEA) Board of Governors,"
Fars News Agency, March 7, 2007. http://english.farsnews.com
/printable.php?nn=8512160500; Khamenei: Ali Khamenei, "Iran
Not Seeking Nuclear Weapons—Leader," trans. BBC Worldwide
Monitoring, Voice of the Islamic Republic of Iran (Radio), February
17, 2008, LexisNexis Academic; Ali Khamenei, "Iran Leader

Criticizes 'Hegemony'' for Monopolising Science' trans. BBC
Worldwide Monitoring," Vision of the Islamic Republic of Iran
(Television), August 26, 2008, LexisNexis Academic; Ali Khamenei,
"Iran Leader: US Language is Hegemonic, 'Fox'-Like Turning
'Wolfish,'" trans. BBC Worldwide Monitoring, Voice of the Islamic
Republic of Iran (Radio), April 21, 2010, LexisNexis Academic; Ali
Khamenei, "Leader Says Iran's Progress Shocked Nuclear Powers,"
trans. BBC Worldwide Monitoring, Vision of the Islamic Republic of
Iran (Television), April 28, 2010, LexisNexis Academic; Ali
Khamenei, "Iran Leader Says Enemy Wants to Reinstate Its 'Evil
Domination,'" trans. BBC Worldwide Monitoring, Vision of the
Islamic Republic of Iran (Television), September 7, 2010, LexisNexis
Academic; Ali Khamenei, "Iran Leader Says US 'Biggest Disaster'
for World of Islam," trans. BBC Worldwide Monitoring, Voice of the
Islamic Republic of Iran (Radio), February 21, 2011, LexisNexis
Academic; Ahmadinejad: Mahmoud Ahmadinejad, "Iran's President
Ahmadinezhad Rules Out Preconditions for Nuclear Talks," trans.
BBC Worldwide Monitoring, June 19, 2006, LexisNexis Academic;
Mahmoud Ahmadinejad, "Iran Not to Give in to Pressures—
Ahmadinezhad," trans. BBC Worldwide Monitoring, Islamic
Republic of Iran News Network, October 23, 2006, LexisNexis
Academic; Ahmadinejad, "Iran President Defends Right"; Mahmoud
Ahmadinejad, "Iran Will Have Nuclear Power by Next Year—
President," Islamic Republic of Iran News Network, trans. BBC
Worldwide Monitoring, January 30, 2008, LexisNexis Academic;
Mahmoud Ahmadinejad, "Iran Brought West to its Knees over the
Nuclear Issue—President," Islamic Republic of Iran News Network,
trans. BBC Worldwide Monitoring, February 20, 2008. http://aca-
demic.lexisnexis.nl/uva/; Mahmoud Ahmadinejad, "Iran Nuclear
Issue Should Be Discussed Against Broader Background—President,"
Vision of the Islamic Republic of Iran (Television), trans. BBC
Worldwide Monitoring, July 14, 2008. http://academic.lexisnexis
.nl/uva/; Ahmadinejad, "Text of the President's Speech, Addressing
African Nations"; Ahmadinejad, "Text of President's Speech at the
1st International Conference"; Mahmoud Ahmadinejad, "Iranian
President Hails Tehran Declaration, Hits at Russia," trans. BBC
Worldwide Monitoring, Vision of the Islamic Republic of Iran
Kerman Provincial TV, May 26, 2010, LexisNexis Academic;
Mahmoud Ahmadinejad, "Ahmadinezhad Says Iran Not to be
Affected by Latest Sanctions—Full Text," trans. BBC Worldwide
Monitoring, Vision of the Islamic Republic of Iran Network, East
Azarbayjan Provincial TV5, July 5, 2010, LexisNexis Academic;
Mahmoud Ahmadinejad, "Iranian President Upbeat Ahead of
Nuclear Talks in Istanbul—Full Text," trans. BBC Worldwide
Monitoring, Yazd Provincial TV, January 19, 2010, LexisNexis
Academic; For Khamenei and Ahmadinejad, excerpts on the subject

of nuclear development from the documents used in chapter 4 were also included.

7. Like chapter 4, the discourse analysis conducted for this chapter focuses on subject and predicates, assigned inductively to excerpts in their original context. These were then positioned in relation to each other to create, as it were, a map of Iranian foreign policy makers view on the nuclear issue.

8. A. A., Larijani, "Iranian Negotiator"; VIRIN, "Foreign Minister Says Iran Wishes to Defuse Tension With UK" (Mottaki); Khamenei, "Leader's Statements at the Tehran Friday Prayers"; IRINN, "Iran Foreign Minister Calls" (Mottaki); Khamenei, "Message to the Hajj Pilgrims from the Whole World," 2006; VIRIN, "Iranian Foreign Minister Threatens to End Nuclear Cooperation" (Mottaki); Larijani, "Iran's Security Chief"; VIRIN, "Iranian Minister Says 'Essence' of Nuclear Incentive Package 'Could Be Positive'"; Ahmadinejad, "Iran's President Ahmadinezhad Rules Out Preconditions"; Soltanieh, "Full Text of Statements"; Al-Arabiya TV, "Iran Foreign Minister Discusses" (Mottaki); Jalili, "Iran: Deputy Foreign Minister"; Soltanieh, "Full Text of Speech"; Al-Arabiya TV, "Iran Minister Downplays" (Mottaki); VIRIN, "Foreign Minister Says Iranian Diplomats to Be Released in June" (Mottaki); Ahmadinejad, "President Ahmadinejad Addressing 62nd UN General Assembly"; Jalili, "Iran's Top Nuclear Negotiator"; VIRI, "If Some Are Unhappy About Iran's Rights that Is a 'Different Matter'" (Jalili); Khamenei, "Leader's Speech to the Residents of Qom"; VIRI, "Top Nuclear Negotiator Defends Iran's 'Rights'" (Jalili); Ahmadinejad, "Iran Will Have Nuclear Power"; Ahmadinejad, "Iran Brought West to Its Knees"; Jalili, "Security Chief Says"; Ahmadinejad, "Iran Nuclear Issue Should Be Discussed"; Khamenei, "Iran Leader Criticizes 'Hegemony'"; Ahmadinejad, "Iran President Tells UN Assembly"; VIRI, "US 'Confrontational Policy' Must Be Changed" (Qashqavi); IRINN, "Spokesman Hopes Obama" (Qashqavi); VIRIN, "New Head of Iran Nuclear Body Says Committed" (Salehi); IRINN, "Iranian Nuclear Negotiator Says 5+1 Talks 'Positive,'" trans. BBC Worldwide Monitoring, October 1, 2009, LexisNexis Academic (Jalili); Al-Alam TV, "Mottaki Rules Out US War" (Mottaki); Salehi, "Head of Iran's Nuclear"; IRNA, "Foreign Minister: G5+1."

9. For example, Larijani, "Iranian Negotiator"; IRINN, "Iranian Nuclear Negotiator Says 5+1 Talks" (Jalili).

10. For example, Larijani, "Iranian Negotiator"; Larijani, "Iran's Security Chief"; Ahmadinejad, "Iran Will Have Nuclear Power"; Khamenei, "Iran Leader Criticizes 'Hegemony.'"

11. For example, Larijani, "Iranian Negotiator"; VIRIN, "Iranian TV Interviews Foreign Minister Mottaki on Qods Day," trans. BBC Worldwide Monitoring, October 27, 2005, Lexisnexis Academic (Mottaki); Larijani, "Iran's Security Chief"; VIRIN, "Foreign Minister

Says Iranian Diplomats to Be Released in June" (Mottaki); Aqazadeh, "Iranian Nuclear Official Says"; Ahmadinejad, "Iran Not to Give In";Ahmadinejad, "Iran Will Have Nuclear Power"; Ahmadinejad, "Iran Brought West to Its Knees"; Khamenei, "Iran Not Seeking Nuclear Weapons"; Khamenei, "Message to the Hajj Pilgrims from the Whole World" (2006); Khamenei, "Leader Receives Air Force Servicemen"; Khamenei, "Leader's Address to the Iranian People"; Khamenei, "Leader's Speech to the Residents of Qom"; Khamenei, "Leader's Speech to the Residents of the Eastern Azarbaijan Province."

12. Aqazadeh, "Iran Willing to Continue"; Ahmadinejad, "Ahmadinejad Proposed Designation"; Khamenei, "Leader's Statements at the Tehran Friday Prayers."

13. Aqazadeh, "Iran Willing to Continue."

14. For example, Larijani, "Iran's Security Chief"; VIRIN, "Foreign Minister Says Iranian Diplomats to Be Released in June" (Mottaki); Aqazadeh, "Iranian Nuclear Official Says"; Ahmadinejad, "Iran President Defends Right."

15. Ahmadinejad, "Text of President's Speech at the 1st International Conference"; Aqazadeh, "Iran Willing to Continue"; Soltanieh, "Full Text of Speech"; Aqazadeh, "Iranian Nuclear Official Says"; IRNA, "Foreign Minister: G5+1" (Mottaki).

16. Larijani, "Iranian Negotiator"; VIRIN, "Foreign Minister Says Iran Wishes to Defuse Tension With UK" (Mottaki); Khamenei, "Leader's Statements at the Tehran Friday Prayers"; VIRIN, "Iranian TV Interviews Foreign Minister Mottaki on Qods Day," trans. BBC Worldwide Monitoring, October 27, 2005, Lexisnexis Academic (Mottaki); IRINN, "Iran Foreign Minister Calls" (Mottaki); Larijani, "Iran's Security Chief"; VIRIN, "Iranian Minister Says 'Essence' of Nuclear Incentive Package 'Could Be Positive.'" (Mottaki); Larijani, "Iran's Nuclear Negotiator"; Al-Arabiya TV, "Iran Foreign Minister Discusses" (Mottaki); Jalili, "Iran: Deputy Foreign Minister"; Soltanieh, "Full Text of Speech"; IRNA, "Installation of Nuclear Centrifuges"; VIRIN, "Foreign Minister Says Iranian Diplomats to Be Released in June"; Larijani, "Security Chief"; Aqazadeh, "Full Text of Iran's Statement"; VIRI, "Top Nuclear Negotiator Defends Iran's 'Rights'" (Jalili); IRINN, "Spokesman Hopes Obama" (Qashqavi); IRINN, "Iranian Nuclear Negotiator Says 5+1 Talks" (Jalili); IRNA, "Foreign Minister: G5+1" (Mottaki); Ahmadinejad, "President Ahmadinejad Addressing 62nd UN General Assembly"; Khamenei, "Iran Leader: US Language Is Hegemonic."

17. For example, Larijani, "Iranian Negotiator"; VIRIN, "Iranian TV Interviews Foreign Minister Mottaki on Qods Day," trans. BBC Worldwide Monitoring, October 27, 2005, LexisNexis Academic (Mottaki); Soltanieh, Jalili, "Iran: Deputy Foreign Minister."

18. For example, IRNA, "Foreign Minister: G5+1" (Mottaki); Khamenei, "Ayatollah Khamenei: The Cardinal Purpose."

19. VIRI, "Iran Spokesman Says No Letter Received From US" (Qashqavi); IRINN, "Iranian Nuclear Negotiator Says 5+1 Talks" (Jalili); "US Admitting to Iran's," PressTV (Mottaki); Ahmadinejad, "Iran President Defends Right"; Ahmadinejad, "Iran President Tells UN Assembly."

20. Aqazadeh, "Full Text of Iran's Statement"; Al-Alam TV, "Iranian Foreign Minister Comments"; Ahmadinejad, "Text of the President's Speech, Addressing African Nations"; Ahmadinejad, "President Ahmadinejad Addressing 62nd UN General Assembly."

21. Larijani, "Iranian Negotiator"; Aqazadeh, "Iran Willing to Continue"; Soltanieh, "Full Text of Statements"; Aqazadeh, "Full Text of Iran's Statement"; VIRI, "Top Nuclear Negotiator Defends Iran's 'Rights'" (Jalili); Jalili, "Security Chief Says"; Qashqavi, "Spokesman Reacts"; VIRIN, "New Head of Iran Nuclear Body Says Committed" (Salehi); Ahmadinejad, "President Ahmadinejad Addressed the U.N. 64rd General Assembly"; IRINN, "Iranian Nuclear Negotiator Says 5+1 Talks" IRINN, "Iranian Nuclear Negotiator Says 5+1 Talks" (Jalili).

22. Al-Arabiya TV, "Iran Foreign Minister Discusses" (Mottaki); Soltanieh, "Full Text of Speech"; Al-Arabiya TV, "Iran Minister Downplays" (Mottaki); VIRI, "US 'Confrontational Policy' Must Be Changed" (Qashqavi); Salehi, "Iran Nuclear Chief"; IRINN, "Iranian Nuclear Negotiator Says 5+1 Talks" (Jalili); IRINN, "Iran Foreign Ministry Spokesman" (Qashqavi); IRINN, "Iran's Nuclear Activities 'Transparent'" (Mottaki); Ahmadinejad, "Iran Not to Give In"; Ahmadinejad, "Iran President Defends Right."

23. Larijani, "Iranian Negotiator"; Soltanieh, "Full Text of Statements"; Soltanieh, "Full Text of Speech"; Larijani, "Security Chief"; Jalili, "Iran's Top Nuclear Negotiator"; VIRI, "If Some Are Unhappy About Iran's Rights that Is a 'Different Matter.'" (Jalili); VIRI, "Top Nuclear Negotiator Defends Iran's 'Rights.'" (Jalili); VIRI, "US 'Confrontational Policy' Must Be Changed" (Qashqavi); VIRIN, "New Head of Iran Nuclear Body Says Committed" (Salehi); Salehi, "Head of Iran's Nuclear"; Ahmadinejad, "Iran President Defends Right"; Ahmadinejad, "Iran Will Have Nuclear Power"; Ahmadinejad, "Iran Brought West to Its Knees"; Ahmadinejad, "President Ahmadinejad Addressing the 11th Summit."

24. Larijani, "Iranian Negotiator"; VIRIN, "Foreign Minister Says Iran Wishes to Defuse Tension with UK" (Mottaki); Larijani, "Iran's Security Chief"; VIRIN, "Iranian Minister Says 'Essence' of Nuclear Incentive Package 'Could Be Positive'" (Mottaki); Soltanieh, "Full Text of Statements"; Soltanieh, "Full Text of Speech"; IRNA, "Installation of Nuclear Centrifuges" (Aqazadeh); Larijani, "Security Chief"; Jalili, "Security Chief Says"; IRINN, "Iranian Nuclear Negotiator Says 5+1 Talks"; Al-Alam TV, "Iranian Foreign Minister Comments" (Mottaki); IRINN, "Iran's Nuclear Activities 'Transparent'" (Mottaki); IRINN,

"Iran Nuclear Official Announces Production" (Salehi); Ahmadinejad, "Iran Not to Give In."

25. Larijani, "Iranian Negotiator"; Aqazadeh, "Iran Willing to Continue"; VIRIN, "Iranian Minister Says 'Essence' of Nuclear Incentive Package 'Could Be Positive'" (Mottaki); Jalili, "Iran: Deputy Foreign Minister."

26. The IAEA itself reports ups and downs in Iran's cooperation. IAEA reports and a chronology of key events are available on their website (International Atomic Energy Agency (IAEA), "Chronology of Key Events," 2011. http://www.iaea.org/newscenter/focus/iaeairan /iran_timeline8.shtml; International Atomic Energy Agency (IAEA), "IAEA and Iran: IAEA Reports," 2011. http://www.iaea.org/news-center/focus/iaeairan/iaea_reports.shtml).

27. Jalili, "Security Chief Says"; VIRIN, "New Head of Iran Nuclear Body Says Committed" (Salehi); Salehi, "Head of Iran's Nuclear"; Ahmadinejad, "Iran Brought West to Its Knees"; Ahmadinejad, "Text of the President's Speech, Addressing African Nations"; Khamenei, "Iran Leader Says US 'Biggest Disaster.'"

28. Aqazadeh, "Iran Willing to Continue"; Ahmadinejad, "Iran Will Have Nuclear Power."

29. Larijani, "Iran's Security Chief"; IRNA, "Installation of Nuclear Centrifuges" (Aqazadeh); IRINN, "Iran Nuclear Official Announces Production" (Salehi).

30. Salehi, "Head of Iran's Nuclear"; IRNA, "Foreign Minister: G5+1" (Mottaki); IRINN, "Iran FM Says Latest Obama Statements" (Mottaki); Ahmadinejad, "Iranian President Hails Tehran Declaration."

31. Aqazadeh, "Iran Willing to Continue"; Jalili, "Security Chief Says" ; VIRI, "Iran Spokesman Dismisses US Efforts to Create Iranophobia in Region," trans. BBC Worldwide Monitoring, December 22, 2008, LexisNexis Academic (Qashqavi); Salehi, "Head of Iran's Nuclear"; Ahmadinejad, "Iran Will Have Nuclear Power"; Ahmadinejad, "Iran Brought West to Its Knees"; Khamenei, "Iran Leader Says US 'Biggest Disaster.'"

32. VIRIN, "Iranian Foreign Minister Threatens to End Nuclear Cooperation" (Aqazadeh); VIRIN, "Iranian Foreign Minister Threatens to End Nuclear Cooperation" (Mottaki); Aqazadeh, "Iran Willing to Continue"; Soltanieh, "Full Text of Statements"; Larijani, "Iran's Nuclear Negotiator"; Soltanieh, "Full Text of Speech"; Larijani, "Security Chief."

33. Ahmadinejad, "Text of President's Speech at the 1st International Conference"; Larijani, "Iran's Nuclear Negotiator"; "Iranian Foreign Minister," Mehr News Agency; IRINN, "Iran FM Says Latest Obama Statements."

34. Aqazadeh, "Full Text of Iran's Statement"; Ahmadinejad, "Text of President's Speech at the 1st International Conference"; Al-Alam

TV, "Mottaki Rules Out US War" (Mottaki); Ahmadinejad, "Iran President Tells UN Assembly."

35. Aqazadeh, "Iran Willing to Continue"; Jalili, "Security Chief Says"; VIRI, "Iran Spokesman Dismisses US Efforts to Create Iranophobia in Region" (Qashqavi); Salehi, "Head of Iran's Nuclear"; Ahmadinejad, "Iran Will Have Nuclear Power"; Ahmadinejad, "Iran Brought West to Its Knees"; Khamenei, "Iran Leader Says US 'Biggest Disaster'" ; VIRIN, "Iranian Minister Says 'Essence' of Nuclear Incentive Package 'Could Be Positive'" (Mottaki); Soltanieh, "Full Text of Statements."; VIRIN, "Foreign Minister Says Iranian Diplomats to Be Released in June" (Mottaki).

36. Larijani, "Iranian Negotiator"; Larijani, "Iran's Nuclear Negotiator"; Aqazadeh, "Full Text of Iran's Statement"; VIRI, "Top Nuclear Negotiator Defends Iran's 'Rights'" (Jalili); Ahmadinejad, "Iranian President Hails Tehran Declaration."

37. Larijani, "Iran's Security Chief"; Aqazadeh, "Iran Willing to Continue"; VIRIN, "Iranian Minister Says 'Essence' of Nuclear Incentive Package 'Could Be Positive'" (Mottaki); Jalili, "Iran: Deputy Foreign Minister"; VIRIN, "Foreign Minister Says Iranian Diplomats to Be Released in June" (Mottaki); Aqazadeh, "Full Text of Iran's Statement"; Salehi, "Head of Iran's Nuclear"; "US Admitting to Iran's," PressTV ; Ahmadinejad, "Iran Not to Give In"; Khamenei, "Iran Not Seeking Nuclear Weapons"; Khamenei, "Iran Leader Says US 'Biggest Disaster.'"

38. Ahmadinejad, "Text of President's Speech at the 1st International Conference"; Larijani, "Iran's Nuclear Negotiator"; IRNA, "Foreign Minister: G5+1"; IRINN, "Iran FM Says Latest Obama Statements"; Aqazadeh, "Full Text of Iran's Statement"; Al-Alam TV, "Iranian Foreign Minister Comments"; Ahmadinejad, "Iran President Tells UN Assembly"; "President Ahmadinejad Addressing 62nd UN General Assembly."

39. Larijani, "Security Chief"; Ahmadinejad, "Iran President Defends Right"; Ahmadinejad, "Iran Will Have Nuclear Power"; Ahmadinejad, "Text of President's Speech at the 1st International Conference"; Khamenei, "Iranian Supreme Leader Criticizes US Nuclear Policies."

40. Soltanieh, "Full Text of Statements"; VIRIN, "Iranian TV Interviews Foreign Minister Mottaki on Qods Day," Trans. BBC Worldwide Monitoring, October 27, 2005, Lexisnexis Academic (Mottaki); IRNA, "Foreign Minister: G5+1" (Mottaki).

41. For example, Larijani, "Iranian Negotiator"; Larijani, "Security Chief"; VIRI, "Top Nuclear Negotiator Defends Iran's 'Rights'" (Jalili).

42. Larijani, "Security Chief"; Jalili, "Iran: Deputy Foreign Minister"; Larijani, "Security Chief."

43. Larijani, "Iranian Negotiator"; Larijani, "Iran's Security Chief"; Larijani, "Iran's Nuclear Negotiator"; VIRIN, "Foreign Minister Says

Iranian Diplomats to Be Released in June" (Mottaki); VIRI, "Top Nuclear Negotiator Defends Iran's 'Rights'"; Ahmadinejad, "Iran Nuclear Issue Should Be Discussed."

44. Fars News Agency, "Iran Foreign Minister-Designate Says" (Mottaki); VIRIN, "Iranian Minister Says 'Essence' of Nuclear Incentive Package 'Could Be Positive'" (Mottaki); Soltanieh, "Full Text of Statements"; Al-Arabiya TV, "Iran Foreign Minister Discusses" (Mottaki); Soltanieh, "Full Text of Speech"; Al-Arabiya TV, "Iran Minister Downplays" (Mottaki); Ahmadinejad, "Iran's President Ahmadinezhad Rules Out Preconditions."

45. Larijani, "Iranian Negotiator"; Larijani, "Iran's Security Chief"; Aqazadeh, "Iran Willing to Continue"; VIRI, "Top Nuclear Negotiator Defends Iran's 'Rights'" (Jalili).

46. Larijani, "Iran's Security Chief"; Aqazadeh, "Iran Willing to Continue"; Jalili, "Iran: Deputy Foreign Minister."

47. Ibid.

48. Larijani, "Iranian Negotiator"; VIRIN, "Foreign Minister Says Iran Wishes to Defuse Tension With UK" (Mottaki); VIRIN, "Iranian TV Interviews Foreign Minister Mottaki on Qods Day," trans. BBC Worldwide Monitoring, October 27, 2005, Lexisnexis Academic (Mottaki); IRNA, "There Is No Legal Basis" (Mottaki); Larijani, "Iran's Security Chief"; VIRIN, "Iranian Minister Says 'Essence' of Nuclear Incentive Package 'Could Be Positive'" (Mottaki); Ahmadinejad, "Iran's President Ahmadinezhad Rules Out Preconditions"; Soltanieh, "Full Text of Statements"; Ahmadinejad, "Iran Nuclear Issue Should Be Discussed"; VIRI, "US 'Confrontational Policy' Must Be Changed" (Qashqavi); VIRI, "Iran Spokesman Dismisses US Efforts to Create Iranophobia in Region" (Qashqavi); IRINN, "Iran Foreign Ministry Spokesman" (Qashqavi); Al-Alam TV, "Mottaki Rules Out US War" (Mottaki).

49. "Head of Nuclear Program," Quds (Salehi); Salehi, "Head of Iran's Nuclear"; Ahmadinejad, "Iran Brought West to Its Knees."

50. Aqazadeh, "Iran Willing to Continue"; Salehi, "Head of Iran's Nuclear."

51. Larijani, "Iranian Negotiator"; VIRIN, "Iranian Foreign Minister Threatens to End Nuclear Cooperation" (Mottaki); Larijani, "Iran's Security Chief"; Aqazadeh, "Iran Willing to Continue"; VIRIN, "Iranian Minister Says 'Essence' of Nuclear Incentive Package 'Could Be Positive'" (Mottaki); Soltanieh, "Full Text of Statements"; Larijani, "Iran's Nuclear Negotiator"; Al-Arabiya TV, "Iran Foreign Minister Discusses" (Mottaki); Jalili, "Iran: Deputy Foreign Minister"; IRNA, "Installation of Nuclear Centrifuges" (Aqazadeh); Larijani, "Security Chief"; VIRI, "Top Nuclear Negotiator Defends Iran's 'Rights'" (Jalili); Jalili, "Security Chief Says"; VIRI, "US 'Confrontational Policy' Must Be Changed" (Qashqavi); VIRI, "Iran Spokesman Says No Letter Received From US" (Qashqavi); IRINN, "Iran Foreign

Ministry Spokesman" (Qashqavi); "Jalili's Bitter Chinese News," *Javan* (Jalili); IRNA, "Foreign Minister: G5+1" (Mottaki); IRINN, "Iran FM Says Latest Obama Statements" (Mottaki); IRINN, "Iran Minister Urges Dialogue" (Mottaki); Ahmadinejad, "Ahmadinezhad Says Iran Not to Be Affected"; Khamenei, "Iran Leader Says Enemy."

52. For example, Larijani, "Iranian Negotiator"; VIRIN, "Iranian TV Interviews Foreign Minister Mottaki on Qods Day," trans. BBC Worldwide Monitoring, October 27, 2005, LexisNexis Academic (Mottaki); Larijani, "Iran's Security Chief"; VIRIN, "Foreign Minister Says Iranian Diplomats to Be Released in June" (Mottaki); Aqazadeh, "Iranian Nuclear Official Says"; Ahmadinejad, "Iran Not to Give In"; Ahmadinejad, "Iran Will Have Nuclear Power"; Ahmadinejad, "Iran Brought West to Its Knees"; Khamenei, "Iran Not Seeking Nuclear Weapons"; Khamenei, "Message to the Hajj Pilgrims From the Whole World" (2006); Khamenei, "Leader Receives Air Force Servicemen"; Khamenei, "Leader's Address to the Iranian People"; Khamenei, "Leader's Speech to the Residents of Qom"; Khamenei, "Leader's Speech to the Residents of the Eastern Azarbaijan Province."

53. Larijani, "Iranian Negotiator"; Jalili, "Security Chief Says"; Ahmadinejad, "Iran Not to Give In"; Ahmadinejad, "Iran Will Have Nuclear Power"; Ahmadinejad, "Text of President's Speech at the 1st International Conference."

54. Larijani, "Iranian Negotiator"; VIRIN, "Foreign Minister Says Iran Wishes to Defuse Tension With UK" (Mottaki); Jalili, "Security Chief Says"; Aqazadeh, "Iranian Nuclear Official Says"; Ahmadinejad, "Iran Not to Give In"; Ahmadinejad, "Iran Brought West to Its Knees"; Ahmadinejad, "Iran Nuclear Issue Should Be Discussed"; Khamenei, "Iran Not Seeking Nuclear Weapons."

55. Larijani, "Iran's Security Chief"; Aqazadeh, "Iran Willing to Continue"; Jalili, "Iran: Deputy Foreign Minister"; IRINN, "Iran Nuclear Official Announces Production" (Salehi); Khamenei, "Iran Not Seeking Nuclear Weapons"; Khamenei, "Iran Leader Criticizes 'Hegemony.'"; Khamenei, "Leader Says Iran's Progress"; Khamenei, "Iran Leader Says Enemy."

56. For example, Larijani, "Iran's Security Chief"; Salehi, "Head of Iran's Nuclear."

57. Larijani, "Iran's Security Chief"; Larijani, "Iranian Negotiator."

58. Khamenei, "Leader's Speech to the Residents of Qom."; Khamenei, "Iran Leader Says US 'Biggest Disaster.'"

59. Khamenei, "Iran Not Seeking Nuclear Weapons"; Jalili, "Security Chief Says"; Ahmadinejad, "Iran Brought West to Its Knees"; Ahmadinejad, "Iran Nuclear Issue Should Be Discussed"; Ahmadinejad, "Iranian President Hails Tehran Declaration."

60. Ahmadinejad, "Iran Nuclear Issue Should Be Discussed."

61. See chapters 3 and 4.

62. Ahmadinejad, "Iran President Defends Right."
63. Khamenei, "Iran Leader Criticizes 'Hegemony.'"
64. Ahmadinejad, "Iran President Defends Right."
65. Ahmadinejad, "Text of President's Speech at the 1st International Conference."
66. Ahmadinejad, "President Ahmadinejad Addressing 62nd UN General Assembly"; Ahmadinejad, "Iran President Tells UN Assembly."
67. Marc Lanteigne, "But There Are Limits: China's UN Security Council Behavior and the Iran Crisis," Unpublished draft presented at ISA convention, 2011.
68. "Jalili's Bitter Chinese News," *Javan* (Jalili).
69. Lanteigne, "But There Are Limits." Perspectives on this differ. Garver, for example, puts emphasis on the mutual effort of China and Iran to counter US hegemony. Despite the importance of this convergence in goals, particularly in the context of a broader global antihegemonic front among developing states, Lanteigne's article shows that cooperation has not as yet moved beyond energy and trade. That China was not ready to side with Iran became evident when China supported a new round of sanctions on Iran in 2010. As US power declines, this however increases possibilities for increased relations. John W. Garver, *China and Iran: ancient Partners in a Post-imperial World* (Washington: University of Washington Press, 2007).
70. IRINN, "Iran Minister Urges Dialogue."
71. One can assume Davutoğlu meant the use of nuclear technology for military purposes.
72. IRINN, "Iran's Nuclear Activities 'Transparent.'"
73. Agence France Presse, "Brazil's Lula Holds 'Last Chance' Nuclear Talks in Iran," May 16, 2006, LexisNexis Academic.
74. Agence France Presse, "Brazil Hails Iran Nuclear Deal, Says Should Avert Sanctions," May 17, 2010, LexisNexis Academic.
75. Agence France Presse, "U.S. Tables Tough Iran Sanctions Draft at UN," May 18, 2010, LexisNexis Academic.
76. United States State Department Documents and Publications, "Remarks by Clinton."
77. Agence France Presse, "English U.S., Europe Welcome Fresh UN Sanctions," June 10, 2010, LexisNexis Academic.
78. Mahmoud Ahmadinejad, "Iranian President Hails Tehran Declaration, Hits at Russia—Text," trans. BBC Worldwide Monitoring, Vision of the Islamic Republic of Iran Kerman Provincial TV, Kerman, May 27, 2010, LexisNexis Academic.
79. Agence France Presse, "UN Slaps Fourth Set of Sanctions on Iran," June 10, 2010, LexisNexis Academic.
80. Agence France Presse, "Brazil's Lula Slams Fresh UN Sanctions on Iran," June 9, 2010, LexisNexis Academic.
81. Agence France Presse, "Turkey Urges World to Support Iran Nuclear," May 18, 2010, LexisNexis Academic.

82. Ahmadinejad, "Iranian President Hails Tehran Declaration."
83. Ibid.
84. Ibid.
85. Kessler and Erdbrink, "Iran Reaches Nuclear Deal."
86. Doty, "Foreign Policy."

7 Foreign Threat and Political Repression

*This chapter was first published as a paper within the framework of the Hivos Knowledge Programme Civil Society in West Asia. It has been altered and updated.

  1. Oliver Schlumberger, "Opening Old Bottles in Search of New Wine: On Nondemocratic Legitimacy in the Middle East," *Middle East Critique* 19, no. 3 (2010): 233–250, 232.
  2. Mahmoud Ahmadinejad, "Iranian President Slams West for Interfering in Presidential Polls," trans. BBC Worldwide Monitoring, Vision of the Islamic Republic of Iran Khorasan Provincial TV, July 16, 2009, LexisNexis Academic.
  3. The Office of the Supreme Leader (OSL) Sayyid Ali Khamenei, the "Friday Prayer," June 20, 2009. http://www.leader.ir/langs/en /index.php?p=contentShow&id=5618.
  4. The British Media, "executive tools of the British government's interventionist policies" ("Keyhan Analytical-News Report: Britain's Role in Recent Disturbances," trans. BBC Worldwide Monitoring, *Keyhan* June 17, 2009, LexisNexis Academic) had a major role to play according to the hardliners ("Playing Yazid in Yiddish English During Ashura," trans. BBC Worldwide Monitoring, *Keyhan* December 28, 2009, LexisNexis Academic; "Wild Cowboys," trans. BBC Worldwide Monitoring, *Keyhan* July 17, 2010, LexisNexis Academic).
  5. "Keyhan Analytical-News Report," *Keyhan.*
  6. Hoseyn Shari'atmadari, "This is the Same," trans. BBC Worldwide Monitoring, *Keyhan* June 30, 2009, LexisNexis Academic.
  7. "CIA and Britain's MI6," trans. BBC Worldwide Monitoring, *Keyhan* July 21, 2009, LexisNexis Academic.
  8. "Ablution of Martyrdom [Preparation for Martyrdom] by the BBC of Britain," trans. BBC Worldwide Monitoring, *Keyhan* June 25, 2009, LexisNexis Academic.
  9. Shaban "Bimokh" (Brainless) Jafari led the counter-uprising in Tehran to reinstate the shah.
 10. Hamid Omidi, "The Curtains Fell," trans. BBC Worldwide Monitoring, *Keyhan* August 26, 2009, LexisNexis Academic.
 11. . H. Mowlana, "Rise and Fall of Velvet Revolutions (Part One)," trans. BBC Worldwide Monitoring, *Keyhan* August 10, 2009, LexisNexis Academic.
 12. Hoseyn Shari'atmadari, "Green Organization or a Red Carpet for America?!" trans. BBC Worldwide Monitoring, *Keyhan* August 17,

2009, LexisNexis Academic; Hoseyn Shari'atmadari, "So Many Similarities!?" trans. BBC Worldwide Monitoring, *Keyhan* June 13, 2009, LexisNexis Academic; Manouchehr Mohammadi, "In Opposing Ahmadinezhad, the Policy of Westerners and Disgraced Domestic Movements Became the Same," trans. BBC Worldwide Monitoring, *Keyhan* June 30, 2009, LexisNexis Academic.

13. Mohammadi, "In Opposing Ahmadinezhad."
14. The color of Islam, now adopted by people who "had nothing in the slightest to do with holiness—most of whom in fact did not even observe the most basic Islamic codes of conduct" (Shari'atmadari, "So Many Similarities!?").
15. "Kiyan Tajbakhsh Revealed: 'Tier 2'; the Project for American Intelligence Organizations," *Keyhan* August 2, 2009, LexisNexis Academic.
16. Hesameddin Borumand, "The Opposite Outcome," trans. BBC Worldwide Monitoring, *Keyhan* February 7, 2009, LexisNexis Academic.
17. Ali Khamenei, "The Message of H. E. Ayatullah Khamenei to the Hajj Pilgrims," The Office of the Supreme Leader Website, November 26, 2009. http://www.leader.ir/langs/en/print.php?sec=content&id=6135.
18. See also: Khamenei, "Leader's Address to the Officials"; Khamenei, "Fourth International Conference for Support"; Khamenei, "Leader's Statements at the Tehran Friday Prayers"; Ahmadinejad, "President Ahmadinejad's Speech Addressing the UN General Assembly."
19. Khamenei, "Message to the Hajj Pilgrims From the Whole World," 2006.
20. Shari'atmadari, "This Is the Same."
21. "Kiyan Tajbakhsh Revealed," *Keyhan.*
22. Hamid Omidi, "Colourful Dreams," trans. BBC Worldwide Monitoring, *Keyhan* June 24, 2009, LexisNexis Academic.
23. "Former Assistant Secretary of the US Treasury in Interview with Keyhan: America Had Reported a Green Coup D'etat in Iran Before the Elections," trans. BBC Worldwide Monitoring, *Keyhan* September 9, 2009, LexisNexis Academic.
24. "Activists Say 'Adventurists' Are Threatening Detente in foreign Policy," trans. BBC Monitoring, *Norooz* February 17, 2002, LexisNexis Academic.
25. Hoseyn Shari'atmadari, "Radical Daily Says Reformists America's "Fifth Column," trans. BBC Worldwide Monitoring, *Keyhan* May 19, 2002, LexisNexis Academic.
26. Mir-Hoseyn Mousavi and Mehdi Karubi.
27. "One can ask why reformists share the same views with America, Israel, super capitalists and the economically corrupt", Shari'atmadari wrote (Hoseyn Shari'atmadari, "Please Believe that We Do not Believe!" trans. BBC Worldwide Monitoring, *Keyhan* May 24, 2009, LexisNexis Academic).

28. Hesameddin Borumand,"Prosecution of the Main Accused in Rigi's Case," trans. BBC Worldwide Monitoring, *Keyhan* February 28, 2010, LexisNexis Academic; see also Omidi, "The Curtains Fell."
29. "The Completely Self-evolving Process of Employing Extremists by America," trans. BBC Worldwide Monitoring, *Keyhan* June 21, 2009, LexisNexis Academic.
30. Matin Mahjub, "Three Crises for a Dying Front," trans. BBC Worldwide Monitoring, *Keyhan* September 23, 2009, LexisNexis Academic.
31. Shari'atmadari, "So Many Similarities!?"
32. Mehdi Mohammadi, "When America Becomes angry," trans. BBC Worldwide Monitoring, *Keyhan* June 8, 2009, LexisNexis Academic.
33. Mahjub, "Three Crises"; "Green Agreement with the Great Satan!" Trans. BBC Worldwide Monitoring, *Keyhan* November 1, 2009, Lexisnexis Academic; Shari'atmadari, "Please Believe That We Do not Believe!"; Shari'atmadari, "Green Organization."
34. "CIA and Britain's MI6," *Keyhan*; Shari'atmadari, "Green Organization."
35. "Keep Saying That We Are Not Supported by foreigners," trans. BBC Worldwide Monitoring, *Keyhan* February 10, 2010, LexisNexis Academic.
36. Sa'd Allah Zare'i, "…and This Is the Same Path," trans. BBC Worldwide Monitoring, *Keyhan* December 21, 2009, LexisNexis Academic.
37. "In a forum Commemorating Commander Shushtari: Full-time Presence of a British Intelligence Agent Alongside Rigi," trans. BBC Worldwide Monitoring, *Keyhan* December 10, 2009, LexisNexis Academic; Fars News Agency, "Minister Criticizes Some Elite over Post-election Events in Iran (BBC Title)," trans. BBC Worldwide Monitoring, December 10, 2009, LexisNexis Academic; Shari'atmadari, "Green Organization"; "Green Agreement," *Keyhan*.
38. In one article the Green Movement is explicitly referred to as the *Mofsed-e Fel'arz*, a term translated by BBC Monitoring as applying to the shah's corrupt politicians (Hoseyn Shari'atmadari, "Iran Paper Wants 'Severe' Punishment for Recent Post-poll Unrest Leaders," trans. BBC Worldwide Monitoring, *Keyhan* August 9, 2009, LexisNexis Academic).
39. "VOA and BBC Are Obviously Ominous But We Dare Not Choose another Way," trans. BBC Worldwide Monitoring, *Keyhan* December 10, 2009, Lexisnexis Academic.
40. "The Completely Self-Evolving Process," *Keyhan*.
41. "Keep Saying," *Keyhan*; "Wild Cowboys," *Keyhan*.
42. Hoseyn Shari'atmadari, "Paper Tigers…!" trans. BBC Worldwide Monitoring, *Keyhan* March 13, 2010, LexisNexis Academic.
43. "VOA and BBC ," *Keyhan*.

44. "Ignominy of Opposition's Stooges that Have Taken Photo with Bush," trans. BBC Worldwide Monitoring, *Keyhan* June 28, 2010, LexisNexis Academic; "CIA Dollars at Service of Provoking Pseudo Clerics," trans. BBC Worldwide Monitoring, *Keyhan* July 15, 2009, LexisNexis Academic; "London Clique Exposed Perhaps Places Like Berlin, Paris or Brussels," *Keyhan* July 22, 2010, LexisNexis Academic; "Green Sedition's Genealogy Reached Cultural NATO and the Hojjatiyeh Society," trans. BBC Worldwide Monitoring, *Keyhan* March 6, 2010, LexisNexis Academic.
45. "Green Sedition's Genealogy," *Keyhan*.
46. "CIA Dollars," *Keyhan*.
47. "Green Agreement," *Keyhan*.
48. H. Mowlana, "Defeat of the Defeated West," trans. BBC Worldwide Monitoring, *Keyhan* July 2, 2009, LexisNexis Academic; Shari'atmadari, "So Many Similarities!?"
49. The West started a "No Ahmadinejad campaign" because of his demanding position around the negotiating table (Shari'atmadari, "This Is the Same") and because of his anti-Israel stance (Akbar Safari, "Studying the Role of foreign Countries in Recent Unrest, They Are not Impartial (Part One)," trans. BBC Worldwide Monitoring, *Keyhan* July 15, 2009, LexisNexis Academic).
50. "Iran's Turn," trans. BBC Worldwide Monitoring, *Keyhan* June 29, 2009, LexisNexis Academic.
51. Safari, "Studying the Role"; "Keyhan Analytical-news Report," *Keyhan*; Hoseyn Shari'atmadari, "Broken Ladder!" Trans. BBC Worldwide Monitoring, *Keyhan* August 6, 2009, LexisNexis Academic.
52. This repetition by the domestic media is emphasized as evidence of the cooperation between the reformist and foreign media ("Kazemianfar in an Interview with Fars: Britain's Position Must be Clarified Once and for All," *Keyhan* June 21, 2009, LexisNexis Academic).
53. Shari'atmadari, "So Many Similarities!?"; Similar: Omidi, "The Curtains Fell."
54. "Keyhan Analytical-News Report," *Keyhan*.
55. Omidi, "Colourful Dreams."
56. Shari'atmadari, "Green Organization."
57. Safari, "Studying the Role."
58. Mehdi Mohammadi, "In Defence of the Truth," trans. BBC Worldwide Monitoring, *Keyhan* July 12, 2009, LexisNexis 2009.
59. "The Completely Self-evolving Process," *Keyhan*.
60. Borumand, "Prosecution of the Main Accused"; "The Completely Self-evolving Process," *Keyhan*.
61. Shari'atmadari, "So Many Similarities!?"
62. "Keyhan Analytical-News Report," *Keyhan*.
63. Ibid.
64. Shari'atmadari, "Broken Ladder!"

65. "Khatami's Suggestion or Michael Ledeen's Guideline?" trans. BBC Worldwide Monitoring, *Keyhan* June 21, 2009, LexisNexis Academic; Shari'atmadari, "Broken Ladder!"
66. "Keep Saying ," *Keyhan.*
67. "Iran's Turn," Trans. BBC Worldwide Monitoring, *Keyhan* June 29, 2009, LexisNexis Academic.
68. Iraj Nezafati, "West's New Strategy of Digital Diplomacy: Revealing America's Covert Objectives in anti-Iranian 'Media Diplomacy'—First Part," trans. BBC Worldwide Monitoring, *Keyhan* August 28, 2010, LexisNexis Academic.
69. "Ablution of Martyrdom," *Keyhan.*
70. "Traces of Terrorists in London's Collapsed Group House," trans. BBC Worldwide Monitoring, *Keyhan* February 17, 2010, LexisNexis Academic; Neda Aqa Soltan became an icon of the 2009 protests after bystanders filmed her death and broadcast it on the internet. According to reformists, she was shot by a member of the *Basij* (Iran's militia of volunteers), but the government claimed her death was a set-up by the West.
71. "Keyhan Analytical-News Report," *Keyhan.*
72. "Iran's Turn," *Keyhan.*
73. Mohammadi, "In Defence of the Truth."
74. Safari, "Studying the Role."
75. Mohammadi, "When America Becomes Angry."
76. H. Mowlana, "Defeat of the Defeated West," trans. BBC Worldwide Monitoring, *Keyhan* July 2, 2009, LexisNexis Academic.
77. Zare'i, "...And This Is the Same Path."
78. See chapter 3.
79. Mohammad Imani, "Intersection of Two Parallel Lines," trans. BBC Worldwide Monitoring, *Keyhan* August 29, 2009, LexisNexis Academic; Hoseyn Shari'atmadari, "The Lord of the Rings?" trans. BBC Worldwide Monitoring, *Keyhan* June 28, 2009, LexisNexis Academic; Shari'atmadari, "Green Organization"; "CIA and Tunnel Digging in Canadian Embassy," trans. BBC Worldwide Monitoring, *Keyhan* August 6, 2009, LexisNexis Academic.
80. Imani, "Intersection."; Omidi, "The Curtains Fell"; "Ignominy," *Keyhan.*
81. Shari'atmadari, "Broken Ladder!"
82. Mowlana, "Defeat."
83. Ali Khamenei, "US, UK 'Opposition' to Iran Government 'Does Not Scare anyone' Supreme Leader," trans. BBC Worldwide Monitoring, *Islamic Republic of Iran News Network* September 11, 2009, LexisNexis Academic.
84. Ahmad Khatami, "Iran Cleric Says Armed Rioters "Waging War Against God"," trans. BBC Monitoring, *Voice of the Islamic Republic of Iran* June 26, 2009, LexisNexis Academic.

85. "Wild Cowboys," *Keyhan*; "The Bells Are Ringing; Will They Capture Us Also?!" trans. BBC Worldwide Monitoring, *Keyhan* March 1, 2010, LexisNexis Academic; "Head of Intelligence Organization of Sistan-Baluchestan Province: Some 180 Crimes of Rigi's Group Have Been Thwarted During Recent Years," trans. BBC Worldwide Monitoring, *Keyhan* July 5, 2010, LexisNexis Academic.

86. Amir Ali Sarayani, "Thoughts on the Nature of the Terrorist Rigi Group," trans. BBC Worldwide Monitoring, *Keyhan* March 3, 2010, LexisNexis Academic.

87. "Head of Intelligence Organization," *Keyhan*; "VOA and BBC," *Keyhan*.

88. Sarayani, "Thoughts on the Nature of the Terrorist Rigi Group."

89. "The Bells Are Ringing," *Keyhan*.

90. BBC News, "Protest at Iran's 'Evil UK' Claim," June 19, 2009. http://news.BBC News.co.uk/2/hi/uk_news/politics/8109303.stm.

91. Roula Khalaf and Najmeh Bozorgmehr, "Diplomats in Tit-for-Tat Expulsion," *The Financial Times* June 24, 2009, LexisNexis Academic; BBC News, "Britain and Iran's Fraught History," June 29, 2009. http://news.BBC News.co.uk/2/hi/uk_news/8116245.stm.

92. BBC News, "UK Fury as Staff Arrested in Iran," June 28, 2009. http://news.BBC News.co.uk/2/hi/middle_east/8122871.stm.

93. Robert F. Worth, "Iran Accuses West of Stirring Protests; U.K. Envoy Summoned as Government Backers Stage Counter-Rallies," *International Herald Tribune* December 30, 2009, LexisNexis Academic.

94. Ibid.

95. Agence France Presse, "Iran Mps Push for Cut in Ties with Britain," December 19, 2010, LexisNexis Academic; Fars News Agency, "Senior Lawmaker: Cutting Ties with Britain Still on Parliament's Agenda," April 4, 2011. http://english.farsnews.com/printable.php?nn=9001220529 15.

96. BBC News, "UK's Iran Ambassador in NATO Move," February 9, 2011. http://www.BBC News.co.uk/news/uk-12405528.

97. Government of the United Kingdom, "Dominick Chilcott," May 11, 2013. https://www.gov.uk/government/people/dominick-chilcott.

98. Julian Borger, "Iran Leaves Ambassador Post Free in Snub to UK," *The Guardian* September 17, 2010, LexisNexis Academic.

99. Ian Black, "Historic Enmity Revived as Relations Between Iran and UK Reach New Low with Expulsions: Rivalry Flared Periodically Since Days of Empire: 'Little Satan' Accused of Backing Election Protests," *The Guardian* June 24, 2009, LexisNexis Academic.

100. BBC News, "UK Culture Body Halts Iran Work," February 5, 2009. http://news.BBC News.co.uk/2/hi/middle_east/7870503.stm;

BBC News, "British Council in Iran 'Illegal,'" February 5, 2009. http://news.BBC News.co.uk/2/hi/middle_east/7872525.stm.

101. Ali Khamenei, "Islamic Revolution Leader in Response to President Mahmoud Ahmadinejad's Letter," The Office of the Supreme Leader, February 4, 2009. http://www.leader.ir/langs/en/print .php?sec=content&id=4746.

102. BBC News, "UK Culture Body Halts Iran Work," February 5, 2009. http://news.BBC News.co.uk/2/hi/middle_east/7870503.stm.

103. BBC News, "UK Culture Body Halts Iran Work," February 5, 2009. http://news.BBC News.co.uk/2/hi/middle_east/7870503.stm.

104. Fars News Agency, "'Ground Set' for Retrieving UK Embassy Compound—Iran Commander," trans. BBC Worldwide Monitoring, July 4, 2009, LexisNexis Academic; VIRI, "Iran Students Call for "Liberation of UK-occupied" Park in Capital," trans. BBC Worldwide Monitoring, August 24, 2009, LexisNexis Academic; "Iranian Newspaper Calls for Return of Qolhak Garden to Iran by Britain," trans. BBC Monitoring, *Resalat* January 17, 2011, LexisNexis Academic.

105. IRINN, "President Says Action Against Iran Will Be Regretted," trans. BBC Worldwide Monitoring, February 17, 2010, LexisNexis Academic.

106. BBC News, "UK Yacht Crew Detained by Iran," December 1, 2009. http://news.BBC News.co.uk/2/hi/uk_news/8387469.stm.

107. Ian Black, "Despite Protests at Home and Abroad, Ahmadinejad Begins His Second Term: Iran's President Sworn in Amid Demonstrations: Reformists and Many Mps Boycott Inauguration," *The Guardian* August 6, 2009, LexisNexis Academic.

108. BBC News, "Iran 'Arrests Four UK-linked Men,'" November 4, 2010, sec. Middle East. http://www.co.uk/news/world-middle -east-11691544.

109. Majid Tafreshi, "Iran-UK Relations: Two Sides of a Coin," April 20, 2011. http://irdiplomacy.ir/en/page/12076/IranUK+Relations +Two+Sides+of+A+Coin.html.

110. "Iran, Britain in Talks to Resume Consular Relations," PressTV April 17, 2013. http://www.presstv.com/detail/2013/03/18/294281 /relations/.

111. Robert F. Worth and Rick Gladstone, "In Tehran, Protesters Storm British Embassy," *The New York Times* November 29, 2011, sec. World/Middle East. http://www.nytimes.com/2011/11/30 /world/middleeast/tehran-protesters-storm-british-embassy.html.

112. Damien McElroy, "British Relations with Iran Sink to Lowest in Decades as Tehran Embassies Are Stormed," *Telegraph.co.uk* November 29, 2011, sec. worldnews. http://www.telegraph.co.uk /news/worldnews/middleeast/iran/8924441/British-relations -with-Iran-sink-to-lowest-in-decades-as-Tehran-embassies-are -stormed.html.

113. Government of the United Kingdom, "Sweden to Represent British Interests in Iran," May 11, 2013. https://www.gov.uk /government/news/sweden-to-represent-british-interests-in-iran.

Conclusion

1. Valerie Hudson, *Foreign Policy Analysis* (Lanham: Rowman & Littlefield Publishers, 2006), 125.
2. Karin M. Fierke, "Besting the West," *International Feminist Journal of Politics* 1, no. 3 (2001): 403–434.
3. Personal conversation with a Tehran-based colleague.
4. Henry R. Nau, and Deepa M. Ollapally, eds. *Worldviews of Aspiring Powers: Domestic Foreign Policy Debates in China, India, Iran, Japan, and Russia* (New York: Oxford University Press, 2012).

Bibliography

Aarts, Paul, and Gerd Nonneman. *Saudi Arabia in the Balance: Political Economy, Society, Foreign Affairs.* London: Hurst, 2005.

Abrahamian, Ervand. *A History of Modern Iran.* Cambridge, UK: Cambridge University Press, 2008.

———. *Khomeinism: Essays on the Islamic Republic.* London: I.B.Tauris, 1993.

Adib-Moghaddam, Arshin. *Iran in World Politics: The Question of the Islamic Republic.* London: Hurst, 2007.

———. *The International Politics of the Persian Gulf: A Cultural Genealogy.* London: Routledge, 2006.

Aftab-e Yazd. "A Number of Principle-ist Representatives Warned Ahmadinezhad: Warnings and Limitations over the 10th Cabinet; Real Warning or Continuation of a Scenario." *Aftab-e Yazd* July 7, 2009, LexisNexis Academic.

Agence France Presse. "Bahrain Fears Fallout from Iran Nuclear Crisis." Agence France Presse, June 2006, LexisNexis Academic.

———. "Brazil Hails Iran Nuclear Deal, Says Should Avert Sanctions." Agence France Presse, May 17, 2010, LexisNexis Academic.

———. "Brazil's Lula Holds 'Last Chance' Nuclear Talks in Iran." Agence France Presse, May 16, 2006, LexisNexis Academic.

———. "Brazil's Lula Slams Fresh UN Sanctions on Iran." Agence France Presse, June 9, 2010, LexisNexis Academic.

———. "English U.S., Europe Welcome Fresh UN Sanctions." Agence France Presse, June 10, 2010b, LexisNexis Academic.

———. "Iran MPs Push for Cut in Ties with Britain." Agence France Presse, December 19, 2010, LexisNexis Academic.

———. "Iranian FM Visits Qatar." Agence France Presse, October 6, 2005, LexisNexis Academic.

———. "Turkey Urges World to Support Iran Nuclear." Agence France Presse, May 18, 2010a, LexisNexis Academic.

———. "U.S. Tables Tough Iran Sanctions Draft at UN." Agence France Presse, May 18, 2010b, LexisNexis Academic.

———. "UN Slaps Fourth Set of Sanctions on Iran." Agence France Presse, June 10, 2010a, LexisNexis Academic.

Aggestam, Liesbeth. "Role Conceptions and the Politics of Identity in Foreign Policy." ARENA Working Papers, 1999. http://www.deutsche -aussenpolitik.de/resources/seminars/gb/approach/document /wp99_8.htm.

Ahmadinejad, Mahmoud. "A Reply to an American Mother's Message." Presidency of the Islamic Republic of Iran News Service, March 18, 2007. http://www.president.ir/en/print.php?ArtID=3555.

———. "Ahmadinejad: Gaza, Sight for Independent Nations and Gov'ts Victory Over Oppressor Powers' Will." Presidency of the Islamic Republic of Iran News Service, January 20, 2009. http://www.president.ir/en /print.php?ArtID=14505&noimage.

———. "Ahmadinezhad Praises Iran's Production Capability—Full Text." Translated by BBC Worldwide Monitoring, IRINN, November 15, 2010, LexisNexis Academic.

———. "Ahmadinejad Proposed Designation of 2011 as Year of Rectifying Consumption Pattern, Reducing Pollution." Presidency of the Islamic Republic of Iran News Service, December 17, 2009. http://www.president.ir/en/print.php?ArtID=19320&noimage.

———. "Ahmadinezhad Says Iran not to be Affected by Latest Sanctions—Full Text." Translated by BBC Worldwide Monitoring, Vision of the Islamic Republic of Iran Network, East Azarbayjan Provincial TV5, July 5, 2010, LexisNexis Academic.

———. "Dr Ahmadinejad in Reply to Imam Al Haj Talib Abd al Rashid's Letter Today All Nations of the World Are Seeking Justice." Presidency of the Islamic Republic of Iran News Service, April 4, 2007. http://www .president.ir/en/print.php?ArtID=3626&noimage.

———. "Full Text of President's Address to APA General Assembly." Presidency of the Islamic Republic of Iran News Service, November 19, 2007. http://www.president.ir/en/print.php?ArtID=7376&noimage.

———. "Full Text of Speech Presented by H.E. Dr. Mahmoud Ahmadinejad." August 30, 2012. http://www.president.ir/en/41317/printable.

———. "Honourable Barack Obama President elect of the United States of America." Presidency of the Islamic Republic of Iran News Service, November 8, 2008. http://www.president.ir/en/print .php?ArtID=13116&noimage.

———. "Iran Brought West to Its Knees Over the Nuclear Issue—President." Islamic Republic of Iran News Network, Translated by BBC Worldwide Monitoring, February 20, 2008, LexisNexis Academic.

———. "Iran Not to Give in to Pressures—Ahmadinezhad." Translated by BBC Worldwide Monitoring, Islamic Republic of Iran News Network, October 23, 2006, LexisNexis Academic.

———. "Iran Nuclear Issue Should be Discussed against Broader Background—President." Translated by BBC Worldwide Monitoring, Vision of the Islamic Republic of Iran (Television), July 14, 2008, LexisNexis Academic.

———. "Iran President Defends Right to Nuclear Fuel, Re-asserts Statement on Holocaust." IRNA, September 25, 2007b, LexisNexis Academic.

———. "Iranian President Hails Tehran Declaration, Hits at Russia—Text." Translated by BBC Worldwide Monitoring, Vision of the Islamic Republic of Iran Kerman Provincial TV, *Kerman* May 27, 2010, LexisNexis Academic.

———. "Iran President Tells UN Assembly that Nuclear Case Is Political." Translated by BBC Worldwide Monitoring, September 23,2008, LexisNexis Academic.

———. "Iran Will Have Nuclear Power by Next Year—President." Translated by BBC Worldwide Monitoring, Islamic Republic of Iran News Network, January 30, 2008, LexisNexis Academic.

———. "Iranian President Slams West for Interfering in Presidential Polls." Translated by BBC Worldwide Monitoring, Vision of the Islamic Republic of Iran Khorasan Provincial TV, July 16, 2009, LexisNexis Academic.

———. "Iranian President Upbeat Ahead of Nuclear Talks in Istanbul—Full Text." Translated by BBC Worldwide Monitoring, Yazd Provincial TV, January 19, 2010, LexisNexis Academic.

———. "Iran's President Ahmadinezhad Rules Out Preconditions for Nuclear Talks." Translated by BBC Worldwide Monitoring, June 19, 2006, LexisNexis Academic.

———. "Message for the Birth of Jesus Son of Mary Word of God the Messenger of Mercy." Presidency of the Islamic Republic of Iran News Service, December 25, 2008b. http://www.president.ir/en/print .php?ArtID=14056&noimage.

———. "President Ahmadinejad Addressed the U.N. 64rd General Assembly." Presidency of the Islamic Republic of Iran News Service, September 25, 2009. http://www.president.ir/en/print .php?ArtID=17937&noimage.

———. "President Ahmadinejad Addresses Students at Columbia University Full Text." Presidency of the Islamic Republic of Iran News Service, September 25, 2007a. http://www.president.ir/en/print .php?ArtID=6747&noimage.

———. "President Ahmadinejad Addressing 62nd UN General Assembly—Full Text." Presidency of the Islamic Republic of Iran News Service, September 26, 2007. http://www.president.ir/en/print .php?ArtID=6781&noimage.

———. "President Ahmadinejad Addressing the 11th Summit of the Organization of the Islamic Conference in Senegal." Presidency of the Islamic Republic of Iran News Service, March 14, 2008. http://www .president.ir/en/print.php?ArtID=9261&noimage.

———. "President Ahmadinejad's Speech Addressing the UN General Assembly." Presidency of the Islamic Republic of Iran News Service, September 24, 2008. http://www.president.ir/en/print .php?ArtID=12188&noimage.

———. "President Congratulates Pope Catholics on Christmas." Presidency of the Islamic Republic of Iran News Service, December 25, 2008a. http://www.president.ir/en/print.php?ArtID=14066&noimage.

Ahmadinejad, Mahmoud. "President: D-8 Can Be Pioneer of Peace, Justice in World." Presidency of the Islamic Republic of Iran News Service, July 8, 2008. http://www.president.ir/en/print.php?ArtID=10647&noimage.

———. "President: Unilateral, Oppressive Ties Must Be Replaced by Just Mechanisms." Presidency of the Islamic Republic of Iran News Service, June 3, 2008. http://www.president.ir/en/print.php?ArtID=10102&noimage.

———. "President's Speech in Durban II." Presidency of the Islamic Republic of Iran News Service, April 21, 2009. http://www.president.ir/en/print.php?ArtID=16845&noimage.

———. "Text of President's Speech at the 1st International Conference on Disarmament and Non-proliferation." Presidency of the Islamic Republic of Iran News Service, April 17, 2010. http://www.president.ir/en/print.php?ArtID=21266&noimage.

———. "Text of the President's Speech, Sddressing African Nations." Presidency of the Islamic Republic of Iran News Service, September 23, 2008b. http://www.president.ir/en/print.php?ArtID=12175&noimage.

Ahram Online. "Egypt's President Morsi to Visit Saudi Arabia on Wednesday." *Ahram Online* July 10, 2012. http://english.ahram.org.eg/News/47362.aspx.

Akram, Fares. "Hamas Supports Syrian Opposition." *The New York Times* February 24, 2012, sec. World, Middle East. http://www.nytimes.com/2012/02/25/world/middleeast/hamas-leader-supports-syrian-opposition.html.

Akram, Fares, and Jodi Rudoren. "Hamas Says Egypt Will Reopen Crossing Into Gaza." *The New York Times* August 25, 2012, sec. World, Middle East. http://www.nytimes.com/2012/08/26/world/middleeast/hamas-says-egypt-will-reopen-crossing-into-gaza.html.

Al Jazeera. "Ahmadinejad Row with Khamenei Intensifies—Middle East—Al Jazeera English." *Al Jazeera* May 6, 2011. http://www.aljazeera.com/news/middleeast/2011/05/201156113955925329.html.

———. "Iran's Standoff: Khamenei vs Ahmadinejad." *Al Jazeera* May 12, 2011. http://www.aljazeera.com/indepth/opinion/2011/05/2011512101644247806.html.

Al-Alam TV. "Iranian Foreign Minister Comments on Stand-off with USA, Nuclear Fuel Swap." Translated by BBC Worldwide Monitoring, Al-Alam TV, February 21, 2010, LexisNexis Academic.

———. "Mottaki Rules Out US War on Iran, Says Iran Will Resume Cooperation with IAEA." Translated by BBC Worldwide Monitoring, Al-Alam TV, February 22, 2010, LexisNexis Academic.

Alamdari, K. "The Power Structure of the Islamic Republic of Iran: Transition from Populism to Clientelism, and Militarisation of the Government." *Third World Quarterly* 26, no. 8 (2005): 1285–1301.

Al-Arabiya TV. "Iran Foreign Minister Discusses Policy on Nuclear, Iraq, Saudi, Lebanon Issues." Translated from Arabic by BBC Worldwide Monitoring, Al-Arabiya TV, December 21, 2006, LexisNexis Academic.

———. "Iran Minister Downplays Brief US Contact on Al-Arabiya." Translated from Arabic by BBC Worldwide Monitoring, Al-Arabiya TV, May 6, 2007, LexisNexis Academic.

Alavi, Nasrin. "Iran: A Blind Leap of Faith." *Open Democracy*, September 19, 2009. http://www.opendemocracy.net/article/iran-a-blind-leap-of-faith.

Albrecht, Holger, and Oliver Schlumberger. "'Waiting for Godot': Regime Change without Democratization in the Middle East." *International Political Science Review* 25, no. 4 (2004): 371–392.

Albright, David, and Andrea Stricker. "Iran's Nuclear Programme." In *The Iran Primer: Power, Politics, and U.S. Policy*, edited by Robin Wright, 115–118. Washington, DC: United States Institute of Peace, 2010..

Alfoneh, Ali. "Iran News Round-up August 2–3, 2009." In *Iran News Round-up*, edited by M. Rubin and A. Majidyar. Washington: American Enterprise Institute, 2009.

Alizadeh, Parvin. "Iran's Quandary: Economic Reforms and the Structural Trap." *Brown Journal of International Affairs* 9, no. 2 (2003): 267–281.

Al-Shibani, S. "A Very Important Visit." Translated from Arabic by BBC Monitoring, Tishrin Website, January 22, 2006, LexisNexis Academic.

Althusser, Louis. "Ideology and Ideological State Apparatuses." 1970. http://www.marxists.org/reference/archive/althusser/1970/ideology.htm.

Amuzegar, Jahangir. "The Ahmadinejad Era: Preparing for the Apocalypse." *Journal of International Affairs* 60, no. 2 (Spring–Summer 2007): 35–53.

Ansari, Ali M. "Civilizational Identity and Foreign Policy: The Case of Iran." In *The Limits of Culture: Islam and Foreign Policy*, edited by Brenda Shaffer, 241–262. Cambridge, Massachusetts: MIT Press, 2006

———. *Iran Under Ahmadinejad: The Politics of Confrontation*. Abingdon, Oxon: Routledge, 2007.

Ansari, Ali M., ed. *Preliminary Analysis of the Voting Figures in Iran's 2009 Presidential Election*. London: Chatham House, 2009. http://www.chathamhouse.org/publications/papers/view/109081/.

Aqazadeh, Gholam Reza. "Full Text of Iran's Statement to IAEA Meeting." Fars News Agency, September 17, 2007. http://english.farsnews.com/printable.php?nn=8606260606.

———. "Iran Willing to Continue Nuclear Talks with West." Translated by BBC Worldwide Monitoring, Vision of the Islamic Republic of Iran (Television), February 16, 2006, LexisNexis Academic.

———. "Iranian Nuclear Official Says the Country Now Has 7,000 Centrifuges." Translated by BBC Worldwide Monitoring, Islamic Republic of Iran News Network, April 10, 2009, LexisNexis Academic.

Associated Press, "AP Interview: Egypt's Tourism Minister Says Iranian Tourists Pose No Threat to Egypt." *Associated Press* March 28, 2013. http://www.foxnews.com/world/2013/03/28/ap-interview-egypt-tourism-minister-says-iranian-tourists-pose-no-threat-to/.

Barkin, J. Samuel. "Realist Constructivism and Realist-constructivisms." *International Studies Review* 6, no. 2 (2004): 348–352.

———. "Realist Constructivism."*International Studies Review* 5, no. 3 (2003): 325–342.

Barnett, Michael. "Identity and Alliances in the Middle East." In *The Culture of National Security*, edited by Peter J. Katzenstein. New York: Columbia University Press, 1996, 400–432.

Barrionuevo, Alexei. "Brazil Defends Iran President's Visit." *International Herald Tribune* November 24, 2009, LexisNexis Academic.

———. "Brazil's President Elbows U.S. on the Diplomatic Stage." *The New York Times* November 23, 2009, LexisNexis Academic.

Barton, Dominic, and Kito De Boer. "Tread Lightly Along the New Silk Road." *Financial Times* January 30, 2007, LexisNexis Academic.

Barzegar, Kayhan. "The Paradox of Iran's Nuclear Consensus." *World Policy Journal* 26, no. 3 (2009): 21–30.

Bayandor, Darioush. *Iran and the CIA: The Fall of Mosaddeq Revisited.* New York: Palgrave Macmillan, 2010.

Bayat, Asef. *Making Islam Democratic: Social Movements and the Post-Islamist Turn.* Stanford, California: Stanford University Press, 2007.

BBC News. "Britain and Iran's Fraught History." BBC News, June 29, 2009. http://news.BBC News.co.uk/2/hi/uk_news/8116245.stm.

———. "British Council in Iran 'Illegal.'" BBC News, February 5, 2009a. http://news.BBC News.co.uk/2/hi/middle_east/7872525.stm.

———. "British Council Statement on Iran." BBC News, February 4, 2009. http://news.BBC News.co.uk/2/hi/middle_east/7870699.stm.

———. "EU Imposes New Sanctions on Iran." BBC News, October 15, 2012, sec. Middle East. http://www.bbc.co.uk/news/world-middle-east-19947507.

———. "Iran 'Arrests Four UK-linked Men.'" BBC News, November 4, 2010, sec. Middle East. http://www.bbc.co.uk/news/world-middle-east-11691544.

———. "Iran Intelligence Minister Sacked." BBC News, July 27, 2009, sec. Middle East. http://news.bbc.co.uk/1/hi/education/8169839.stm.

———. "Iran Leader Dismisses US Currency." BBC News, November 18, 2007, sec. Americas. http://news.bbc.co.uk/2/hi/7101050.stm.

———. "Iran President Ahmadinejad Begins Historic Egypt Visit." BBC News, February 5, 2013. http://www.bbc.co.uk/news/world-middle-east-21336367.

———. "Iran Rial Drop Dents Border Trade." BBC News, October 3, 2012, sec. Middle East. http://www.bbc.co.uk/news/world-middle-east-19815103.

———. "Iran Rial Hits Record Dollar Low." BBC News, October 1, 2012, sec. Business. http://www.bbc.co.uk/news/business-19786662.

———. "Iran Says It Could Attack First." BBC News, February 21, 2012, sec. Middle East. http://www.bbc.co.uk/news/world-middle-east-17116588.

————. "Iranian Leader Targeted with Shoe." BBC News, February 6, 2013, sec. Middle East. http://www.bbc.co.uk/news/world-middle-east-21348630.

————. "Iranian Oil Revenues 'Plunge 45%.'" January 8, 2013, sec. Middle East. http://www.bbc.co.uk/news/world-middle-east-20942138.

————. "Israeli FM 'Boycotts Brazil Head.'" BBC News, March 16, 2010, sec. Middle East. http://news.bbc.co.uk/2/hi/middle_east/8569471.stm.

————. "Nuclear Fuel Declaration by Iran, Turkey and Brazil." BBC News, Text of Tehran Declaration, May 17, 2010. http://news.BBCNews.co.uk/2/hi/middle_east/8686728.stm.

————. "On Board US Carrier in Strait of Hormuz." BBC News, February 14, 2012, sec. Middle East. http://www.bbc.co.uk/news/world-middle-east-17034496.

————. "Police Oversee Iran Subsidy Cuts." BBC News, November 9, 2010, sec. Middle East. http://www.bbc.co.uk/news/world-middle-east-11685293.

————. "Protest at Iran's 'Evil UK' Claim." BBC News, June 19, 2009. http://news.BBC.co.uk/2/hi/uk_news/politics/8109303.stm.

————. "Q&A: Iran Sanctions." BBC News, October 16, 2012, sec. Middle East. http://www.bbc.co.uk/news/world-middle-east-15983302.

————. "Q&A: Petrol Rationing in Iran." BBC News, June 27, 2007, sec. Middle East. http://news.bbc.co.uk/1/hi/world/middle_east/6244574.stm.

————. "Sanctions Detonate Iran Currency." BBC News, October 2, 2012, sec. Business. http://www.bbc.co.uk/news/business-19800532.

————. "Talabani 'Trusts in Iran Support.'" BBC News, November 21, 2005, LexisNexis Academic.

————. "UK Culture Body Halts Iran work." BBC News, February 5, 2009b. http://news.BBC News.co.uk/2/hi/middle_east/7870503.stm.

————. "UK Fury as Staff Arrested in Iran." BBC News, June 28, 2009. http://news.BBC News.co.uk/2/hi/middle_east/8122871.stm.

————. "UK Yacht Crew Detained by Iran." BBC News, December 1, 2009b. http://news.BBC News.co.uk/2/hi/uk_news/8387469.stm.

————. "UK's Iran Ambassador in NATO Move." BBC News, February 9, 2011b. http://www.BBC News.co.uk/news/uk-12405528.

Beeman, William O. *The Great Satan vs. the Mad Mullahs: How the United States and Iran Demonize Each Other.* Chicago: University of Chicago Press, 2008.

Behravesh, Maysam. "Revolt in Syria: An Alternative View from Iran." October 3, 2011. http://www.irdiplomacy.ir/en/page/16724/Revolt+in+Syria+An+alternative+view+from+Iran.html.

Bieler, Andreas, and Adam D. Morton. "The Gordian Knot of Agency—Structure in International Relations." *European Journal of International Relations* 7, no. 1 (2001): 5–35.

Black, Ian. "Despite Protests at Home and Abroad, Ahmadinejad Begins his Second Term: Iran's President Sworn in Amid Demonstrations: Reformists and Many MPs Boycott Inauguration." *The Guardian* August 6, 2009, LexisNexis Academic.

———. "Historic Enmity Revived as Relations Between Iran and UK Reach New Low with Expulsions: Rivalry Flared Periodically Since Days of Empire: 'Little Satan' Accused of Backing Election Protests." *The Guardian* June 24, 2009, LexisNexis Academic.

———. "Iran's Supreme Leader Backs Ahmadinejad: Hardline President to Be Sworn in Tomorrow: Reformists and Moderates Boycott Ceremony." *The Guardian* August 4, 2009, LexisNexis Academic.

———. "The U.S. Embassy Cables: Reaction: Iran Dismisses Arab Worries as Psychological Warfare: Middle East Reaction." *The Guardian* November 30, 2010, LexisNexis Academic.

Borger, Julian. "Iran Leaves Ambassador Post Free in Snub to UK." *The Guardian* September 17, 2010, LexisNexis Academic.

Borger, J. "Middle East: Strategy: Surprising Partners among Tehran's Layer of Alliances." *The Guardian* February 10, 2007, LexisNexis Academic.

Borumand, Hesameddin. "Prosecution of the Main Accused in Rigi's Case." Translated by BBC Worldwide Monitoring, *Keyhan* February 28, 2010, LexisNexis Academic.

———. "The Opposite Outcome." Translated by BBC Worldwide Monitoring, *Keyhan* February 7, 2009, LexisNexis Academic.

Bozorgmehr, Najmeh. "Iran Praises Lula for his Mediator Role." *Financial Times* May 17, 2010, LexisNexis Academic.

———. "Iran Says Saudis Seized Atom Expert." *Financial Times* December 9, 2009, LexisNexis Academic.

Bronson, Rachel. *Thicker than Oil: America's Uneasy Partnership with Saudi Arabia*. Oxford: Oxford University Press, 2008.

Buchta, Wilfred *Who Rules Iran? The Structure of Power in the Islamic Republic*. Washington: Washington Institute for Near East Policy and Sankt Augustin: Konrad Adenauer Stiftung, 2000.

Bulliet, Richard. W. "Iran between the East and the West." *Journal of International Affairs* 60, no. 2 (2007): 1–14.

Burns, Nicholas. "India's Support for Iran Threatens Its US Relationship and Global Leadership Role." *Christian Science Monitor* February 14, 2012. http://www.csmonitor.com/Commentary/Opinion/2012/0214/India-s-support-for-Iran-threatens-its-US-relationship-and-global-leadership-role.

Buzan, Barry, Ole Wæver, and Jaap de Wilde. *Security: A New Framework for Analysis*. London: Lynne Rienner Publishers, 1998.

Campbell, David. *Writing Security: United States Foreign Policy and the Politics of Identity*. Minneapolis: University of Minnesota Press, 1998.

Carabine, Jane. "Unmarried Motherhood: 1830–1990: A Genealogical Analysis." In *Discourse as Data*, edited by Margaret Wetherell, Simeon Yates, and Stephanie Taylor, 267–310. London: Sage, 2001.

Carroll, Rory. "Brazil Stands up to U.S. Over Iran Sanctions." *The Guardian Unlimited* March 4, 2010, LexisNexis Academic.

———. "Nicaragua Defies U.S. with Iran Trade Deal: Tehran to Fund Projects in Exchange for Coffee, Meat Washington Warns of 'Dangerous Partner.'" *The Guardian* August 6, 2007, LexisNexis Academic.

———. "Venezuela Sells Petrol to Iran to Reinforce Front against U.S." *The Guardian* July 4, 2007, LexisNexis Academic.

Chimbelu, Chiponda. "Iran Makes Inroads in Parts of Africa." *Deutsche Welle* February 28, 2010, LexisNexis Academic.

Chubin, Shahram. *Iran's Nuclear Ambitions.* Washington: Carnegie Endowment for International Peace, 2006.

CIA World Factbook. "Iran." 2006. https://www.cia.gov/library /publications/the-world-factbook/geos/ir.html.

Clark, Ian. *Legitimacy in International Society.* Oxford: Oxford University Press, 2005.

Clawson, Patrick. "US Sanctions." In *The Iran primer: Power, Politics, and U.S. Policy,* edited by Robin Wright, 115–118. Washington, DC: United States Institute of Peace, 2010.

CNN. "Venezuela Defends Controversial Flights to Iran and Syria—CNN. com." CNN, August 22, 2010. http://edition.cnn.com/2010/WORLD /asiapcf/08/21/venezuela.flights.iran/index.html.

Cooper, Helene. "Voices of Discontent: Anti-U.S. Leaders Seek Allies." *The New York Times* September 23, 2006, LexisNexis Academic.

Cordesman, Anthony H., Bryan Gold, Sam Khazai, and Bradley Bosserman. "U.S. and Iran Strategic Competition; Sanctions, Energy, Arms Control, and Regime Change." Centre for Strategic and International Studies, January 22, 2013. http://csis.org/files/publication/130122 _IranVSanctions_Final_AHC_1_22_13.pdf.

Cottam, Martha L., Beth Dietz-Uhler, Elena Mastors, and Thomas Preston. *Introduction to Political Psychology.* Mahwah, New Jersey: Lawrence Erlbaum Associates, 2004.

Cottam, Richard. "Inside Revolutionary Iran." In *Iran's Revolution: The Search for Consensus,* edited by R. K. Ramazani and Middle East Institute (Washington, DC). Bloomington, Indiana: Indiana University Press, 1990.

Cox, Robert W. "Gramsci, Hegemony and International Relations: An Essay in Method." *Millennium Journal of International Studies* 12, no. 2 (1983): 162–175.

———. "Social Forces, States and World Orders: Beyond International Relations Theory." *Millennium Journal of International Studies* 10, no. 2 (1981): 126–155.

David, Steven R. "Explaining Third World Alignment." *World Politics* 43, no. 2 (1991): 233–256.

Dehghan, Saeed Kamali. "Non-aligned Movement Summit: 'You'd Think Iran Was Hosting the Olympics.'" *The Guardian* August 30, 2012, sec. World News. http://www.guardian.co.uk/world/2012/aug/30/iran -non-aligned-movement-summit.

Dehghani Firouz Abadi, S. J. "Emancipating Foreign Policy: Critical Theory and Islamic Republic of Iran's Foreign Policy." *The Iranian Journal of International Affairs* XX, no. 3 (Summer 2008): 1–26.

Devine, James. "Understanding Iranian Foreign Policy: Combining Ideological and Realist Explanations." Paper prepared for the International Studies Association Annual Conference 2011, Montreal, March 16–19, 2011.

DG Trade Statistics. "Iran: EU Bilateral Trade and Trade with the World." April 26, 2013. http://trade.ec.europa.eu/doclib/docs/2006/september/tradoc_113392.pdf.

Dombey, Daniel, and Wheatley Jonathan. "Brazil Ends Its Role as Mediator." *Financial Times* June 21, 2010, LexisNexis Academic.

Dorraj, Manouchehr. "Neo-populism in Comparative Perspective: Iran and Venezuela." *Comparative Studies of South Asia, Africa and the Middle East* 29, no. 1 (2009): 137–151.

Doty, Roxanne Lynn. "Foreign Policy as Social Construction: A Post-positivist Analysis of U.S. Counterinsurgency Policy in the Philippines." *International Studies Quarterly* 37, no. 3 (1993): 297–320.

Dunne, Tim, Milya Kurki, and Steve Smith. *International Relations Theories: Discipline and Diversity.* Oxford: Oxford University Press, 2007.

Eagleton, Terry. *Ideology: An Introduction.* London: Verso, 1991.

Egypt Independent. "Egyptian Official Says Cairo May Open Embassy in Iran Soon, Reports Iranian Media." *Egypt Independent* August 28, 2012. http://www.egyptindependent.com/news/egyptian-official-says-cairo-may-open-embassy-iran-soon-reports-iranian-media.

———. "Hamas Military Wing Denies Planning Deadly Attack on Rafah Army Camp | Egypt Independent." *Egypt Independent* March 14, 2013. http://www.egyptindependent.com/news/hamas-military-wing-denies-planning-deadly-attack-rafah-army-camp.

———. "Iran Plans US$5 Bln Worth of Investments in Egypt." *Egypt Independent* February 19, 2012. http://www.egyptindependent.com/news/iran-plans-us5-bln-worth-investments-egypt.

———. "Protests Outside Iranian Embassy." *Egypt Independent* February 2, 2013. http://www.egyptindependent.com/news/protests-outside-iranian-embassy.

———. "Salafis Plan Tahrir Demo to Protest Iran, Shia Relations." *Egypt Independent* March 3, 2013. http://www.egyptindependent.com/news/salafis-plan-tahrir-demo-protest-iran-shia-relations.

Ehteshami, Anoushiravan. "Failure of Khatami Reformers, not Reform Movement." *Journal of Iranian Research and Analysis* 18, no. 2 (2002): 69–72.

———. "Iran's New Order: Domestic Developments and Foreign Policy Outcomes". *Global Dialogue* 3 no. 2–3, 2001. http://www.worlddialogue.org/print.php?id=1460.

Ehteshami, Anoushiravan, and Mahjoob Zweiri, eds. *Iran and the Rise of Its Neoconservatives: The Politics of Tehran's Silent Revolution.* London: I.B. Tauris, 2007.

————. *Iran's Foreign Policy from Khatami to Ahmadinejad.* Reading: Ithaca Press, 2008.

Elman, Colin. "Horses for Courses: Why not Neorealist Theories of Foreign Policy?" *Security Studies* 6, no. 1 (1996): 7–53.

Engstrom, Par. "Brazilian Foreign Policy and Human Rights: Change and Continuity Under Dilma." *Critical Sociology* 38, no. 6 (2012): 835–849.

Erdbrink, Thomas. "Iran Enters Nuclear Talks in a Defiant Mood." *The New York Times* February 25, 2013, sec. World/Middle East. http://www.nytimes.com/2013/02/26/world/middleeast/iran-enters-nuclear-talks-in-a-defiant-mood.html.

————. "Nonaligned Nations Back Iran on Nuclear Bid, but not on Syria." *The New York Times* August 31, 2012, sec. World/Middle East. http://www.nytimes.com/2012/09/01/world/middleeast/iran-criticizes-egypts-mohamed-morsi-over-syria-comments.html.

Fadel, Leila. "Iranian Nobel Winner Urges Obama to stress Human Rights." *McClatchy-Tribune News Service* October 14, 2009, LexisNexis Academic.

Fairclough, Norman. "The Discourse of New Labour: Critical Discourse Analysis." In *Discourse as Data*, edited by M. Wetherell, S. Yates, and S. Taylor, 229–266. London: Sage, 2001.

Fars News Agency. "'Ground Set' for Retrieving UK Embassy Compound—Iran Commander." Translated by BBC Worldwide Monitoring, Fars News Agency, July 4, 2009, LexisNexis Academic.

————. "Iran after Opening Embassy in Egypt." Fars News Agency, April 16, 2012. http://english.farsnews.com/newstext.php?nn=9101142029.

————. "Iran Agency Publishes Interview with UK Spokesman on Regional Issues." Translated by BBC Worldwide Monitoring, Fars News Agency, December 29, 2010, LexisNexis Academic.

————. "Iran Foreign Minister-Designate Says No Pre-conditions in Nuclear Talks with EU." Translated by BBC Worldwide Monitoring, Fars News Agency, August 21, 2005, LexisNexis Academic.

————. "Minister Criticizes Some Elite over Post-election Events in Iran (BBC Title)." Translated by BBC Worldwide Monitoring, Fars News Agency, December 10, 2009, LexisNexis Academic.

————. "MPs: Severing Ties with Britain Incurs No Harm on Iran." Fars News Agency, April 12, 2011. http://english.farsnews.com/printable.php?nn=9001230706.

————. "President Ahmadinejad to Go on Tour of Africa in Days." Fars News Agency, April 6, 2012. http://english.farsnews.com/newstext.php?nn=9107158026.

————. "Senior Lawmaker: Cutting Ties with Britain Still on Parliament's Agenda." Fars News Agency, April 4, 2011. http://english.farsnews.com/printable.php?nn=9001220529 15.

Fattah, H. M. "Iran's Growing Power Has Saudis Worried; Riyadh Weighs How to Confront Tehran." *International Herald Tribune* December 22, 2006, LexisNexis Academic.

Feigenbaum, Evan A. "India's Rise, America's Interest," *Foreign Affairs*
    March 1, 2010. http://www.foreignaffairs.com/articles/65995/evan-a
    -feigenbaum/indias-rise-americas-interest.
Fierke, Karin M. "Besting the West: Russia's Machiavella Strategy."
    International Feminist Journal of Politics 1, no. 3 (2001): 403–434.
———. "Constructivism." In *International Relations Theories: Discipline and
    Diversity*, edited by Timothy Dunne, Milja Kurki, and Steve Smith, 166–
    184. Oxford: Oxford University Press, 2007.
———. *Critical Approaches to International Security*. Cambridge: Polity,
    2007a.
Fifield, Anna. "For Oil-rich Iran, Friends Are not Proving Hard to Find."
    Financial Times May 28, 2008, LexisNexis Academic.
Figes, Orlando. *The Whisperers: Private Life in Stalin's Russia*. New York:
    Metropolitan Books, 2007.
Financial Times. "A Dodgy Dossier on Iran's Activity in Iraq: The U.S.
    Should Start a More Diplomatic Offensive against Tehran." *Financial
    Times* February 13, 2007, LexisNexis Academic.
Forbes, Mark. "Indonesia Offers Summit on Iran Crisis: Jakarta Says Muslim
    Nations Must Be Involved in Finding Peaceful Solution to Deepening
    Nuclear Stand-off." *The Age* May 11, 2006, LexisNexis Academic.
Foreign Ministry of the People's Republic of China. "Foreign Ministry
    Spokesperson Hong Lei's Regular Press Conference on November 13,
    2012." Foreign Ministry of the People's Republic of China, November 13,
    2012. http://www.fmprc.gov.cn/eng/xwfw/s2510/2511/t988806.htm.
———. "Foreign Ministry Spokesperson Hong Lei's Regular Press
    Conference on November 6, 2012." Foreign Ministry of the People's
    Republic of China, November 6, 2012. http://www.fmprc.gov.cn/eng
    /xwfw/s2510/2511/t986346.htm.
———. "Foreign Ministry Spokesperson Hong Lei's Regular Press
    Conference on December 14, 2012." Foreign Ministry of the People's
    Republic of China, December 14, 2012. http://www.fmprc.gov.cn/eng
    /xwfw/s2510/2511/t998567.htm.
———. "Foreign Ministry Spokesperson Ma Zhaoxu's Remarks on Iran
    Building a Uranium Enrichment Factory." Foreign Ministry of the People's
    Republic of China, September 27, 2009. http://www.fmprc.gov.cn/eng
    /xwfw/s2510/t607387.htm.
Freyberg-Inan, Annette, Ewan Harrison, and Patrick James. *Rethinking
    Realism in International Relations: Between Tradition and Innovation*.
    Baltimore, Maryland: Johns Hopkins University Press, 2009.
Ganji, Akbar. "The Latter-day Sultan." *Foreign Affairs* 87, no. 6 (2008):
    45–65.
Garver, John W. *China and Iran: Ancient Partners in a Post-imperial World*.
    Seatlle: University of Washington Press, 2007.
Gee, John. "Behind Indonesia's Warm Welcome for Iranian President
    Ahmadinejad." *Washington Report on Middle East Affairs* August, 2006,
    LexisNexis Academic.

Gerring, J. "Ideology: A Definitional Analysis." *Political Research Quarterly* 50, no. 4 (1997): 957–994.

Giddens, Anthony. *The Constitution of Society: Outline of the Theory of Structuration*. Cambridge: Polity Press, 1984.

Gladstone, Rick. "Iran: Oil Exports Rose, Report Says." *The New York Times* March 13, 2013, sec. World/Middle East. http://www.nytimes .com/2013/03/14/world/middleeast/iran-oil-exports-rose-report-says .html.

———. "Iran's Double-digit Inflation Worsens." *The New York Times* April 1, 2013, sec. World/Middle East. http://www.nytimes.com/2013/04/02 /world/middleeast/irans-double-digit-inflation-worsens.html.

———. "Iran's Oil Exports and Sales Down 40 Percent, Official Admits." *The New York Times* January 7, 2013, sec. World/Middle East. http:// www.nytimes.com/2013/01/08/world/middleeast/irans-oil-exports -and-sales-down-40-percent-official-admits.html.

———. "U.S. Imposes Sanctions on Those Aiding Iran." *The New York Times* May 9, 2013, sec. World/Middle East. http://www.nytimes .com/2013/05/10/world/middleeast/us-imposes-sanctions-on-those -aiding-iran.html.

Glaser, Bonnie S., and Evan S. Medeiros. "The Changing Ecology of Foreign Policy-making in China: The Ascension and Demise of the Theory of 'Peaceful Rise.'" *The China Quarterly* 190 (2007): 291–310.

Glasius, Marlies. "Dissident Writings as Political Theory on Civil Society and Democracy." *Review of International Studies* 37, no. 1 (2011): 1–22.

Goldstein, Judith, and Robert O. Keohane. *Ideas and Foreign Policy: Beliefs, Institutions, and Political Change*. Ithaca, New York: Cornell University Press, 1993.

Government of the United Kingdom. "Dominick Chilcott." Government of the United Kingdom, May 11, 2013. https://www.gov.uk/government /people/dominick-chilcott.

———. "Sweden to Represent British Interests in Iran." Government of the United Kingdom, May 11, 2013. https://www.gov.uk/government /news/sweden-to-represent-british-interests-in-iran.

The Guardian Unlimited. "Iran Sought Turkey's Help to Mend Links with U.S., Says Erdogan." *The Guardian Unlimited* February 24, 2009, LexisNexis Academic.

The Guardian. "Historic Enmity Revived as Relations between Iran and UK Reach New Low with Expulsions: Rivalry Flared Periodically Since Days of Empire: 'Little Satan' Accused of Backing Election Protests." *The Guardian* June 24, 2009, LexisNexis Academic.

———. "Non-aligned Movement: A Two-edged Summit in Tehran." *The Guardian* August 29, 2012, sec. Comment is free. http://www.guardian .co.uk/commentisfree/2012/aug/29/non-aligned-movement-two -edged-summit-tehran.

———. "Turkey to Site Nato Missile Shield Radar in Its South-east." *The Guardian* September 14, 2011, sec. World news. http://www.guardian .co.uk/world/2011/sep/14/turkey-nato-missile-shield-radar.

Halaby, Jamal. "Iran Foreign Minister Visits Jordan." *Associated Press* May 17, 2006, LexisNexis Academic.

Hall, Stuart. "The Spectacle of the Other." In *Discourse Theory and Practice: A Reader*, edited by Margaret Wetherell, Simeon Yates, and Stephanie Taylor, 324–344. London: Sage, 2001.

Halliday, F. *The Middle East in International Relations: Power, Politics and Ideology.* Cambridge: Cambridge University Press, 2005.

Hansen, Lene. *Security as Practice: Discourse Analysis and the Bosnian War.* London: Routledge, 2006.

Hen-Tov, Elliot. "Understanding Iran's New Authoritarianism." *The Washington Quarterly* 30, no. 1 (2006): 163–179.

Herszenhorn, David M., and Rick Gladstone. "Iran Expands Nuclear Fuel Production After Talks." *The New York Times* April 9, 2013, sec. World /Middle East. http://www.nytimes.com/2013/04/10/world/middleeast/iran-expands-nuclear-fuel-production-after-talks.html.

Hinnebusch, Raymond A. "Does Syria Want Peace?" *Journal of Palestine Studies* 26, no. 1 (1996): 42–57.

———. "Identity in International Relations: Constructivism versus Materialism and the Case of the Middle East." *Review of International Affairs* 3, no. 2 2003: 358–362.

———. "Omni-balancing Revisited; Syrian Foreign Policy between Rational Actor and Regime Legitimacy." Unpublished article, n.d.

———. "Syria: The Politics of Peace and Regime Survival." *Middle East Policy* 3, no. 4 (1995): 74–87.

———. *The International Politics of the Middle East.* Manchester: Manchester University Press, 2003.

Hinnebusch, R. A., and A. Ehteshami, eds. *The Foreign Policies of Middle East States.* Boulder, Colorado: Lynne Rienner Publishers, 2002.

Holliday, Shabnam J. *Defining Iran.* Farnham: Ashgate, 2011.

Holsti, Kal J. "National Role Conceptions in the Study of Foreign Policy." *International Studies Quarterly* 14, no. 3 (1970): 233–309.

Hoseyni, Omid. " Rigi's Capture Knocked Out the BBC." Translated by BBC Worldwide Monitoring, *Keyhan* March 7, 2010, LexisNexis Academic.

Hudson, Valerie. *Foreign Policy Analysis.* Lanham: Rowman & Littlefield Publishers, 2006.

Hunter, Shireen. *Iran's Foreign Policy in the Post-Soviet Era: Resisting the New International Order.* Santa Barbara, California: Praeger, 2010.

Hurriyet Daily News. "Turkey-Iran Gold-for-gas Hits $120 Million in a Month." *Hurriyet Daily News* April 1, 2013. http://www.hurriyetdailynews.com/turkey-iran-gold-trade-resumes-after-stopping-in-january.aspx?pageID=238&nID=43982&NewsCatID=344.

Hurst, Steven R., and Diana Elias. "Arab Distrust of Iran Gains Momentum." *Associated Press* May 3, 2006, LexisNexis Academic.

Idiz, Semih. "Turkey-Iran Ties Strained by Iraq, Syria—Al-Monitor: The Pulse of the Middle East." *Al-Monitor* February 19, 2013. http://www

.al-monitor.com/pulse/originals/2013/02/turkey-iran-tensions-rise
-syria.html.

Imani, Mohammad. "Intersection of Two Parallel Lines." Translated by
    BBC Worldwide Monitoring, *Keyhan* August 29, 2009, LexisNexis
    Academic.

———. "Nostalgia for a Strategy." Translated by BBC Worldwide Monitoring,
    Keyhan March 8, 2010, LexisNexis Academic.

———. "Oh Pious Man! You and Wine." Translated by BBC Worldwide
    Monitoring, *Keyhan* June 30, 2009, LexisNexis Academic.

International Atomic Energy Agency (IAEA). *Chronology of Key Events.*
    Vienna: IAEA, 2011. http://www.iaea.org/newscenter/focus/iaeairan
    /iran_timeline8.shtml.

———. *IAEA and Iran: IAEA Reports.*Vienna: IAEA, 2011. http://www
    .iaea.org/newscenter/focus/iaeairan/iaea_reports.shtml.

International Bank for Reconstruction and Development (IBRD). *Iran
    Country Brief.* Washington: IBRD, 2009. http://siteresources.worldbank
    .org/INTIRAN/Resources/IRAN-web-brief-June2009.pdf.

International Crisis Group (ICG). *Iran: Ahmadi-Nejad's Tumultuous
    Presidency.* Brussels: ICG, 2007, http://www.crisisgroup.org/home
    /index.cfm?id=4647&l=1.

———. *Spider Web: The Making and Unmaking of Iran Sanctions.* Brussels:
    ICG,February25,2013.http://www.crisisgroup.org/en/regions/middle
    -east-north-africa/iraq-iran-gulf/iran/138-spider-web-the-making-and
    -unmaking-of-iran-sanctions.aspx.

———. *What Does Ahmadi-Nejad's Victory Mean?* Brussels: ICG, 2005,
    http://www.crisisgroup.org/home/index.cfm?id=3604&l=1.

International Herald Tribune. "Sinopec Signs Deal to Develop Iranian Oil; $2
    Billion Pact Firms Beijing-Tehran Links." *International Herald Tribune*
    December 11, 2007, LexisNexis Academic.

International Montary Fund (IMF). "Islamic Republic of Iran: Selected
    Issues." *IMF Country Report No. 08/285,* 2008. http://www.imf.org
    /external/pubs/cat/longres.aspx?sk=22282.0.

Iran Diplomacy. "Iran-Egypt Relations Enters a New Phase." *Iran Diplomacy*
    February 18, 2010. http://www.irdiplomacy.ir/en/page/1471/IranEgy
    pt+Relations+Enters+a+New+Phase.html.

Iran Pulse. "Chinese Investment in Iran Said to Drop from $3 Billion to $400
    Million." *Iran Pulse* March 15, 2013. http://iranpulse.al-monitor.com
    /index.php/2013/03/1555/chinese-investment-in-iran-said-to-drop
    -from-3-billion-to-400-million/.

IRINN. "Iran FM Says Latest Obama Statements 'Propaganda,' Criticizes UN
    Security Council." Translated by BBC Worldwide Monitoring, IRINN,
    April 7, 2010, LexisNexis Academic.

———. "Iran Foreign Minister Calls for Purposeful Nuclear Talks with EU3."
    Translated by BBC Worldwide Monitoring, IRINN, December 21, 2005,
    LexisNexis Academic.

IRINN. "Iran Foreign Minister Urges West to Give Up on 'Biased' Views." Translated by BBC Worldwide Monitoring, IRINN, April 7, 2010, LexisNexis Academic.

———. "Iran Foreign Ministry Spokesman's Weekly News Conference." Translated by BBC Worldwide Monitoring, IRINN, October 12, 2009, LexisNexis Academic.

———. "Iran Minister Urges Dialogue, Trust Building—TV." Translated by BBC Worldwide Monitoring, IRINN, April 20, 2010, LexisNexis Academic.

———. "Iran Nuclear Official Announces Production of Yellow Cake." Translated by BBC Worldwide Monitoring, IRINN, December 5, 2010, LexisNexis Academic.

———. "Iran Says Nuclear Talks 'Escape Route for Other Side.'" Translated by BBC Worldwide Monitoring, IRINN, December 5, 2010, LexisNexis Academic.

———. "Iran's Nuclear Activities 'Transparent'—Foreign Minister." Translated by BBC Worldwide Monitoring, IRINN, April 20, 2010, LexisNexis Academic.

———. "Iranian Nuclear Negotiator Says 5+1 Talks 'Positive.'" Translated by BBC Worldwide Monitoring, IRINN, October 1, 2009, LexisNexis Academic.

———. "Minister Says Turkey Shares Iran's Views on Nuclear Weapons." Translated by BBC Worldwide Monitoring, IRINN, April 20, 2010, LexisNexis Academic.

———. "President Says Action Against Iran Will Be Regretted." Translated by BBC Worldwide Monitoring, IRINN, February 17, 2010, LexisNexis Academic.

———. "Spokesman Hopes Obama Remarks on Iran's Nuclear Rights Become Reality." Translated by BBC Worldwide Monitoring, IRINN, April 6, 2009, LexisNexis Academic.

———. "Spokesman Says Iran Ready For Talks on Its Nuclear Programme." Translated by BBC Worldwide Monitoring, IRINN, June 29, 2009, LexisNexis Academic.

IRNA. "Algerian-Lebanon-Israel." IRNA, August 14, 2006, LexisNexis Academic.

———. "Day of Public Mourning Announced in Iran for Hugo Chavez." IRNA, March 6, 2013. http://www.irna.com/en/News/80572936/Politic/Day_of_public_mourning_announced_in_Iran_for_Hugo_Chavez.

———. "Foreign Minister: G5+1 Lack Political Will to Resolve Dispute on Iran Nuclear Programme." Translated by BBC Worldwide Monitoring, IRNA, April 7, 2010, LexisNexis Academic.

———. "Fuel Swap a Chance for Mutual Trust-building—Iran Minister." Translated by BBC Worldwide Monitoring, IRNA, April 20, 2010, LexisNexis Academic.

———. "Iraqi President Arrives in Tehran." IRNA, November 21, 2005, LexisNexis Academic.

————. "President-Ahmad-Bahrain." IRNA, March 1, 2006, LexisNexis Academic.

————. "Riyadh-Visit-Iran." IRNA, April 12, 2006, LexisNexis Academic.

————. "Speaker Criticizes U.S. for Involvement in Iran's Bombing Attack." IRNA, October 29, 2009, LexisNexis, Academic.

ISNA. "Installation of Nuclear Centrifuges Continues in Natanz—Iran Nuclear Official." ISNA, April 17, 2007, LexisNexis Academic.

————. "There is No Legal Basis for UN Referral." Translated by BBC Worldwide Monitoring, ISNA, January 31, 2006, LexisNexis Academic.

Jackson, Patrick T., and Daniel H. Nexon. "Constructivist Realism or Realist-constructivism?" *International Studies Review* 6, no. 2 (2004):337–341.

Jalali-Naini, Ahmad R. "Capital Accumulation and Economic Growth in Iran: Past Experience and Future Prospects." *Iranian Studies* 38, no. 1 (2005): 91–116.

Jalili, Saeed. "Iran: Deputy Foreign Minister Defends Nuclear Policy; Outlines Foreign Policy." Translated by BBC Worldwide Monitoring, Fars News Agency, March 7, 2007, LexisNexis Academic.

————. "Iran's Top Nuclear Negotiator Jalili Speaks of 'a Positive Climate.'" Translated By BBC Worldwide Monitoring, Vision of the Islamic Republic of Iran (Television), December 1, 2007, LexisNexis Academic.

————. "Security Chief Says Nuclear Watchdog Report Confirms Iran's Truthfulness." Translated by BBC Worldwide Monitoring, Islamic Republic of Iran News Network, February 22, 2008, LexisNexis Academic.

Javan. "Head of Iran's Nuclear Organization on Nuclear Policy and Enrichment." Translated by BBC Worldwide Monitoring, *Javan* March 17, 2010, LexisNexis Academic.

————. "Jalili's Bitter Chinese News for the US." Translated by BBC Worldwide Monitoring, *Javan* April 3, 2010, LexisNexis Academic.

Jedinia, Mehdi. "Iranian President Gunning for Foreign Minister." *Mianeh* September 22, 2010. http://mianeh.net/article/iranian-president-gunning-foreign-minister.

————. "Iran's Hardliners Fall Out." *Mianeh* September 22, 2010. http://mianeh.net/article/iran%E2%80%99s-hardliners-fall-out.

Johnson, Stephen. "Iran's Influence in the Americas: Full Report." Washington: Centre for Strategic and International Studies, March 12, 2012. http://csis.org/files/publication/120312__Johnson_Iran%27sInfluence_web.pdf.

Kandemir, Asli. "Exclusive: Turkey-Iran Gold Trade Wiped Out by New U.S. Sanctions." *Reuters* February 16, 2013. http://www.reuters.com/article/2013/02/16/us-iran-turkey-sanctions-idUSBRE91F01F20130216.

Karimi, Nasser. "Iran Blames U.S., Britain for Bombings." *Associated Press* January 26, 2006, LexisNexis Academic.

————. "Iranian President Blames U.S., Israel for Destruction of Samarra Shrine's Golden Dome." *Associated Press Worldstream* February 23, 2006, LexisNexis Academic.

Karshenas, Massoud, and Hassan Hakimian "Oil, Economic Diversification and the Democratic Process in Iran." *Iranian Studies* 38, no. 1 (2005): 67–90.

Katzenstein, Lawrence, and Jason Strakes. *Omnibalancing and Substitutability in Analyzing Middle East Foreign Policies: Applications to Post-2005 Iraq.* Unpublished draft presented at the 2011 ISA Annual Conference, Montreal, 2010.

Katzenstein, Peter J., ed., *The Culture of National Security.* New York: Columbia University Press, 1996.

Keddie, Nikki R., and Yann Richard. *Roots of Revolution: An Interpretive History of Modern Iran.* First Edition. New Haven: Yale University Press, 1981.

Kessler, Glenn, and Thomas Erdbrink. "Iran Reaches Nuclear Deal with Brazil and Turkey; U.S. Reacts with Caution to Accord that Could Imperil Sanctions Effort." *The Washington Post* May 18, 2010, LexisNexis Academic.

Keyhan. "Ablution of Martyrdom [Preparation for Martyrdom] by the BBC of Britain." Translated by BBC Worldwide Monitoring, *Keyhan* June 25, 2009, LexisNexis Academic.

———. "Are We Dead that the BBC Should Select a Source of Emulation for Us?" Translated by BBC Worldwide Monitoring, *Keyhan* January 11, 2010, LexisNexis Academic.

———. "Candidate and the Spear." Translated by BBC Worldwide Monitoring, *Keyhan* April 8, 2009, LexisNexis Academic.

———. "CIA and Britain's MI6." Translated by BBC Worldwide Monitoring, *Keyhan* July 21, 2009, LexisNexis Academic.

———. "CIA and Tunnel Digging in Canadian Embassy." Translated by BBC Worldwide Monitoring, *Keyhan* August 6, 2009, LexisNexis Academic.

———. "CIA Dollars at Service of Provoking Pseudo Clerics." Translated by BBC Worldwide Monitoring, *Keyhan* July 15, 2009, LexisNexis Academic.

———. "CIA's Useless Instructions for Soft Warfare and Velvet Coup." Translated by BBC Worldwide Monitoring, *Keyhan* July 4, 2010, LexisNexis Academic.

———. "Detecting the Best Foot Scrub in the Web." Translated by BBC Worldwide Monitoring, *Keyhan* June 14, 2010, LexisNexis Academic.

———. "Electoral Deception Under the Cover of Protecting Votes." Translated by BBC Worldwide Monitoring, *Keyhan* May 27, 2009, LexisNexis Academic.

———. "Foreign Minister: UK Supports Those Who Insult Islamic Holy Beliefs." Translated by BBC Worldwide Monitoring, *Keyhan* January 3, 2010, LexisNexis Academic.

———. "Former Assistant Secretary of the US Treasury in Interview with Keyhan: America had Reported a Rreen Coup d'Etat in Iran Before the Elections." Translated by BBC Worldwide Monitoring, *Keyhan* September 9, 2009, LexisNexis Academic.

———. "Green Agreement with the Great Satan!" Translated by BBC Worldwide Monitoring, *Keyhan* November 1, 2009, LexisNexis Academic.

———. "Green Sedition's Genealogy Reached Cultural NATO and the Hojjatiyeh Society." Translated by BBC Worldwide Monitoring, *Keyhan* March 6, 2010, LexisNexis Academic.

———. "Head of Intelligence Organization of Sistan-Baluchestan Province: Some 180 Crimes of Rigi's Group Have Been Thwarted During Recent Years." Translated by BBC Worldwide Monitoring, *Keyhan* July 5, 2010, LexisNexis Academic.

———. "Ignominy of Opposition's Stooges that Have Taken Photo with Bush." Translated by BBC Worldwide Monitoring, *Keyhan* June 28, 2010, LexisNexis Academic.

———. "In a Forum Commemorating Commander Shushtari: Full-time Presence of a British Intelligence Agent Alongside Rigi." Translated by BBC Worldwide Monitoring, *Keyhan* December 10, 2009, LexisNexis Academic.

———. "Iran's Turn." Translated by BBC Worldwide Monitoring, *Keyhan* June 29, 2009, LexisNexis Academic.

———. "Kazemianfar in an Interview with Fars: Britain's Position Must Be Clarified Once and for All." *Keyhan* June 21, 2009, LexisNexis Academic.

———. "Keep Saying that We Are Not Supported by Foreigners." Translated by BBC Worldwide Monitoring, *Keyhan* February 10, 2010, and LexisNexis Academic.

———. "Keyhan Analytical-news Report: Britain's Role in Recent Disturbances." Translated by BBC Worldwide Monitoring, *Keyhan* June 17, 2009, LexisNexis Academic.

———. "Khatami's Suggestion or Michael Ledeen's Guideline?" Translated by BBC Worldwide Monitoring, *Keyhan* June 21, 2009, LexisNexis Academic.

———. "Kiyan Tajbakhsh revealed: 'Tier 2'; The Project for American Intelligence Organizations." *Keyhan* August 2, 2009, LexisNexis Academic.

———. "Location of Torture and Rape in the House of Mr Director, as Ordered by Foreigners!" Translated by BBC Worldwide Monitoring, *Keyhan* April 27, 2010, LexisNexis Academic.

———. "London Clique Exposed Perhaps Places Like Berlin, Paris or Brussels." *Keyhan* July 22, 2010, LexisNexis Academic.

———. "Majlis National Security Committee: Ties with Britain Must be Reviewed." Translated by BBC Worldwide Monitoring, *Keyhan* June 23, 2009, LexisNexis Academic.

———. "Mistake by a Clumsy MI6 Agent or...!" Translated by BBC Worldwide Monitoring, *Keyhan* February 1, 2010, LexisNexis Academic.

———. "Musavi: If Mirza Kuchek Khan Was in His Right Mind, He Would not Fight against the British and Reza Khan." Translated by BBC Worldwide Monitoring, *Keyhan* June 27, 2010, LexisNexis Academic.

Keyhan. "Musavi's New Statement; A Copy of the CIA Version." Translated by BBC Worldwide Monitoring, *Keyhan* September 7, 2009, LexisNexis Academic.

———. "On the Threshold of another Dawn." Translated by BBC Worldwide Monitoring, *Keyhan* March 18, 2009, LexisNexis Academic.

———. "Playing Yazid in Yiddish English during Ashura." Translated by BBC Worldwide Monitoring, *Keyhan* December 28, 2009, LexisNexis Academic.

———. "Summoning Ghosts in the Election." Translated by BBC Worldwide Monitoring, *Keyhan* March 9, 2009, LexisNexis Academic.

———. "The Bells Are Ringing; Will They Capture Us Also?!" Translated by BBC Worldwide Monitoring, *Keyhan* March 1, 2010, LexisNexis Academic.

———. "The Completely Self-evolving Process of Employing Extremists by America." Translated by BBC Worldwide Monitoring, *Keyhan* June 21, 2009c, LexisNexis Academic.

———. "Three weeks in a Coma and the Repetition of the Jokes of Three Idiots." Translated by BBC Worldwide Monitoring, *Keyhan* February 28, 2010, LexisNexis Academic.

———. "Traces of Terrorists in London's Collapsed Group House." Translated by BBC Worldwide Monitoring, *Keyhan* February 17, 2010, LexisNexis Academic.

———. "Until Yesterday It Was Enemy's Voice; Now It Is Civil Behaviour?!" Translated by BBC Worldwide Monitoring, *Keyhan* June 22, 2009, LexisNexis Academic.

———. "VOA and BBC Are Obviously Ominous but We Dare Not Choose Another Way." Translated by BBC Worldwide Monitoring, *Keyhan* December 10, 2009, LexisNexis Academic.

———. "Wild Cowboys." Translated by BBC Worldwide Monitoring, *Keyhan* July 17, 2010, LexisNexis Academic.

———. "Zadsar: Sedition Leaders' Children Give Information to the Enemies." Translated by BBC Worldwide Monitoring, *Keyhan* January 3, 2010, LexisNexis Academic.

Khalaf, Roula. "Iran-Saudi Talks Aim to Reduce Tensions." *Financial Times* March 3, 2007, LexisNexis Academic.

———. "Resurgent Iran Sets Challenge For Arab Rulers in Troubled Gulf Sunni Regimes Are Struggling to Formulate a Strategy to Deal with a Shift in the Balance of Power, Reports Roula Khalaf." *Financial Times* January 2, 2007, LexisNexis Academic.

———. "Sunni Arab States Wary of Role for Iran Jordan, Egypt and Saudi Arabia Are Keen to Head Off Any Move by the U.S. to Talk to Tehran, Reports Roula Khalaf." *Financial Times* November 30, 2006, LexisNexis Academic.

Khalaf, Roula, and Najmeh Bozorgmehr. "Diplomats in Tit-for-tat Expulsion." *Financial Times* June 24, 2009, LexisNexis Academic.

Khalaji, Mehdi. "Apocalyptic Politics: On the Rationality of Iranian Policy." *Policy Focus*, no. 79, The Washington Institute for Near East Policy, 2008.

Khamenei, Ali. "A Message Friday to Ismail Haniya." The Office of the Supreme Leader, January 17, 2009. http://www.leader.ir/langs/en/print.php?sec=content&id=4688.

———. "Announces General Policies of Fifth Development Plan." The Office of the Supreme Leader, November 12, 2009. http://www.leader.ir/langs/en/print.php?sec=content&id=4677.

———. "Ayatollah Khamenei Thanks Nation." The Office of the Supreme Leader, December 23, 2006. http://www.leader.ir/langs/en/print.php?sec=content&id=3585.

———. "Ayatollah Khamenei: The Cardinal Purpose of Hajj is to Show the United Identity of the Muslim Ummah." The Office of the Supreme Leader, December 29, 2006. http://www.leader.ir/langs/en/print.php?sec=content&id=3586.

———. "Ayatollah Khamenei Condemns Qana Tragedy." The Office of the Supreme Leader, August 2, 2006. http://www.leader.ir/langs/en/print.php?sec=content&id=3541.

———. "Fourth International Conference for Support of Palestine, the Model of Resistance, and Ghaza, the Victim of War Crimes." The Office of the Supreme Leader, March 4, 2009. http://www.leader.ir/langs/en/print.php?sec=content&id=4858.

———. "Friday Prayer." Translated by BBC Worldwide Monitoring, VIRIN, June 17, 2009, LexisNexis Academic.

———. "IR Leader Condoles Shiraz Mishap." The Office of the Supreme Leader, April 14, 2008. http://www.leader.ir/langs/en/print.php?sec=content&id=3770.

———. "IR Leader Condoles with Ayatollah Montazeri's Demise." The Office of the Supreme Leader, December 20, 2009. http://www.leader.ir/langs/en/print.php?sec=content&id=6238.

———. "IR Leader Endorses Vote to President-elect Mahmoud Ahmadinejad." The Office of the Supreme Leader, August 3, 2009. http://www.leader.ir/langs/en/print.php?sec=content&id=5723.

———. "IR Leader Receives Cinema Directors." The Office of the Supreme Leader Sayyid Ali Khamenei, June 13, 2006. http://www.leader.ir/langs/en/print.php?sec=bayanat&id=3531.

———. "IR Leader Salutes Basiji Students." The Office of the Supreme Leader, August 23, 2006. http://www.leader.ir/langs/en/print.php?sec=content&id=3549.

———. "IR Leader Sends Congrats Message to Nasrallah." The Office of the Supreme Leader, August 17, 2006. http://www.leader.ir/langs/en/print.php?sec=content&id=3545.

———. "IR Leader's New Year's Day Message." The Office of the Supreme Leader, March 20, 2006. http://www.leader.ir/langs/en/print.php?sec=content&id=3511.

Khamenei, Ali. "Iran Leader Criticizes 'Hegemony' for Monopolising Science". Translated by BBC Worldwide Monitoring, Vision of the Islamic Republic of Iran (Television), August 26, 2008, LexisNexis Academic.

———. "Iran Leader Says Enemy Wants to Reinstate Its 'Evil Domination.'" Translated by BBC Worldwide Monitoring, Vision of the Islamic Republic of Iran (Television), September 7, 2010, LexisNexis Academic.

———. "Iran Leader Says US 'Biggest Disaster' for World of Islam." Translated by BBC Worldwide Monitoring, Voice of the Islamic Republic of Iran (Radio), February 21, 2011, LexisNexis Academic.

———. "Iran Leader Says US 'Trick' to Divide People from State." Translated by BBC Worldwide Monitoring, Voice of the Islamic Republic of Iran, September 24, 2009, LexisNexis Academic.

———. "Iran Leader Sees 'Hyperactive' Opposition as 'Aimless.'" Translated by BBC Worldwide Monitoring, Vision of the Islamic Republic of Iran Khorasan Provincial TV, September 16, 2010, LexisNexis Academic.

———. "Iran Leader: US Language Is Hegemonic, 'Fox'-like Turning 'Wolfish.'" Translated by BBC Worldwide Monitoring, Voice of the Islamic Republic of Iran (Radio), April 21, 2010, LexisNexis Academic.

———. "Iran Not Seeking Nuclear Weapons—Leader." Translated by BBC Worldwide Monitoring, Voice of the Islamic Republic of Iran (Radio), February 17, 2008, LexisNexis Academic.

———. "Iranian Supreme Leader Criticizes US Nuclear Policies." Translated by BBC Worldwide Monitoring, The Office of the Supreme Leader, April, 17, 2010, LexisNexis Academic.

———. "Islamic Republic, Modern Example of Religious Democracy." The Office of the Supreme Leader, February 20, 2007. http://www.leader.ir/langs/en/print.php?sec=content&id=3598.

———. "Islamic Revolution Leader in Response to President Mahmoud Ahmadinejad's Letter." The Office of the Supreme Leader, February 4, 2009. http://www.leader.ir/langs/en/print.php?sec=content&id=4746.

———. "Islamic Revolution Leader Issued a Statement Sunday on the Horrendous Tragedy of Gaza Bloodbath in the Hand of the Zionists." The Office of the Supreme Leader, December 28, 2008. http://www.leader.ir/langs/en/print.php?sec=content&id=4603.

———. "Islamic Umma Must Generate Waves of Wrath." The Office of the Supreme Leader, March 2, 2008. http://www.leader.ir/langs/en/print.php?sec=content&id=3716.

———. "Leader Appoints CSDS Director and Deputy Chief of General Staff of the Armed Forces for Inspection Affairs." The Office of the Supreme Leader, September 26, 2005. http://www.leader.ir/langs/en/print.php?sec=content&id=3469.

———. "Leader Appoints New Director of the Defense Ministry's Information Security Organization." The Office of the Supreme Leader, October 30, 2005. http://www.leader.ir/langs/en/print.php?sec=content&id=3475.

———. "Leader Appreciates Armed Forces." The Office of the Supreme Leader, December 21, 2005. http://www.leader.ir/langs/en/print.php?sec=content&id=3488.

————. "Leader Designates New Representative in IRGC." The Office of the Supreme Leader, December 24, 2005. http://www.leader.ir/langs/en/print.php?sec=content&id=3489.

————. "Leader Receives Air Force Servicemen." The Office of the Supreme Leader, February 7, 2006. http://www.leader.ir/langs/en/print.php?sec=content&id=3500.

————. "Leader Says Iran's Progress Shocked Nuclear Powers." Translated by BBC Worldwide Monitoring, Vision of the Islamic Republic of Iran (Television), April 28, 2010, LexisNexis Academic.

————. "Leader Urges End to Protests, Says Poll Results Can Be Investigated Legally. Second Friday sermon delivered by Ayatollah Ali Khamenei, leader of Iran's Islamic revolution, at Tehran University—Live." Islamic Republic of Iran News Network Television (IRINN), June 19, 2009. http://www.juancole.com/2009/06/supreme-leader-khameneis-friday-address.html.

————. "Leader's Address at the Graduation and Oath-taking Ceremony of IRGC Cadets." The Office of the Supreme Leader, November 25, 2006. http://www.leader.ir/langs/en/print.php?sec=bayanat&id=3578.

————. "Leader's Address to Air Force Servicemen." The Office of the Supreme Leader Sayyid Ali Khamenei, February 7, 2006. http://www.leader.ir/langs/en/print.php?sec=bayanat&id=3500.

————. "Leader's Address to Executive Officials." The Office of the Supreme Leader, June 30, 2007. http://www.leader.ir/langs/en/print.php?sec=bayanat&id=3617.

————. "Leader's Address to the Iranian People from Various Social Strata." The Office of the Supreme Leader Sayyid Ali Khamenei, December 13, 2006. http://www.leader.ir/langs/en/print.php?sec=bayanat&id=3583.

————. "Leader's Address to the Officials and Executives of the Islamic Republic." The Office of the Supreme Leader Website, April 6, 2007. http://www.leader.ir/langs/en/print.php?sec=bayanat&id=3603.

————. "Leader's Address to the Participants in the 2nd Congress in Commemoration of IBN Maytham Bahrani." The Office of the Supreme Leader, January 15, 2007. http://www.leader.ir/langs/en/print.php?sec=bayanat&id=3588.

————. "Leader's Address to University Professors and Elite Academics." The Office of the Supreme Leader, October 13, 2005. http://www.leader.ir/langs/en/print.php?sec=bayanat&id=3472.

————. "Leader's Address to War-disabled Veterans." The Office of the Supreme Leader, October 26, 2005. http://www.leader.ir/langs/en/print.php?sec=bayanat&id=3474.

————. "Leader's Condolatory Message on the Demise of Hajji Ali Mohammadi-Doost." The Office of the Supreme Leader, November 12, 2005. http://www.leader.ir/langs/en/print.php?sec=content&id=3479.

————. "Leader's Message in Commemoration of Martyrs and Devotees of the Sacred Defense Era." The Office of the Supreme Leader, September 22, 2005. http://www.leader.ir/langs/en/print.php?sec=content&id=3468.

Khamenei, Ali. "Leader's Message of Condolence on Tragic Pakistan Earthquake." The Office of the Supreme Leader, October 10, 2005. http://www.leader.ir/langs/en/print.php?sec=content&id=3471.

———. "Leader's Message on Sammara Tragedy." The Office of the Supreme Leader, February 22, 2006. http://www.leader.ir/langs/en/print .php?sec=content&id=3505.

———. "Leader's Speech on Feast of Mab'ath." The Office of the Supreme Leader, September 2, 2005. http://www.leader.ir/langs/en/print .php?sec=content&id=3467.

———. "Leader's Speech to Government Officials on the Eid-al-Fitr." The Office of the Supreme Leader, November 4, 2005. http://www.leader.ir /langs/en/print.php?sec=bayanat&id=3477.

———. "Leader's Speech to Governor-generals." The Office of the Supreme Leader, February 27, 2006. http://www.leader.ir/langs/en/print .php?sec=bayanat&id=3506.

———. "Leader's Speech to Residents of the Holy City of Qom." The Office of the Supreme Leader Sayyid Ali Khamenei, January 9, 2006. http:// www.leader.ir/langs/en/print.php?sec=bayanat&id=3492.

———. "Leader's Speech to the Residents of Qom." The Office of the Supreme Leader, January 8, 2007. http://www.leader.ir/langs/en/print. php?sec=bayanat&id=3587.

———. "Leader's Speech to the Residents of Qom." The Office of the Supreme Leader, Sayyid Ali Khamenei, August 1, 2007. http://www. leader.ir/langs/en/print.php?sec=bayanat&id=3587.

———. "Leader's Speech to the Residents of the Eastern Azarbaijan Province." The Office of the Supreme Leader, February 17, 2007. http:// www.leader.ir/langs/en/print.php?sec=bayanat&id=3595.

———. "Leader's Statements at the Funeral of Major General Kazemi and His Colleagues." The Office of the Supreme Leader, January 11, 2006. http://www.leader.ir/langs/en/print.php?sec=content&id=3493.

———. "Leader's Statements at the Graduation Ceremony of Army Cadets." The Office of the Supreme Leader, September 28, 2005. http://www .leader.ir/langs/en/print.php?sec=bayanat&id=3470.

———. "Leader's Statements at the Tehran Friday Prayers." Office of the Supreme Leader Website, October 21, 2005. http://www.leader.ir /langs/en/print.php?sec=content&id=3473.

———. "Leader's Statements in a Meeting with Residents of Dasht-e-Azadegan, Sousangerd, Bostan, Hamidiyeh and Hovayzeh." The Office of the Supreme Leader, March 25, 2006. http://www.leader.ir/langs/en /print.php?sec=bayanat&id=3513.

———. "Leader's Statements on the Day of Elections for the Experts Assembly and Islamic Councils." The Office of the Supreme Leader, December 15, 2006. http://www.leader.ir/langs/en/print.php?sec=bayanat&id=3584.

———. "Leadership Assembly of Experts Stands Essential Beacon of the System." The Office of the Supreme Leader, September 6, 2007. http:// www.leader.ir/langs/en/print.php?sec=content&id=3634.

————. "Message to the General Meeting of the United Islamic Students Association in Europe." The Office of the Supreme Leader, September 23, 2006. http://www.leader.ir/langs/en/print .php?sec=content&id=3557.

————. "Mughniyeh's Blood Would Double the Resistance." The Office of the Supreme Leader, February 14, 2008. http://www.leader.ir/langs /en/print.php?sec=content&id=3707.

————. "New Members of System Interests Council Appointed." The Office of the Supreme Leader, February 27, 2007. http://www.leader.ir/langs /en/print.php?sec=content&id=3600.

————. "Palestinian Issue, at Focal Point." The Office of the Supreme Leader, April 14, 2006. http://www.leader.ir/langs/en/print .php?sec=content&id=3515.

————. "President Elect is President of All Iranians." The Office of the Supreme Leader, June 13, 2009. http://www.leader.ir/langs/en/print .php?sec=content&id=5566.

————. "Scientific Progress Vital for Country." The Office of the Supreme Leader, September 24, 2008. http://www.leader.ir/langs/en/print .php?sec=content&id=4058.

————. "Supreme Leader Thanks Iranian Nation for Impressive Bahman 22 Rallies." The Office of the Supreme Leader, February 12, 2010. http:// www.leader.ir/langs/en/print.php?sec=content&id=6459.

————. "Supreme Leader's Public Address on Eid ul-Fitr." The Office of the Supreme Leader, October 1, 2008. http://www.leader.ir/langs/en /print.php?sec=bayanat&id=4074.

————. "Supreme Leader's Speech to Air Force Staff." The Office of the Supreme Leader, February 8, 2008. http://www.leader.ir/langs/en /print.php?sec=bayanat&id=3703.

————. "Supreme Leader's Speech to Government Officials on Eid ul-Fitr." The Office of the Supreme Leader, October 1, 2008. http://www.leader .ir/langs/en/print.php?sec=bayanat&id=4079.

————. "The Message of H. E. Ayatullah Khamenei to the Hajj Pilgrims from the Whole World." Office of the Supreme Leader Website, January 9, 2006. http://www.leader.ir/langs/en/print.php?sec=content&id=349.

————. "The Message of H. E. Ayatullah Khamenei to the Hajj Pilgrims from the Whole World." The Office of the Supreme Leader, December 7, 2008. http://www.leader.ir/langs/en/print.php?sec=content&id=4460.

————. "The Message of H. E. Ayatullah Khamenei to the Hajj Pilgrims." Office of the Supreme Leader Website, November 26, 2009. http://www .leader.ir/langs/en/print.php?sec=content&id=6135.

————. "The Message of H.E. Ayatullah Khamenei to the Hajj Pilgrims from the Whole World." The Office of the Supreme Leader, December 18, 2007. http://www.leader.ir/langs/en/print.php?sec=content&id=3657.

————. "US Forces, Prime Suspect in Iraqi Bombings." The Office of the Supreme Leader, April 25, 2009. http://www.leader.ir/langs/en/print .php?sec=content&id=5193.

Khamenei, Ali. "US, UK 'Opposition' to Iran Government 'Does Not Scare Anyone' Supreme Leader." Translated by BBC Worldwide Monitoring, Islamic Republic of Iran News Network, September 11, 2009, LexisNexis Academic.

———. "Your Islamic Republic Threw Challenge to All Anti-religion or Anti-people Models of Government." The Office of the Supreme Leader, March 15, 2008. http://www.leader.ir/langs/en/print .php?sec=content&id=3739.

Khatami, Ahmad. "Iran Cleric Says Armed rioters 'Waging War against God.'" Translated by BBC Monitoring, Voice of the Islamic Republic of Iran, June 26, 2009, LexisNexis Academic.

Khosrokhavar, Farhad. "The New Conservatives Take a Turn." *Middle East Report* 233 (2004): 24–27.

Kirkpatrick, David D. "Egyptian President Seeks Regional Initiative for Syria Peace." *The New York Times* August 26, 2012, sec. World / Middle East. http://www.nytimes.com/2012/08/27/world/middleeast/egyptian -president-seeks-regional-initiative-for-syria-peace.html.

Korany, Bahgat, and Hillal Dessouki. *The Foreign Policies of Arab States: The Challenge of Globalization.* Cairo: American University in Cairo Press, 2008.

Kramer, Andrew E. "Despite Price Drop, Oil Cartel Keeps Production Limit." *The New York Times* June 14, 2012, sec. Business Day / Global Business. http://www.nytimes.com/2012/06/15/business/global/opec-is-said -to-leave-production-steady.html.

Krane, Jim. "Many Gulf Arabs Uneasy about Iran." *Associated Press* April 6, 2006, LexisNexis Academic.

Kuchins, Andrew C., and Igor Zevelev. "Russia's Constested National Identity and Foreign Policy." In *Worldviews of Aspiring Powers: Domestic Foreign Policy Debates in China, India, Iran, Japan, and Russia*, edited by Henry R. Nau and Deepa M. Ollapally, 181–209. New York: Oxford University Press, 2012.Landler, Michael. "Tehran Casts Its Shadow on Clinton Mideast Trip; Iran Is on the Agenda, If not the Itinerary." *International Herald Tribune* March 6, 2009, LexisNexis Academic.

Lanteigne, Marc. *But There Are Limits: China's UN Security Council Behaviour and the Iran Crisis.* Unpublished draft presented at ISA convention, 2011.

Larijani, Ali A. "Iran's Security Chief Explains Tehran's Nuclear Strategy in TV Interview." Translated by BBC Worldwide Monitoring, Vision of the Islamic Republic of Iran (Television), January 1, 2006, LexisNexis Academic.

———. "Iran's Nuclear Negotiator on Failure of Western Policy—Text of Interview." Translated by BBC Worldwide Monitoring, Mehr News Agency, October 18, 2006, LexisNexis Academic.

———. "Iranian Negotiator Gives Press Conference on Nuclear Issue." Translated by BBC Worldwide Monitoring, Islamic Republic of Iran News Network, September 21, 2005, LexisNexis Academic.

————. "Security Chief Warns West not to Seek Adventurism on Iran's Nuclear Case." Translated by BBC Worldwide Monitoring, Islamic Republic of Iran News Network, September 12, 2007, LexisNexis Academic.

Lee, Min-Jeong. "South Korea's Iran Imports Fall While China's Increase." *Wall Street Journal* March 22, 2013. http://online.wsj.com/article/SB1 0001424127887324103504578375653102125928.html.

Mahdavikhah, Sa'id. "The Enemy Is Awake." Translated by BBC Worldwide Monitoring, *Keyhan* March 11, 2009, LexisNexis Academic.

Mahjub, Matin. "Three Crises for a Dying Front." Translated by BBC Worldwide Monitoring, *Keyhan* September 23, 2009, LexisNexis Academic.

Maloney, Suzanne. "Identity and Change in Iran's Foreign Policy." In *Identity and Foreign Policy in the Middle East*, edited by Shibley Telhami and Michael Barnett, 88–116. New York: Cornell University Press, 2002.

————. "Sanctioning Iran: If Only It Were So Simple." *Washington Quarterly* 33, no. 1 (2010): 131–147.

Maloney, Suzanne, and the United States Institute of Peace. *Iran's Long Reach: Iran as a Pivotal State in the Muslim World*. Washington, DC: United States Institute of Peace Press, 2008.

Mândrăşescu, Valentin. "Turkey Trade with Iran to Resume Despite the US Sanctions." Radio the Voice of Russia, March 31, 2013 http://english.ruvr.ru/2013_03_31/Turkey-trade-with-Iran-to-resume-despite-the-US-sanctions/.

Mardom Salari. "Pursuing the Policy of Détente in the New Government." Translated by BBC Worldwide Monitoring, September 23, 2009, LexisNexis Academic.

Marlowe, Lara. "Syria and Iran Take a Stand Against U.S. and the West." *The Irish Times* January 21, 2006, LexisNexis Academic.

Martin, Vanessa. *Creating an Islamic State: Khomeini and the Making of a New Iran*. London: I.B. Tauris, 2000.

Mashayekhi, Mehrdad. "The Rise and Fall of the Really-Existing Reform Movement in Iran." *Journal of Iranian Research and Analysis* 18, no. 2 (2002): 79–83.

Mattern, Janice B. "Power in Realist-constructivist Research." *International Studies Review* 6, no. 2 (2004): 343–346.

Macfarquhar, Neil. "Elections in Iran Favor Ayatollah's Allies, Dealing Blow to President and His Office." *The New York Times* March 4, 2012. http://www.nytimes.com/2012/03/05/world/middleeast/iran-elections-deal-blow-to-ahmadinejad-and-the-presidency.html?pagewanted=all&_r=1&.

McElroy, Damien. "British Relations with Iran Sink to Lowest in Decades as Tehran Embassies Are Stormed." *Telegraph.co.uk* November 29, 2011, sec. worldnews. http://www.telegraph.co.uk/news/worldnews/middleeast/iran/8924441/British-relations-with-Iran-sink-to-lowest-in-decades-as-Tehran-embassies-are-stormed.html.

McGreal, Chris. "Zimbabwe Bans Western Observers from Ballot: Fears of Rigging as Mugabe Faces Strong Challenges: China and Iran Among Few

Foreign Teams Allowed in." *The Guardian* March 8, 2008, LexisNexis Academic.

McLellan, David. *Ideology*. Buckingham: Open University Press, 1995.

Mehr News Agency. "Iran Guards Warns US, UK, Israel against Interference in Iran's Affairs." Translated by BBC Worldwide Monitoring, Mehr News Agency, June 22, 2009, LexisNexis Academic.

———. "Iranian Foreign Minister: Nuclear Disarmament an Achievable Goal." Translated by BBC Worldwide Monitoring, Mehr News Agency, April 7, 2010, LexisNexis Academic.

Memarian, Omid. "Ahmadinejad Alienates Key Protector." *Mianeh* January 28, 2011, http://mianeh.net/article/ahmadinejad-alienates-key-protector.

Milani, Mohsen M. "Tehran's Take." *Foreign Affairs* 88, no. 4 (2009): 46–62.

———. *The Making of Iran's Islamic Revolution: From Monarchy to Islamic Republic*. Boulder: Westview Press, 1994.

Ministry of External Affairs, Government of India. "External Affairs Minister's Speech at Global India Foundation Conference on 'Iran's Eurasian Dynamic: Mapping Regional and Extra-Regional Interests.'" Government of India, February 13, 2013. http://www.mea.gov.in/Speeches-Statements.htm?dtl/21246/External+Affairs+Ministers+speech+at+Global+India+Foundation+Conference+on+Irans+Eurasian+Dynamic+Mapping+Regional+and+ExtraRegional+Interests.

———. "Joint Statement on the 13th India-Russia Annual Summit: 'Partnership for Mutual Benefit and a Better World.'" Government of India, December 24, 2012. http://mea.gov.in/bilateral-documents.htm?dtl/20993/Joint+Statement+on+the+13th+IndiaRussia+Annual+Summit+Partnership+for+mutual+benefit+and+a+better+world.

Moaddel, Mansoor. *Class, Politics, and Ideology in the Iranian Revolution*. New York: Columbia University Press, 1992.

Mohammadi, Manouchehr. "In Opposing Ahmadinezhad, the policy of Westerners and Disgraced domestic Movements Became the Same." Translated by BBC Worldwide Monitoring, *Keyhan* June 30, 2009, LexisNexis Academic.

Mohammadi, Mehdi. "In Defence of the Truth." Translated by BBC Worldwide Monitoring, *Keyhan* July 12, 2009, LexisNexis 2009.

———. "The Other Undertaking." Translated by BBC Worldwide Monitoring, *Keyhan* June 8, 2009, LexisNexis Academic.

———. "When America Becomes Angry." Translated by BBC Worldwide Monitoring, *Keyhan* June 8, 2009, LexisNexis Academic.

———. "Wishful Thinking." Translated by BBC Worldwide Monitoring, *Keyhan* September 30, 2010, LexisNexis Academic.

Moj News Agency. "Iran Absorbed $34bln of FDI." December 7, 2008 LexisNexis Academic.

Moshirzadeh, Homeira. "Discursive Foundations of Iran's Nuclear Policy." *Security Dialogue* 38, no. 4 (2007): 521–543.

Moslem, Mehdi. *Factional Politics in Post-Khomeini Iran*. Syracuse: Syracuse University Press, 2002.

Mottaki, Manouchehr. "Iran's Foreign Policy under President Ahmadinejad." *Discourse: An Iranian Quarterly* 8, no. 2 (2009): 10–15.

Mouffe, Chantal. *Gramsci and Marxist Theory*. London: Routledge and Kegan Paul, 1979.

Mowlana, Hamid. "Defeat of the Defeated West." Translated by BBC Worldwide Monitoring, *Keyhan* July 2, 2009, LexisNexis Academic.

———. "Rise and Fall of Velvet Revolutions (part one)." Translated by BBC Worldwide Monitoring, *Keyhan* August 10, 2009, LexisNexis Academic.

Namazikhah, Sahar. "Khamenei Challenged by Senior Cleric." *Mianeh* October 29, 2010. http://mianeh.net/article/khamenei-challenged-senior-cleric.

National Iranian American Council. "Summary of Iran Human Rights Legislation in 111th Congress." http://www.niacouncil.org/site/DocServer/Guide_to_Iran_Human_Rights_Legislation.pdf?docID=302.

Nau, Henry R., and Deepa M. Ollapally, eds. *Worldviews of Aspiring Powers: Domestic Foreign Policy Debates in China, India, Iran, Japan, and Russia*. New York: Oxford University Press, 2012.

Naylor, Hugh. "U.S. Sanctions Drive Iranian Businesses and Exports to Syria." *International Herald Tribune* October 4, 2007, LexisNexis Academic.

The New York Times. "Nonaligned Nations Back Iran on Nuclear Bid, But Not on Syria." *The New York Times* September 1, 2012. http://www.nytimes.com/2012/09/01/world/middleeast/iran-criticizes-egypts-mohamed-morsi-over-syria-comments.html?_r=0.

———. "Russia Resists U.S. Position on Sanctions for Iran." *The New York Times* October 14, 2009. http://www.nytimes.com/2009/10/14/world/europe/14diplo.html?_r=1&.

Nezafati, Iraj. "West's New Strategy of Digital Diplomacy: Revealing America's Covert Objectives in Anti-Iranian 'Media Diplomacy'—First Part." Translated by BBC Worldwide Monitoring, *Keyhan* August 28, 2010, LexisNexis Academic.

Nia, Mehdi Mohammad. "Discourse and Indentity in Iran's Foreign Policy." *Iranian Review of Foreign Affairs* 3, no. 3 (Fall 2012): 29–64.

Noori, V. "Status-Seeking and Iranian Foreign Policy: The Speeches of the President at the United Nations." *Iranian Review of Foreign Affairs* 3, no. 1 (Spring 2012): 157–152.

Norooz. "Activists Say 'Adventurists' Are Threatening Detente in Foreign Policy." Translated by BBC Monitoring, *Norooz* February 17, 2002, LexisNexis Academic.

O'Connor, Anne Marie, and Mary Beth Sheridan. "Iran's Invisible Nicaragua Embassy; Feared Stronghold Never Materialized." *The Washington Post* July 13, 2009, LexisNexis Academic.

Office of the Supreme Leader Sayyid Ali Khamenei. "Feb 11 Rallies, Great Divine Miracle." Office of the Supreme Leader Sayyid Ali

Khamenei, February 17, 2010. http://www.leader.ir/langs/en/index .php?p=contentShow&id=6477 7.

———. "Friday Prayer." Office of the Supreme Leader Sayyid Ali Khamenei, June 20, 2009. http://www.leader.ir/langs/en/index .php?p=contentShow&id=5618.

———. "Imam Khomeini, Father of Islamic Awakening." Office of the Supreme Leader Sayyid Ali Khamenei, June 3, 2012. http://www.leader .ir/langs/en/?p=contentShow&id=9483.

———. "Supreme Leader Meets with Participants of International Conference on Islamic Awakening." Office of the Supreme Leader Sayyid Ali Khamenei, December 11, 2012. http://www.leader.ir/langs /en/?p=contentShow&id=10215.

Ogilvie-White, Tanya. "The Non-proliferation Diplomacy of the Non-nuclear-weapon States: Understanding International Responses to Iran's Nuclear Defiance." *European Journal of International Law* 18, no. 3 (2007): 453–476.

Ollapally, Deepa M., and Rajesh Rajagopalan. "India: Foreign Policy Perspectives of an Ambiguous Power." *Worldviews of Aspiring Powers: Domestic Foreign Policy Debates in China, India, Iran, Japan, and Russia*, edited by Henry R. Nau and Deepa M. Ollapally, 73–113. New York: Oxford University Press, 2012.

Omelicheva, Mariya Y. "Russia's Foreign Policy Toward Iran: A Critical Geopolitics Perspective." *Journal of Balkan and Near Eastern Studies* 14, no. 3 (2012): 331–344.

Omidi, Hamid. "Colourful Dreams." Translated by BBC Worldwide Monitoring, *Keyhan* June 24, 2009, LexisNexis Academic.

———. "Crossing over from a Defensive Role to an Aggressive One." Translated by BBC Worldwide Monitoring, *Keyhan* September 2, 2009, LexisNexis Academic.

———. "The Curtains Fell." Translated by BBC Worldwide Monitoring, *Keyhan* August 26, 2009, LexisNexis Academic.

Onderco, Michal. "South Africa's Iran Policy: 'Poster Child' Meets Renegade." *South African Journal of International Affairs* 19, no. 3 (2012): 299–318.

Parsa, Misagh. *Social Origins of the Iranian Revolution*. New Brunswick, London: Rutgers University Press, 1989.

Parsi, Trita. *Treacherous Alliance: The Secret Dealings of Israel, Iran, and the United States*. New Haven: Yale University Press, 2008.

Pew Research Center. "A Rising Tide Lifts Mood in the Developing World." Pew Global Attitudes Project, July 24, 2007. http://www.pewglobal .org/2007/07/24/a-rising-tide-lifts-mood-in-the-developing-world/.

———. "America's Image Slips, but Allies Share U.S. Concerns over Iran, Hamas." Pew Research Center, 2006. http://pewglobal. org/2006/06/13/americas-image-slips-but-allies-share-us-concerns -over-iran-hamas/.

————. "Global Unease with Major World Powers." Pew Global Attitudes Project, June 27, 2006. http://www.pewglobal.org/2007/06/27/global-unease-with-major-world-powers/.

Pomeroy, Robin. "Iran Tells Turkey: Change Tack or Face Trouble." *Reuters* October 8, 2011. http://www.reuters.com/article/2011/10/08/us-iran-turkey-khamenei-idUSTRE7970XI20111008.

Presidency of the Islamic Republic of Iran News Service. "Dr.Ahmadinejad Downplays Effects of Western Oil Embargos Against Iran." Presidency of the Islamic Republic of Iran News Service, May 8, 2013. http://www.president.ir/en/48531.

PressTV. "75% Principlists Win Majlis Vote." PressTV, March 3, 2013. http://www.presstv.ir/detail/229714.html.

————. "Chinese Supertanker Gets Oil at Iran Port." PressTV, April 7, 2013. http://www.presstv.ir/detail/2013/03/28/295493/chinese-supertanker-gets-oil-at-iran-port/.

————. "Italy to Be Iran's Top EU Trade Partner." PressTV, January 30, 2013. http://www.presstv.ir/detail/2013/01/30/286279/italy-to-be-irans-top-eu-trade-partner/.

————. "Enemy Seeking to Divide Clergy, Officials—Iranian Cleric." PressTV, October 4, 2010, LexisNexis Academic.

————. "Foreign Minister Says Iran Committed to Nuclear Disarmament." Transcribed by BBC Worldwide Monitoring, PressTV, August 21, 2010, LexisNexis Academic.

————. "Iran Attacks Turkey's NATO Shield, If Hit." PressTV, November 26, 2011. http://www.presstv.ir/detail/212321.html.

————. "Iran Warns UK Against Further Meddling." PressTV, March 14, 2012. http://www.presstv.ir/detail/175612.html.

————. "Iran, Britain in Talks to Resume Consular Relations." PressTV, April 17, 2013. http://www.presstv.com/detail/2013/03/18/294281/relations/.

————. "Principalists Win Majority of Seats." PressTV, March 15, 2008. http://edition.presstv.ir/detail/47596.html.

————. "Russia Stresses Iran's Right to Peaceful Nuclear Energy." PressTV, December 28, 2012. http://www.presstv.com/detail/2012/12/28/280565/russia-stresses-iran-right-to-nenergy/.

————. "US Admitting to Iran's Nuclear Right Positive—Foreign Minister." PressTV, December 5, 2010, LexisNexis Academic.

Pruzan-Jørgensen, Julie E. "Analyzing Authoritarian Regime Legitimation: Findings from Morocco."*Middle East Critique* 19, no. 3 (2010): 269–286.

Qashqavi, Hassan. "Spokesman Reacts to US Claims on Iran's Nuclear Programme, Hollywood Films." Translated by BBC Worldwide Monitoring, Vision of the Islamic Republic of Iran (Television), March 2, 2009, LexisNexis Academic.

Quds. "CIA Channel in the Canadian Embassy." Translated by BBC Worldwide Monitoring, *Keyhan* August 8, 2009, LexisNexis Academic.

Quds. "Head of Nuclear Program Says Iran Ready to Find Way Out of Impasse." Translated by BBC Worldwide Monitoring, March 7, 2010, LexisNexis Academic.

Radio Zamaneh. "Opposition Leader says Revolutionary Guards will Benefit from Iran Sanctions." *Payvand* July 10, 2010, http://www.payvand.com /news/10/jul/1092.html.

Rafsanjani, Ali Hashemi. "Iran's Rafsanjani Offers Suggestions for Resolving Post-election 'crisis'—More." Translated by BBC Worldwide Monitoring, VIRIN, July 17, 2009, LexisNexis Academic.

Raghavan, Sudarsan. "Yemen Denounces Iran's 'Interference'; Sunni Government Says Shiite Tehran Meddling in Conflict with Rebels." *The Washington Post* November 12, 2009, LexisNexis Academic.

Rahimi, Babak. "Iran's Declining Influence in Iraq." *The Washington Quarterly* 5, no. 1 (Winter 2012): 25–40.

Rakel, Eva Patricia. "The Political Elite in the Islamic Republic of Iran: From Khomeini to Ahmadinejad." *Comparative Studies of South Asia, Africa and the Middle East* 29, no. 1 (2009): 105–125.

———. *Power, Islam, and Political Elite in Iran: A study on the Iranian Political Elite from Khomeini to Ahmadinejad.* Leiden: Brill, 2009.

Ramazani, R. K., and Middle East Institute (Washington, DC). *Iran's Revolution: The Search for Consensus.* Bloomington, Indiana: Indiana University Press, 1990.

———. "Iran's Foreign Policy: Independence, Freedom and the Islamic Republic." In *Iran's foreign Policy from Khatami to Ahmadinejad*, edited by M. Zweiri and A. Ehteshami. Reading: Ithaca Press, 2008.

Resalat. "Iranian Newspaper Calls for Return of Qolhak Garden to Iran by Britain." Translated by BBC Monitoring, *Resalat* January 17, 2011, LexisNexis Academic.

Reuters. "Egypt Suspends Commercial Flights from Iran after Protests." *Reuters* April 8, 2013. http://www.reuters.com/article/2013/04/08 /egypt-iran-idUSL5N0CV0NL20130408.

———. "India Asks EU to Clarify Stance on Iran Oil Insurance." *Reuters* March 22, 2013. http://www.reuters.com/article/2013/03/22/india-iran-idUSL3N0CE0PE20130322.

———. "Iran Renews Hormuz Closure Threats." *Reuters* July 15, 2012. http://www.reuters.com/article/2012/07/15/us-iran-hormuz -idUSBRE86E0CN20120715.

———. "Russia Criticizes EU Iran Sanctions, Urges Talks." *Reuters* October 17, 2012. http://www.reuters.nl/article/2012/10/17/us-iran-nuclear -russia-idUSBRE89G1FM20121017.

———. "Shell Reveals Iranian Oil Trade Loss, $2.3 Bln Iran Debt." *Reuters* March 20, 2013. http://www.reuters.com/article/2013/03/20/shell -iran-idUSL6N0CCCL220130320.

———. "U.S. Extends Waivers on Iran Sanctions to China and India." *Reuters.* December 7, 2012.http://www.reuters.nl/article/2012/12/07/us-usa -iran-sanctons-idUSBRE8B615M20121207.

————. "UPDATE 1-Ahmadinejad Labels Iran Sanctions Worthless Paper."
    Reuters June 11, 2010. http://www.reuters.com/article/2010/06/11
    /nuclear-iran-china-idAFSGE65A0AY20100611.
Robins, Robert S., and Jerrold. M. Post. "The Paranoid Political Actor."
    Biography 10, no. 1 (1987): 1–19.
Romero, Simon. "Iranian President Visits Venezuela to Strengthen Ties." *The
    New York Times* January 14, 2007, LexisNexis Academic.
————. "Venezuela and Iran Strengthen Ties with Caracas-to-Tehran Flight."
    The New York Times March 3, 2007, LexisNexis Academic.
————. "Venezuela Says Iran Is Helping It Look for Uranium." *The New
    York Times* September 26, 2009, LexisNexis Academic.
Rudoren, Jodi. "Netanyahu Strikes Tough Tone on Possible Iran Strike." *The
    New York Times* November 5, 2012, sec. World / Middle East. http://
    www.nytimes.com/2012/11/06/world/middleeast/netanyahu-uses-
    tough-tone-on-possible-iran-strike.html.
Sadjadpour, Karim. "Setting the Scene: Iran's Presidential Elections." 2009.
    http://www.carnegieendowment.org/publications/?fa=view&id=23210.
Saeidi, Ali A. "The Accountability of Para-Governmental Organisations
    (Bonyads): The Case of Iranian Foundations." *Iranian Studies* 37, no. 3
    (2004): 479–498.
Safari, Akbar. "Studying the Role of Foreign Countries in Recent Unrest,
    They Are not Impartial (Part One)." Translated by BBC Worldwide
    Monitoring, *Keyhan* July 15, 2009, LexisNexis Academic.
Saleh, Heba. "Saudi Arabia Offers Counterweight to Resurgent Iran."
    Financial Times February 7, 2007, LexisNexis Academic.
Salehi, Ali Aakbar. "Head of Iran's Nuclear Organization on Nuclear Policy
    and Enrichment." Translated by BBC Worldwide Monitoring, *Javan*
    March 18, 2010, LexisNexis Academic.
————. "Iran Nuclear Chief slams Western Leaders Stance on New Nuclear
    Enrichment Plant." Islamic Republic of Iran News Network, September
    25, 2009, LexisNexis Academic.
Salek, Sajjad. "Ahmadinezhad's Purgatorial Week." Translated by BBC
    Worldwide Monitoring, *E'temad* July 28, 2009, LexisNexis Academic.
Sanandaji, Kaveh-Cyrus. "The Eighth Majles Elections in the Islamic Republic
    of Iran: A Division in Conservative Ranks and the Politics of Moderation."
    Iranian Studies 42, no. 4 (2009): 621–648.
Sarayani, Amir Ali. "Thoughts on the Nature of the Terrorist Rigi Group."
    Translated by BBC Worldwide Monitoring, *Keyhan* March 3, 2010,
    LexisNexis Academic.
Schlumberger, Oliver. "Opening Old Bottles in Search of New Wine: On
    Nondemocratic Legitimacy in the Middle East." *Middle East Critique* 19,
    no. 3 (2010): 233–250.
Schmitt, Thom, Eric Shanker, and David E. Sanger. "U.S. Adds Forces in
    Persian Gulf, a Signal to Iran." *New York Times* July 3, 2012, sec. World
    /Middle East. http://www.nytimes.com/2012/07/03/world/middlee-
    ast/us-adds-forces-in-persian-gulf-a-signal-to-iran.html.

Scott, James C. *Weapons of the Weak: Everyday forms of Peasant Resistance.* New Haven, London: Yale University Press, 1985.

Sedaei, Sam. "The biggest Lie told to the American People: Ahmadinejad's Alleged Remarks on Israel." *Huffington Post* October 29, 2007. http://www.huffingtonpost.com/sam-sedaei/the-biggest-lie-told-to-t_b_70248.html.

Sedgwick, Mark. "Measuring Egyptian Regime Legitimacy." *Middle East Critique* 19, no. 3 (2010): 251–267.

Shaffer, Brenda, ed. *The Limits of Culture: Islam and Foreign Policy.* Cambridge, Massachusetts: MIT Press, 2006.

Shambaugh, David, and Ren Xiao "China: The conflicted Rising Power." In *Worldviews of Aspiring Powers: Domestic Foreign Policy Debates in China, India, Iran, Japan, and Russia,* edited by Henry R. Nau and Deepa M. Ollapally, 36–72. New York: Oxford University Press, 2012.

Shari'atmadari, Hoseyn. "A Political Party or a Fifth Column?" Translated by BBC Worldwide Monitoring, *Keyhan* July 4, 2009, LexisNexis Academic.

———. "Broken Ladder!" Translated by BBC Worldwide Monitoring, *Keyhan* August 6, 2009, LexisNexis Academic.

———. "Coconut and…!" Translated by BBC Worldwide Monitoring, *Keyhan* November 5, 2009, LexisNexis Academic.

———. "Green Organization or a Red Carpet for America?!" Translated by BBC Worldwide Monitoring, *Keyhan* August 17, 2009, LexisNexis Academic.

———. "Iran Paper Wants 'Severe' Punishement for Recent Post-poll Unrest Leaders." Translated by BBC Worldwide Monitoring, *Keyhan* August 9, 2009, LexisNexis Academic.

———. "Paper Tigers…!" Translated by BBC Worldwide Monitoring, *Keyhan* March 13, 2010, LexisNexis Academic.

———. "Please Believe that We Do Not Believe!" Translated by BBC Worldwide Monitoring, *Keyhan* May 24, 2009, LexisNexis Academic.

———. "Radical Daily Says Reformists America's 'Fifth Column.'" Translated by BBC Worldwide Monitoring, *Keyhan* May 19, 2002, LexisNexis Academic.

———. "So Many Similarities!?" Translated by BBC Worldwide Monitoring, *Keyhan* June 13, 2009, LexisNexis Academic.

———. "The Lord of the Rings?" Translated by BBC Worldwide Monitoring, *Keyhan* June 28, 2009, LexisNexis Academic.

———. "This Is the Same." Translated by BBC Worldwide Monitoring, *Keyhan* June 30, 2009, LexisNexis Academic.

———. "Watch Your Shoes!" Translated by BBC Worldwide Monitoring, *Keyhan* February 27, 2010, LexisNexis Academic.

———. "When the Dust from Sedition Settles." Translated by BBC Worldwide Monitoring, *Keyhan* August 2, 2009, LexisNexis Academic.

———. "Who Have You Turned Your Back on and with Whom Have You Started Cooperation?" Translated by BBC Worldwide Monitoring, *Keyhan* June 6, 2010, LexisNexis Academic.

————. "Why You?!" Translated by BBC Worldwide Monitoring, *Keyhan* March 14, 2010, LexisNexis Academic.

Sharifian, Farzad. "Figurative Language in International Political Discourse: The Case of Iran." *Journal of Language and Politics* 8, no. 3 (2009): 416–432.

Slackman, Michael, and Robert F. Worth. "Arab Leaders on Edge as Iran Stretches Its Sway; Welcome Mat Isn't Out for Tehran Officials at League Summit in Qatar." *International Herald Tribune* March 31, 2009, LexisNexis Academic.

Soltanieh, Ali Ashgar. "Full Text of Speech Delivered by Iran's Envoy the International Atomic Energy Agency (IAEA) Board of Governors." Fars News Agency, March 7, 2007. http://english.farsnews.com/printable. php?nn=8512160500.

————. "Full Text of Statements of Iran's Representative to Board of Governors." Fars News Agency, September 13, 2006. http://english .farsnews.com/printable.php?nn=8506220617 24.

Sterling-Folker, Jennifer. "Realism and the Constructivist Challenge: Rejecting, Reconstructing, or Rereading." *International Studies Review* 4, no. 1 (2002): 73–97.

————. "Realist-constructivism and Morality." *International Studies Review* 6, no. 2 (2004): 341–343.

Tafreshi, Majid. "Iran-UK Relations: Two Sides of a Coin." April 20, 2011. http://irdiplomacy.ir/en/page/12076/IranUK+Relations+Two+Sides +of+A+Coin.html.

Takeyh, Ray. *Guardians of the Revolution: Iran and the World in the Age of the Ayatollahs.* Oxford: Oxford University Press, 2009.

Tavernise, Sabrina. "Russia, Turkey and Iran Meet, Posing Test for U.S." *The New York Times* June 8, 2010, sec. World. http://www.nytimes .com/2010/06/09/world/09iran.html.

————. "Turkey Offers to Mediate Between U.S. and Iran." *International Herald Tribune* November 12, 2008, LexisNexis Academic.

Tazmini, Ghoncheh. "Russian-Iranian Relations in the Context of the Tehran Declaration." *Iranian Review of Foreign Affairs* 1, no. 3 (2010): 7–32.

Tehrani, Mania. "Sanctions Help Iran Limit Internet Use." *Mianeh Website* February 16, 2010. http://mianeh.net/article/sanctions-help-iran-limit -internet-use.

Telhami, Sibley, and Michel N. Barnett. *Identity and Foreign Policy in the Middle East.* New York: Cornell University Press, 2002.

Tendi, Blessing-Miles. "Iran's Africa Foray No Cause for Panic." *Guardian Unlimited* April 28, 2010, LexisNexis Academic.

Teti, Andrea. "Bridging the Gap: IR, Middle East Studies and the Disciplinary Politics of the Area Studies controversy." *European Journal of International Relations* 13, no. 1 (2007): 117–145.

Thaler, David E. *Mullahs, Guards, and Bonyads: An Exploration of Iranian Leadership Dynamics.* Santa Monica, California: RAND, 2010.

Thompson, John B. *Ideology and Modern Culture: Critical Social Theory in the Era of Mass Communication.* Cambridge: Polity, 1990.

Tisdall, Simon. "Can the Brics Create a New World Order?" *The Guardian* March 29, 2012, sec. Comment is free. http://www.guardian.co.uk/commentisfree/2012/mar/29/brics-new-world-order?INTCMP=SRCH.

Trading Economics. "Crude Oil Latest Data." *Trading Economics.* http://www.tradingeconomics.com/commodity/crude-oil (Accessed May 13, 2013).

Turner, Mark. "Pretoria Jeopardises New UN Deal on Iran Sanctions Security Council." *Financial Times* March 20, 2007, LexisNexis Academic.

United States State Department Documents and Publications. "Remarks by Clinton, Treasury Secretary Geithner in Beijing; Answer Questions on North Korea, U.S.-China Dialogue, Iran and More." United States State Department Documents and Publications, May 25, 2010, LexisNexis Academic.

VIRI, "If Some Are Unhappy About Iran's Rights that Is a 'Different Matter.'" Translated by BBC Worldwide Monitoring, VIRI, December 1, 2007, LexisNexis Academic.

———. "Iran Spokesman Dismisses US Efforts to Create Iranophobia in Region." Translated by BBC Worldwide Monitoring, Voice of the Islamic Republic of Iran (Radio), December 22, 2008, LexisNexis Academic.

———. "Iran Spokesman Says No Letter Received from US." Translated by BBC Worldwide Monitoring, Voice of the Islamic Republic of Iran (Radio), September 2, 2009, LexisNexis Academic.

———. "Iran Students Call for 'Liberation of UK-occupied' Park in Capital." Translated by BBC Worldwide Monitoring, Voice of the Islamic Republic of Iran (Radio), August 24, 2009, LexisNexis Academic.

———. "Radio Says No Talks with U.S. as Long as It 'Threatens or Humiliates' Iran." Voice of the Islamic Republic of Iran External Service, in English, May 31, 2002, LexisNexis Academic.

———. "Top Nuclear Negotiator Defends Iran's 'Rights' in European Parliament." Translated by BBC Worldwide Monitoring, Voice of the Islamic Republic of Iran (Radio), January 23, 2008, LexisNexis Academic.

———. "US 'Confrontational Policy' Must be Changed—Iran Spokesman." Translated by BBC Worldwide Monitoring, Voice of the Islamic Republic of Iran (Radio), December 8, 2008, LexisNexis Academic.

VIRIN, "Foreign Minister Says Iran Ready to Resume Nuclear Talks ASAP." Translated by BBC Worldwide Monitoring, Vision of the Islamic Republic of Iran (Television), July 26, 2010, LexisNexis Academic.

———. "Foreign Minister Says Iran Wishes to Defuse Tension with UK." Translated by BBC Worldwide Monitoring, Vision of the Islamic Republic of Iran (Television), October 19, 2005, LexisNexis Academic.

———. "Foreign Minister Says Iranian Diplomats to be Released in June." Translated by BBC Worldwide Monitoring, Vision of the Islamic Republic of Iran (Television), May 10, 2007, LexisNexis Academic.

———. "Iran Foreign Minister and Russian President Discuss Tehran's Nuclear Policy." Translated by BBC Worldwide Monitoring, Vision of the Islamic Republic of Iran (Television), January 11, 2006, LexisNexis Academic.

———. "Iran Ready to Stop 20-per-cent Enrichment If West 'Comes to Its Senses.'" Translated by BBC Worldwide Monitoring, Vision of the Islamic Republic of Iran (Television), February 8, 2010, LexisNexis Academic.

———. "Iran TV Airs 'Press Conference' of Reformist Detainees." Translated by BBC Worldwide Monitoring, Vision of the Islamic Republic of Iran (Television), August 1, 2009, LexisNexis Academic.

———. "Iranian Foreign Minister Threatens to End Nuclear Cooperation If Case Referred to UN." Translated by BBC Worldwide Monitoring, Vision of the Islamic Republic of Iran (Television), January 31, 2006, LexisNexis Academic.

———. "Iranian Minister Says 'Essence' of Nuclear Incentive Package 'Could be Positive.'" Translated by BBC Worldwide Monitoring, Vision of the Islamic Republic of Iran (Television), June 7, 2006, LexisNexis Academic.

———. "Iranian TV Interviews Foreign Minister Mottaki on Qods Day." Translated by BBC Worldwide Monitoring, Vision of the Islamic Republic of Iran (Television), October 27, 2005, LexisNexis Academic.

———. "Mass Production of New Centrifuges to Start in 2011 Iran Nuclear Chief." Translated by BBC Worldwide Monitoring, Vision of the Islamic Republic of Iran (Television), January 9, 2010, LexisNexis Academic.

———. "New Head of Iran Nuclear Body says Committed to International Obligations." Translated by BBC Worldwide Monitoring, Vision of the Islamic Republic of Iran (Television), July 18, 2009, LexisNexis Academic.

Vries, Stephan de. "Dynamics and Dilemmas of 'Democratization': Non-democratic Rule, Democratization and U.S. efforts to 'Democratize' Iran." Master thesis, University of Amsterdam, Amsterdam, 2010.

Walt, Stephen M. *Revolution and War*. Ithaca, New York: Cornell University Press, 1996.

———. *The Origins of Alliances*. Ithaca, New York: Cornell University Press, 1987.

Wedeen, Lisa. *Ambiguities of Domination: Politics, Rhetoric, and Symbols in Contemporary Syria*. Chicago: University of Chicago Press, 1999.

Wehrey, Frederic, Jerrold D. Green, Brian Nichiporuk, Alireza Nader, Lydia Hansell, Rasool Nafisi, and S. R. Bohandy. *The Rise of the Pasdaran: Assessing the Domestic Roles of Iran's Islamic Revolutionary Guards Corps*. Santa Monica: RAND National Defense Research Institute, 2009.

Weinthal, Benjamin. "Deutsche Firmen Weiter Im Iran Aktiv." Welt Online, October 3, 2010, sec. Home. http://www.welt.de/welt_print/wirtschaft/article6711136/Deutsche-Firmen-weiter-im-Iran-aktiv.html.

Wendt, Alexander. "Anarchy Is What States Make of It: The Social Construction of Power Politics." *International Organization* 46, no. 2 (1992): 391–425.

Wetherell, M., S. Yates, and S. Taylor. *Discourse Theory and Practice: A Reader*. London: Sage, 2001.

Williams, Daniel. "Tehran Courts Support of Arabs; Officials Seek Alliances, Backing for Nuclear Program." *The Washington Post* March 20, 2006, LexisNexis Academic.

Worth, Robert F. "As Iran Gets Ready to Vote, Economy Dominates." *The New York Times* June 10, 2009, sec. International / Middle East. http://www.nytimes.com/2009/06/10/world/middleeast/10iran.html.
———. "In Iran Rivalry, Khamenei Takes on Presidency Itself." *The New York Times* October 26, 2011, sec. World / Middle East. http://www.nytimes.com/2011/10/27/world/middleeast/in-iran-rivalry-khamenei-takes-on-presidency-itself.html.
———. "Iran Accuses West of Stirring Protests; U.K. Envoy Summoned as Government Backers Stage Counter-Rallies." *International Herald Tribune* December 30, 2009, LexisNexis Academic.
Worth, Robert F., and Rick Gladstone. "In Tehran, Protesters Storm British Embassy." *The New York Times* November 29, 2011, sec. World / Middle East. http://www.nytimes.com/2011/11/30/world/middleeast/tehran-protesters-storm-british-embassy.html.
Wright, Robin. "As Pressure for Talks Grows, Iran and Syria Gain Leverage." *The Washington Post* November 16, 2006, LexisNexis Academic.
———. "Iran Is Critical as U.S. Unveils Arms Sales in the Middle East." *The Washington Post* July 31, 2007, LexisNexis Academic.
———. *The Iran Primer: Power, Politics, and U.S. Policy.* Washington, DC: United States Institute of Peace Press, 2010.
Xinhua General News Service. "Iran FM Expresses Keenness to Further Cooperate with GCC, Iraq." Xinhua General News Service, October 7, 2005, Lexis Nexis Academic.
Xinhua News Agency. "China Urges Conditions for Resolving Iran Nuclear Issue." Xinhua News Service April 10, 2013. http://news.xinhuanet.com/english/china/2013-04/10/c_124564922.htm.
Zacharia, Janine. "U.S. Finds an Antagonist in a Country on the Rise; Letter from South Africa." *International Herald Tribune* June 27, 2007, LexisNexis Academic.
Zakaria, Fareed. "For Iran, a Policy of Patience." *The Washington Post* September 25, 2006, LexisNexis Academic.
Zare'i, Sa'd Allah. "…and This is the Same Path." Translated by BBC Worldwide Monitoring, *Keyhan* December 21, 2009, LexisNexis Academic.
———. "If the Guards Didn't Exist…" Translated by BBC Worldwide Monitoring, *Keyhan* April 21, 2009, LexisNexis Academic.
———. "Sedition in the Service of Power-seeking." Translated by BBC Worldwide Monitoring, *Keyhan* June 18, 2009, LexisNexis Academic.
Zhdannikov, Dmitry, and Claire Milhench. "Oil Bull Goldman Sees End to Rising Prices." *Reuters* October 18, 2012, http://www.reuters.com/article/2012/10/18/us-goldman-crude-research-idUSBRE89H0LC20121018.
Zweiri, Mahjoob. "Arab-Iranian Relations: New realities?" In *Iran's Foreign Policy from Khatami to Ahmadinejad,* edited by Anoushiravan Ehteshami and Mahjoob Zweiri. (Reading: Ithaca Press, 2008), 115–128.

Index

Note: Locators in **'boldface'** refer to tables and the locators followed by 'n' refer to notes.

relations with Iran, 114,
118–19, 126
see also Iran-Iraq War, Gulf War
(1991), Gulf War (2003)
Islam, 86
in Iranian identity, 97–9
Islamic Jihad, 71, 119
Israel, 65, 78
and nuclear weapons, 78, 86, 116
destruction of, 106, 215n. 99
in Iranian discourse, 82, 86,
105–6, 108, 111, 213–14, 171
relations with Iran, 7, 20–3,
183n. 66

jame'e-ye rowhaniyat-e mobarez, see
combatant clergy society
jebhey-e mosharekat-e Iran-e eslami,
see participation party
Jordan, 115, 120
Jundallah, 162, 163
juxtapositioning, 26, 81, 82, 83,
89, 90, 99, 102, **104,** 111,
146, 163

Karubi, Mehdi, 55
Keyhan, 154
Khamenei, Ayatollah Ali, 45–7,
52, 81
Kharazi, Kamal, 46
Khatami, Ahmad, 163
Khatami, Mohammed, 2, 3, 4, 35,
72, 127, 157, 165
Khomeini, Ayatollah Ruhollah, 20,
31, 67, 69, 45, 46, 58, 171
Korean War, 102
Kuwait, 115, 121

Larijani, Ali, 4, **49,** 50, 115, 116
Latin America, 30, 74, 100, 101,
102, 170, 171
relations with Iran, 129–31
Lebanon, 133, 149
in Iranian discourse, 87, 100,
102, 107, 109, 111, 209n. 5,
213n. 80, 213–14n. 81

relations with Iran, 114, 115,
117, 119
legitimacy, 27, 39–43, 172
and foreign policy, 172–3
institutional legitimacy, 44–53
international legitimacy, 63–80
material legitimacy, 53–7
revolutionary legitimacy, 57–60
letter to American mother, 83
Libya, 43, 73, 115
linking and differentiation: processes
of, 90, 111
see also juxtapositioning
Lula da Silva, *see* Silva, Lula da

Mahdi, imam, 98
majles, 44, 47, **49,** 50, 130, 118
majma'e-ye rohaniyun-e mobarez, see
combatant clerics association
Makhmalbaf, Mohsen, 159
marja-e taqlid, 45
Mashaei, Esfandiar Rahim, 47, 52,
165, 189n. 54
media, 35, 41–2, 52, 58, 59,
154, 167
MEK *see mujahedin-e khalq*
Merkel, Angela, 139
Meshkini, Ayatollah Ali Akbar
Feyz, 57
Middle East
in Iranian discourse, 109
relations with Iran, 114–26
Ministry of Foreign Affairs, 46, 47
MI6, 68, 155, 158
MKO, *see mujahedin-e khalq*
Moin, Mostafa, 51
monarchists, 158
Morales, Evo, 129
moral identity, *see* identity
Morsi, Mohammed, 124
Mosaddeq, Mohammed, 68, 69, 70,
155, 162
see also Coup of 1953
Mottahari, Morteza, 31
Mottaki, Manouchehr, 2, 47, 113–14,
115, 116, 121, 128, 148